The Khmer Rouge Tribunal

Critical Human Rights

Scott Straus and Tyrell Haberkorn, Series Editors;
Steve J. Stern, Editor Emeritus

Books in the series Critical Human Rights emphasize research that opens new ways to think about and understand human rights. The series values in particular empirically grounded and intellectually open research that eschews simplified accounts of human rights events and processes.

The Khmer Rouge Tribunal

Powers, Politics, and Resistance in Transitional Justice

Julie Bernath

The University of Wisconsin Press

The University of Wisconsin Press
728 State Street, Suite 443
Madison, Wisconsin 53706
uwpress.wisc.edu

Gray's Inn House, 127 Clerkenwell Road
London EC1R 5DB, United Kingdom
eurospanbookstore.com

Printed in the United States of America
This book may be available in a digital edition.

Library of Congress Cataloging-in-Publication Data
Names: Bernath, Julie, author.
Title: The Khmer Rouge tribunal : powers, politics, and resistance in transitional justice / Julie Bernath.
Other titles: Critical human rights.
Description: Madison, Wisconsin : The University of Wisconsin Press, [2023] | Series: Critical human rights | Includes bibliographical references and index.
Identifiers: LCCN 2022058155 | ISBN 9780299343606 (hardcover)
Subjects: LCSH: Extraordinary Chambers in the Courts of Cambodia. | Transitional justice—Cambodia. | Trials (Crimes against humanity)—Cambodia. | Justice, Administration of—Political aspects—Cambodia.
Classification: LCC KZ1208.C36 B47 2023 | DDC 345/.59605046—dc23/eng/20230420
LC record available at https://lccn.loc.gov/2022058155

Contents

Illustrations

Charts

Maps

Tables

Acknowledgments

This book is the result of a long journey of engaging with the Khmer Rouge tribunal. It would not have been possible without the support of many people. First and foremost, I am deeply grateful to my interview partners, in both the capital city and rural areas in Cambodia, named and anonymous, who have taken their time to meet me, at times repeatedly over years, and generously shared their insights and experiences.

My original research benefited from the encouragement and feedback of Briony Jones, Laurent Goetschel, and Caroline Hughes. I am particularly indebted to Briony Jones for her initial invitation to think of transitional justice in Cambodia through the lens of resistance, and her generous support and feedback, and to Caroline Hughes for inspiration to locate my work within research on Cambodian politics.

In conducting the empirical research that lies at the heart of this book, I have been lucky to have received assistance from many colleagues, who have not stopped surprising me with their tireless support and resourcefulness. I warmly thank Hing Sendy, Phann Chandara, Socheat, and Hin Dilen. My thanks also go to Tim Minea and Sonja Meyer. Some of the empirical data in this book is the result of a collaborative research project titled "Victimhood after mass atrocity in Cambodia," which I conducted jointly with Timothy Williams, Tann Boravin, and Kum Somaly, with support from Soy Kimsan and his team at the Centre for the Study of Humanitarian Law (CSHL) at the Royal University of Law and Economics, and a team of exceptionally dedicated interns. The project also received the kind support of the Victims Support Section (VSS) at the ECCC, particularly Hang Vannak and Eng Sokmeng, as well as Kranh Tony, Helen Jarvis, Christoph Sperfeldt, Laura McGrew, Keo Duong, Theresa De Langis, Rachel Killean, and Daniel Mattes. For this book, I have also drawn inspiration from a year-long collaboration with Ly Ratana on a Special Issue on transitional justice in Cambodia.

Over the years, I have written earlier drafts of this book while being hosted at various institutions. For the beginning and the end of this writing journey, I thank my colleagues at swisspeace then and now. This includes Elisabeth Baumgartner, Lisa Ott, the entire Dealing with the Past team, including former colleagues Sandra Rubli, Adou Djané Dit Fatogoma, Ulrike Lühe, and Adam Kochanski. My thanks also go to the larger research community at swisspeace, including Sara Hellmüller, Stefan Bächtold, Dana Landau, Farooq Yousaf, Metka Herzog, Toon Dirkx, Julia Palmiano Federer, Jamie Pring, and Claske Dijkema. I also thank Resmy Paracherry for her research assistance. At the Center for Conflict Studies of the University of Marburg in Germany, I warmly thank Susanne Buckley-Zistel and her team for feedback and wonderful support, with a special note of gratitude to Timothy Williams and Mariam Salehi. Other important writing stations, for which I am grateful, included the Research Institute on Contemporary Southeast Asia (IRASEC), the Southeast Asian Studies Institute at Thammasat University in Bangkok, and the Cambodian Centre for Peace and Conflict Studies in Siem Reap. Finally, I cannot thank Katrin Travouillon enough for her unwavering encouragement and her invaluable feedback on various drafts of this manuscript.

I owe special thanks to the editorial staff at the University of Wisconsin Press, for their patience, encouragements, and guidance, especially to Amber Rose Cederström, as well as her predecessors Gwen Walker and Ivan Babanovski, the series editors Tyrell Haberkorn and Scott Straus, managing editor Sheila McMahon, and art director Jennifer Conn. I am very grateful to the two anonymous reviewers who provided detailed feedback to an earlier version of this manuscript that greatly improved this work.

I end with warm thanks to my parents, who first brought us to Phnom Penh in 1995, after which Cambodia became a home for us, to my partner, and to my sister, for their incredible support throughout this writing journey.

The research for this book was funded by the Swiss National Science Foundation (project number 140289) and the Research Fund of the University of Basel. Empirical research conducted for the "Victimhood after mass atrocity in Cambodia" project was funded by the German Federal Ministry for Economic Cooperation and Development (BMZ).

Earlier writings on the themes in this book have appeared in Briony Jones and Julie Bernath, eds., *Resistance and Transitional Justice* (Routledge, 2017) and "Political Violence as a Time That Is Past? Engaging With Non-Participation in Transitional Justice in Cambodia," *Social & Legal Studies* 28, no. 5 (2019): 600–24. I am grateful for permission to reproduce this material here, and to the anonymous reviewers of my article published in *Social & Legal Studies*.

Abbreviations

ADHOC	Cambodian Human Rights and Development Association (French acronym)
CCHR	Cambodian Center for Human Rights
CNRP	Cambodia National Rescue Party
CPK	Communist Party of Kampuchea
CPP	Cambodian People's Party
DK	Democratic Kampuchea
ECCC	Extraordinary Chambers in the Courts of Cambodia
ELC	economic land concession
FUNCINPEC	United National Front for an Independent, Neutral, Peaceful and Cooperative Cambodia (French acronym)
KPNLF	Khmer People's National Liberation Front
LICADHO	Cambodian League for the Promotion and Defense of Human Rights (French acronym)
NGO	nongovernmental organization
OSJI	Open Society Justice Initiative
PRK	People's Republic of Kampuchea
SLC	social land concession

UN	United Nations
UNDP	United Nations Development Program
UNTAC	United Nations Transitional Authority for Cambodia
VSS	Victims Support Section of the ECCC

The Khmer Rouge Tribunal

Introduction

In January 2016, a man in his midsixties from the Cham Muslim minority in Cambodia had agreed to meet me near his village in the southwestern province of Kampot. Balancing on his bicycle along narrow sand paths, he arrived at the wooden hut where we had arranged to meet. He enthusiastically started to share his experience of participating in the Khmer Rouge tribunal, as a survivor of the Khmer Rouge regime. He was a civil party at the Extraordinary Chambers in the Courts of Cambodia (ECCC) established by the United Nations (UN) and the Royal Government of Cambodia in 2004 to try the senior leaders and those most responsible for crimes committed under the Khmer Rouge regime from 17 April 1975 until 6 April 1979. This hybrid tribunal allows victims to participate not only as complainants or witnesses but also as civil parties to the proceedings. Although the tribunal was located in the capital city of Phnom Penh, more than a hundred kilometers away from his village, he was aware of the latest developments at the tribunal, and some of the more complicated details of its legal proceedings. During our conversation, he was explaining his point of view on the tribunal to me, while at the same time seizing the opportunity to share some updates with the few other civil parties who started gathering with us. The research interview quickly turned into an engaged discussion on the tribunal, on this otherwise quiet afternoon in the village.

At some point, we started discussing the protests of civil parties for individual financial reparations that had taken place more than a year before in the capital city. Between 150 and 200 civil parties had staged a demonstration at the gates of the tribunal on 18 October 2014, during the opening of the evidentiary hearings in Case 002/02, holding signs in both Khmer and English reading "We are the civil parties. We need individual reparations."[1] Threatening to withdraw their civil party applications if their claims for individual financial reparations remained unheard, the civil parties tried to enter the tribunal's compound to submit their petition. Security officers prevented them from doing so. Finally, the Cambodian co-lead civil party lawyer went outside to receive the petition from the protest group. A significant number of civil parties from across the country had signed the petition, in which they were asking for US$13,500 for each family member lost during the Khmer Rouge regime. After delivering the petition to the tribunal, a group of civil parties continued with a tour across town to the embassies of the ECCC's main donors, to the UN office, and to the Cambodian Council of Ministers to submit their petition and make their grievances heard by these actors in the transitional justice process.

From the outset, the Khmer Rouge tribunal's mandate had been limited to providing only collective and moral reparations to civil parties, excluding any avenue for individual, financial reparations. Over time, this had become a central issue of contention for civil parties. During our encounter more than a year after these protests, the man I met in Kampot province explained that he had supported the protests but had been unable to travel to Phnom Penh to join them. He did not explain in further detail why he was unable to do so—whether it was because of the large costs incurred with traveling to the capital city, or because with the information economy in rural areas, such a journey would necessarily come to the attention of local authorities, who may suspect him of being involved in opposition politics. Jokingly, yet also cautiously looking at me, he concluded: "But you won't tell my lawyer that I said this, [that I supported the protests], right? Otherwise, I won't be invited anymore [to join civil party activities at the tribunal]."

This conversation became a central moment in my own research journey and reflection process on how the ongoing transitional justice process at the Khmer Rouge tribunal is endowed with various layers of meaning. It illustrates whose views had prevailed when it came to setting up the mandate of the transitional justice process: the views of those present at the table of the negotiations between the UN and the Cambodian government rather than of the victims of the Khmer Rouge regime to whom the tribunal was dedicated. It further showed how victims who were later allowed to participate in the proceedings did not act as passive beneficiaries—thereby questioning essentialist readings of Cambodian culture that portray passivity as one of its central characteristics.

Civil parties did stage a public protest in the capital city, and repeatedly claimed for individual, financial reparations. While doing so, they had to navigate the expectations they felt transitional justice professionals were having toward them. This man's concern with his lawyer's reaction shows that he felt that protesting for individual, financial reparations was not seen as acceptable for civil parties. This could be because money is not necessarily deemed as an ethical claim for justice, especially when raised in relation to the loss of loved ones, or because the invisibility of economics in the field of transitional justice sidelines demands of socioeconomic justice as a legitimate form of justice. It could also be linked to how voicing dissent as a civil party possibly questions the new patron-client relations in which civil parties are invested with their lawyers, other ECCC staff members, or intermediary actors, which may require them to publicly display loyalty rather than contestation. It may also be because dissent challenges the prevailing image of victims benefiting from a transitional justice process as necessarily grateful, satisfied, and therefore easy to manage—expectations that overlap with rationales of containing contestation in an authoritarian setting.

Finally, this moment of contention also illustrates how the civil parties protesting for individual, financial reparations were drawing from practices of contestations existing beyond the transitional justice arena. They made use of petitions, protests, and visits to embassies of donor countries identified as key stakeholders. These all represented central and common elements of the "repertoire" of resistance in Cambodia. While many of the protesters came from a rural background, they furthermore staged their protest in the capital city as urbanized protesters, thereby explicitly making use of the urban environment for the public expression of their discontent and grievances. This, again, is a common practice in a context where villages are more tightly surveilled political environments.

Mapping the Politics of Transitional Justice through Resistance

This book takes such instances of contestations of transitional justice as a starting point to analyze the politics of transitional justice at the ECCC. It aims to address the following questions: How is the transitional justice process in Cambodia embedded in, and in turn shaping, existing practices of power? How is it affected by, and affecting, longer-term political struggles and ongoing contestations over imaginaries of justice, peace, and the political order?

The primary aim of this book is thus not to study resistance in and of itself, in order either to condemn those spoilers who resist transitional justice, or on the contrary to celebrate the agency of those who come to oppose it. Nor is the purpose of this book to develop a typology, an explanation, or a causal model of resistance to transitional justice, based on the case of Cambodia.

Instead, it aims to use the lens of resistance for an empirical study of the politics of transitional justice in Cambodia. While certainly not the only avenue to study power and politics in transitional justice, the analysis of empirical moments of resistance constitutes a fruitful approach to analyze how power relations both shape and are being shaped by transitional justice. As the example of civil party protests discussed above illustrates, resistance can render visible the politics of transitional justice processes, in the specific political context in which they are taking place. They show how these processes are perceived through, and mediated by, preexisting relations of power, and how they participate in the contestation, transformation, or consolidation of these relations of power. An analysis of resistance further brings to the fore imaginaries of justice, peace, and the political order that are negotiated in transitional justice processes and shows how these processes are embedded within longer-term political and social struggles.

This book thereby adopts an understanding of transitional justice processes as inherently political. By this I mean that transitional justice processes are necessarily contested, as they prioritize certain sets of practices, discourses, and actors over others. Here I draw from the critical turn in the study of transitional justice, which has shed light on the ontological, epistemological, and methodological biases of transitional justice interventions (see, e.g., N. Palmer, Clark, and Granville 2012; D. Sharp 2018; Jones and Lühe 2021). This scholarship has shown how transitional justice processes produce teleological discourses on the past, the present, and the future of societies. Transitional justice processes prioritize certain approaches, institutional mechanisms, types of knowledges, and experts who come to speak on behalf of victims. They (re)define what counts as a crime, who may count as a perpetrator or as a victim, and what may count as a legitimate claim for justice. Transitional justice processes assign guilt and attribute blame across a selected number of individuals. They thereby validate certain narratives on the past, while silencing other experiences. They (re)distribute legitimacy to domestic political actors involved in nation-building processes, or to foreign actors invested in quests for self-legitimation in countries in which they had been deeply involved in the past violence. Starting with an understanding of transitional justice processes—including criminal justice proceedings—as inherently political also speaks to critical approaches to international criminal justice, which deconstruct legalistic views that claim that after the (geo)politics leading to the establishment of international(ized) criminal tribunals, politics will end at the door to the Courtroom (see, e.g., Schwöbel 2014; De Vos, Kendall, and Stahn 2015).

Finally, this book's focus on resistance is an attempt to decenter the study of transitional justice in Cambodia both conceptually and methodologically.

Conceptually, rather than taking transitional justice as the starting point, I start with contestations of transitional justice in Cambodia. Rather than conceiving of resistance as an exception, or a form of deviance from the transitional justice norm, the book sees resistance as a necessary element of the empirical story of transitional justice. Starting with resistance, then, locates the Khmer Rouge tribunal within a larger sociopolitical context, in which it is not necessarily always a central actor. Methodologically, this approach translates into an engagement with justice demands and claims-making that exceed established normative frameworks. This means taking into account alternative views on transitional justice and forms of resistance that otherwise are considered to be irrelevant for exceeding established transitional justice mandates and toolkits. It implies listening to claims related to violations that are either not entirely past or not part of the selected past that features in formal transitional justice institutions, or to claims voiced by actors who do not formally participate or signal any interest in these institutions.[2] It also requires engaging with those forms of resistance that are readily dismissed as illegitimate in normative approaches to transitional justice, including resistance from those commonly seen as the "bad guys" and "spoilers." This is not about abandoning the commitment to acknowledge one's positionality as a researcher: research on how to address massive human rights violations of the past necessarily raises ethical questions. However, this book proposes to take a step back to study resistance as a heuristic method to better understand the dynamics of power, processes of legitimation and imaginaries of justice, and peace and political order that are negotiated in transitional justice processes.

Transitional Justice in Cambodia

In 2004, the Cambodian government and the United Nations jointly established the Khmer Rouge tribunal, formally known as the ECCC. Its mandate is to try the senior leaders and those most responsible for crimes committed between 17 April 1975 and 6 January 1979, which is the period during which the Communist Party of Kampuchea (CPK), also known as the Khmer Rouge, held central command over the country. This book focuses on the ECCC as the central transitional justice process in Cambodia. This is not to isolate the Khmer Rouge regime from the longer-term history of conflict, violence, and war in which it took place. Nor is it to say that the Khmer Rouge past has not been central to memory politics or practices of dealing with the past prior to the establishment of the ECCC (see, e.g., Chandler 2008). Anthropologist Anne Yvonne Guillou (2012) has, for instance, criticized how local practices of remembrance and mourning have remained under the radar of policy debates on transitional justice, although they constitute central, culturally embedded ways of dealing with the past, which may even hold more significance or relevance to large parts of the population than the ECCC ever had. Other scholars such as Sok-Kheang Ly (2017) and Craig Etcheson (2005) have also shown how important social and political processes of dealing with the Khmer Rouge past have taken place at various levels, long before the ECCC came into existence.

In this book, however, I decidedly focus on the ECCC because I understand transitional justice as the specific set of internationally legitimized practices of dealing with past massive human rights violations that emerged in the context of the political transitions in Latin America and Eastern Europe at the end of the Cold War. The specific historical origins of the contemporary field of transitional justice have linked the quest for justice to the delivery of liberal goods—the rule of law, human rights, and liberal democracy (D. Sharp 2018), thereby tying the "transitional justice imaginary" to a linear teleology of progress (Hinton 2018). By the end of the 1990s, transitional justice consolidated into a professionalized "industry" of experts, donors, and researchers (Buckley-Zistel and Oettler 2011, 27) based on a standardization—some would argue, the bureaucratization (Rubli 2012)—of a set of practices that rely on normative aspirations regarding truth, justice, reconciliation, and transition (Arthur 2009; Bell 2009). Transitional justice has thereby expanded into a global phenomenon, promoted by the UN, and funded by international donors. It has become increasingly deployed as a response to massive human rights violations not only in paradigmatic cases of regime change from authoritarianism to democracy but also in the absence of political transitions, in the aftermath of civil war, during conflict and occupation, or in contexts of ongoing violence (see, e.g., Hansen 2014). After initial divides over what institutions and goals should be prioritized—which crystallized in the polarized debates on peace versus justice, and justice versus truth—transitional justice advocates have increasingly embraced a holistic approach that conceive of transitional justice as a set of judicial and nonjudicial mechanisms.

The ECCC is linked to the emergence and evolution of the field of transitional justice. The formal negotiations for its establishment started in the late 1990s, following the creation of international ad hoc tribunals and post–Cold War liberal enthusiasm. Resembling the other mixed tribunals established in the early 2000s, the ECCC's hybrid nature is more the result of "politically contingent compromises" and "haphazard bargains to fill pressing impunity gaps in emergency situations" than a conscious process of experimentation in international criminal justice (McAuliffe 2011, 2). Nonetheless, the ECCC's establishment has been associated with the promise that, as a hybrid tribunal, it could contribute to developing judicial capacity and contribute to the rule of law in Cambodia (see, e.g., OHCHR 2008; Staggs Kelsall 2009; Ryan and McGrew 2016; Kum 2019). The ECCC's hybrid nature has further been praised for offering the possibility to address a key shortcoming of international ad hoc tribunals—the distance to the affected population and victims—even if this never translated into sufficient funding for outreach or victim participation. In particular, the ECCC has been widely celebrated for its unprecedented scheme for victim participation—even if this resulted from Cambodia's civil law system and provisions for civil party participation, inherited from French colonial rule, rather than consistent planning from all parties involved during the negotiations. Moreover, the ECCC has been mandated with achieving both justice and national reconciliation, thereby reflecting not only the priorities of the Cambodian government but also the holistic language that characterizes UN policymaking on transitional justice since the early/mid-2000s. The ECCC's establishment has further led to the arrival in Cambodia of international practitioners in international criminal justice (A. Kent 2013; Christensen 2019) along with professionals in civilian peacebuilding, media, arts, and memory work who have contributed to a circulation of knowledges, norms, and practices characteristic of the field of transitional justice. The ECCC's creation has finally spurred interest in the field of transitional justice among Cambodian nongovernmental organizations (NGOs) who have been able to tap into a new interest for transitional justice in Cambodia of donors who already had a previous relationship to Cambodia (McGrew 2018). These initiatives, developed in the ECCC's orbit, significantly complemented and broadened the ECCC's focus on individual criminal accountability through, for example, artistic, memorialization, or educational projects. However, they have not fundamentally disrupted the selective, temporal focus set solely on the Khmer Rouge regime (Manning 2017; Hinton 2018; Kochanski 2021).

While being embedded in the "transitional justice imaginary," the ECCC challenges some of the ambitions and claims that lie at its very core: that transitional justice, including retributive justice, is an essential part of transitions from authoritarianism to liberal peace and democracy (Peou 2017), and that hybrid tribunals are particularly significant in this regard as they can directly contribute to the rule of law (see, e.g., Dickinson 2003; Horsington 2004). As discussed in more detail in chapter 1, and throughout this book, the ECCC has operated in a dynamic political context. The ECCC was established in 2004—that is, almost ten years after the UN peacebuilding mission in Cambodia and the UN Transitional Authority in Cambodia (UNTAC). However, civil war in Cambodia continued until 1998. Moreover, after the UN-supervised elections in 1993, Cambodia's political system has been characterized as one of electoral or competitive authoritarianism, as the Cambodian People's Party (CPP)—whose leadership had run the government throughout the 1980s—continued to consolidate its power. Since 2017–18, the country further transitioned toward hegemonic authoritarianism (Un 2019; Loughlin and Norén-Nilsson 2021). After having faced unexpected and unprecedented political contestation in the 2013 legislative elections and in the streets, the CPP outlawed the political opposition. This has been accompanied by a crackdown on civil society, the dismantling of independent media, the digital extension of repressive practices, and an increasingly sophisticated instrumentalization of the judiciary. The CPP, in its transition to hegemonic authoritarianism, has also relied upon China, which has become Cambodia's main foreign partner, with an increasing presence in Cambodia's economic, diplomatic, and military spheres (Loughlin 2021b).

The Late Establishment of a Highly Selective Criminal Justice Process

Under the CPK's rule, an estimated 1.75 to 2.2 million people died from starvation, torture, execution, forced labor, and malnutrition—that is, at least one in five of the 1975 population (Tabeau and Kheam 2009). However, decades of political violence, war, and authoritarian rule preceded and followed this regime. This includes massive bombing campaigns from 1969 until 1973 of large parts of the countryside by the US government in the context of the US-Vietnam War; a coup and the establishment of a repressive, US-supported government in 1970; and the subsequent civil war that lasted for five years until the Khmer Rouge seized power in April 1975. After remaining in power for almost four years, the Khmer Rouge were toppled by the Vietnamese army, which "liberated" the country in December 1978 (or "invaded" it, depending on one's political reading of these events). While the CPK leadership and most of the revolutionary forces fled to the northwestern provinces of Cambodia, the Soviet-oriented Vietnamese government established the People's Republic of Kampuchea (PRK). This newly established socialist dictatorship enforced conscription and violent policies, while exercising tight control and surveillance of the population down to the local level (Gottesman 2004). In the context of the Cold War, a proxy war developed. It opposed the PRK, supported by the Soviet Union and Vietnam, to the Khmer Rouge forces, who received the support of China and Thailand but also the US, the UK, Australia, and several other ASEAN member countries (Fawthrop and Jarvis 2004, 52–69; Ciorciari 2009, 40–41). The international support they received allowed the Khmer Rouge to transform into an insurgent army, the National Army of Democratic Kampuchea, which continued to pose a military threat until the mid-1990s. The war in Cambodia only ended in 1998, long after Vietnam had withdrawn its troops in 1989 and after the UN-overseen peace negotiations, which led to the Paris Peace Agreements in October 1991 and the UN peacebuilding mission to Cambodia in 1992–93. In this context, demands for accountability for crimes committed under the Khmer Rouge regime were sidelined and did not form part of the mandate of the UN peacebuilding mission (Power 2003; Heder 2011). The involvement of external powers in Cambodia not only prolonged the civil war following the fall of the Khmer Rouge regime in 1979 but also led to the absence, throughout the 1980s and 1990s, of internationally sanctioned accountability mechanisms.

Given this geopolitical constellation of the Cold War, as well as the political priorities of successive Cambodian governments following the fall of the Khmer Rouge regime, the negotiations for an internationalized accountability mechanism for Khmer Rouge crimes only started in 1997—that is, almost twenty years after the end of the Khmer Rouge regime. The UN Special Representative for Human Rights in Cambodia, Thomas Hammarberg, made efforts to push for UN involvement in judicial accountability for Khmer Rouge crimes. Following the mention of possible international assistance to address Khmer Rouge crimes in the April 1997 resolution of the UN Human Rights Commission, the then two co–prime ministers of Cambodia asked the UN secretary-general for international assistance to investigate crimes committed under the Khmer Rouge. The Group of Experts appointed by the UN to assess the feasibility of a Khmer Rouge tribunal recommended the establishment of an international ad hoc tribunal. It considered the national judicial system to lack guarantees for the respect of international standards (UN Group of Experts 1999). The Cambodian government, however, refused the scenario of an international tribunal. Negotiations started when the UN proposed the option of a mixed or "hybrid" tribunal (Etcheson 2006). During the difficult negotiations, the balance between international and national control over the trials emerged as a core issue of contention, and it has continued to shape the ECCC until today.

After its establishment in 2004 by the Cambodian government and the UN, the ECCC finally became operational by 2006. The ECCC has been "clearly the most national of any hybrid courts set up" (Petit 2010, 195). It applies international and national law and is of international and national composition. It features a majority of Cambodian judges in all three judicial chambers. A supermajority rule, however, requires at least one international judge to be part of a vote for a decision to be valid. As such, it is very much the product of the complicated negotiations between the Cambodian government and the UN.

The ECCC is highly selective in its scope: it only focuses on the period during which the CPK held central control over Cambodia. During the negotiations between the UN and the Cambodian government, it became clear that efforts to widen the temporal scope would thwart the establishment of a tribunal (Hammarberg 2001). The US wanted to avoid any consideration of crimes before 1975, as this could include its mass bombing of neutral Cambodia and the abuses of the US-backed Lon Nol regime (Fawthrop and Jarvis 2004, 5–6; Ciorciari 2009). Although the Cambodian government tried several times to widen the temporal scope (Hammarberg 2001), the issue of temporal jurisdiction did not become too controversial, as the Cambodian government was itself concerned about drawing attention to crimes committed during the Third Indochina War (Ciorciari 2009, 73).

In terms of its personal jurisdiction, the ECCC can try senior leaders and those most responsible for crimes committed under the Khmer Rouge regime. While the UN Group of Experts (1999, §110) initially considered that twenty to thirty defendants could be tried, the Cambodian prime minister indicated from early on his interest to limit the trials to "only four or five of the people responsible" (Ciorciari 2009, 72). The Cambodian government's position of personal jurisdiction has been interpreted as an attempt to divert attention from both the Khmer Rouge past of senior officials of the ruling party and the defection deals negotiated by the ruling party with high-ranking Khmer Rouge officials (Ciorciari and Heindel 2014, 30). An in-depth accountability process with a broader personal jurisdiction could indeed disrupt the ruling party's "narrative of rescue" (UN Group of Experts 1999, §98; Ainley 2013). The Cambodian People's Party (CPP) is made of dissident Khmer Rouge members who became part of the Kampuchean People's Revolutionary Party that governed during the 1980s and transformed into the CPP ahead of the peace negotiations. Ever since the first democratic elections overseen by the UN in 1993, the "moral claim to be the party that liberated Cambodians from the murderous Khmer Rouge regime" has been a central feature of CPP rhetoric and electoral campaigns (Un 2011, 555; see also McCargo 2011, 73; Un 2013b; LICADHO 2014, 4). Through this self-legitimizing discourse, the CPP uses the Khmer Rouge regime as a "yardstick for its own achievements" (Un 2013b). With this comparison, the present becomes discursively constructed in antithesis to what is portrayed as the country's darkest period.

The ECCC first tried Kaing Guek Eav, alias Duch, the former deputy and chairman of the S-21 Khmer Rouge security center, in Case 001. More than twelve thousand detainees were interrogated, tortured, and killed at S-21 and its execution site, Choeung Ek.[3] S-21 initially targeted former cadres of the previous Khmer Republic, as well as intellectuals, but soon turned its focus to internal purges within the Khmer Rouge, against high-level military and political cadres. Case 001 was considered to be a relatively simple start for the ECCC's work, given the availability of documentation and witnesses, the accused's partial recognition of his acts, and the fact that his trial was not perceived to be politically sensitive (Ciorciari and Heindel 2014, 104–5). After an appeal procedure, Duch was sentenced to life imprisonment in February 2012 for crimes against humanity and grave violations of the 1949 Geneva Conventions. Duch died in prison in September 2020.

Case 002, which consists of charges against four senior Khmer Rouge leaders, is often considered to be the ECCC's landmark case. Three of the accused, however, died before completion of the case. Ieng Thirith,[4] former minister for social affairs, was released in November 2011 after being declared unfit to stand trial because of Alzheimer's and died in August 2015. Her husband, Ieng Sary, former foreign minister, died while in ECCC detention in March 2013. From 2013 onward, only two accused remained in Case 002: Nuon Chea, former deputy secretary of the Communist Party of Kampuchea, also known as "Brother Number 2" after Pol Pot; and Khieu Samphan, former head of state. Because of their denial of any responsibility for crimes committed under their rule, and a weaker evidence base than in Case 001, Case 002 has often been described as the most complex case since the Nuremberg trial (Ciorciari and Heindel 2014, 134). It was subsequently divided into two portions dedicated to different sets of charges. Case 002/01 focused on charges of crimes against humanity in the form of the forced transfer of the population and execution of soldiers of the Khmer Republic immediately after the Khmer Rouge seized power. Both accused were sentenced to life imprisonment in November 2016 after completion of the appeals proceedings in Case 002/01. Case 002/02 focused on a larger set of charges: genocide against Vietnamese and Cham (Muslim) minorities, crimes against humanity in the form of forced marriages and rape, internal purges, the persecution of Buddhists, and forced labor in work camps and cooperatives. The Trial Chamber sentenced both accused to life imprisonment in November 2018. However, after Nuon Chea died in August 2019, only Khieu Samphan was still alive and in the courtroom when a summary of the appeal judgement in Case 002/02 was pronounced on 22 September 2022. The end of the appeal proceedings in Case 002/2 signaled the ECCC's move to its three-year residual functions, as it was the last case that would come to trial at the ECCC.

Cases 003 and 004, introduced by the international co-prosecutor and several successive international co-investigating judges at the ECCC, met with the consistent opposition of their national colleagues and of the national Pre-Trial Chamber and Trial Chamber judges. These cases focused on the criminal responsibility of a set of accused at lower ranks than those in Case 002. This included Meas Muth, former commander of the Khmer Rouge navy; Ao An, former deputy secretary of the Central Zone; Yim Tith, former acting secretary of the Northwest Zone; and Im Chaem, former district secretary in the Northwest Zone. However, none of these accused was in the end tried or sentenced at the ECCC. The national prosecutors and judges at the ECCC consistently sided with the CPP government's opposition to these cases. Trial monitors, NGO representatives, scholars, and journalists have interpreted this as "circumstantial evidence" for a lack of "judicial independence" and for "political interference" by the government, in connection also with the allegations of corruption that emerged early on (see, e.g., OSJI 2011b, 11–12). In February 2017, the case against Im Chaem was dismissed because the international co-investigating judge in the end agreed with his national counterpart that Im Chaem did not fall under the Court's personal jurisdiction. After repeated split rulings opposing international and national judges over whether to move the remaining cases to trial (discussed in more detail in chapter 2), the Supreme Court Chamber finally terminated the remaining cases against Ao An, Meas Muth, and Yim Tith in August 2020 and December 2021.

Researching Transitional Justice in Cambodia: Contributions of the Book

Almost twenty years after the establishment of the ECCC, a very rich body of literature exists on the ECCC and Cambodia's transitional justice process. Large parts of this literature are characterized by a close intertwining of scholarship, practice, and policymaking. Many authors published while, or after, holding positions at the ECCC (e.g., Mohan 2009; Petit 2010; Studzinsky 2011; Lemonde 2013; Jarvis 2014; Etcheson 2019) or within international and Cambodian NGOs (e.g., Ryan and McGrew 2016; Sperfeldt and Oeung 2019). This reflects more generally the blurred lines among research, policy, and practice in the fields of international criminal justice and transitional justice. Epistemic communities of actors move fluidly in and out of academia, NGOs, and transitional justice institutions, and thereby engage in analysis, advocacy, and implementation simultaneously or consecutively. This intertwining of scholarship, practice, and policymaking on the ECCC is also reminiscent of how previous international interventions in Cambodia—most prominently the UN's peacebuilding mission—has led to a longer-term scholarly engagement with Cambodian politics of some of the foreign professionals involved in these interventions. In the context of the highly polarized assessments and negative media coverage of the ECCC, scholars at this policy-research-practice nexus foreground the ECCC's positive legacies and defend its relevance for international criminal justice (S. M. Meisenberg and Stegmiller 2016; Lobba and Pons 2020).

Much of the literature on the ECCC has analyzed it in terms of international criminal law, including from critical and feminist perspectives (see, e.g., Killean 2015; E. Palmer and Williams 2017; Grey 2019; DeFalco 2022). Over the years, the literature on the ECCC has, however, become increasingly interdisciplinary. It now includes contributions from sociology (e.g., Abe 2019), anthropology (e.g., Kent 2013; Emde 2014; Hinton 2014), geography (Tyner, Sirik, and Henkin 2014; R. Hughes 2015), history (Gidley 2019), or psychiatry (S. Chhim 2014). It also features an increasing visibility of a new generation of scholars from Cambodia (e.g., L. Sok and Abe 2019; Soy and Hing 2019; Huy 2019; Sirik 2020).

This book analyzes the politics of the ECCC at the intersection of transitional justice and Cambodian politics. To do so, it draws from the scholarship focusing on the politics of the ECCC. Many works have dissected the politics of the ECCC's establishment, from the geopolitics of the Cold War that isolated criminal accountability efforts for atrocities committed under the Khmer Rouge to the complicated history of negotiations between the UN and the Cambodian government (see, e.g., Etcheson 2004; Fawthrop and Jarvis 2004; Ciorciari 2009; McGrew 2009). Some works have also analyzed the role of donors, UN representatives, and the Cambodian government in shaping the ECCC's proceedings (McCargo 2011; Ciorciari and Heindel 2014; Etcheson 2019; Gidley 2019), or examined how the ECCC or NGO initiatives in the ECCC's orbit have intersected with memory politics and political framings of the past in Cambodia (Ainley 2013; Manning 2017; Hinton 2018; Kochanski 2021).

This scholarship is important as it questions legalistic portrayals of politics at the ECCC, which isolate its politics to the past—the protracted negotiations between the UN-mandated team of negotiators and the Cambodian government's assigned task force—and/or to the "political interference" of the Cambodian government. This book similarly attempts to offer a more nuanced understanding of the politics of transitional justice in Cambodia. It sees legalistic portrayals of the ECCC as a missed opportunity to understand how transitional justice processes, including international(ized) tribunals, are unfolding in the specific contexts in which they are taking place. Such views bring our attention away from how the political context shapes perceptions and experiences of the transitional justice process as it unfolds in specific places and times. They gloss over the previous involvement of international actors in the conflicts that are being investigated in transitional justice institutions. Finally, such views reproduce problematic, ahistorical binaries of international versus national actors, which homogenously portray the international as neutral, apolitical, and moral in its pursuit of justice.

This book enters into conversation with these existing works on ECCC's politics, yet it also differs in several key respects. First, this book engages explicitly with studies of Cambodian politics, the political, and power relations in Cambodia. It reflects upon the intersections between on the one hand, transitional justice at the ECCC, and on the other hand, neo-patrimonial and authoritarian practices, the ruling party's discursive claims for legitimacy, and power dynamics across urban-rural divides.

Second, this book analyzes the politics of the ECCC with a multisite and multiactor approach. Instead of focusing on international diplomacy or national party politics as the central sphere of politics that is shaping the transitional justice process in Cambodia, the book engages with intersections of the ECCC with politics at the national and community levels. To do so, it takes into account a broad range of actors. This includes the political elite, representatives of the UN and donor countries, foreign and national staff members at the ECCC, victims participating at the ECCC as civil parties (including former low-level Khmer Rouge cadres), and citizens who do not formally participate in the ECCC proceedings and continue to face political violence today. My analysis, which moves beyond the compound of the ECCC, thereby adds to existing research that examines how the political context is shaping NGOs' transitional justice initiatives at the local level (Kochanski 2021). It complements works studying the ECCC as a political endeavor (Ciorciari 2009; Etcheson 2019) in an illiberal context (Gidley 2019) but do so mainly with a focus on elite actors, such as the political elite or key UN officials, and ECCC staff members.

Third, this book is primarily an *empirical* study of resistance to transitional justice. As discussed in the next section in more detail, it draws upon a wide range of primary data, spanning over more than a decade. This allows us to capture, over a long period, intersections between the ECCC and a dynamic domestic political context, which saw unprecedented contestation of the ruling party's power in 2013/14, followed by a turn to increasingly overt authoritarian practices. It can thereby complement earlier empirical studies conducted on memory politics at the intersection of transitional justice at the ECCC and domestic politics (Manning 2017), as well as more recent research conducted after Cambodia's transition to hegemonic authoritarianism (A. Kent 2022).

Beyond research on Cambodia, this book connects with academic efforts to better understand the political dimension of transitional justice processes and international(ized) criminal tribunals (see, e.g., Krever 2014; Clark 2018;

Salehi 2022). While following the "local turn" in the field of transitional justice, many works have examined how culture mediates understandings of transitional justice, including in the context of Cambodia (see, e.g., Hinton 2018; Huy 2019), but this book highlights the need to analyze more explicitly how power relations mediate local experiences and perceptions of formal transitional justice processes. Such an analysis can be a valuable contribution from political scientists embracing a broader epistemology of power and the political to ongoing discussions in the field on the disconnections between international legal norms and local realities. This can better help us to assess whether, and to what extent, transitional justice can deliver upon its emancipatory promise of a transformation of those power relations that initially led to massive human rights violations, and contribute to a more just, peaceful, and equal society. The book thereby also speaks to a core concern, in scholarship on peacebuilding, transitional justice, and international criminal justice, to better understand how the multifaceted interactions between foreign and domestic actors shape interventions for peace and justice (Millar and Lecy 2016; McAuliffe 2017a; McAuliffe and Schwöbel-Patel 2018). This concern has seen multiple iterations in debates spanning various concepts, such as local ownership, hybridity, frictions, or the everyday, and with varying normative pulls toward either the "local" or the "international" side of these interactions (see, e.g., Arnould 2016; Kochanski 2018).

An Empirical Study

This book draws from a large range and depth of primary data, gathered between 2008 and 2022, and based on a sustained and ongoing interest in Cambodia and its politics in a broad sense. The book primarily draws from qualitative research, including 270 qualitative interviews,[5] but also participant observation; a collaborative, large-scale quantitative survey conducted with 439 respondents; and numerous informal conversations conducted over the years with various respondents. This book does not draw from ethnographic work in the classical sense of an intensive, long-term immersion in a single site of ethnographic observation and participation. Nonetheless, the research that lies at the heart of this book emerges from a commitment to an "ethnographic sensibility"—the epistemological commitments of an "approach that cares to glean the meanings that the people under study attribute to their social and political reality" (Schatz 2009, 5).

If not mentioned otherwise, I conducted all interviews in person in Khmer, French, English, or German, when needed with the help of an interpreter. While the main interview method chosen was that of individual interviews, the communal aspect of everyday life in rural Cambodia sometimes required the adaptation of this method to that of group interviews, with neighbors, spouses, or family members spontaneously joining in the exchange. In such settings, I made sure to avoid raising particularly sensitive topics that could have potentially been detrimental for respondents to discuss. Whenever possible, I attribute quotes and reference interviews to named respondents. However, most statements are anonymized to protect respondents' security or because they only agreed to speak to me on this basis.

The book primarily draws from a set of 163 formal, qualitative interviews with 170 respondents conducted between November 2013 and February 2016. Table 1 provides an overview of the various categories of respondents I met during that time in the cities of Siem Reap and Phnom Penh, and in villages across the provinces of Kandal, Takeo, Kampot, Prey Veng, Svay Rieng, Kratie and Kampong Cham.

I conducted repeat interviews with several of these respondents, which are not counted in Table 1. The majority of the Cambodian respondents from this field research are ethnic Khmer, but I also met some members of the Kachok, Krung, and Tampuan ethnic minorities that make up approximately 4 percent of the population (Blot and Guillou 2016), as well as members of the Cham and ethnic Vietnamese minorities who are civil parties at the ECCC.

I identified respondents through key informant interviews and fieldwork encounters. A focus on purposive sampling, in combination with snowball sampling, allowed the maintenance of direction and coherence as well as the openness and flexibility to experiences in the field that are difficult to predict.

Table 1. Overview of qualitative interviews, 2013–2016

ECCC staff members (national and UN-appointed, across judicial and administrative offices, at various hierarchy levels)	37
Civil society actors, journalists, analysts based in Cambodia	25
Members of the political elite (CPP and political opposition)	9
Civil parties (including 2 rejected civil party applicants)	48
Witnesses at the ECCC (former Khmer Rouge cadres at S-21)	4
Neighbors, village chiefs, former Khmer Rouge cadres, local civil society actors living in villages next to civil parties	29
Respondents facing political violence in land grabbing cases (from Borei Keila and Boeung Kak in Phnom Penh, and from Rattanakiri) and in repression of the protests after the 2013 national elections	18
Total	170

Both within and across the different respondent groups, I made sure to allow for a variation according to gender, urban/rural livelihoods, and social class. A variation in terms of urban/rural locations is particularly relevant to capture the experiences of the majority of the population, which still lives in rural areas (75 percent),[6] with almost half of them relying on farming as a main source of income, earning an average farm income of US$108 per month.[7] As Caroline Hughes and Vanessa Pupavac (2005, 876–78) have argued, representations of Cambodia in media, research, and policy reports have long had a tradition of dismissing the political agency of "ordinary Cambodians." Making sure to include the voices of those who are beyond the usual reach of journalists and researchers is also important in the study of transitional justice more generally, which routinely sees experts or "transitional justice entrepreneurs" speaking on behalf of the affected population and/or victims (Madlingozi 2010; see also Millar 2010; Robins 2012; Jones 2015).

Most of these interviews were in-depth interviews. For the small set of interviews conducted with citizens facing political violence today (discussed in chapter 4), I chose the method of narrative interviews with a focus on life stories in relation to one specific category of respondents. This method provides the opportunity for the respondents to select and order events in ways they feel is relevant and reflects their own meanings. It is particularly relevant for the study of transitional justice processes since the analytic boundaries used by researchers, including the designated time frame, can clash significantly with subjective experiences of political violence and victimization (see, e.g., Fujii 2010).

In addition to this empirical material gathered between 2013 and 2016, this book also draws upon a mixed-methods study conducted as part of a collaborative project on victim participation and nonparticipation in the transitional justice process in Cambodia.[8] This study consisted of a large-scale quantitative survey with 439 respondents across all provinces; the follow-up qualitative interviews with 65 of those respondents; and interviews with 21 ECCC officers and NGO representatives working on transitional justice in Cambodia. The tables included here provide an overview of the survey sampling (table 2) and the qualitative follow-up interviews (table 3) conducted after the quantitative survey.

The 439 respondents for the quantitative survey were selected based on a stratified random sampling strategy, in which participation constituted our theoretically core category. Our survey differed from most previous surveys conducted on civil party participation, as we made sure to include civil parties beyond the group of easily accessible civil parties that had registered with the Cambodian human rights NGO ADHOC.[9] The 65 respondents for the follow-up interviews were drawn from all categories of respondents. We selected these

Table 2. Overview of quantitative survey, 2018

Civil parties		255
including	24 rejected civil party applicants	
	29 civil party applicants in Cases 003 and 004	
	28 civil parties with little attendance in ECCC and NGO outreach activities	
	88 Case 002 civil parties	
	30 civil parties consulted in reparation projects	
	11 civil parties who had testified at the ECCC	
	29 civil party representatives or focal points	
	16 civil parties in Case 001	
Complainants at the ECCC		59
Participants in NGO projects related to the ECCC or the Khmer Rouge past		67
Respondents who did not participate in any transitional justice activity of the ECCC or NGOs		58
Total		439

Table 3. Overview of qualitative interviews, 2018

Civil parties and civil party applicants	44
Complainants at the ECCC	6
Participants in NGO projects related to the ECCC or the Khmer Rouge past	10
Respondents who did not participate in any transitional justice activity of the ECCC or NGOs	5
ECCC staff members and civil society actors based in Cambodia (international and national)	21
Total	86

respondents based on their survey responses, including those whose views reflected broader trends in the survey, as well as those whose views markedly departed from most survey responses.

Finally, this book also draws from document analysis of gray literature, key speeches of senior members of the ruling party, international and national media reporting, and public transcripts of ECCC trial proceedings. I also made use of the method of overt, nonparticipant and semistructured observations, whenever possible, for the observation of key events. This includes the observation of regional civil party forums organized by the Victims Support Section of the ECCC in the capital city and different regions,[10] of public trial hearings at the ECCC and conferences organized by the ECCC,[11] and of workshops and events organized by national or international civil society organizations. I also observed key political events such as the celebrations of the ruling Cambodian People's Party (CPP) of the thirty-fifth anniversary of "Victory Day" on 7 January 2014, protests in the context of the contested 2013 national elections, and demonstrations of communities facing political violence in contemporary Cambodia.

Defining Resistance to Transitional Justice

As evident from this introduction, my approach to resistance is broad. I propose to define resistance to transitional justice as an act intended by an actor to negotiate, question, or reject the power relations exercised in state-sanctioned transitional justice processes, or to mitigate the specific effects of these power relations upon her or him. With such a definition, I explicitly draw from poststructuralist and agonistic understandings of power and the political, which relocate power away from institutions to practices and beyond the "fetishism of the state" that has traditionally been prevalent in studies on the Global South (Rajagopal 2003, 14). I see power as diffuse, multiple, and inscribed in specific relationships and contexts. As a result, resistance is also relational, localized, and manifold (Escobar 1984, 381). It is inherent to any political order and a reaction to the specific power relations that run through it.

From this viewpoint, resistance is a necessary element in the unfolding of transitional justice processes. This stands in stark contrast to normative approaches to transitional justice. As they start from the premise that transitional justice is necessarily doing good, these approaches often imply that resistance to transitional justice will mainly come from the so-called spoilers (Jones and Bernath 2017). It is expected that it is those who were previously involved in massive human rights violations who will resist transitional justice, because they have something to lose in the political transition: the "old-regime loyalists" (Subotić 2014, 135) and the former political elite, or the direct perpetrators of violence. Resistance is also often seen in connection with "recalcitrant" victims who are unable to let go of the past (Jones and Bernath 2017). Instead, I adopt a multiactor approach and analyze how multiple actors engage and/or resist the transitional justice process.

What forms can resistance to transitional justice then take? Resistance may not only take the form of public acts of protests, such as the protest of civil parties for individual, financial reparations already mentioned briefly in the introduction. Ever since James Scott's (1985) seminal work on everyday resistance in the Southeast Asian context of Malaysia, scholars in the social sciences and the prolific and interdisciplinary field of resistance studies[12] have reached a more comprehensive understanding of resistance. Its analysis goes beyond the study of revolutions and public, confrontational, or collective forms of resistance and attends to subtle, nonorganized and individual forms of resistance.

In my work, I have thus come to conceive of resistance as a continuum of diverse forms that move between the collective and the individual, the organized and the sporadic, the public and the private spheres, rather than referring only to a single selection thereof. Resistance may include public and collective protests, as well as forms of resistance that are short of collective action, that are subtle and unorganized. Resistance may include material and physical resistance but also symbolic acts and discursive strategies. Finally, resistance may refer both to acts of *commission*, that is, doing something one should not be doing; and acts of *omission*, that is, refusing to do something (G. Sharp 2005, 547). One form of resistance may further feed into another: everyday resistance may feed into public and collective protests, or vice-versa.

In addition to drawing from resistance studies for my analytical framework, I also borrow from the literature on concepts alternative to that of resistance—namely, works on contentious politics and social movements. In particular, I propose to use the analytical tools of "repertoires" and "performances" to think of resistance. Repertoires can be defined as the whole set of means those who resist transitional justice can draw from in a specific context. The study of contentious politics has shown how this is shaped not only by "what [those who resist] know how to do" but also by "what society has come to expect them to choose to do within culturally sanctioned and empirically limited set of options" (Tilly 1978, 151). The specific performances of resistance to transitional justice will therefore depend not only on "how people make claims but what they know about making claims and the reception by targets of their claims" (Tarrow 2013, 2). In other words, resistance to transitional justice will be informed by how groups or individuals usually resist or make claims toward powerful (state) actors. It is necessarily connected to the broader context of struggles and claims making that takes place beyond the orbit of transitional justice.

Although these concepts were developed for the analysis of collective movements that necessarily involve the state as either a target, an initiator of claims, or a third party (see, e.g., Tarrow 2013), they are helpful for the purposes of researching resistance to transitional justice. They enrich such an analysis with a focus on the dynamism and fluidity of forms of resistance across different sites of resistance. They help identify the ways in which those who resist transitional justice draw from the culturally sanctioned forms of resistance in the specific context in which they operate. They thereby show that we need to analyze transitional justice in constant connection to what may be conceived of as "normal politics" in a specific society.

With this broad approach to resistance, the forms of resistance investigated in this book are of varying visibility. The burden of interpretation thereby shifts in my analysis. Here, the combination of various methods—in-depth interviews, narrative interviews with a focus on life stories, observation, and a large-scale quantitative survey—has informed the analysis of both subtle forms of resistance (and their underlying meanings) and more public forms of resistance. Moreover, while some acts appear more straightforwardly as being intended to negotiate, question, or reject the power relations defined in the transitional justice process, others have required more interpretation on my side as a researcher. My commitment to an empirical approach over a long period has also allowed me to balance my aspiration of drawing a purposeful analysis of empirical moments of resistances with caution against too readily equating acts with resistance when they clearly exceeded such an interpretative frame.

Overview of the Book

Chapter 1 provides an overview of the long-term conflicts that preceded and followed the Khmer Rouge regime and of the international interventions to which the ECCC is the latest addition. I briefly discuss the establishment of the ECCC, outline the key issues of contention that emerged during the negotiations between the UN and the Cambodian government, and offer an overview of the ECCC's operations after its establishment until 2022 and the political context in which it operated. Finally, I engage with contemporary academic debates on the study of power, agency, social movements, and resistance in Cambodia that are of relevance for the study of transitional justice.

In the three subsequent chapters, I explore the three sites of resistance to transitional justice that constitute the core of my empirical approach. Chapter 2 analyzes the resistance of senior members of the ruling party against an in-depth accountability process at the ECCC. This chapter shows that the discursive dimension of the ruling party's resistance to an in-depth accountability process is part not only of its efforts to consolidate its power and claims to legitimacy as the party that has saved the country from the genocidal Khmer Rouge regime but also, more recently, of a personalized peace narrative that portrays the prime minister as father of peace. Beyond its discursive dimension, the ruling party's resistance to an in-depth accountability process at the ECCC has also translated into political control of the tribunal's national side. While resistance has been selective rather than obstructive of all legal proceedings, the chapter shows that the ruling party's control has taken place through practices of patronage and coercion, which have embedded the ECCC in the neo-patrimonial structures of power shaping the domestic judiciary. This chapter's analysis, however, does not bring to light a neat binary opposition between international versus national actors. Instead, it shows a split among the involved international actors, between legalists and pragmatists. This split has shaped international actors' investments in, and assessments of, the ECCC ever since its creation was negotiated between the UN and the Cambodian government.

Chapter 3 turns to resistance from victims of the Khmer Rouge regime who are participating as civil parties in the ECCC proceedings. This chapter shows how the intersections of politics at the local and domestic level with the transitional justice politics at the ECCC shaped who could come forward as a victim, what types of claims could be voiced, how claims could be pursued, and what section of the past could be discussed. This chapter analyzes victim participation as a spatially embedded experience: through their participation, civil parties navigated different places, from the village to the courtroom in the capital city, and these places offered various options for mobilizing, resisting, and voicing their grievances. The chapter discusses the early stages of victim participation when villagers first encountered the ECCC and decided to apply for participation, and how these initial encounters were mediated by preexisting power relations and shaped by experiences of fear. The chapter then analyzes civil party resistances against the limitation of the ECCC's reparations mandate and temporal jurisdiction. Civil parties have resisted the marginalization of socioeconomic forms of justice as well as the depoliticization of civil party participation and its relegation to the realm of suffering. The analysis of their resistance shows how civil parties, when participating in transitional justice, have become exposed to a new set of power relations at the intersection of domestic politics and transitional justice politics.

Chapter 4 examines the nonparticipation in the ECCC proceedings of citizens facing political violence in contemporary Cambodia. It discusses perceptions of, and engagements with, the ECCC of respondents who have recently experienced, or continue to experience, human rights violations. This chapter thereby brings into focus actors who often remain at the margins of transitional justice discussions for opting out of a process that is also dedicated to them as victims of the Khmer Rouge regime. This chapter analyzes the multidimensionality of their nonparticipation in the ECCC proceedings, which resulted from a lack of knowledge on the ECCC, a lack of the necessary resources to participate, or, simply, an absence of interest. But the chapter also shows that nonparticipation often stemmed from everyday experiences of the law. Citizens who are subject to human rights violations and publicly dissent CPP rule have come to experience the judiciary as an agent of injustice and repression. These experiences can lead to mistrust of the ECCC as it is perceived as being embedded in the political status quo. Nonparticipation is thus also about the disappointment that the transitional justice process is not going far enough and does not address claims for nonrepetition and structural reforms. Finally, the chapter also discusses nonparticipation as a form of temporal resistance of the ruling party's and the ECCC's teleological temporalities, which both posit a rupture between a time of political violence, relegated to the Khmer Rouge past, and a time of democracy, development, and peace, equated with the present.

The book concludes by bringing together the analysis of these different sites of resistance and sets of actors. The ECCC thereby emerges as a site of contestations taking place between diverse foreign and national actors who are shaping the trajectories of Cambodia's multiple transitions. These contestations pertain to what the transitional justice process at the ECCC should look like, and who is allowed to take an active role in it. They also connect to various political struggles in Cambodia that exist beyond the sphere of the transitional justice "industry," in the context of an increasingly overt authoritarian setting.

1

Transitional Justice, Politics, and Resistance in Cambodia

Before the book moves to the empirical analysis of different sites of resistance to transitional justice, this chapter offers a detailed overview of the context of transitional justice in Cambodia. The chapter comprises three sections. The first section discusses the Khmer Rouge regime and locates it within the larger context of the national, regional, and geopolitical conflicts that preceded and followed it. This is essential to understand the belated establishment of the ECCC twenty-five years after the end of the Khmer Rouge rule and the selective scope of the transitional justice process. The section further discusses how Cambodia, after having been caught up in the geopolitical machinations of the Cold War, became an experiment of liberal interventionism in the early 1990s. This foregrounds the history of international interventions in Cambodia, to which the ECCC was the latest addition. It also showcases how the UN, from its peacebuilding mission in 1992–93 until the establishment of the ECCC in 2004, operated a temporal sequencing of peace and justice. The second section introduces the political history of the ECCC's establishment. Starting in 1997, the difficult negotiations between the UN and the Cambodian government revolved around several issues of contentions, most importantly questions of control over the tribunal. Once the ECCC was finally established in 2004, these issues would continue to shape its operations. The second section also provides an overview of the ECCC's operative years from 2006 to 2022. Finally, the third section turns to the dynamic political context in which the ECCC has taken place, which has included unprecedented and unforeseen contestation in 2013–14 before Cambodia's turn to increasingly overt authoritarian practices. The third section ends with a discussion of the implications for researching resistance in this political context.

Cambodia's Long-Term Conflicts and Multiple Transitions

The ECCC and the transitional justice process in Cambodia have focused on the period during which the Khmer Rouge held control over the entire country, from 17 April 1975 to 6 January 1979. While the Khmer Rouge rule has led to atrocities of an unprecedented scale in Cambodia and beyond, decades of political violence, war, and authoritarian rule took place both prior to and after this regime. The fall of the Khmer Rouge regime in 1979 did not mark the end of the Khmer Rouge military power. The involvement of foreign powers played a crucial role in prolonging the Khmer Rouge's existence, and the ensuing civil war only ended in 1998. The question of accountability for Khmer Rouge atrocities was also sidelined in the context of the Cold War throughout the 1980s and also later, as Cambodia became an experiment for liberal interventionism.

From the Emergence of the Khmer Rouge to Democratic Kampuchea

The Cambodian communist movement originates in the 1940s fight against French colonial rule in Cambodia (1867–1946) and Indochina. Established in 1951 as a Cambodian branch of the Vietnamese-led Indochinese communist party, the Khmer People's Revolutionary Party was renamed the Communist Party of Kampuchea (CPK) in 1966 and progressively distanced itself from the Vietnamese movement. Saloth Sar, later known as Pol Pot, was elected party secretary in 1963 (Dy 2007). The CPK remained relatively weak in the 1950s and 1960s. Shortly after independence in 1953, King Sihanouk abdicated from the throne to play a more active role in politics as prime minister and later head of state with his newly founded political party, the People's Socialist Community (Sangkum Reastr Niyum). Sihanouk's relations to North Vietnam and his stark repression of opponents did not allow the CPK to become a strong political force. He coined the French term "Khmer Rouge" (red Khmers) to differentiate the CPK from the republican "blue" and royalist "white Khmers" (Dy 2007).

Toward the end of the 1960s, the economic situation became increasingly unstable, and opposition grew. Often nostalgically portrayed as Cambodia's golden era, Sihanouk's rule was characterized by repression, narcissism, and patronage (Chandler 2018). Intellectuals, the urban-based elite, and students faced limited opportunities for social upward mobility, and freedom of expression was increasingly restricted (Peou 2000, 40–47). The country became entangled in the escalating US-Vietnam war, despite Sihanouk's efforts to preserve neutrality. To cut off the Vietcong supply route known as the Ho Chi Minh trail that ran through northeastern Cambodia, US commanders launched a bombing campaign, which quickly escalated into B-52s carpet bombing large parts of the Cambodian countryside (Owen and Kiernan 2006, 2010). From 1969 until 1973, the US military dropped around five hundred thousand tons of bombs on Cambodia. While the total number of US bombs dropped and the resulting deaths are still subject to controversy (see, e.g., High, Curran, and Robinson 2013; Owen and Kiernan 2015), the estimated casualties, ranging between 50,000 and 150,000, exceeded the Allied bombing of Germany and Japan in World War II in per capita terms (Kiernan 1989; Owen and Kiernan 2015).

In March 1970, while Sihanouk was outside of the country, Prime Minister and General Lon Nol took power through a military coup and proclaimed the Khmer Republic. A five-year-long civil war ensued, during which up to 600,000 died (Peou 2000). Lon Nol's US-backed government fought against Sihanouk's government in exile. Sihanouk formed an unlikely alliance with his previous opponent—the CPK—and gained China's and North Vietnam's support. The CPK received unprecedented support, as Sihanouk called his "brothers and sisters" to join their movement, while the devastating US bombings and Lon Nol's corrupt and repressive military rule also fueled grievances in the countryside (Heder and Ledgerwood 1996a; Chandler 2018). Between 1970 and 1973, the CPK revolutionary army grew from only 3,000 soldiers to more than 40,000 (Dy 2007). In early 1973, the CPK already controlled 90 percent of the territory (Peou 2000). On 17 April 1975, they seized power over the capital city. They were initially cheered by Phnom Penh's population, who had grown from 0.5 to approximately 2 to 2.5 million because of internal displacement,[1] and was desperately hoping for an end to the devastating civil war. Under the CPK's rule, however, an estimated 1.75 to 2.2 million people, that is, at least one in five of the 1975 population, would die from starvation and malnutrition, overwork and forced labor, torture or execution.

The CPK's regime, known as Democratic Kampuchea (DK), was characterized by extreme secrecy. The DK leaders remained unknown for a long time. Ordinary people were required to blindly obey "Angkar" (អង្គការ),[2] the "organization"—an obfuscatory term dating back to the early days of the communist movement. Only in 1977 did Pol Pot publicly confirm his position as prime minister and the existence of the party. In September 1975, Sihanouk returned to Cambodia as the official head of state until his resignation in March 1976, after which he remained under house arrest. The constitution adopted in January 1976 foresaw a National Assembly, yet it only held one session (Dy 2007). The Standing Committee held effective control. It consisted of seven members of the CPK Central Committee, including Pol Pot, Ieng Sary, and Nuon Chea. The DK leaders divided the country administratively into zones, which comprised sectors (or regions), themselves made up of districts, communes, and cooperatives. Zone secretaries were usually members of the CPK Central Committee, while some were also members of the Standing Committee (e.g., Sao Phim or Ta Mok).[3] The DK leaders further controlled the administrative hierarchy through three-member committees assigned at each level to overview politics, the economy, and military issues.

The DK leaders introduced radical policies that aimed to establish a new people and a communist agrarian utopia within the time frame of a single generation. They aspired for a "Super Great Leap Forward" that was to surpass Mao Tse Tung's policies (Chandler 1991). This was to be achieved through repeated forcible population transfers, starting with the forced transfer of Phnom Penh's population to the countryside immediately after the CPK forces had seized the capital city. The CPK adopted a "four-year plan to build socialism in all fields 1977–1980" at the 1976 party congress, which foresaw the collectivization of all property and the production of an impossible average of three tons of rice per hectare (CPK Party Centre 1988). Most of the harvest was destined for the army, the few factory workers, or for exports to China and other communist countries. The population starkly suffered and died from malnutrition and hunger. People were reduced to their mere "muscular strength" (Ponchaud 2001, 117) and the entire country was transformed into a labor camp (Chandler 1991). The CPK further abolished religion, schools, modern medicine, tribunals, money, markets, freedom of movement, and traditional family structures. All aspects of public and private life became collectivized and controlled by Angkar (*badevat*), the "(revolutionary) organization" (អង្គការ[បដិវត្តន៍]). The population was redistributed in cooperatives and subjected to close surveillance by "espionage troops" (*kâng chlob*, កងឈ្លប). These operated at the lowest level of the administrative structure with the support of ordinary people and youth (Quinn 1989; Ponchaud 2001; Kane 2009). The CPK further introduced forced marriages and subsumed matrimony to the production of new children for the revolution (Dy 2007). Sexual and gender-based violence by Khmer Rouge cadres and officers took place both within and outside of forced marriage and were rarely punished (Mam 2001; Nakagawa 2008; Natale 2011; Savorn 2011; De Langis 2014b; Ye 2014). This included gang rapes and mass rapes, rape prior to execution or as part of the "re-education" process, and rape against the Vietnamese, Khmer Krom, or Cham minorities (Natale 2011; Braaf 2014).

Despite its communist rhetoric of building a classless society, the CPK introduced a strict social hierarchy. Those who had lived in a CPK-controlled rural area before 17 April 1975 were designated as "old" or "base people." If they did not have any relatives who had worked for Lon Nol's Khmer Republic, they were categorized as "full rights candidates" and could access leading positions within cooperatives (Becker 1989). The rest, classified as "trial candidates," were subject to particular scrutiny (Dy 2007). Those forcibly evicted from cities in April 1975 were classified as "new people" or "April 17 people." They were considered to be "parasites" (31) or "prisoners of war," had little access to proper food rations or to Khmer Rouge cadres' "benefit of the doubt" in what often amounted to life-and-death situations (Ponchaud 2001, 74, 132).

During the CPK rule, minorities were targeted for discrimination and elimination. In the early months of the DK regime, around 150,000 to 170,000 ethnic Vietnamese were forced to leave Cambodia, while almost all the ethnic Vietnamese who remained in the country were killed (Tabeau and Kheam 2009). The Cham Muslim were prohibited to practice their religion; those who refused or protested were imprisoned or killed (Osman 2006). The CPK further prohibited the Cham culture, language, and dress, and as of 1977 adopted a policy of destroying the Cham as a group, leading to mass executions (F. So 2010). The Khmer Krom community, inhabiting the Mekong River delta that became part of southern Vietnam over the course of the twentieth century, was also specifically targeted for extermination. The CPK accused them of having "Khmer bodies with Vietnamese minds" and considered them to be Vietnamese enemies (Mohan 2008, 47).

The CPK ideology relied on constant class warfare and revolution, which required a permanent provision of enemies (Chandler 2002), either external, such as the US, the Soviet Union, or Vietnam, or internal. In February 1975, the CPK leadership had decided to exterminate the former cadres of the Khmer Republic (Chandler 1991), while anyone being associated with the vague category of "intellectuals" was also targeted during the forced population transfers. In January 1976, the party leadership moved to the "second stage of revolution," which entailed the elimination of the "remaining bourgeois elements" (Becker 1989, 246–47). This led to a second wave of executions, during which the Buddhist clergy and the Vietnamese and Cham minorities were specifically targeted. When the ordered agrarian "miracle" did not materialize, the search for enemies was extended to infiltrated elements within the movement (259). As from April 1976, inner party purges increasingly targeted CPK cadres (Chandler 1991). The "flux and reflux agitating the high spheres of power" would arbitrarily define "guilt and innocence" (Chandler 2002, 69). It became increasingly difficult to strictly differentiate between perpetrators and victims.

These internal struggles ultimately led to an end of the DK regime, along with clashes with Vietnam that developed into a full-fledged war by 1978 (Dy 2007). In 1977 and 1978, provincial Khmer Rouge commanders and soldiers fled to Vietnam and formed the Kampuchean United Front for the National Salvation. The original members of the Front include Cambodia's current prime minister Hun Sen. On 25 December 1978, the Vietnamese army launched the "liberation"[4] of Cambodia, with the support of the Salvation Front. Phnom Penh was liberated on 7 January 1979. The CPK leadership and most of the CPK's highest-ranking cadres and its revolutionary forces fled to northwestern provinces.

Cambodia after 1979 in the Geopolitics of the Cold War

While 7 January 1979 signified the end to centralized Khmer Rouge rule over the entire country, it did not bring an end to political violence, war, the humanitarian crisis, or economic deprivation. Moreover, Cold War geopolitics and the political priorities of the successor regime determined how crimes committed under the Khmer Rouge were dealt with.

After the fall of DK, the People's Republic of Kampuchea (PRK) was proclaimed. The Vietnamese-backed socialist dictatorship would last until 1989. The PRK leadership was mainly composed of former Khmer Rouge *déserteurs*, including Hun Sen, as well as Cambodian communists who had stayed in Vietnam since the 1950s (Chandler 2008, 357). Since only very few educated and trained Cambodians had survived DK, many former Khmer Rouge cadres were also integrated in the new government (359). Ideologically retaining the principles of Marxism-Leninism, the PRK leadership attempted to distance itself from the DK ideology. Its official narrative was therefore that the newly reconstituted communist party, renamed Kampuchean People's Revolutionary Party, had defeated the imperialist US in April 1975. Its victory, however, had been stolen by the Khmer Rouge, a small group of murderous criminals who proceeded to decimate the true revolutionaries (Ledgerwood 1997; Chigas 2000). The PRK introduced a shift from Maoist-oriented to Soviet-oriented communism and a mix of planned and market economy, while also allowing cultural and religious freedoms and the reintroduction of Buddhism. It exercised tight control and surveillance of the population down to the local level, more than any other Cambodian government except for the DK regime (Pak et al. 2007). The PRK's "perhaps most resented policy" was the conscription of Cambodians known as the K5 plan, a radical defense policy and mass labor program inspired by the idea of the Berlin Wall (Gottesman 2004, 231). Half a million Cambodians are estimated to have been conscripted and sent to the Cambodia-Thai border for forced labor, consisting of clearing forests, building defensive fortifications, or laying landmines (Gottesman 2004). They faced starvation and deplorable living conditions, which reminded many of the Khmer Rouge regime. This policy led to ten thousand deaths from diseases such as malaria or land mines (Gottesman 2004).

In the context of the Cold War, a proxy war developed in Cambodia. The PRK fought against the remaining Khmer Rouge forces, with the support of Vietnam and the Soviet Union. Although Khmer Rouge atrocities had become known in the West as early as 1976, countries from the Western bloc—the US, UK, and Australia—supported the Khmer Rouge forces, alongside China and ASEAN countries, most prominently Thailand (Power 2003; Fawthrop and Jarvis 2004; Ciorciari 2009). The Khmer Rouge became partners for those foreign powers aspiring for the defeat of Vietnam and the Soviet bloc in the region, with the US fearing the spread of communism in Southeast Asia until 1989 (Ciorciari 2009). The Khmer Rouge leadership was even granted the representative seat of Cambodia in the UN General Assembly.[5] It was also able to (re)build an insurgent army, the National Army of DK, which would continue to pose a military threat until the mid-1990s. In 1982, the Khmer Rouge formed the Coalition Government of Democratic Kampuchea in an unlikely alliance with two weaker Cambodian factions: the royalist United National Front for an Independent, Neutral, Peaceful and Cooperative Cambodia (FUNCINPEC), led by former King Sihanouk; and the republican, pro-US Khmer People's National Liberation Front (KPNLF), established by former Lon Nol officials.

Throughout the 1980s, the Western bloc isolated the PRK politically and economically, seeing Vietnam as an illegal foreign occupation force (Ciorciari 2009). The Western bloc further prohibited any delivery of aid despite Cambodia's dire humanitarian situation, and only a few nongovernmental aid organizations made efforts to circumvent this ban (Fawthrop and Jarvis 2004). Cold War geopolitics thus had a devastating impact in Cambodia, with war remaining the main arbiter for political power in a country trapped "in a bloody, but internationally and regionally convenient, stalemate" (C. Hughes 2003, 87). The PRK's repeated calls, starting from 1981, to bring the Khmer Rouge leaders to trial before an international jurisdiction were also ignored (Heder 2011).

This international legitimation of the Khmer Rouge stood in stark contrast with their demonization under the PRK (Chandler 2008). The PRK's memory politics aimed at sustaining the population's hostility toward the Khmer Rouge, justifying the persisting civil war and portraying the PRK as the country's "liberator" (Hinton 1998). In July 1979, just a few months after the fall of DK and before a Ministry of Justice could be established, the PRK created the People's Revolutionary Tribunal to "try the acts of genocide committed by the Pol Pot-Ieng Sary clique" (De Nike, Quigley, and Robinson 2000).

Singling out Pol Pot and his brother-in-law Ieng Sary, DK's foreign minister, allowed the PRK regime to distinguish between leaders responsible for crimes committed under DK and the thousands of former DK soldiers and cadres it hoped would eventually defect (Gottesman 2004). The indictment also left out other prominent DK leaders such as CPK deputy secretary Nuon Chea or DK minister of defense Son Sen who, given their previous ties to Vietnam, were seen as more likely to be co-opted (Heder 2002). The tribunal thus enforced the PRK's emerging narrative of "a handful of absent, demonic perpetrators and millions of victims" (Chandler 2000, 73). But the tribunal was also to serve the PRK's international legitimization and discrediting of the Khmer Rouge.

To bring international attention and legitimacy to the trial, representatives of socialist countries and lawyers sympathetic to the Indochinese revolution were invited to participate. Public hearings were held for five days from 15 to 19 August 1979 at the Chaktomuk theater in Phnom Penh. Even if politically used by the PRK, the trial allowed survivors to make sense of their horrifying experiences under the regime that just ended and provided an immediate and public acknowledgment of the Khmer Rouge crimes (see, e.g., Affonço 2005). US lawyer John Quigley, who had been invited to testify to the commission of genocide, recalls: "Around the auditorium where the trial was held, an overflow audience milled, anxious to talk with anyone who would listen about what they and their families suffered under the Khmer Rouge" (Quigley 2000, 1). Witnesses testified with raw emotions during the public hearings, which were broadcast on the radio throughout Cambodia (Quigley 2000; see also Hinton 2018, 45–46). The People's Revolutionary Tribunal moreover constituted the first tribunal to try crimes of genocide since the 1948 adoption of the Genocide Convention, although it used a much broader definition of "genocide" (Fawthrop and Jarvis 2004). It was, however, strongly criticized in the West and ever since for being a "show trial." Some of the criticisms resulted from unfamiliarity with civil law procedure (47). But the tribunal clearly operated in disregard of international fair trial standards, as the ECCC judges would later also conclude.[6] The defense lawyers did not exonerate the defendants and were invited to extend the blame to China (Chandler 2008). After only five days of public hearings, both accused were found guilty of genocide, and sentenced in absentia to death, and to the confiscation of their property.

The PRK's memory politics also included the opening of a museum on the "genocidal crimes" of the Khmer Rouge as early as July 1980 in the former security center S-21, known as Tuol Sleng. The museum aimed at showcasing the DK atrocities to prove to "the outside world" that the Vietnamese army invasion had indeed been a liberation (Ledgerwood 1997, 87). For this purpose, and in contrast to Khmer funerary traditions (Guillou 2012; Jarvis 2015), the museum displayed a "skull map" of Cambodia until 2002, made up of 300 skulls and bones found by the Vietnamese army in the "killing fields" of Choeung Ek (K. Chhim 2012, 26). Choeung Ek, the execution site of S-21, also became a significant site of official remembrance. Across the country, local authorities also constructed state-run memorials at the location of mass graves, which were often excavated upon the initiative of private citizens (K. Chhim 2012). As from 1983, the state-led national "Day of Anger"[7] was celebrated on May 20[8] at these memorials (Emde 2014). It also aimed to sustain hate toward the remnants of Khmer Rouge forces in the ongoing civil war.

Cambodia as an Experiment of Liberal Interventionism in the Early 1990s

In 1989, with the dissolution of the Soviet Union, Vietnam withdrew its troops from Cambodia. The main PRK leaders remained in power. They changed the name of the PRK regime to State of Cambodia, while the Kampuchean People's Revolutionary Party was renamed the Cambodian People's Party (CPP); it still rules the country today. The CPP officially abandoned its Marxist-Leninist orientation, driven by key political leaders who anticipated ideological transformation, such as Hun Sen and Chea Sim (Etcheson 2005; Chandler 2008). "Ideologically rigid leaders" such as PRK president Heng Samrin were left behind (Gottesman 2004, 349). The State of Cambodia reinstated Buddhism as the state religion, introduced a free-market economy as well as private ownership of land. It slowly started to transform itself from a socialist dictatorship into a mixed authoritarian system (Peou 2000). Gottesman (2004, 348–49) describes the specificities of this political transition: "No Berlin Wall ever fell in Cambodia. No Vaclav Havel or Lech Walesa came to power. The regime did not collapse; it negotiated the terms of its survival. Impoverished and isolated, the [State of Cambodia] understood that it needed legitimacy and assistance from the United Nations and from the West."

With the end of the Cold War, the permanent five members of the UN Security Council and major regional powers became invested in an end to the Vietnam-Cambodia conflict. Peace negotiations led to the adoption of the Comprehensive Peace Agreement in Paris on 23 October 1993. The four acknowledged factions—the State of Cambodia, the Khmer Rouge, the FUNCINPEC and the KPNLF—signed the Accords, agreed to disarm, and allowed the UN's deployment to Cambodia. In line with post–Cold War liberal interventionism, the Paris Peace Accords envisaged Cambodia's transformation into a liberal democracy, based on the Wilsonian assumption that free political competition creates the best conditions for a stable and lasting peace (Paris 2009).

Since the Khmer Rouge were considered indispensable partners for the consolidation of peace, the Paris Agreements prioritized negative peace over accountability (Ciorciari 2009). The Peace Agreements did not condemn the Khmer Rouge crimes. In fact, the term of "genocide" was deleted from the text because of opposition from the US, China, and the Khmer Rouge (Power 2003). The State of Cambodia's initial demands included judicial accountability through an international tribunal for "Khmer Rouge leaders" in conformity with the UN's Genocide Convention (Heder 2011). However, the Khmer Rouge and their Cambodian allies rejected these demands, as did most foreign governments involved in the peace negotiations, most prominently China and ASEAN countries. The Agreements nonetheless required that Cambodia undertakes "effective measures to ensure that the policies and practices of the past shall never be allowed to return."[9] This reflects the promotion of liberalism at the end of the Cold War but also involved countries' concerns that they would face a "backlash from liberal constituencies at home" if the Khmer Rouge were strengthened through the peace process or if further atrocities were to be committed (C. Hughes 2015b, 123).

In 1992, the UN set up the UN Transitional Authority in Cambodia (UNTAC) to oversee the implementation of the Paris Agreements. It pursued two main goals: establishing peace and establishing a government through democratic elections. UNTAC was to take over official interim governing duties until the ratification of a new constitution and the conduct of national elections. Such a mandate for a UN peacekeeping mission was "both revolutionary and unprecedented with regard to the mission aims and the intrusive methods it employed to achieve them" (Richmond and Franks 2007, 28). As Michael Doyle (1995, 13) points out, "Not since the colonial era and post–World War II Allied occupations of Germany and Japan had a foreign presence held so much formal administrative jurisdiction over the civilian functions of an independent country." Lasting from March 1992 to September 1993, the UN mission deployed 22,600 police, military, and civilian staff members from more than one hundred countries with a total cost of US$1.7 billion. As UNTAC chief of mission Yasushi Akashi (2012, 165) recalls, the mission took place in a unique context of "heady optimism in the post-Cold War era and generous voluntary contributions by donor countries." Although UNTAC's mandate did not foresee any accountability for Khmer Rouge crimes, the mission was the UN's first peacekeeping operation to include a human rights component. This led to the establishment of human rights monitoring institutions that still exist today, albeit in different forms, such as the OHCHR Cambodia Country Office and the UN Special Rapporteur on the situation of human rights in Cambodia. The extent to which UNTAC was able to reach its objectives, and its legacies for Cambodia's political trajectory ever since, remain the subject of fierce debates among Cambodian politicians, civil society actors, signatories of the Paris Peace Agreements, donor countries, international professionals of the human rights and development industries in Cambodia, as well as scholars (Öjendal and Ou 2013).

The national elections supervised by UNTAC were held in May 1993 and were largely considered a success, even though the Khmer Rouge announced in May 1992 their refusal to disarm and to participate in the election. Ninety-six percent of the eligible population registered to vote and almost 90 percent of the registered voters polled their votes during the six-day election, despite high levels of intimidation and violence from the Khmer Rouge and from the CPP (Ledgerwood 1994; McGrew and Worden 2017). The elections, however, did not lead to a real transfer of power. The CPP received an unexpectedly low 38 percent of the votes, while the royalist FUNCINPEC party earned 44 percent of the votes. A coalition government was adopted, as the constitution required a two-thirds majority for the winning party to govern alone. But as the CPP threatened a return to civil war if not granted an equal share in government, an awkward system of two co–prime ministers was introduced. FUNCINPEC's Ranariddh became the first prime minister and CPP's Hun Sen the second prime minister. Formally, each controlled equal shares of ministerial and provincial portfolios. However, the CPP, which had been in power for twelve years since the fall of DK, continued to maintain its de facto control over the public and local administration, the military, and the police (Öjendal and Ou 2013). The subsequent power struggles between the two prime ministers culminated in a violent coup in July 1997, from which Hun Sen emerged victorious.

In addition to the compromised legacies of the elections it supervised, UNTAC's ability to deliver upon its mandate of securing stability has been questioned. The mission was unprepared for the Khmer Rouge's unforeseen return to armed resistance. Even though the Khmer Rouge finally became "political pariahs on the world stage" with their boycott of the 1993 election process (Chigas 2000, 250), the immediate memory of the US-Vietnam war prevented the West from engaging in a peace enforcement mission in the region (Power 2003). UNTAC remained unable to maintain the ceasefire, disarm combatants, and end the civil war that ensued between the newly established Royal Government of Cambodia and the Khmer Rouge (Sanderson 2001; C. Hughes 2015b). When the UN mission withdrew in September 1993, the Khmer Rouge still controlled about one sixth of the territory. They would remain a strong military threat until 1998, funding themselves through the illegal trade of timber and gems (Chigas 2000; Le Billon 2000; Diepart and Schoenberger 2016).

The civil war was only ended due to Pol Pot's death in 1998, internal conflicts within the remnant Khmer Rouge factions, and domestic policies. Hun Sen successfully co-opted Khmer Rouge leaders into his patronage networks (Path 2017). He did so based on the CPP's so-called win-win policy of national reconciliation, which granted defecting Khmer Rouge members de facto amnesties, the maintenance of ranks and positions after integration into the Royal Government of Cambodia, and the guarantee of their property and wealth. This policy signaled a move toward "collective amnesia," which stood in stark contrast to the PRK's previous demonization of the Khmer Rouge (Chandler 2008).

Two main waves of defection signaled the end of the Khmer Rouge movement. In August 1996, after striking a deal with Hun Sen, former DK foreign affairs minister Ieng Sary led factions from the western zones to turn themselves in to the CPP (Bultmann 2019). This included former commander of the DK navy Meas Muth and former commander of the DK air force Sou Met. In return for their defection, they received a certain degree of political autonomy, land, and positions in the military and government. Ieng Sary was further granted a royal pardon for his 1979 death sentence pronounced by the 1979 PRK trial. He also received an amnesty from prosecution under the 1994 law prohibiting Khmer Rouge membership.[10] The second main wave of defection followed Pol Pot's death, Hun Sen's violent coup, and the CPP's victory in the 1998 elections. It included the defection of five senior Khmer Rouge intellectuals in June 1998; eight high-ranking Khmer Rouge military commanders in early December 1998, along with five thousand soldiers; and finally, at the end of December 1998, former CPK deputy secretary Nuon Chea and former DK head of state Khieu Samphan (Etcheson 2019). In March 1999, the only remaining high-level leader, former CPK standing committee member and Southwest Zone secretary Ta Mok, was arrested. The success of Hun Sen's win-win policy would become a central element in his claim to power (see chapter 2).

The ECCC: A Negotiated Instrument of Transitional Justice

This overview of the emergence of the communist movement in the 1940s until the end of the civil war in 1998 emphasizes how particularly complex, malleable, and shifting alliances of (inter)national actors shaped the conflicts in Cambodia. Cold War geopolitics, the priorities of successor governments, and the entanglements of the new political elite with the Khmer Rouge regime all contributed to sidelining accountability efforts. It is only in 1997 that a new momentum for accountability for Khmer Rouge crimes emerged. The establishment of the ECCC would still take longer than any other internationalized tribunal in the post–Cold War era (Scheffer 2012). This section starts with a brief discussion of the efforts that led to the ECCC's establishment, drawing from the analyses of political scientists and legal scholars as well as published accounts from those involved in the negotiations.[11] The section ends with an overview of the ECCC's main years of operation, from 2006 until 2022.

The Political History of the ECCC's Establishment: A Brief Overview

In the mid-1990s, the imminent end of the civil war in Cambodia, the creation of ad hoc tribunals for the former Yugoslavia and Rwanda, and a shift in US policy led to an unprecedented momentum for accountability for Khmer Rouge crimes on the international scene (Power 2003; Ciorciari 2009).[12] The UN's human rights office in Cambodia seized this opportunity. After having initially, yet unsuccessfully, explored possibilities of a truth commission, Thomas Hammarberg, UN Special Representative for Human Rights in Cambodia from 1996 to 2000, tried to involve the UN in judicial accountability efforts (Ciorciari and Heindel 2014). In April 1997, he secured the adoption of a clause in a resolution passed by the UN Human Rights Commission, which mentioned the possibility of international assistance to address Khmer Rouge crimes. In June 1997, he then lobbied the co–prime ministers Hun Sen and Norodom Ranarridh to sign a letter to the UN secretary-general. The letter, drafted by the UN Human Rights Office in Phnom Penh, requested "the assistance of the United Nations and the international community in bringing to justice those persons responsible for the genocide and crimes against humanity during the rule of the Khmer Rouge from 1975 to 1979."[13] It further recognized that "Cambodia does not have the resources or expertise to conduct this very important procedure. [. . .] We are aware of similar efforts to respond to the genocide and crimes against humanity in Rwanda and the former Yugoslavia, and ask that similar assistance be given to Cambodia."

The drafting of the letter coincided with a unique window of opportunity at the domestic level. At that time, the two co–prime ministers were facing the task of neutralizing the remnant Khmer Rouge units. In their competition for power, each attempted to attract the remaining Khmer Rouge forces to rally their political parties and thereby outnumber their rival's political force (Heder

2011). The co–prime ministers were easily convinced to sign the letter. Publicly pursuing accountability for Khmer Rouge crimes allowed them to shield their ongoing negotiations with the Khmer Rouge from international attention and claim moral credence. It also provided them with a useful tool—the threat of prosecutions—in their attempts to convince commanders to defect.

The submission of the letter to the UN secretary-general was immediately followed by tumultuous events. This included Hun Sen's violent coup against Ranariddh and the FUNCINPEC in July 1997, which put into question his political legitimacy on the international scene, as well as Pol Pot's death under house arrest in April 1998 amid US efforts to capture him for prosecution (Etcheson 2019). Hun Sen's government was able to secure international endorsement with the 1998 elections. Despite the year-long political crisis, the 1997 letter still set the path forward for UN involvement in a Khmer Rouge tribunal. Given China's opposition if the matter was to be raised at the UN Security Council, Hammarberg turned to the UN General Assembly. In December 1997, the UN General Assembly adopted a resolution requesting the UN secretary-general to appoint a Group of Experts to assess the evidence and recommend further measures. This procedure had also been used prior to the establishment of the International Criminal Tribunals for ex-Yugoslavia and Rwanda. The December 1997 resolution represented the first time the UN ever acknowledged the serious human rights violations that had taken place under the DK regime (Fawthrop and Jarvis 2004).

In July 1998, the UN secretary general appointed the Group of Experts.[14] While no comprehensive survey was conducted to systematically assess the views of survivors, the experts observed an "unambiguous demand for trials" during their consultations (UN Group of Experts 1999, §94). In February 1999, they concluded that sufficient evidence existed but deemed the national judicial system to be lacking guarantees for the respect of international standards (UN Group of Experts 1999). They recommended the establishment of an ad hoc international tribunal outside of Cambodia, in the Asia-Pacific region. Prime Minister Hun Sen categorically opposed this option and withdrew his support for the establishment of a tribunal with UN assistance in March 1999, his government briefly exploring the establishment of a truth commission with South African assistance (Etcheson 2019). For analysts and those involved in the negotiations, this reaction confirmed that the prime minister had not pursued accountability as an end in itself but had rather used the threat of a trial to defeat the Khmer Rouge (Hammarberg 2001; Ciorciari 2009). By the end of 1998, once he had succeeded in achieving this, he did not have any further incentive to partake in the negotiations. Hun Sen's withdrawal from the negotiations at the time is also read in connection with opposition from the

Chinese government to an international Khmer Rouge tribunal, coupled with offers of increased bilateral aid (Etcheson 2004; Fawthrop and Jarvis 2004). In spring 1999, a new UN proposal to establish a "mixed" or "hybrid" tribunal succeeded to bring back Hun Sen's government to the negotiations (Etcheson 2006, 7–8).

These early negotiations show how the Cambodian government was performing a careful balancing act between, on the one hand, further consolidating its power and, on the other hand, keeping international respectability and accessing aid through negotiating for a tribunal (Chigas 2000; McGrew 2009). For Etcheson (2004, 202–3), the prime minister thereby engaged in "an important technique of 'weak power diplomacy,'" through which he told China, the UN and Western countries "what they want[ed] to hear" to make sure Cambodia would continue to receive gifts and foreign aid from all sides. In this context, Hun Sen was seen to be more responsive to interventions of foreign governments such as, for example, the US or Japan rather than the UN, which had less to offer (Gidley 2019, 91–96). Yet as negotiations started almost twenty years after the end of the Khmer Rouge rule, the Cambodian government was also in a unique position to impose its priorities to the UN regarding the design of the tribunal, unlike other governments who saw the establishment of internationalized tribunals immediately after the end of conflicts (Ciorciari 2009, 78–79).

Even though the Cambodian government and the UN eventually agreed on a mixed tribunal, distrust on both sides continued to shape the negotiations, also because the two negotiating parties rarely met face-to-face (Fawthrop and Jarvis 2004). The question of who would control the tribunal emerged as a central issue of contention (Fawthrop and Jarvis 2004). The UN, Western officials, Cambodian and international human rights organizations, and domestic opposition parties believed that the ruling party lacked both the competence and commitment to human rights needed to conduct fair trials and deliver credible justice (Ciorciari 2009). The Cambodian government, however, repeatedly demonstrated its determination for the tribunal to remain domestic. Hun Sen explicitly framed this as an issue of national sovereignty. In a meeting with Hammarberg in October 1999, for example, he stated: "I do not wish a foreign woman to come to Cambodia and dress up in a Khmer dress. I want a Khmer woman to dress in a Khmer dress and for foreigners to come and help put on the make-up" (Hammarberg 2001, 18).

Hammarberg (2001, 9) pointed out that the CPP's emphasis on local ownership also reflects its long-standing animosity toward the UN and its criticism of the UN's betrayal of Cambodia for supporting the Khmer Rouge after 1979 (see also Gidley 2019, 97–104). This can be illustrated with the following quote of Foreign Minister Hor Nam Hong from a meeting among Hammarberg, Hun Sen, and senior CPP officials in March 1999: "The international community talks about finding justice for the Cambodian people. [. . .] But what has the international community been doing vis-à-vis the Khmer Rouge lately? Once the genocidal Khmer Rouge regime was toppled, the so-called international community continued to support the Khmer Rouge. The so-called international community forced Cambodia to accept the Khmer Rouge as partners in the Paris peace talks and in the Supreme National Council (SNC). It said nothing about responsibility of the Khmer Rouge, let alone prosecution of them. But now that Cambodia has achieved peace and reconciliation, they call for an international tribunal. Can we trust them?" (Hammarberg 2001, 11).

CPP officials also seemed to fear that foreign powers—in particular the US—and opposition domestic political parties would use a UN-dominated process to undermine the CPP (Gidley 2019, 84). In the end, the UN negotiators and the Cambodian government reached a compromise on the dividing issue of the relative power of Cambodians versus UN staff, agreeing on a suggestion put forward by David Scheffer, then US ambassador-at-large for war crimes. Two pairs of UN-appointed and Cambodian co-prosecutors and co-investigating judges would work alongside each other. Moreover, the three judicial chambers would all feature a majority of Cambodian judges, in exchange for a supermajority rule. This rule required an affirmative vote of at least four of the five judges at the Pre-Trial or Trial Chamber, or at least five of the seven Supreme Court Chamber judges.[15] Effectively, this rule provided a veto to the international judges: at least one international judge had to be part of a vote for a decision to be valid. If unable to reach a supermajority vote, the default provision foreseen in the legal framework was that a prosecution or investigation shall proceed. Finally, to address the risk that prosecutions could be blocked by Hun Sen, a special judicial chamber—the Pre-Trial Chamber—was foreseen. The Pre-Trial Chamber would address any disagreements between the international and Cambodian co-prosecutors, or the international and Cambodian co-investigating judges. If the co-investigating judges disagreed on opening an investigation, or if the co-prosecutors disagreed on indicting a suspect, the investigation or indictment would proceed unless a supermajority of Pre-Trial Chamber judges voted against it—that is, a vote including at least one international judge.

The tribunal's personal jurisdiction also constituted a core issue of the negotiations. In their 1999 report, the UN Group of Experts (1999, §110) recommended to focus on two categories of suspects: "senior leaders with responsibility over the abuses" and "those at lower levels who are directly implicated in the most serious atrocities." They indicated that this could encompass twenty to thirty suspects. During the negotiations, while discussing at length the specific wording of the tribunal's personal jurisdiction, the UN and the Cambodian government agreed that it should encompass both senior leaders and second-tier figures (Heder 2011). Hun Sen emphasized that this would shield from prosecution the rank-and-file Khmer Rouge cadres at the lowest echelons as well as those who had defected and "helped to overthrow the genocide"—such as himself, then–CPP president Chea Sim, and CPP honorary chairman Heng Samrin (37). The UN remained concerned that the Cambodian government was not genuinely committed to prosecuting suspects beyond senior leaders, and that the UN would therefore come to be "seen to collaborate in a process of selective justice for a few politically convenient indictees" (32).

During the negotiations, the Cambodian government also criticized the limiting of the tribunal's temporal jurisdiction to 1975–79. Hun Sen repeatedly raised the possibility of widening the temporal scope to include crimes such as the US bombing or the Chinese support for the Khmer Rouge, thereby reminding all involved parties of the risks of "an uncontrolled trial" (Gidley 2019, 89). However, as Hammarberg (2001, 6) observed, it had been clear from the outset of the negotiations that "to widen the scope would be a recipe for no result." The US in particular was keen to avoid any consideration of crimes before 1975, as this would include the abuses of the US-backed Lon Nol regime and the US carpet bombing of Cambodia (Fawthrop and Jarvis 2004, 5–6). In the end, the issue of temporal jurisdiction would not become too controversial, since the Cambodian government was also concerned with drawing too much attention to the crimes committed during the Third Indochina War (Ciorciari 2009, 73).

In 2000, the UN and the Cambodian government reached a first agreement. However, the draft law subsequently introduced in the Cambodian National Assembly differed in several points from the UN understanding, most importantly regarding the power to appoint foreign personnel, the validity of Ieng Sary's previous amnesty and pardon, and the possibility of enacting amnesties for indicted suspects (Etcheson 2006, 15). In early 2002, the frustrated UN mission led by Hans Corell, under-secretary general for legal affairs, ended the negotiations, arguing that it had "come to the conclusion that the Extraordinary Chambers, as currently envisaged, would not guarantee the independence, impartiality and objectivity that a court established with the support of the UN must have" (UN Department of Public Information 2002). International and Cambodian human rights organizations applauded this decision (Ciorciari 2009, 76). The UN's withdrawal from negotiations would not last long. In December 2002, the UN General Assembly pushed the UN secretary general to renew the negotiations, through a resolution sponsored by Japan and France, with the support of the US and Australia (UN General Assembly 2003). The UN and the Cambodian government finally reached a framework agreement, which they signed in June 2003.

The Agreement, however, would not be ratified until October 2004, as Cambodia faced a year-long domestic political crisis that prevented the convening of the National Assembly. In the July 2003 parliamentary elections, the CPP did not reach the two-thirds majority required to govern alone and was unable to form a coalition government as the royalist FUNCINPEC and the Sam Rainsy Party rejected the election results. In July 2004, the CPP finally reached an agreement with FUNCINPEC to form a new government. In October 2004, the newly constituted National Assembly passed the revised ECCC Law, formally establishing the ECCC.[16]

This brief overview reveals the heterogeneity of the actors involved in the negotiations, which cannot be subsumed within a monolithic binary of international versus national actors. Among international actors, a divide between pragmatists and legalists came to the fore during the negotiations, which would continue to shape the ECCC's operations (see chapter 2). In the context of the ECCC's establishment, this divide can be most vividly illustrated with the different positions of David Scheffer, who was closely involved in the negotiations for the establishment of the ECCC in his function as President Clinton's ambassador-at-large for war crimes issues and later privately, and Hans Corell, who led the UN's negotiations as under-secretary general for legal affairs and the UN's Legal Counsel. While Scheffer (2012, 341) believed that "international justice is the art of the possible," Corell refused the establishment of a tribunal that would not fully respect international standards, and returned to the negotiations table only because his hands were tied by the UN General Assembly resolution. This divide can be seen from Scheffer's perspective, as he recalls discussions with Corell in 1999 (2012, 392): "Sitting in that room, I wondered: does anyone here give a damn about 1.7 million dead, or is this just a game of who can win the prize for arguing the perfect formula for justice rather than building a court that can *deliver* such justice? The easiest point to make at the table is the cautious one that cynically demands a perfect outcome. The real challenge is how to make an imperfect world work reasonably well."

Mikkel Jarle Christensen and Astrid Kjeldgaard-Pedersen (2018) have argued that this divide also reflects a competition between, on the one hand, legal professionals invested in the development of the then-still-emerging field of international criminal justice and, on the other, a transnational network of actors with deep ties to Cambodia, the emergence of genocide studies, and early efforts for bringing the Khmer Rouge to justice.

Regarding domestic actors, it is important to note that even though the "CPP is still little known to the outside world" (Pak 2011, 18) and its internal divisions are particularly difficult to discern, given strict rules of party discipline, the CPP's approach to the ECCC's establishment was not homogeneous. Etcheson (2004, 183–84) observed that CPP views included a complex mix of differentiated positions of both support and opposition to the establishment of a Khmer Rouge tribunal. Among opposers, viewpoints ranged from a systematic rejection of external interference in the country's affairs and fears it could harm national reconciliation and threaten stability, to expressions of solidarity to core CPP members who could potentially become suspects. CPP supporters of a tribunal included those advocating for access to increased aid and political credibility through an internationally legitimized tribunal, those interested in internal benefits for the domestic fight against impunity, and finally, those who saw the tribunal as the confirmation of the party's narrative as savior of the country, and as a final act of revenge against those who betrayed Cambodia's communist revolution. Bound to lobby for their party's interests, senior CPP officials have also themselves been victims of the Khmer Rouge rule (see, e.g., Scheffer 2012, 389–90).

The ECCC's Operations: 2006–2022

The ECCC, formally established in October 2004, was set up on the outskirts of Phnom Penh in a reconverted area of the Royal Cambodian Armed Forces headquarters (Gidley 2018). It became operational in 2006, after sufficient funds had been raised to cover the initially planned budget of three years (Jarvis 2016).

As a result of the lengthy negotiations between the UN and the Cambodian government, the ECCC structure has been a divided one. The ECCC is the only internationalized tribunal to have consisted of parallel Cambodian and international structures at all levels of the court, with separate recruitment, reporting, and funding streams. The personnel working on the so-called international side was nominated or recruited by the UN. Although routinely referred to as "international," it in fact also includes Cambodian nationals. The personnel working on the Cambodian side was appointed or recruited by the Cambodian government. At the height of its operations, the ECCC was employing up to 520 staff members (344 on the national side).[17] This number has been significantly reduced as the ECCC slowed down its work. The ECCC has been operating in Khmer, English, and French. This use of three official working languages was starkly underestimated in early budget provisions and contributed to significant delays in the Court's operation (Ciorciari and Heindel 2014, 96–97; Jarvis 2016).

In the pursuit of its mandate, the ECCC had authority to apply both national and international criminal law. Its substantive jurisdiction covered international crimes and domestic crimes.[18] As the first internationalized tribunal to investigate international crimes in the 1970s, the ECCC needed to fill a gap between the Nuremberg trials of the 1940s, which introduced the basic principles of modern international criminal law, and the international criminal tribunals for ex-Yugoslavia and Rwanda, which continued the development of international criminal law in the 1990s (Ciorciari and Heindel 2014, 50). A central aspect of the ECCC's work has thus been to determine what crimes were recognized in international customary law between 1975 and 1979, and whether crimes covered in the 1956 Cambodian Penal Code could still be tried, given its ten-year statute of limitations.

Regarding procedural law, Cambodian law prevailed, following the Cambodian government's insistence on domestic ownership. International law was only to provide guidance when the interpretation of Cambodian procedural law remained unclear, lied in opposition to international standards, or did not treat the specific questions raised at the ECCC. However, a comprehensive criminal code of procedure was only adopted in Cambodia in 2007, after the ECCC's establishment. A plenary session of national and international judicial officers therefore drafted and enacted Internal Rules in June 2007, and revised them nine times since.[19] This lack of clear procedures was criticized for significantly delaying the start of the ECCC's operations and later leading to challenges of the Internal Rules' legitimacy (see, e.g., Ciorciari and Heindel 2014, 59–69; Torrens 2016, 394–95).

Both the Internal Rules and the Cambodian criminal code of procedure draw from the French system, as Cambodia's judicial system originates in French colonial rule. The ECCC thus featured essential elements of the civil law system, including most prominently judicial investigation and civil party participation. The ECCC thereby became the first internationalized tribunal to allow victims to participate as civil parties, a feature discussed in greater length in chapter 3. Civil party status afforded victims the right to formally participate as parties in the proceedings and to seek collective and moral reparations. Over time, civil party rights would be increasingly curtailed, amid concerns of efficiency and equality of arms. Given the common law background of many international staff members and the inclusion of standards borrowed from the practice of other internationalized courts, the ECCC would also eventually adopt a "complicated mélange of civil law and common law practices" (Ryan and McGrew 2016, 19). This complexity led to conflicts between staff with different legal cultures and significant delays (see, e.g., Bates 2010, paras. 132–35; Ciorciari and Heindel 2014, 46–48; Torrens 2016, 402–6). In particular, the inclusion of co-investigating judges has been criticized for duplicating investigations and for being inadequate for mass atrocities trials.

At the ECCC, the office of the co-prosecutors, headed by a Cambodian and a foreign prosecutor, initiated proceedings by conducting preliminary investigations into crimes falling under the ECCC's jurisdiction. They made introductory submissions to the co-investigating judges, outlining the facts, suspects, and alleged offenses to be investigated.[20] The office of the co-investigating judges, also headed by a Cambodian and a foreign judge, could only investigate the facts included in these submissions. At the end of their judicial investigation, the co-prosecutors filed a final submission, requesting to send the case to trial or dismiss it. The co-investigating judges would then issue a closing order, deciding whether to indict the defendant or to dismiss the case.

The ECCC further consisted of three judicial chambers—the Pre-Trial Chamber, Trial Chamber, and Supreme Court Chamber—each staffed with a majority of Cambodians and a minority of foreign officials. As we have seen, a super-majority was required for any decisions to investigate, try, or convict. The Pre-Trial Chamber was responsible for resolving disagreements between the co-prosecutors or co-investigating judges, and additionally for hearing appeals by the parties of decisions of the co-prosecutors or co-investigating judges during the pre-trial phase. If the Pre-Trial Chamber judges failed to reach a super-majority vote, any proposed prosecution, investigation, or indictment was to proceed. The Trial Chamber was tasked with the conduct of trials and the pronouncement of judgments. The Supreme Court Chamber heard appeals from decisions and judgments of the Trial Chamber.

While nominally, the ECCC was part of the Cambodian court system, it was funded as a separate entity. By the end of October 2022, the ECCC had cost a total of US$337.8 million (ECCC 2022b). The ECCC's residual functions, expected to last for three years after completion of Case 002/02 proceedings, are estimated to cost an additional US$9 million.[21] The ECCC's overall budget therefore far exceeded the initial budget of 56.3 million USD planned for only three years of operations. By October 2022, the main donors having contributed to the ECCC's overall budget were Japan (27 percent), Cambodia (14 percent), Australia (11 percent), the US (10 percent) and the EU (10 percent), with European states also contributing bilaterally (ECCC 2022b).

Ahead of the ECCC's establishment, UN secretary-general Kofi Annan had advocated for a system of assessed contributions, given negative experiences made with voluntary contributions at the Special Court for Sierra Leone (UN Secretary-General 2003, paras. 74–75). The major UN donors ruled this option out, in fear of "being caught in ever spiraling demands for funds" as with the international criminal tribunals for ex-Yugoslavia and Rwanda (Jarvis 2016, 36).

As predicted, the reliance on voluntary contributions caused chronic financial crises and significantly delayed and affected its core judicial operations. Challenges to secure donor contributions arose in the context of the European debt crisis, the 2011 Japanese tsunami, and most recently the COVID-19 pandemic, as well as in relation to allegations of corruption and political interference at the ECCC (see, e.g., Wolfe-Robinson 2012; Ciorciari and Heindel 2014; Jarvis 2016; UN Secretary-General 2020). Donor conditionality and earmarking also made it difficult to process funds (Ciorciari and Heindel 2014, 101; Etcheson 2019). The Court resorted to various strategies to address funding shortages, including reducing weekly hearing days, letting go of staff, recruitment freezes, employing international judges part-time and remotely, or renewing contracts on a monthly or three-months basis only. This resulted in higher staff turnover, problematic losses in institutional memory, and a negative impact on "staff morale and health" (UN Secretary-General 2013, para. 30; see also Bates 2010, para. 33; Ciorciari and Heindel 2014, 100; Etcheson 2019). The Court's financial insecurity also led to resignations and strikes. This included a "work boycott" of interpreters in March 2013, during Case 002/1 trial hearings, and a large-scale walkout of 134 Cambodian staff in September 2013 after they had been working for months without pay (Crothers 2013; UN Secretary-General 2013). These were noticeable incidents of collective action when considering the CPP's control of domestic courts and routine repression of labor strikes. The ECCC's financial insecurity arguably also affected perceptions of the ECCC among the general population, as media coverage often focused on its difficulties to secure funding, thereby foregrounding its large budget in the Cambodian context.[22]

The ECCC funding scheme is also split along its national and UN components,[23] although disagreements arose regarding who was responsible for paying what (Jarvis 2016, 35–38). In the first years of operation, the Cambodian government refused to provide much funding besides its in-kind contributions.[24] Financial insecurity therefore particularly affected the national side until 2014. Donors repeatedly stepped in just before funds for the national side expired (Ciorciari and Heindel 2014, 98). In the first years of operation, 80 percent of the national side's budget was thereby funded by voluntary contributions (UN Secretary-General 2021, para. 25). Since 2014, perhaps in response to staff strikes and/or international pressure (Etcheson 2019), the Cambodian government finally increased its contributions. Between 2016 and 2021, it covered 70 percent of the budget of the national side, thereby eventually becoming the Court's second largest donor after Japan (UN Secretary-General 2021, para. 25).

From early on, it had been clear that the ECCC was working against time in a "race against mortality," given the aging suspects and Khmer Rouge survivors (Mydans 2006). Most of the senior DK leaders and those deemed to be most responsible for crimes committed under DK had died prior to the ECCC's establishment.[25] In July 2006, only eleven days after the ECCC's Office of the Co-prosecutors launched its work, Ta Mok died in a military hospital. In government custody since 1999, he was expected to become one of the ECCC's main defendants, as former CPK standing committee member and Southwest Zone secretary.

In the end, the ECCC opened investigations against a total of ten individuals, divided into four cases, known as Cases 001 through 004.[26] Only

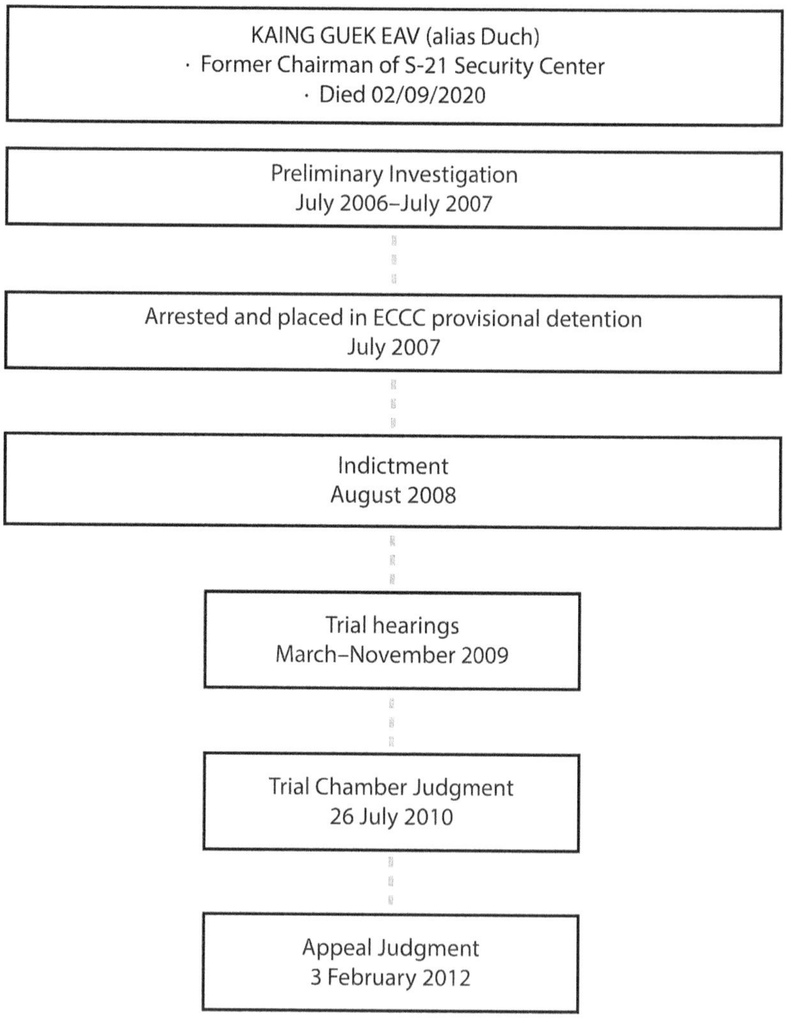

Chart 1. Case 001 timeline

two cases reached trial and three defendants died before completion of appeal proceedings.

Case 001 focused on Kaing Guek Eav, alias Duch, the former deputy chairman of the S-21 Khmer Rouge security center. The accused was charged with crimes against humanity and grave breaches of the 1949 Geneva Conventions, and the national crimes of premeditated murder and torture. Evidence hearings lasted from 30 March until 27 November 2009, featuring the testimonies of thirty-three witnesses and twenty-two civil parties, including from the Cambodian diaspora. As the Court's first case, it captured the attention of national and international media, as well as of national audiences. More than thirty-five thousand visitors attended the public trial proceedings in the courtroom's public gallery,[27] while trial summaries were broadcast weekly on one of Cambodia's largest television networks in the popular TV series *Duch on Trial* (Sperfeldt 2014).[28] Duch's case was unique in that after cooperating in the investigation, he also offered testimony on key factual issues during the trial. Up to the final days of the trial, he admitted his responsibility for many of the crimes charged, although he did so while minimizing his responsibility. In his closing statements, Duch surprisingly asked to be acquitted and released, leading to a split between his international and national defense lawyers. For the civil parties and their lawyers, this turnaround only confirmed their view that Duch's admissions of guilt during the trial had been insincere (Cruvellier 2011, 347–57).

On 26 July 2010, the Trial Chamber found Duch guilty of crimes against humanity and war crimes via direct and superior responsibility. The Trial Chamber sentenced Duch to thirty-five years in prison, to be reduced to nineteen years due to his time served in pre-trial detention in the Cambodian Military Court between 1999 and 2007 and violation of his fair trial rights during the unlawful pre-trial detention. Human Rights organizations, in particular the Cambodian Center for Human Rights (CCHR),[29] welcomed Duch's sentence reduction as setting an important precedent in the context of Cambodia's worrying pre-trial detention practices and disregard of fair trial rights (see also Soy and Hing 2019). Many civil parties and Cambodians felt the sentence to be far too lenient (see, e.g., Mydans 2010a; Pham et al. 2011). In February 2012, the Supreme Court Chamber issued its appeal verdict, extending Duch's sentence to life imprisonment. Civil parties and many Cambodians expressed their satisfaction over this increased sentence (see, e.g., Sirik 2012; Soy 2016). Observers, however, argued that the Chamber had given in to victims' expectations of a harsh punishment after reports of strong dissatisfaction in Cambodia and diaspora communities abroad. Human rights organizations also criticized the life sentence, with Amnesty International (2012) calling it "a case of public opinion trumping human rights." Regarding the issue of reparations, the Supreme

Court Chamber upheld the Trial Chamber's decision. Finding the accused to be indigent, it awarded only two reparation measures: the compilation and publication of statements of apology made by the accused during the trial, and the inclusion of civil parties' names and those of the immediate victims in the judgment. This decision was widely criticized for not being very creative or courageous and for not responding meaningfully to civil party requests (see, e.g., Ciorciari 2010; Kroker 2010).[30] Monitoring organizations nonetheless concluded that Duch's trial met basic international standards of due process (Ryan and McGrew 2016, 22). The trial also served as a testing ground for civil party participation. In 2013, Duch was transferred to the Kandal Provincial Prison, where he died in September 2020.

Case 002 has often been viewed as the ECCC's landmark case. It involves the most senior DK leaders still alive following Pol Pot's and Ta Mok's deaths and covers crimes that affected a very large number of victims throughout Cambodia. The accused initially indicted in September 2010 were Ieng Sary, former DK foreign minister; his wife, Ieng Thirith, former DK minister for

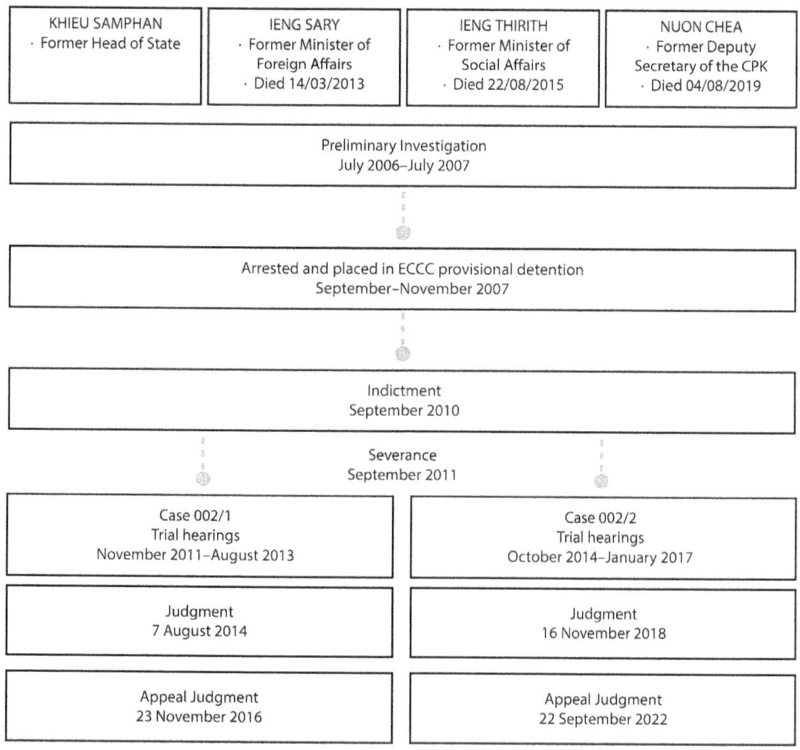

Chart 2. Case 002 timeline

social affairs; Nuon Chea, former CPK deputy secretary; and Khieu Samphan, former DK head of state. They were each charged for crimes against humanity, genocide, and grave breaches of the Geneva Conventions, as well as murder, torture, and religious persecution in violation of the 1956 Cambodian Penal Code. At the time of their indictment, the youngest of the four defendants was seventy-eight years old, the oldest eighty-five. From the start, Case 002 presented itself as much more challenging and complex than Case 001. The case is extremely large, even in comparison to cases at other international criminal courts. Less evidence connecting the accused to the alleged crimes was available than in Case 001. Moreover, none of the defendants ever admitted any responsibility for the crimes committed under their rule, instead blaming deviant elements and lower-level cadres. Their defense lawyers, in particular Nuon Chea's international lawyers, also adopted a much more disruptive approach than their peers in Case 001, drawing from Jacques Vergès's rupture strategy (Baaz and Lilja 2016; Hinton 2018, 40–59; Etcheson 2019; Hassellind and Baaz 2020). Finally, the previous deals the accused had engaged in with foreign powers and Hun Sen's government after the end of DK made this a more politically sensitive case. The 1996 royal pardon and amnesty granted to Ieng Sary also posed a jurisdictional challenge. Ieng Sary's defense team relentlessly raised this issue, however the Pre-Trial Chamber and Trial Chamber ruled that this did not prevent Ieng Sary's prosecution and trial.[31]

In September 2011, before the start of evidentiary hearings, the Trial Chamber severed the Case 002 trial into several portions.[32] Case 002/01 covered charges related to the April 1975 evacuation of Phnom Penh's population, subsequent forced population transfers in late 1975 and 1976, and targeting of former Khmer Republic officials for execution immediately after the Khmer Rouge seized power. Case 002/02 concerned crimes committed across Cambodia according to four CPK policies: the operation of cooperatives and worksites, the torture and execution of perceived enemies in security centers and execution sites, the persecution of specific groups (Buddhist monks, the Cham and Vietnamese, and officials of the former Lon Nol regime), and the regulation of marriage. Case 002/02 was therefore considered to be more representative of the harms suffered by many victims and thus believed to be of greater relevance to Cambodians (Ciorciari and Heindel 2014, 156).[33] In severing Case 002, the Trial Chamber aimed to expedite the proceedings and reach a verdict on at least some of the charges while the accused were still alive. This was, however, a controversial decision. According to trial monitors, the Trial Chamber's decision on severance led to lengthy trials in Case 002/01. It further led to procedural uncertainty, evidentiary confusion, bias against the accused, and a lack of representativity considering the enormity and gravity of DK crimes, especially if it were to remain the only case ever tried in Case 002 (Cohen, Hyde, and Van Tuyl 2015; Heindel 2016). By the time the Trial Chamber reached its judgment in August 2014, two defendants had been removed from trial. Ieng Thirith had been released in November 2011 after being declared unfit to stand trial because of Alzheimer's and died in August 2015. Her husband, Ieng Sary, died in ECCC detention in 2013.

In August 2014, the Trial Chamber unanimously found the remaining two accused, Nuon Chea and Khieu Samphan, guilty of crimes against humanity and sentenced them to life imprisonment. The UN, the Cambodian government, donor embassies, and NGOs welcomed the judgment (see, e.g., Saling 2014). Trial monitors criticized it for being poorly written and displaying "questionable foundations in law, an extremely weak approach to factual findings, and a totally misguided application of law to facts" (Cohen, Hyde, and Van Tuyl 2015, 41). The Trial Chamber endorsed eleven of the thirteen reparations measures requested by the civil party co-lead lawyers. In its appeal judgment of November 2016, the Supreme Court Chamber upheld the crimes against humanity conviction and life sentences for both accused. However, it reversed the conviction for extermination in relation to forced population movements and the conviction for persecution on political grounds. The Chamber further found the available evidence to be insufficient to establish the existence of a policy to kill Lon Nol regime soldiers and therefore ruled that the defendants could not be held criminally liable.

Evidentiary hearings in Case 002/02 started in October 2014. In November 2018, the Trial Chamber sentenced both accused to life imprisonment. Based on the doctrines of joint criminal enterprise, aiding and abetting, and superior responsibility, it convicted Nuon Chea of genocide against the Cham and Vietnamese minorities, war crimes, and crimes against humanity; and Khieu Samphan of all charges except for genocide against the Cham minority group, for which he was found to have lacked the relevant intent. The Trial Chamber further endorsed thirteen out of the fifteen reparation projects requested by civil parties and their lawyers. The Trial Chamber judgment was welcomed by the UN, the Cambodian government, donor embassies, and NGOs. It had been much awaited, particularly for its verdict on genocide and forced marriages.

The question of genocide has long been at the core of historiographical and legal debates on the Khmer Rouge regime (see, e.g., Vianney-Liaud 2016; Thun and Keo 2021; vs. Schabas 2001; Kiernan 2021; vs. Heder 1997; Stanton 2001; vs. Kiernan 1993). Despite civil party lawyers' attempts to broaden the charges to include genocide against the Khmer national group,[34] the Trial Chamber, following the co-prosecutors and co-investigating judges, only examined charges of genocide against the Cham Muslim (as an ethnic and religious group) and the Vietnamese (as an ethnic, national, and racial group).[35] This restrictive legal use differs from the widespread sociopolitical use of the term in Cambodia (Bernath 2018; Giry 2014). The Khmer term for "genocide" (ប្រល័យពូជសាសន៍) has indeed become a shorthand description for the population's suffering under the Khmer Rouge, while featuring at the heart of successive governmental policies ever since 1979. For those arguing for a broader interpretation of genocide charges, the Trial Chamber judgment is seen as a missed opportunity to give "their proper meaning" to the Khmer Rouge crimes.[36] Following the Trial Chamber verdict, many civil society actors, civil parties, Cambodians, and the Cambodian government remained undeterred in their broad use of the term "genocide."

Given the scant attention granted to sexual and gender-based crimes in Case 001 and Case 002/01,[37] the judgment was also awaited for its decision on forced marriages (De Langis 2014a; Elander 2018b). At first, sexual and gender-based violence remained largely invisible in the ECCC's investigations. It is only through the advocacy of civil party lawyers and civil society actors that sexual and gender-based crimes were belatedly included in Case 002 investigations, although only in the form of forced marriages and rape within forced marriages (Studzinsky 2011; E. Palmer and Williams 2017). Scholars and involved actors explained this invisibility by the prevalence of a myth that sexual and gender-based violence was absent or strongly punished under DK, the lack of gender balance and gender expertise among key ECCC international and national staff members, a focus on killings in the initial indictments, and the fact that some Cambodians—including ECCC national judges—who continue to live in these marriages until today did not necessarily perceive forced marriages as a crime (Studzinsky 2011; Lilja 2013; De Langis 2014b; Killean 2015; E. Palmer and Williams 2017; Grey 2019). The Trial Chamber's judgment on the nationwide policy of forced marriages was applauded for addressing marriage-related crimes nationally and against both male and female victims, although it was criticized for omitting sexual violence against men, forced pregnancies, and the experiences of gender-nonconforming persons (Grey 2019).

In August 2019, Nuon Chea died before the Supreme Court Chamber could reach its appeal judgment. On 22 September 2022, the Supreme Court Chamber upheld Khieu Samphan's life sentence and conviction for war crimes, crimes against humanity, and genocide against the ethnic Vietnamese. The Chamber further added the conviction of the crime against humanity of other inhumane acts through forced sexual intercourse in the context of forced marriages with regard to male victims. The judges thereby upheld the co-prosecutor's appeal of the Trial Chamber's failure to recognize sexual violence against male victims in forced marriages.

Case 002/02 was the last case to reach trial at the ECCC. Cases 003 and 004 have all been either dismissed or terminated by the end of 2021. As discussed in more detail in chapter 2, these cases featured at the heart of allegations of political interference. Case 003 initially included three suspects: Meas Muth, former commander of the DK navy; Sou Met, former commander of the DK air force; and Van Rith, former DK minister of commerce. Van Rith and Sou Met died in 2008 and 2013 respectively, before being charged at the ECCC. Case 004 focused on a group of second-rank provincial CPK leaders: Ao An, former deputy secretary of the Central Zone; Yim Tith, former acting secretary of the Northwest Zone; and Im Chaem, former district secretary in the Northwest Zone.

In 2015, the international co-investigating judge charged Meas Muth with genocide against the Vietnamese, crimes against humanity, war crimes, and murder; Im Chaem with crimes against humanity and murder; Ao An with genocide against the Cham, crimes against humanity, and murder; and Yim Tith with genocide against the Khmer Krom, crimes against humanity, war crimes, and murder. Among these charges, civil parties and their lawyers, NGO representatives, monitors, and scholars particularly welcomed those related to forced marriages and sexual and gender-based violence outside of forced marriages, including rape,[38] and the charges of genocide against the Khmer Krom (see, e.g., Crothers 2014; Ye 2014; Oosterveld and Viseur Sellers 2016). However, hopes that the ECCC could thereby redress its earlier failures to account for these crimes remained limited, given doubts that these cases would ever reach trial. In 2016, Case 004 was severed into Case 004 against Yim Tith, Case 004/1 against Im Chaem, and Case 004/2 against Ao An.[39] In February 2017, the international co-investigating judge finally dismissed the case against Im Chaem, agreeing with the national judges that Im Chaem fell outside the ECCC's personal jurisdiction. In the remaining cases, the national and international co-investigating judges maintained their disagreement and, in a scenario unforeseen by the Internal Rules, issued contradictory closing orders. The Cambodian judge dismissed the cases, while his international counterpart issued orders to send them to trial. After years of procedural deadlocks, the Supreme Court Chamber finally terminated the case against Ao An (Case 004/2) in August 2020, and the cases against Meas Muth (Case 003) and Yim Tith (Case 004) in December 2021, bluntly noting that "judicial purgatory is not an option."[40]

The completion of the appeal proceedings in Case 002/02 in 2022 thus signaled the end of the ECCC's main years of operation and its move toward its residual functions. These functions are outlined in the UN General Assembly resolution, sponsored by Cambodia and Australia, which was adopted in

July 2021.[41] The Addendum to the Agreement between the UN and the Cambodian government was promulgated into Cambodian law in November 2021. Planned for an initial period of three years, extendable upon agreement between the Cambodian government and the UN, the residual functions encompass the protection of victims and witnesses; the monitoring of enforcement of reparations awarded to civil parties; the enforcement of sentences and monitoring of the treatment of convicted prisoners; the maintenance, preservation, and management of its archives, including public access; and the dissemination of information to the public on the ECCC.

The ECCC in Political Context: Between Consolidation and Contestation of the Ruling Party

This final section turns to the Cambodian political context in which the ECCC has taken place, and implications for research on resistance. As this chapter has so far illustrated, when the negotiations for the establishment of the ECCC started in 1997, the country had already undergone significant political, social, and economic transformations since the fall of DK in 1979. Once established and operational, the ECCC's work unfolded in a dynamic context during which the CPP gradually consolidated its power and transitioned toward overt authoritarian practices, despite an intermittent and unprecedented episode of popular contestation in 2013–14.

Neopatrimonialism or the Co-optation of Cambodia's Multiple Transitions since 1991

Since the 1991 Paris Peace Agreements and subsequent UN peacebuilding mission, the CPP—more precisely Hun Sen—successfully co-opted the multiple transitions foreseen for Cambodia in the context of post–Cold War liberal interventionism: a transition from war to (negative) peace, from authoritarianism to liberal democracy, and from command economy to free market capitalism.

Regarding the country's transition from war to negative peace, as discussed above, in the aftermath of the Khmer Rouge's return to armed resistance and boycott of the 1993 UN-organized elections, the CPP secured the most important defections of senior former Khmer Rouge leaders and integrated them into its patronage networks. The CPP thereby successfully outmaneuvered the competing royalist party of FUNCINPEC from power and put an end to the civil war in 1998. Until today, Hun Sen's national reconciliation policy, the so-called win-win policy, provides the foundation for his and his party's claim to legitimacy for having achieved peace against all odds for the Cambodian people. Hun Sen was further able to consolidate his centralized control over the military forces, which prior to the 1997 coup were fragmented and included military loyal to FUNCINPEC or to other senior CPP members (Human Rights Watch 2018; Un 2019). Hun Sen also built his own military elite forces, consisting of a bodyguard unit of two thousand to four thousand soldiers answerable only to him, in addition to the reserve unit Brigade 70 of two thousand soldiers established in 1994 (Global Witness 2007; Morgenbesser 2018; Un 2019). In recent years, his personal control of the country's military forces has been increasingly visible. Senior commanders of the army and gendarmerie, for instance, have publicly pledged allegiance to him rather than the state after the 2013 elections (Human Rights Watch 2018, 29–30). Since 2015, there has also been a militarization of the CPP's Central Committee, while Hun Sen's sons have been appointed to key positions in the military as part of efforts to retain military power within his family (Loughlin 2021a). Any removal of Hun Sen and his dynasty from power thus comes with a tangible threat of civil war, as Hun Sen himself does not tire of repeating (Global Witness 2007; Un 2019).

Regarding the country's aimed transition from authoritarianism to democracy, the CPP successfully co-opted the executive, legislative, and judiciary organs to consolidate its power. Apart from the 1993 UN-organized national elections, the CPP repeatedly won elections until 2013. Research suggests that this success of the CPP at the polls was not only the expression of a preference of the electorate for the CPP's promise of political stability and economic development (Un 2011). Nor could it be only explained by specific political developments that took place ahead of the elections, such as, for example, the rise of nationalist anti-Thai sentiment at the height of the Preah Vihear border dispute, which the CPP captured in the 1998 elections (C. Hughes 2015a). The CPP's electoral victories are also attributed to its established practices of social control in rural areas, where the majority of the population lives; to its use of violence and tactics of fearmongering; and to vote-buying and other forms of electoral fraud in all elections (C. Hughes 2015a).

In 2013, the parliamentary elections suggested a break in the CPP's grip over the electorate. Ahead of the 2013 elections, the opposition parties—Kem Sokha's Human Rights Party and Sam Rainsy's Party—merged into the Cambodia National Rescue Party (CNRP). The CNRP won 44.5 percent of the votes (fifty-five seats at the National Assembly), while the CPP secured 49 percent of the votes (sixty-eight seats). For the first time, the political opposition, because it was unified, could seriously challenge the CPP at the polls (C. Hughes 2015a).

As the CNRP rejected the election results for alleged electoral fraud, the elections were followed by unprecedented and largely unforeseen public protests, which took place over several weeks in 2013, mainly in Phnom Penh.[42] These demonstrations were the public expression of discontent over critical issues involving the CPP—including corruption, land disputes, deforestation, socio-economic inequalities, and lack of government services—which Cambodians had become aware of at an unprecedented scale through increasing access to internet and social media (Un 2019). The protests also reflected the demographic change that had taken place. In 2013, an estimated 1.5 million young Cambodians were eligible to vote for the first time (McCargo 2014; C. Hughes 2015a; Un 2019). This younger population does not buy into the CPP's decade-old rhetoric of bringing peace after the Khmer Rouge (McCargo 2014). It encompasses urban workers, a highly mobile population who is able to escape the CPP's social-control strategies in rural areas (McCargo 2014; C. Hughes 2015a; Un 2019). Garment workers indeed played a key role in the contestation of CPP power in the wake of the 2013 contested elections, successfully transforming localized grievances into a coordinated, nation-wide movement (Lawreniuk 2020). These unprecedented demonstrations led to emboldened hopes for political change through a "Cambodian Spring." However, the protests and a unified CNRP opposition failed to undermine the CPP's and Hun Sen's hold onto power. The CPP reacted with the use of violence and tactics of coercion and consent. Since then, it has turned to increasingly overt repressive practices. These have included the "weaponization" of the judiciary,[43] the use of the legislative to crack down on independent media and civil society, and the authoritarian co-optation of digital space (see, e.g., Un 2019; Beban, Schoenberger, and Lamb 2020). Ahead of the 2018 parliamentary elections, the CPP neutralized the political opposition. The CPP-controlled Supreme Court dissolved the CNRP, arrested and exiled its leaders and banned 118 parliamentarians from any political activity for a period of five years. Unsurprisingly, Hun Sen emerged victorious at the ballots, the CPP capturing 77.5 percent of the votes and claiming all 125 National Assembly seats.

Finally, the transition from command economy to free market capitalism has also been central to the CPP's consolidation of power, even though it has often merely been considered as "a function of the country's political trajectory" (C. Hughes 2003, 19). Already in 1979, Hun Sen cultivated the loyalty of state officials and anticipated economic liberalization to allow the political elite to maintain its power after the withdrawal of the Vietnamese and after UNTAC's arrival (Gottesman 2004, 277). The economic reforms that Hun Sen promoted did not correspond to market capitalism but to "a kind of state capitalism in which [state] officials were prone to consider the resources at their disposal—land, factory parts, timber, vehicles, soldiers—as assets to be exploited for profit" (300). As a result, the transition to market economy has been both brutal and predatory: "Elite groups and foreign investors associated with the military and the state" have devastated the country's natural resources and dispossessed large parts of the population by violent means (C. Hughes 2015b, 128). A particular vivid example of this is the illegal trade in timber, through which the political elite, the army, and police forces, as well as local authorities, destroyed Cambodia's primary tropical forests for personal enrichment and the consolidation of power (Le Billon 2002; Global Witness 2007). Since the early 2000s, the country's economy has moved away from such a short-term, "asset-stripping rationale of a post-conflict economy" characterized by "illicit conflict trades in timber, gems and narcotics" (C. Hughes and Un 2011, 9). It has embraced "more respectable" industries and services with the country's increasing integration into regional and global markets. But Prime Minister Hun Sen continues to use the economy to strengthen his power through the extension of his patronage networks into the private sector. This can be seen in the proliferation of the title of Oknha (ឧកញ៉ា) since its reintroduction in the 1990s, which signifies a deepening of intra-elite patronage networks between the CPP leadership and the business elite, often based on family ties (Verver and Dahles 2014).[44] The title of Oknha is granted by the king to Cambodian businesspeople identified by the CPP leadership as contributing at least US$500,000 to national development projects.[45] This system allows the CPP elite to enrich itself, finance the state apparatus, and buy political legitimacy from the rural population (Verver and Dahles 2014). In recent years, foreign direct investment from China has increasingly played a role as an avenue for elite patronage (Loughlin 2021a).

In light of these developments since the 1993 UN-organized elections, political scientists have read Cambodia's political trajectory in relation to the contestation of transitology and the transitions paradigm that accompanied the initial study of the "third wave of democratizations." Discussions often revolved around the "gray zone" Cambodia has found itself in, after the disillusion of the post–Cold War liberal promises of a linear transition from authoritarianism and dictatorship to liberal democracy (Carothers 2002; Diamond 2002). One strand of analysis has drawn upon the notion of hybridity to characterize Cambodia's political system after 1993 and until the early 2010s. Here, reference is mainly made to postcolonial debates on hybridity that draw upon Homi Bhabha's or Iris Marion Young's work (Lilja 2010), and the subsequent use of the concept of hybridity in critiques of the liberal peace (Öjendal and Lilja 2009; Öjendal and Ou 2013), rather than to discussions on hybridity in typologies of transitional regimes. For these scholars, characterizing Cambodia as a "hybrid political system" allowed them to make sense of the contradictions of its trajectory since the 1991 Peace Agreements, with, on the one hand, the end of civil war, relative political stability, economic growth and constitutional democracy; and on the other hand, sustained human rights violations and intermittent political violence, social inequalities, weak governance and patronage (Öjendal and Ou 2013, 370–71). This notion further captured the necessary friction and subfrictions that came with a massive peacebuilding intervention such as UNTAC. Other scholars have assessed political developments in Cambodia as variations in degrees of "electoral authoritarianism"—for example, from "unstructured competitive authoritarianism" to "hegemonic party authoritarianism" (Un 2011, 2019). The 2018 elections, in which the CPP competed effectively unopposed, has been seen as signaling "a new era of hegemonic authoritarian rule" (Loughlin and Norén-Nilsson 2021, 225).

What clearly emerges from the CPP's co-optation of the country's multiple transitions since 1991 is that the consolidation of CPP power is entrenched in the deployment of patron-client relationships, which pervade and structure the state, society, and the economy. From this perspective, Cambodia's political system can be described as one of neo-patrimonialism. Neo-patrimonialism refers to a system of organization that relies upon both the existence of formal, bureaucratic state institutions, which give the appearance of legal and rational bureaucracy, and informal networks of patron-clientelism, which determine where state power truly lies (Gottesman 2004; Heder 2005; Hinton 2005, 100–116; Pak et al. 2007; Un 2011). Patronage bonds, which are "informal, uncodified and unpoliced policies" (Un 2011, 548), determine how power is built, perpetuated, and legitimized and run parallel to the realm of legally based and transparent policies, which the government rhetorically commits to (see also Pak 2011, 3). In such a regime, distinctions between the public and private realm, as well as among supposedly separate organs of government—the executive, legislative, judiciary, military—become blurred (Young 2021).

In his ethnographic work on Southeast Asia, Scott (1972, 93) provided the following seminal definition of patron-client relationships: "[A] special case of dyadic (two person) ties involving a largely instrumental friendship in which an individual of higher social-economic status (patron) uses his influence and resources to provide protection or benefits, or both, for a person of lower status (client) who, for his part, reciprocates by offering general support and assistance, including personal services to [the] patron."

These unequal, yet complementary, relationships are embedded in the disparities in relative wealth, power, and status that are present in society (Scott 1972, 92–93). In Cambodia, these relationships are commonly referred to as a *khsae* (ខ្សែ), or network (literally, a string or rope), with a *khnâng* (ខ្នង), or patron (literally, a back). Inherently instrumental, since mainly driven toward exchange and wealth accumulation, patron-client relationships are also underpinned by interpersonal obligations and affections based on personal loyalties, friendships, and kinships (Pak et al. 2007, 39–42).

The legitimacy of such unequal relationships arguably draws from religious understandings of social positioning. In particular, the central Buddhist notion of *karma*—that is, the sum of one's good and bad deeds in current, previous and future lives—implies a belief that "merit accumulated in previous lives [goes] a long way toward explaining a person's social position" (Chandler 1991, 4; see also Jacobsen and Stuart-Fox 2013). This does not exclude forms of constraints and accountability. In the Cambodian context, this reciprocity is arguably derived from the Buddhist notion of *dharma*—that is, the prescribed duty for a person of high status to act as a generous and righteous leader in redistributing goods and providing protection to his client (Ledgerwood 2002).

Drawing out how patron-client relationships function through cultural and religious practices of meaning-making does not mean that patron-client relationships are an ingrained, monostructural, cultural feature that has homogenously existed across time. Patron-clientelism networks instead constitute a "dynamic institution" (Un 2019, 6), even though they are historically rooted in Cambodia in precolonial and religious traditions, and shaped power in previous regimes such as the Sangkum Reastr Niyum (1955–70), the Lon Nol rule (1970–75) or the PRK (1979–89) (see, e.g., Gottesman 2004; Hinton 2005; Jacobsen and Stuart-Fox 2013).

Scholarship on Cambodia highlights the transformations that the institution of patron-client relationship has undergone over time. First, research shows that patron-client relationships have been significantly affected by the decades of conflict since the 1970s. Heightened security threats have, for instance, led to stronger needs for a patron for ordinary citizens, as well as to an increased exposure to coercion, given the limited availability of options for investing into relationships with a patron (Pak et al. 2007). Second, with the deployment of modern tactics of power, patron-client relationships have been reinvented by those in power in such a way as to disempower the population with respect to its own cultural traditions. As Caroline Hughes (2006, 470–71) has shown, the CPP has rationalized patron-client relationships as "a means of domination operating across the national territory and placed at the service of the Cambodian state," which precisely plays upon the "familiarity and persuasiveness" of traditional forms of political relation yet differ substantially from them in that they are "not open for negotiation." With Hun Sen's increased concentration of power since 1993, patron-client relationships, while remaining localized and personal, have become harnessed under the umbrella of the CPP into "a national system of effective and symbolic power, encompassing the military and the government, with the 'strongman,' Hun Sen, at the head" (C. Hughes 2003, 215–16). This system builds upon the CPP political elite's and Hun Sen's narratives of moral legitimacy and "righteous leadership" (see, e.g., Norén-Nilsson 2016, 39–64; Petersson 2021). This system has resulted in a "systematic and nation-wide policy of exclusion of both rival members of the elite and marginalized sections of the poor from engagement in political and economic life" (C. Hughes 2003, 215–16). Finally, patron-client relationships have been constantly redefined in interaction with domestic and international economic and political changes. Sedara Kim (2012) has argued that the increased importance of linkages beyond the village for a patron's power and wealth accumulation has led to patrons becoming less responsive to their clients. Joakim Öjendal and Kim (2006) have shown how the introduction of democratic decentralization processes led to a renegotiation of the expected attitudes of respect, admiration, and fear toward patrons and local authorities. Neoliberal globalization has also significantly shaped patron-clientelism, with patronage ties increasingly extending to external economic actors (Un 2019; Young 2021).

The Study of Resistance in Cambodia's Political Context

These insights are important for the purposes of this book, which is to understand the politics of transitional justice in Cambodia through the lens of resistance. Reflecting upon how power differentials are embedded in culture (C. Hughes and Öjendal 2006) can provide deeper insights into the "forms, moments and absences" of resistance (Ortner 1995, 183), or help avoid framing acts in terms of a ready-made politics of opposition, which privileges Western individualist ideologies of self (Hoffman 1999). Understanding how features of the political context and culture are mobilized and reinvented can thus address critiques that studies of resistance tend to be ethnographically thin (Ortner 1995). This is even more important for the study of resistance in the Cambodian context since, until recently, essentialized approaches to Cambodian culture and a lack of research on the agency of the ordinary citizen have led to little research and understandings of existing practices of resistance.

Research on Cambodia has long been defined by monolithic and static approaches equating Cambodian culture with the characteristics of unquestioned obedience to authoritarian rule, docility, excessive deference, and conservatism (C. Hughes and Öjendal 2006). Caroline Hughes (2003, 25), for instance, observed a tendency, in research on the 1980s and the PRK, to "view the Cambodian population as oppressed by a powerful and overbearing state."

This dismisses the fact that despite limited "organized social forces that openly opposed the constitution or policy making of the 1980s state or party from within the territory under Phnom Penh's control," the PRK nonetheless faced "considerable, if diffuse, resistance, sufficient to derail economic policies and to perpetuate state vulnerability to external attack" (C. Hughes 2003, 25). In some academic works, the impression even emerges that Cambodia's tragic decades of war, violence, authoritarian and even totalitarian rule could be "understood as a 'natural' consequence of this culturally defined history" (Öjendal and Kim 2006, 508). This is closely linked to the long neglect of the agency of the vast majority of the population—peasants—in many discussions of political and economic development, which ultimately led to a denial of their "ability or desire to change" (C. Hughes and Öjendal 2006, 417). Questions of whether these essentialized characteristics of a "Cambodian culture" enabled war, violence, and authoritarian and totalitarian rule, or instead were reinforced as a result thereof, become entangled in a problematic circular rationality.

Such readings of Cambodian culture do not enable us to grasp the profound social and political changes that have been ongoing in contemporary Cambodia (Öjendal and Kim 2006, 508), as well as the extent to which Cambodian culture always "was, and remains, a dynamic field of change" (Edwards 2007, 8). Such approaches are also problematic as they are instrumental to the legitimation of foreign interventions. Portrayals of Cambodians as "changeless, suspended in cultural time and political space" have been central to colonial propaganda under the French protectorate (9), not least because the portrayal of Cambodians as inherently docile "suited the French colonial administration" (Chandler 2018, 3). Such a framing of Cambodia's population, in connection with characterizations of the country in a "post-conflict context" (Öjendal and Kim 2006) or as a "fragile state," have also participated in its pathologization (C. Hughes and Pupavac 2005), which ultimately serves to justify and define external interventions of social engineering. The misappreciation of, and blindness toward, everyday resistance of so-called ordinary citizens can also be linked to an unequivocal endorsement of external interventions. It leads to locating the limits of development or peace only at the domestic level, rather than the international level. As Hughes and Öjendal (2006, 417) have argued, for instance, framing the reluctance of rural Cambodians to enthusiastically rally around participatory development projects as merely "fatigue" and withdrawal from the opportunity of political reform conceals the ways in which their reluctance can be "an expression of 'everyday resistance' to external politics that do not make sense to the rural population."

More recent scholarship on Cambodia has moved away from such essentialized approaches to culture, as the study of agency, activism, protests, social movements, and resistance emerged as a burgeoning field of interdisciplinary research since the 2010s. Resistance has most prominently been studied in relation to land conflicts (see, e.g., Diepart, Ngin, and Oeur 2019; Young 2021). Scholars have examined grassroots movements' alliances with civil society organizations (Norén-Nilsson and Bourdier 2019; Young 2019); the transnational dimensions of contestations in the context of a globalized world, neoliberalism, and international interventions (Hennings 2018; Young 2019); or the gendered effects of resistance (see, e.g., Brickell 2014; Lamb et al. 2017; Hennings 2019). This scholarship on land conflicts also includes ethnographic works. These offer rich accounts of how the layering of the past—in particular, the Khmer Rouge past—and the present can reinforce subjective experiences of intense fear and inhibit resistance (see, e.g., Schoenberger and Beban 2018), or to the contrary provide individual motivations to resist (see, e.g., Brickell 2014). Scholarship on resistance, protests, and social movements in Cambodia has further explored labor activism (Arnold 2017; Arnold and Chang 2017; Lawreniuk and Parsons 2018) and its crucial role in the unprecedented protests following the 2013 elections (Lawreniuk 2020). It also covers, for example, the study of resistance to gendered norms (Lilja 2013), community activism for LGBT rights (Hoefinger, Ly, and Srun 2017), or civil society resistance in the Preah Vihear border conflict (Baaz and Lilja 2017). Taken together, this body of research demonstrates the existence of diverse forms of resistance and activism: from discursive and everyday resistance to public protests, or provocative and violent confrontations with state authorities and security forces. This certainly questions earlier accounts of Cambodians as essentially passive and docile. Some of this research also considers the specific context of neo-patrimonialism. Sokphea Young's work (2020, 2021) in particular shows how the success or failure of social movements to reach their goals depends on whether they target actors strongly embedded in CPP patron-client networks or actors with weak ties to the CPP political elite.

In this book, I draw from this dynamic field of interdisciplinary research. My approach nonetheless differs to the extent that I analyze the resistance of a larger set of actors, rather than only that of "ordinary citizens" or activists engaged in struggles against abusive actors in a neo-patrimonial and authoritarian context. This derives from my specific object of enquiry. Studying resistance in the context of transitional justice interventions requires moving beyond the diametrically opposed moral economies of resistance studies and transitional justice studies (see also Arnould 2016). On the one hand, resistance studies often see resistance as emancipatory and as a part of struggles against inequality, even though geographies and anthropologies of resistance have increasingly examined the ambiguities of resistance and the mutual imbrication of power and resistance in the wake of critiques of the romanticization of resistance (Abu-Lughod 1990; Ortner 1995; Brown 1996; Moore 1998; Hollander and Einwohner 2004). On the other hand, normative approaches to transitional justice will often cast resistance to these processes as necessarily problematic and deviant, as these approaches start from the premise that transitional justice processes are inherently "doing good" (Jones and Bernath 2017). Those resisting transitional justice are usually seen as powerful spoilers who have something to lose, or perhaps victims who become labeled as "recalcitrant" or "bad" for not being able to let go of the past and reconcile.

The following chapters do not exclusively embrace either one or the other of these normative approaches, which tend to either glorify or condemn resistance. Instead, the next chapters take a step back to study resistance from a varied set of actors: the CPP political elite and national staff members at the ECCC, survivors of the Khmer Rouge participating as civil parties in the trial proceedings, and finally, citizens engaged in struggles against CPP power, albeit not participating in the transitional justice process.

2

The Khmer Rouge Tribunal

Patronage, Coercion, and Pragmatism

Ever since the complicated negotiations between the UN and the Cambodian government to establish a Khmer Rouge tribunal, resistance to transitional justice in Cambodia has been primarily associated with the ruling party's attempts to control the tribunal and to limit its scope. Senior officials of the Cambodian People's Party (CPP) have repeatedly, often provocatively, expressed their opposition to a far-reaching transitional justice process at the ECCC. The CPP's resistance has come into play when the ECCC threatened to expose the Khmer Rouge past of senior CPP officials—by summoning them as witnesses—and to expand the scope of investigations to a larger number of suspects. CPP officials also vehemently opposed Cases 003 and 004, arguing that these prosecutions could lead former Khmer Rouge members to take up arms again, and thereby threaten peace, security, and national reconciliation. Over time, Cambodian officials in the ECCC's administrative and judicial offices have echoed the government's positions.

Scholars, rights activists, as well as senior UN-appointed staff at the ECCC considered that a return to civil war was not a realistic scenario. Analysts have therefore generally offered two explanations for CPP's resistance: senior CPP officials' previous involvement in the Khmer Rouge political and military chains of responsibility, and the consolidation of CPP power in the 1990s through the co-optation of Khmer Rouge leaders into its patronage networks (see, e.g., Giry 2012; Path 2017; Etcheson 2019; Gidley 2019). CPP's resistance to an in-depth transitional justice process has been seen as illustrating concerns that internationals at the ECCC could investigate suspects linked to the CPP government—directly charging senior CPP officials or revealing their Khmer Rouge past. An in-depth transitional justice process on the Khmer Rouge regime could thereby unsettle the CPP's power as well as its claims to legitimacy, as these have consistently relied on a glorification of its role as "savior" of Cambodia from the devastating Khmer Rouge rule.

This chapter analyzes CPP resistance at the ECCC, drawing from various sources. Concrete evidence supporting allegations of political interference has been difficult to obtain when it first emerged. This was due to the confidential nature of the investigations, as well as the fact that those at the source of such allegations were often not able to share evidence publicly or to disclose their identities for fear of personal or political repercussions,[1] as well as fear of providing ammunition to defense lawyers in Case 002 who would use it in their combative strategy of rupture. In this context, trial monitors, commentators, rights activists, and scholars often relied upon so-called circumstantial evidence and drew comparisons with the domestic judiciary (see, e.g., DeFalco 2018; West 2019). Public statements of senior CPP officials on the ECCC's work particularly fueled allegations of political interference, as in domestic courts, such declarations are "followed to the letter" and amount to instructions to judicial officials.[2] Interference was further deducted from the alignment of the ECCC national prosecutor's and judges' decisions with the government's positions, as well as from the similarity in the reasoning and justifications provided (see, e.g., OSJI 2011b, 11–12). Over time, a few UN-appointed staff at the ECCC commented on these allegations, either publicly or in conversations later leaked to the press. Former staff members have also published accounts of their work at the ECCC, thereby offering insights into CPP control of key offices at the ECCC. This includes Marcel Lemonde's 2013 book on his tenure as international co-investigating judge (2006–10), as well as Craig Etcheson's 2019 book, which features insights from his time as chief of investigations for the Office of Co-prosecutors (2006–12). This chapter relies on these sources, as well as on trial monitoring and media reports, academic works, public and recently declassified ECCC documents, and speeches of CPP officials. It also draws from qualitative interviews with Cambodian and UN-appointed ECCC staff and civil society actors conducted between 2013 and 2022.

The chapter is organized into three sections. The first section analyzes the discursive nature of CPP resistance against a far-reaching transitional justice process at the ECCC. It locates statements made on the ECCC, especially by the prime minister, within the larger context of discursive claims for legitimacy developed by the CPP and the prime minister during the ECCC's existence. The second section moves to the ECCC legal proceedings as a site of CPP resistance. It focuses on the two instances at the core of allegations of CPP interference: resistance to senior CPP officials providing testimonies as witnesses in Case 002, and resistance to the extension of the list of suspects beyond those in Cases 001 and 002. The third section asks what this resistance tells us about power structures within the hybrid setting of the ECCC. Examining the ECCC as a site of CPP resistance shows the Court's entrenchment within existing neo-patrimonial power structures, as national staff members faced similar patterns of CPP control and constraint as in the national judiciary. However, the story of CPP resistance at the ECCC is also one of compromise and pragmatism from international actors invested and investing in the ECCC. This analysis therefore questions simplistic binaries of internationals actors pursuing justice versus domestic justice spoilers.

The Ruling Party's Discursive Resistance

Public comments of high-level CPP figures have been a key feature of the CPP resistance to the ECCC. However, these comments have most often been interpreted merely as an indication for political interference at the ECCC, rather than being analyzed as part of the CPP's discursive claims for power and legitimacy. This section proposes an analysis of the CPP's discursive resistance within the larger context of statements given on the ECCC. It draws primarily on speeches delivered by Prime Minister Hun Sen between the ECCC's establishment in 2004 and the ECCC final verdict in September 2022.[3] These speeches were given during various public events such as international conferences, graduation ceremonies, or the inauguration of company buildings and construction sites. This analysis shows that Hun Sen's discursive resistance to Cases 003 and 004 and its emphasis on peace has been part of a peace narrative that glorifies not only the party as savior of the Cambodian nation but also, more recently, himself as "father of peace." This resistance is thereby part of the prime minister's claims for legitimacy against competing political rivals within and without the CPP, as well as toward the UN and foreign powers intervening in Cambodia.

Consecrating the CPP as "Savior of the Nation" and Hun Sen as "Father of Peace"

As discussed in chapter 1, the CPP government's opposition to a long list of suspects had already been a matter of concern for the UN during the negotiations for the ECCC's establishment. After the ECCC was established, senior CPP officials repeatedly voiced their opposition to Cases 003 and 004. This includes Prime Minister Hun Sen, Council of Ministers spokesperson Phay Siphan, Minister of Information Khieu Khanarith, late senate and CPP president Chea Sim, and foreign minister Hor Nam Hong (see, e.g., OSJI 2011b, 11–13; Ciorciari and Heindel 2014, 177). Hun Sen voiced his opposition in diverse arenas such as speeches and bilateral diplomatic meetings, as, for instance, in France in July 2009 with President Nicolas Sarkozy (Lemonde 2013, 205). Most notably, during a visit by UN secretary-general Ban Ki-Moon in Phnom Penh in the autumn of 2010, which reportedly left the secretary-general furious (Etcheson 2019), Hun Sen informed him that "Case 003 will not be allowed [. . .] The court will try the four senior leaders successfully and then finish with Case 002" (Sokha and O'Toole 2010).

The main argument put forward by the prime minister and CPP officials is that any prosecutions beyond Cases 001 and 002 would cause unrest or even civil war and disrupt peace, stability, national unity, and national reconciliation. In September 2009, for instance, Hun Sen warned of a return to a war that would kill between two and three hundred thousand people if the ECCC would neglect "national reconciliation and peace" when trying the Khmer Rouge.[4] Years later, Hun Sen still made similar comments. In February 2015, a few days before the international co-investigating judge charged two of the suspects in absentia, he observed in "off the cuff comments" on the ECCC: "Now that the trial of the regime is underway, they have expanded their work almost to scare people to run back into [the] forest. Please think about the value of peace and human life. If the war were to come back, how many would die?"[5]

Evocations of a risk of a return to civil war cannot be taken lightly. With his comments, the prime minister tapped into fears of a return of war, which were tangible among Khmer Rouge survivors during the negotiations for the establishment of the tribunal, and in early years of the ECCC's operation (see, e.g., Ly 2017, 173). However, such fears did not translate into a general lack of support for additional prosecutions at the ECCC. In the survey we conducted in 2018 with 439 respondents who had participated to varying degrees in the transitional justice process, we found that 80.2 percent supported the completion of Cases 003 and 004 (Williams et al. 2018, 63; see also Chy 2009).

In fact, the threat of civil war is a rhetorical trope of the CPP's self-legitimation discourses. Ever since the 1979 ousting of the Khmer Rouge from central power, the ruling party has portrayed itself as "liberator" of the country from the grip of the murderous Khmer Rouge, while silencing the involvement of CPP officials in that regime, as well as in violations that took place after. The CPP thereby claims legitimacy for having defeated the Khmer Rouge regime through armed rebellion, and for having achieved peace through its "win-win policy." These discourses portray the CPP as the "savior" of the country from the genocidal and murderous Khmer Rouge. But they also equate any alternative to CPP rule with insecurity, chaos, or a return of war. Emphasizing peace is a way to deflect any criticism directed to the CPP (see, e.g., Ngoun 2022). This is also a strategy used regarding criticism of the CPP's role at the ECCC. In May 2006, for instance, following NGO criticism of the appointment of Cambodian judges at the ECCC, Hun Sen rebutted that trying the Khmer Rouge was only possible because of his success in defeating the Khmer Rouge in the first place: "The process does not start right here in 2006, but from the time when Cambodia was liberated from the genocide. [. . .] As we are to try the Khmer Rouge, again some people are judgmental on [the] issue of guaranteeing justice. As I said the trial has been a new progress on the foundation achieved from the previous stage—the source of the current achievement. If one neglects its source, one would not be any different from animals that do not know where they are from and where they are going."[6]

Analysts have argued that the CPP's self-legitimation discourse has outlasted its relevance as new generations, not yet alive during the Khmer Rouge regime, outnumbered their elders who had personally experienced Khmer Rouge rule and decades of war. This has been interpreted as having contributed to the erosion of political support for the CPP and the unprecedented contestation surrounding the 2013 national elections (McCargo 2014; Strangio 2014b). Nonetheless, the CPP continued to hold onto these legitimacy claims, although it developed strategies to adapt these in its targeted efforts to mobilize the youth population (M. Vong 2022). The CPP's self-legitimation discourse is rehearsed during electoral campaigns and ritually performed around key dates such as that of January 7 (as discussed in greater detail in chapter 4). An explanation often put forward for the CPP's resistance to Cases 003 and 004 is thus that it aims at preventing an erosion of its savior's discourse.[7] Prosecutions of Khmer Rouge cadres further down the hierarchy in Democratic Kampuchea, even if not directly targeting senior CPP officials as suspects at the ECCC, could uncover their involvement in atrocities committed under Democratic Kampuchea. This could affect popular support and lead voters to cast their ballots for the political opposition.

Despite the CPP's persistent hold onto power, its constant quest for legitimacy should not be underestimated (Ngoun 2022). Highlighting the Khmer Rouge past of senior CPP officials, as well as their responsibility for human rights violations in the 1980s and 1990s, has certainly played a key role in electoral and party politics. It has been a common feature of opposition politicians' attempts—particularly Sam Rainsy's—at discrediting the CPP, including through the combative use of various legal and judicial avenues abroad.[8] The

CPP government countered with defamation lawsuits, characteristic of its instrumentalization of the domestic judiciary. The political history of the ECCC's establishment had also been accompanied by speculations over who within the CPP political elite a Khmer Rouge tribunal could indict. For instance, a Resolution submitted to the US Congress in December 1998 by a Republican Congressman representing an area featuring the largest Cambodian diaspora in the US claimed that Hun Sen, as one of the "leaders of the Cambodian genocide," should be indicted for genocide and crimes against humanity before an international tribunal—claims that were refuted by Cambodian genocide scholars (J. Smith 1998). Such speculations, perceived as character assassinations of key CPP leaders, fueled concerns that the Khmer Rouge tribunal would be used to undermine the CPP's hold onto power in Cambodia (Fawthrop and Jarvis 2004, 151–53). After the ECCC's establishment, foreign lawyers who had been involved at the ECCC as international defense lawyers, also used legal avenues outside of Cambodia to address crimes committed by the CPP government in recent decades. In 2014 and 2015, Richard Rogers submitted an article 15 communication to the Prosecutor of the International Criminal Court with the support of the International Federation for Human Rights (FIDH) and Global Witness. They argue that in pursuing its "twin-objectives of self-enrichment and maintaining power at all costs," the crimes committed by the "Ruling Elite" in its land grabbing since 2002 amounted to crimes against humanity (Global Diligence 2014).

In this context, Sorpong Peou (2018) has argued that the CPP's opposition to a far-reaching criminal accountability process at the ECCC reflects its deep sense of insecurity and fear of (actual or perceived) retribution. The threat of judicial punishment only plays into the CPP's deep-seated "politics of survival." The CPP further consolidates its power and control over security forces and the judiciary to avoid contestation of its rule and any transfer of its power, although these security politics often tend to be underestimated (Peou 2017).

The CPP's discursive portrayal of the pursuit of Cases 003 and 004 at the ECCC as a threat to peace, however, has not only been tied to its self-legitimation claims as savior of the nation. It has also featured in Hun Sen's efforts to glorify himself as "father of peace." While arguing that Cases 003 and 004 could pose a threat to peace, Hun Sen portrays himself as the main architect of peace, national unity, and stability. He foregrounds his role in the past, in personally ending civil war through his successful "win-win policy," and also positions himself as the sole guarantor for peace in Cambodia's present and future. In his September 2009 speech, Hun Sen, for instance, highlighted how he had been ready to sacrifice his own life to secure "peace and national unity":

> In [the] context of a fragile peace if trial of the Khmer Rouge were to be conducted in negligence of national reconciliation and peace, and if another war were to take place, who would stand to be responsible? Would some people who made comments [. . .] about this be staying and dying in Cambodia if such a war takes place? It was the opposition who had challenged many junior leaders of the Khmer Rouge that it would soon be their turn to get arrested at the time when their top leaders like Nuon Chea and Khieu Samphan were taken into custody. If they were to take to the forest, this time who is going to call them off? I have traded my life for this land. My mother and my aunt warned me of going into the Khmer Rouge controlled area as though I was not afraid of death. I explained them if I were to die, only a few people died with me but *if I were to survive, the whole country will get the land back and be united. I have done this with success. I would not stand to let this land be destroyed or this people be brought to instability at all.* The prize of peace is enormous, while justice is being sought for within a justifiable legal framework. [. . .] *I am to defend the country's peace and to allow no one to destroy it.*[9]

In December 2021, amid debates on the nature of peace achieved thirty years after the Paris Peace Agreements, Hun Sen similarly framed his opposition to further prosecutions at the ECCC as a measure to defend his "hard-won peace." He therefore recalled a conversation with the UN secretary-general held at the so-called Peace Palace, the Office of the Prime Minister inaugurated in 2010:

> What has been the driving force that attracts favorable investment and growth of our country? It is the hard-won peace factor. We must not overlook and/or allow anyone to destroy it. [. . .] Our country has already had enough experience of losing peace. [. . .] *What I must do first is ensuring the right to life.* With this right to life ensured, we must not allow this country to fall into war. That is why I always say that we must maintain peace at all costs.
>
> [. . .] The UN Secretary-General Ban Ki-moon during his visit to Cambodia [in 2010], he spoke about this and that, in connection with the imminent hybrid tribunal. I told HE Ban Ki-moon that *I am willing for this court to fail, but I am not willing to let my country to go to war again.* These are the statements recorded by both the UN and the Cambodian side. It was a negotiation in the Peace Palace [. . .] in the course of discussion, there were talks about cases 001, 002, 003, 004 and 005 and I said "no." We were not interfering with the court, but we had to give it a thought. *I can honestly say that I am willing for the court to fail, but I do not want my country to go to war again.* Please do not take 4 to 5 convicts to intimidate and lead to a repeat of the civil war. How many would die[?] I have to bring this up to tell our compatriots about our hard-earned national pride.[10]

With such a peace narrative, Hun Sen has long challenged the late King Sihanouk. Sihanouk's role in the peace process in the early 1990s had led to his portrayal as the "father of peace and national reconciliation" and provided a central legitimacy claim for royalists (Norén-Nilsson 2016). Hun Sen gradually developed a competing peace narrative, building on his role in ending Democratic Kampuchea on 7 January 1979 and later the civil war through his win-win policy. After the CPP's successful co-optation of the royalist party, this peace narrative has remained a central element in Hun Sen's claim to power. Astrid Norén-Nilsson (2021) has argued that following the 2017 dissolution of the Cambodia National Rescue Party, this peace narrative has played an essential role in Hun Sen's turn to "regal authoritarianism," through which he consolidates his power against political rivals both outside and inside the CPP. This peace narrative has been further enshrined in the adoption of 29 December as a national day to commemorate and celebrate Hun Sen's win-win policy and the construction of "win-win monuments" across the country, starting with the "Win-Win Monument" on Win-Win boulevard in the northeast of Phnom Penh (Niem 2019). Costing more than US$12 million, this monument was inaugurated on 29 December 2018 during a massive three-day ceremony on the twentieth anniversary of the surrender of the last senior Khmer Rouge leaders. The monument symbolizes the three core elements of the win-win policy, which were offered to Khmer Rouge forces for their defection to the CPP: political amnesty; the maintenance of military ranks after their integration into the Cambodian Royal Armed Forces; and the guarantee of their property and wealth (Norén-Nilsson 2021).

Opposing further prosecutions at the ECCC is thus in line with Hun Sen's win-win policy, which remains central to the prime minister's claim to power (Path 2017; Bultmann 2020). This is what the minister of information Khieu Kanharith argued when I interviewed him in 2014. He explained that the CPP government needed to uphold its promise toward former Khmer Rouge, even if he acknowledged that they were indeed too old to reignite a war: "Because when we finished the Khmer Rouge, it's not by war. We negotiated with them, they accepted to come back, and we need to keep our promise too. [. . .] When they come back, we say that we guarantee your property, your life, and your function. [. . .] And you know, the promise, we keep the promise. [It] is more important, because now they are old, they could not stage a war again."[11]

As Alexandra Kent (2022) has observed, Hun Sen's peace narrative, with its focus on the win-win policy, certainly sits oddly with the ECCC. It foregrounds the date of December 29, in reference to the day that marked the end of the civil war with the defection of Nuon Chea and Khieu Samphan in 1998. Both, however, ended in the dock at the ECCC. As Daniel Bultmann (2020) explains, Nuon Chea and Khieu Samphan have long been losers of Hun Sen's win-win policy. They defected late to the CPP, after Khieu Samphan had unsuccessfully attempted to strike a deal with Norodom Ranariddh, Hun Sen's rival from the royalist party. The CPP did not reward them with access to significant positions in military units or provincial governments as they did in the case of Ieng Sary, or Khmer Rouge middle-rank military cadres who defected earlier. In contrast, the two initial suspects in Case 003, Meas Muth and Sou Met (who died in 2013) had defected to the CPP during the first wave of defections in 1996 and were rewarded with positions in the state military (A. Kent 2013). By the time he became a suspect, Meas Muth was a retired one-star general and military advisor to the CPP government and was involved in the CPP in Battambang's province Samlot district, where he led a wealthy life (Sun 2019).[12] Case 004 suspect Yim Tith is also a former two-star general.

The CPP's opposition to further prosecutions at the ECCC has thus also been interpreted as an attempt to avoid an erosion of political support for Hun Sen and the CPP among those former Khmer Rouge cadres and soldiers who had been key for the consolidation of his power in the 1990s, and who had supported the CPP government during border clashes with Thailand.[13] As an international ECCC officer explained, Cases 003 and 004, if allowed to move forward, would amount to a "loss of face in some of the ex-Khmer Rouge communities": "[In] places like Anlong Veng, I have seen former cadres which have spoken out very strongly saying that they were promised in 1999 when [. . .] they laid down their weapons and agreed to reintegrate, that they would be reintegrated and that they wouldn't be prosecuted and that they would be part of society and the government. Basically, saying that they are confident that the prime minister and the other two Samdechs would not violate this [. . .] promise."[14] Im Chaem, Case 004/1 suspect, for instance, repeatedly intervened in ECCC outreach forums in Anlong Veng, where she used to be a CPP commune chief, to point out that she had been promised reintegration and amnesty when she surrendered in the 1990s.[15] In a 2016 interview, a national ECCC officer often traveling to former Khmer Rouge strongholds also described a widespread sentiment of abandonment and anger among former Khmer Rouge: "[They] [. . .] feel that the government has forgotten them. [. . .] They are very angry at the government because the government does not allow the Court to be strong enough to call the former Khmer Rouge who are within the government, but the Court can call them as former Khmer Rouge to testify as witnesses."[16]

Justice for the CPP: Criticizing the Hypocrisy of the UN and Foreign Powers

A second feature of the CPP discursive resistance to the ECCC is the CPP's questioning of the terms of engagement of foreign actors. As Kirsten Ainley (2013, 23) has observed, the situation in Cambodia is much more complex than merely being one of an "uneasy tension" between international liberalism and local authoritarianism: "The UN and a series of powerful, occasionally liberal states did business with the Khmer Rouge and are keen to forget having done so." The CPP's emphasis on peace takes aim at the hypocrisy of the UN and of external powers who portray themselves as neutral, apolitical, and moral actors in their pursuit of justice for Cambodia, after having been involved in the country's conflict and war, most notably in maintaining Khmer Rouge forces alive after 1979.

The CPP's criticism of international actors' hypocrisy when pushing for a Khmer Rouge tribunal is not new. It is a continuation of its rhetoric during the negotiations for the ECCC's establishment (see chapter 1). As Kosal Path (2017, 129) has argued, in the eyes of the CPP political elite, the UN and Western powers' interest for retributive justice reflects a "neo-colonial attitude toward international justice in post-genocide Cambodia," as their interest is seen as only serving to redeem "their sense of guilt for not only failing to intervene to prevent the mass killing by the Khmer Rouge regime, but also supporting the Khmer Rouge movement after the regime was toppled in 1979." Here the CPP's criticism related to the ECCC echoes its larger criticism of the role of the UN and Western powers and of their claims to moral authority, impartiality, and superiority (Travouillon 2021). As Katrin Travouillon (2021, 379) has shown, this criticism serves the dual purpose of "assert[ing] Hun Sen's ownership over Cambodia's peace and economic development, thus strengthening the CPP's claim to rule," and deflecting criticisms over the CPP's dire human rights and democratic records.

The CPP's anger and resentment toward the UN and external powers pushing for the ECCC were palpable in speeches in which the prime minister and senior CPP officials reject accusations of political interference at the ECCC (see also Lemonde 2011). In December 2007, for instance, while the UN special representative of the secretary-general for human rights in Cambodia was visiting the country, Hun Sen emphasized that the UN did not have any moral legitimacy to criticize his government's work on the ECCC: "They may in the past support the Khmer Rouge but they have been criticizing the Government about the court process for the trial of the remaining leaders of the Khmer Rouge. [. . .] Whatever they did wrong in the past is never compensated. [. . .]

In the past they supported the Khmer Rouge to occupy the Cambodian seat at the United Nations and today they demand the Khmer Rouge trial. It is indeed a slap in their face but they never say that their policy in the past supporting the Khmer Rouge was wrong."[17]

In February 2009, amid allegations of corruption at the ECCC, Hun Sen rebutted that those criticizing him should "seek forgiveness from the Cambodian people" for having supported the Khmer Rouge, while the CPP and himself were the ones who had already tried, and successfully defeated the Khmer Rouge:

> Yesterday I received a report that the conflict in the [ECCC] has come to an end. . . . I do not care. . . . There is a verdict from the court in 1979 but they did not accept it while continuing to recognize the Khmer Rouge at the [UN] and now they wanted to go through the court case again [. . .] . . . To be correct, I have done my jobs already—Firstly, I have led and cooperated in toppling the Pol Pot regime, and [s]econdly, I have done the job of preventing the return of Pol Pot regime . . . [. . .] Thirdly, with support of the people and armed forces as well as unity among leaders of the [CPP], I have led the implementation of the win-win policy which has unified the country [. . .]
>
> Some people who in the past have supported the Khmer Rouge could not by any standard [be] judged to be human right champions. . . . I think it is *their unpaid duty to seek forgiveness from the Cambodian people for their kowtow to the Khmer Rouge* . . . [. . .] They never even once beg us for an excuse when they did things wrong on us.[18]

In February 2021, while commenting on the upcoming closing of the ECCC, Hun Sen again criticized the lack of remorse shown by countries who had previously supported the Khmer Rouge: "We are victims of genocide, but we came under punishment by countries calling themselves democratic. Those countries supported the Lon Nol's military coup that overthrew the Head of State, Samdech Preah Norodom Sihanouk, and later supported the Khmer Rouge at the United Nations. Fortunately, they later provided assistance to the Khmer Rouge tribunal, which is now nearing its end. However, they have never expressed any remorse for past wrongdoing. This is the history of Cambodia."[19]

The CPP's grievances toward the UN and Western powers can be further illustrated with an interview that I conducted in 2014 with a CPP secretary of state. Using analogies popular in Khmer songs, this senior CPP official equated the UN's involvement in bringing the Khmer Rouge to trial to an act of cowardice, when read in correct historical perspective: "If the buffalo is eating the rice paddy, you do not dare to chase him, but if the buffalo is away [from the rice paddy], you chase after him. Or if the crocodile is in the water, you do not dare to chase him, but if the crocodile is on the land, you dare to chase him!"[20] He explained:

> [The] prime minister has built peace on his own, without the support from other countries, through his successful win-win policy [. . .]. But after the Khmer Rouge regime, the UN did not recognize the PRK but rather even gave the Cambodian seat at the UN to the Khmer Rouge. So, when Cambodia was at war against the Khmer Rouge until 1998, the UN did not care about establishing a tribunal. But afterwards, when there is peace, the UN comes in and wants to try the Khmer Rouge. They should have caught these people in the 1980s! It's a world game, it is cheating the Cambodian people and cheating the victims. When we said the Khmer Rouge are wrong, they said they are good. Now that there is peace, they say they are wrong! At that time, nobody came to support Cambodia. Why can they do this? Because we are poor, because Cambodia is a poor country. They are not Cambodian people, and they want to catch [arrest] Cambodian people! They need to appreciate that we have moved from war to peace, that we have moved from war to less weapons in the streets, to no weapons at all and to peace and stability. [. . .] We have moved from the "rule of life," from survival and death, to the "rule of law." Don't expect too fast, you need to acknowledge the achievements in Cambodia.[21]

From this perspective, the ECCC becomes a form of justice rendered not only—or primarily—for the Cambodian people: it is also a form of justice for the CPP. This can be seen in the following excerpt of a 2005 speech by Hun Sen: "Some people blamed the slow process for the trial on Hun Sen by claiming that Hun Sen does not want such a trial. The Khmer Rouge leaders were tried in 1979 but no one recognized the effort. And I am glad that our people will enjoy justice this time. *As for the Cambodian People's Party and Hun Sen, such a trial is of great significance as it will prove that punishment on Cambodia in the past was wrong or render the CPP with a justice it deserves, so to speak.*"[22]

Here Hun Sen frames the ECCC's existence as retroactively proving the illegitimacy of the isolation and criticism that he and his government suffered from in the 1980s—including through the dismissal of the 1979 People's Revolutionary Tribunal. In August 2014, after the ECCC Trial Chamber pronounced its verdict in Case 002/01, Hun Sen similarly commented that justice had already been served in 1979. The ECCC verdict validated his earlier accountability efforts ex post facto:

> I am happy with the verdict reached by the hybrid court. Sitting down to have lunch with my wife, after watching the court delivering verdicts to the former leaders (of the Khmer Rouge), I talked to my wife that we had to wait for thirty-five years and exactly eight months for this day. We

> toppled the genocide on 7 January 1979. No one recognized it. They even blamed us for bringing them down. [. . .] Even in the Paris Peace Agreement, we had been refrained from referring to them as the regime of genocide but the prevention of the recent past. In 1979, the court of the former People's Republic of Kampuchea, already gave the regime's leaders a sentence. Yesterday, *justice is served again. It proved that what we did 35 years ago was correct. It is a relief.* Though those ageing leaders would not live long enough to serve the term, but the trial should please our people.[23]

The temporality herewith constructed relativizes the role of the UN and other involved countries: the ECCC only serves justice a second time, after it had long been delivered in 1979. It is important to note, here, that this relativization of the role of the UN is not necessarily reflected in other comments of CPP officials. In particular, the chairman of the Cambodian government task force on Khmer Rouge trials has celebrated the ECCC for achieving justice and ending impunity for Khmer Rouge crimes, highlighting these achievements as the result of a convergence of the efforts of the Cambodian government with those of the UN and donor countries.[24] Nonetheless, here Hun Sen's subversion of the UN's and the West's normative power combines a critique of its "lack of 'genuine morality'" (Path 2017, 130) with an effacement of their role in bringing justice to Cambodians. This seems to echo the temporality enshrined in Hun Sen's peace narrative, which refers to the Paris Peace Agreements as a mere "stepping stone" along Cambodia's journey to peace, at the center of which he stands (Norén-Nilsson 2021, 10).

"Political Interference" at the ECCC: A Case Study of CPP Discipline and Control?

After having reviewed the discursive dimension of CPP resistance, I now turn to the legal proceedings at the ECCC as a site of resistance. At the Court, CPP resistance has come into play whenever the work of UN-appointed staff members threatened to tarnish the reputation of senior CPP officials through exposing their Khmer Rouge past, and to extend the list of suspects beyond Cases 001 and 002.

The Untouchables: Senior CPP Officials and Their Khmer Rouge Past

In Case 002, allegations of CPP interference emerged as senior officials refused to testify as witnesses. In September 2009, following an investigative request submitted by Nuon Chea's defense lawyers, the international co-investigating judge Marcel Lemonde summoned six high-ranking CPP officials and former low- to mid-level Khmer Rouge cadres to appear in a closed session. This included late senate and CPP president Chea Sim, CPP honorary president and National Assembly president Heng Samrin, then–minister of economy and finance Keat Chhon, then–minister of foreign affairs Hor Nam Hong and CPP senators Ouk Bunchhoen and Sim Ka.[25] Nuon Chea's and Ieng Sary's defense lawyers also requested that Hun Sen be summoned, but Lemonde rejected this, arguing that the prime minister's testimony would not be useful (Ciorciari and Heindel 2014, 148).

Most of the six subpoenaed witnesses did not answer—including Keat Chon, who had in the past publicly indicated his willingness to testify at the ECCC. Apparently, Lemonde only ever heard back from the cabinet director of one witness. The director explained that summoning such a high-level leader could "harm [the leader's] political career"—a comment that national co-investigating Judge You Bunleng reportedly requested to erase from the minutes (Lemonde 2013, 176). Lemonde decided to render the summons public. However, the ECCC's Court Management Section refused to do so, arguing that this required the signature of both co-investigating judges. The acting director of administration reportedly warned Lemonde (2013, 177): "Your attitude risks to give arguments to those who, in the high spheres, think that we have started an infernal machine with these trials which we can't control anymore."

In October 2009, Lemonde finally succeeded in rendering his summons public, thereby drawing criticism from senior CPP officials, including the prime minister. The minister of information Khieu Kanharith publicly stated that "though the individuals could appear in court voluntarily, the government's position was that they should not give testimony," adding that the international judges could "pack their bags and return home" if they were not satisfied (Strangio and Sokha 2009). Ultimately, Lemonde decided to abandon the issue, concluding that insisting would be too difficult and would unduly delay the judicial investigation.

Analysts interpret the CPP officials' refusal to appear as witnesses as an attempt to avoid shedding light on their Khmer Rouge past (see, e.g., Gidley 2019). A senior member of the ECCC's national administration explained to me that the CPP officials' refusal to testify was also a result of the "culture of secrecy" of the "old guard" within the CPP political elite.[26] A former national staff member of the ECCC office of administration argued that appearing at the ECCC would provide ammunition to the political opposition "to accuse the government that there are former Khmers Rouges in the government," and thereby "question their political credibility."[27] This was because in Cambodia, unlike in the West, being called to testify would automatically lead to suspicions that one committed a crime or did something wrong.[28]

The defense teams would not let the matter rest. Ieng Sary's and Nuon Chea's defense both appealed Lemonde's decision not to insist on the summons. Nuon Chea's defense among others requested that Hun Sen himself be summoned and questioned on the matter. In its June 2010 decision, the Pre-Trial Chamber sided with Judge Lemonde. They found that proceedings could be significantly delayed, since the government officials could invoke parliamentary immunity. The judges therefore argued that the decision on whether to summon them as witnesses should be deferred to the trial stage. Given the government statements to the press, they nonetheless advised the co-investigating judges to assess "whether or not a nexus exists" between discouragements by government representatives and "the actual failure of the summoned witnesses to provide statements."[29] The co-investigating judges, however, responded that they did not believe such an investigation to be necessary.

In September 2010, seized with a second appeal, the Pre-Trial Chamber did not reach a supermajority—that is, an affirmative vote by at least four of the five judges.[30] The two international judges argued that there was reason to believe that government officials interfered with witnesses, and that an investigation was therefore necessary. The three national judges concluded that there was no reason to believe any interference had happened. They argued that the comments made by Khieu Kanharith did not constitute an absolute order, and that he did not make these comments explicitly as a government spokesperson. Interestingly, they also argued that the summoned witnesses were of "higher rank, status and title" than Khieu Kanharith and could therefore not be coerced by him.[31] In the absence of a supermajority decision, the co-investigating judges' decision not to investigate stood by default.

The defense, especially Nuon Chea, insisted. Nuon Chea's lawyers requested to call CPP officials as witnesses throughout the Case 002 trial proceedings.[32] They focused on Heng Samrin, whom they argued to be the most important witness for Case 002 as former deputy division commander of the Eastern Zone, as one of the highest-ranking individuals still alive to have been involved in Phnom Penh's evacuation, and for his knowledge of a May 1975 meeting during which key CPK policies were disseminated. However, the Trial Chamber split along international-national lines.[33] The international judges agreed with the defense that it was necessary to call Heng Samrin and other high-ranking CPP officials as witnesses, while their national colleagues refused to do so. In the absence of a supermajority, the bench did not call them as witnesses during both Case 002 trials.[34] The consistent divergence between national and international judges on the issue—across the co-investigating judges' office,

Pre-Trial and Trial Chambers—fueled perceptions of political interference to the extent that it came to be considered "the quintessential emblem of the Court's failure to act independently" (Lobba and Pons 2020, 4–5).

In its appeal of the Trial Chamber Case 002/01 judgment, Nuon Chea argued that the Trial Chamber's failure to call key witnesses could only be explained by "the absence of judicial independence and integrity"; it therefore violated not only his right to present a defense but also his right to trial by an independent tribunal.[35] In November 2016, the Supreme Court Chamber rendered a unanimous decision on this matter.[36] The bench agreed that Heng Samrin's testimony would have been relevant. However, they dismissed Nuon Chea's claim that his testimony would have been only exonerating or that it would have produced new exonerating information. The co-prosecutors were also of the view that Heng Samrin's testimony in Case 002/01 would be neither unique nor exculpatory.[37] The bench further disagreed with Nuon Chea's view that the reasoning of the national Trial Chamber judges could only be explained by a lack of independence. They argued that it "might be taken at face value, as an acknowledgement of the ECCC's weak enforcement powers vis-à-vis non-cooperative witnesses, a problem generally not uncommon to international(ized) criminal courts and tribunals."[38] Finally, the bench found the decision not to summon Heng Samrin because it would delay proceedings to be unreasonable, as this was merely a supposition. As a remedy, the bench drew inferences in favor of the accused where relevant.

This unanimous decision of the Supreme Court Chamber in Case 002/01 was celebrated as bringing this long-standing controversy at the Court to a "dignified close" (Lobba and Pons 2020, 5). The fact that the national judges sided alongside their international counterparts to safeguard fair trial rights when it came to the thorny issue of summoning Heng Samrin was also seen by some international staff as a sign that the ECCC was able to provide national judges certain wiggle room to act independently.[39] However, from a more critical perspective, one could point out that the Supreme Court Chamber decision ultimately did not change the outcome: senior CPP officials were successfully shielded from testifying at the ECCC. Gidley (2019, 134), for instance, has argued that the decisions not to pursue the summons of Heng Samrin and other CPP leaders contributed to "enforcing the government's preferred silences": the narrative emerging from the ECCC did not threaten, or even reinforced, the CPP's efforts to distance itself from the Khmer Rouge and to portray itself as savior of the Cambodian nation.

Such conclusions, however, do not account for the heterogeneity of the ECCC as an institution, more specifically the defense's combative use of the judicial proceedings. Highlighting the Khmer Rouge past of Heng Samrin and other high-ranking CPP officials was indeed a central element of Nuon Chea's defense. Drawing upon a strategy of rupture, Nuon Chea's international lawyers unabatingly questioned the trial's fairness and the government's political interference, insisting that the broader geopolitical context needed to be considered.[40] Even if CPP officials and Heng Samrin never testified as witnesses, and even if they were unable to delve into Heng Samrin's past extensively during public hearings,[41] they still made very strong accusations. In their appeal against the Case 002/01 judgment, they argued: "Heng Samrin is to the evacuation of Phnom Penh what Duch is to S-21: the person tasked with guiding the implementation of policies which the Co-prosecutors say were adopted by the CPK at one of the most important crime sites alleged in the Closing Order. If Duch is among those "most responsible," Heng Samrin is no less deserving of the attention of this Tribunal."[42]

In November 2011, Nuon Chea's international defense lawyers even brought the issue of political interference to the domestic judiciary (Aun 2016).[43] They filed a criminal complaint at the Phnom Penh Municipal Court, requesting an investigation into the alleged interference by senior CPP officials—including then–CPP leadership triumvirate Hun Sen, Chea Sim, and Heng Samrin—for preventing witnesses to testify, ignoring court summonses to appear as witnesses in Case 002, and blocking Cases 003 and 004. Even though the case never moved forward, such a use of judicial avenues was unheard of in Cambodia.[44] Raising the Khmer Rouge past of CPP officials has certainly long been part of the political opposition's strategy to discredit the CPP. However, domestic courts, when coming into play, were consistently used to shield CPP officials and suppress political opponents rather than the other way around.

Limiting the Number of Suspects: The Saga of Cases 003 and 004

While the refusal of senior CPP officials fueled allegations of political interference at the ECCC, it is the CPP government's opposition to Cases 003 and 004 that has been at the heart of these allegations. At the ECCC, senior national officials replicated the CPP's opposition to Cases 003 and 004, as the cases moved through the foreseen motions and offices. The national co-prosecutor and judges here echoed the government's arguments that proceeding with Cases 003 and 004 would threaten peace, stability, and national reconciliation. Their international counterparts did not consider this to be a plausible scenario in contemporary Cambodia. The international co-prosecutor, for instance, argued: "The Khmer Rouge has ceased to exist as a political or military organization, former cadres are now elderly, the Pol Pot regime is almost universally reviled, and there is no evidence of any support for a resurgence of the movement. A revived Khmer Rouge armed insurrection is simply not a plausible possibility in Cambodia today."[45] The legal dispute centered on how to define the category of "most responsible" and whether the suspects in Cases 003 and 004 would fall under this category. However, the main arguments put forward by Cambodian judicial officials would come to be considered "shaky in fact and unsupported by law."[46]

This section offers an overview of the complicated story of CPP resistance to Cases 003 and 004. As Etcheson (2019) has argued, delaying tactics played an important role.[47] Investigations in Cases 001 and 002 required slightly more than one year and three years respectively, from the co-prosecutors' first introductory submission to the co-investigating judges' Closing Order. Investigations in Cases 003 and 004—not remotely as complex as Case 002—took between seven and ten years. As Diane Orentlicher (2020, 627) observed, given the advanced age of suspects, "such delays can defeat justice just as surely as rulings that bend to political pressure."

Resistance to investigations beyond the five accused in Cases 001 and 002 first emerged within the office of the co-prosecutors, as it is the office responsible for conducting preliminary investigations and putting forward a list of witnesses, suspects, and charges to the co-investigating judges. The work of the international co-prosecutors' team was of such interest to the CPP government that the international investigators' office was apparently put under surveillance. Etcheson (2019) reported noticing regular nocturnal visits of their desks, as well as the copying of the international co-prosecutor's hard disk to a modem apparently linked to the Ministry of the Interior.

In July 2007, the co-prosecutors and their national and international staff finished the first introductory submission. The national co-prosecutor Chea Leang did not prevent the internationals to work on this first submission, nor did she ask her investigators not to participate (Etcheson 2019). However, she refused to co-sign the first introductory submission alongside her international colleague Robert Petit, asking for more time. According to Etcheson (2019), Chea Leang was then still awaiting instructions from Sok An. Until his death in 2017, Sok An chaired the Task Force on the Khmer Rouge trials. Since 2004, he was also deputy prime minister and minister in charge of the Office of the Council of Ministers, a core of Hun Sen's power (Strangio 2014a).

The introductory submission initially included charges against six suspects: Nuon Chea, Ieng Sary, Ieng Thirith, Khieu Samphan, Van Rith, and Duch. In the end, Chea Leang agreed to sign the introductory submission once the charges against Van Rith were taken out (Ciorciari and Heindel 2014, 178). Van Rith, who died in 2008, was allegedly "a central player in the economic catastrophe" of the Khmer Rouge regime, as its former minister of commerce

(Etcheson 2019, 220). While removing Van Rith from the first introductory submission allowed what would subsequently become Cases 001 and 002 to move forward, the national side's opposition to charging additional suspects persisted. Chea Leang refused to participate in the investigations for additional suspects (OSJI 2020). In May 2008, she was reportedly summoned by Sok An, who also happened to be her uncle, to be reminded that the CPP government's position was that only five suspects would be tried at the ECCC (Etcheson 2019). To no avail, her deputy co-prosecutor, also present at the meeting, had tried to convince Sok An that the additional suspects deserved to be punished for the crimes they had committed, that they were not important to the CPP, and that their trials would not threaten Cambodia's peace (Etcheson 2019).

In November 2008, Robert Petit filed a notice of disagreement before the Pre-Trial Chamber, as foreseen in the ECCC rules, since Chea Leang disagreed to his filing of introductory submissions for two new investigations in Cases 003 and 004. The submissions named five additional suspects: Meas Muth, Sou Met, Ao An, Yim Tith, and Im Chaem. Chea Leang put forward a series of arguments to explain her disagreement. First, she argued that new submissions were unnecessary: they were redundant since the facts and crimes were already covered in the first introductory submission. Second, she asserted that given the ECCC's limited personal and temporal jurisdiction it was "neither intended to—nor is it able to—fulfil the principle of perfect justice and bring to trial all those who committed crimes."[48] In her view, the additional suspects identified were neither senior leaders nor most responsible. Moreover, "current considerations of peace, stability and national reconciliation in Cambodia" argue against initiating new prosecutions. Additional prosecutions might change the "perception that the ECCC's mandate is limited to senior leaders and those most responsible" and could therefore potentially lead "ex-members and those who have allegiance to the Khmer Rouge leaders" to "commit violent acts." According to her, the danger of escalation into violence was particularly stark among former Khmer Rouge officials of ranks equivalent to the Cases 003 and 004 suspects. This could introduce a "frightening situation of unrest in Cambodian society." To support these claims, she referred to the Thai-Cambodian border conflict regarding the Preah Vihear temple area, in which she claimed that former Khmer Rouge soldiers were "at the forefront of protecting [Cambodia's] territorial integrity." Chea Leang had earlier argued to her international colleagues in the Office of Co-prosecutors that one of the suspects was even leading troops at the border, although they found no evidence that it was true.[49]

Chea Leang argued that taking into account peace, stability, and national reconciliation in her decision was in accordance with the purpose and spirit of the ECCC Law, the Agreement and the Preamble of the Internal Rules, which is to "promote national unity, reconciliation, stability, security and peace in Cambodia."[50] The Preamble to the Internal Rules indeed specifies that "the General Assembly recognized the legitimate concern of the Government and the people of Cambodia in the pursuit of justice and national reconciliation, stability, peace and security."[51] The inclusion of this clause had been subject to some controversy. In his account of the 2007 Rules drafting process, Lemonde (2013, 38) suggests that the inclusion of these "non-judicial" principles was central to the CPP government's strategy of resistance:

> One morning, the Cambodians arrive in the meeting, declaring that the obligation for the judges to take into consideration in their decisions the principles of 'internal peace' and 'national reconciliation' needed to be integrated into the Internal Rules. I tried to explain that these non-judicial notions had no place in the document we were trying to draft. They insisted. The discussion dragged on. I would understand much later that, in reality, they were a step ahead of us, anticipating the possibility to block prosecutions that were deemed politically inappropriate. On this point, the question would finally be settled through a compromise: only the Preamble of the Rules, whose binding force is not obvious, referred to internal peace and national reconciliation.[52]

In Lemonde's (2011, 599) view, the inclusion of this clause allowed national judicial officers to use the "alibi of peace" and "joker of reconciliation" to avoid undesirable political side effects of the tribunal whenever it was getting out of control for the government. An international judge who had also been part of the Rules Committee, however, pointed out that adding the notions of reconciliation and peace was neither a contested nor controversial issue. Seeing retributive justice and peace as complementary goals merely reflected the UN's policy approach: "That's the mantra that the UN uses. And it's something that we all subscribe to: let's hope that if you observe the rule of law and try to avoid impunity for [. . .] terrible crimes, which involve a lot of people, that you will promote reconciliation and peace. [. . .] I don't think we even debated it. We all said yes, fine, yes, good idea!"[53] The reference to peace, stability, and reconciliation would nonetheless remain essential to Chea Leang's opposition to Cases 003 and 004; and her national colleagues in the co-investigating office and Pre-Trial Chamber would later also repeat it in their opposition to these Cases.

The third and final argument Chea Leang put forward was that the international co-prosecutor had unilaterally conducted the preliminary investigations of the Cases 003 and 004 suspects without her knowledge. The investigations were thus illegal: they violated the ECCC Law and Internal Rules. Robert Petit, however, refuted this version of the nature of their collaboration.[54]

The Pre-Trial Chamber, tasked with settling the disagreement, rendered its considerations in August 2009, after deliberating for almost a year.[55] The Pre-Trial Chamber did not reach any supermajority and split along national-international lines. The national judges voted against the investigations. They agreed with Chea Leang that the preliminary investigation was illegal for having been conducted unilaterally by the international co-prosecutor, and that additional cases were unnecessary as acts and crimes were already covered in the previous cases. The international judges disagreed on all these points. The bench, however, did not address the remainder of Chea Leang's arguments. Since the judges could not reach a supermajority, the default mechanism foreseen in the Internal Rules, which favored prosecution, was triggered. The international co-prosecutor's request for additional judicial investigations would thus proceed. In September 2009, Cases 003 and 004 were transferred to the office of the co-investigating judges, which would become the next stage for the CPP's resistance at the Court.

At first, the issue of additional suspects was put aside. The international co-investigating judge Marcel Lemonde initially concentrated efforts on investigating Case 002. Knowing that Cases 003 and 004 would lead to a confrontation with his national counterpart You Bunleng, he did not want this to jeopardize their work on Case 002.[56] In January 2010, with Case 002 investigations completed, the international investigation team finally moved to Cases 003 and 004. They drafted a rogatory letter—that is, written instructions for investigators or the police to collect evidence. However, You Bunleng repeatedly requested more time for consideration before signing the letter. Lemonde finally gave him an ultimatum, and both judges signed the letter on Friday, 4 June 2010 (Lemonde 2013, 194–99). On Sunday, 7 June 2010, however, You Bunleng withdrew his signature after a communication with Sok An,[57] and yet another public comment by a government spokesperson that the government was opposed to any further trials beyond "the five top leaders" (Gillison 2010). When withdrawing his signature, You Bunleng explained that, in the end, it did not seem "opportune to him to immediately start with the investigations in these new files" given that the Closing Order in Case 002, the ECCC's core case, was not to be completed before September.[58]

Trial monitors, rights activists, and commentators interpreted this incident as another indication of the CPP government's pressure, given both the timing and reasoning of Judge You's un-signing of the rogatory letter (see, e.g., Ciorciari and Heindel 2014, 179). You Bunleng's appointment at the ECCC had been welcomed by civil society organizations and legal analysts: he was considered to be one of the "best picks" among Cambodian jurists (see, e.g., US Embassy 2006). This event, however, signaled that he would not be working independently. Lemonde (2013, 197–98) recalled how You Bunleng commented to him at that time that "the tribunal had been created by political will, and could also be closed by political will": it would be useless to pursue the investigation knowing in advance that the Pre-Trial Chamber national judges would oppose it.

As part of their defense strategy in Case 002, Nuon Chea's defense lawyers did not let this matter rest. In mid-June 2010, they applied for the disqualification of You Bunleng. They accused him of using his judicial power improperly, in furtherance of the government's agenda, given his earlier refusal to sign letters and summonses to high-ranking government officials and this "unsigning" of rogatory letters. In September 2010, the Pre-Trial Chamber judges unanimously rejected Nuon Chea's request.[59] In their view, the allegations were too vague, false, and lacking in evidence to establish that You Bunleng had acted, or appeared to have acted, without impartiality or independence. Following the Chamber's decision, You Bunleng mentioned to Lemonde (2013, 197) that he had actually come "to wish that the request would have been accepted" so that he "could finally be left in peace."

The office of the co-investigating judges would remain the central stage for the international-national disagreements on Cases 003 and 004. After Lemonde resigned in September 2010, he was followed by a total of four international co-investigating judges. Most of them also attempted to pursue Cases 003 and 004, while You Bunleng persisted in his opposition to these cases. One noticeable—and to this day rather puzzling—exception was the controversial German co-investigating judge Siegfried Blunk. Soon after he was appointed to replace Lemonde in 2010, he agreed with You Bunleng to close the investigation in Case 003. Cambodian and international civil society organizations strongly criticized this decision (OSJI 2011b). The international co-prosecutor, American Andrew Cayley, disclosed information on the Case 003 crime sites to demonstrate his intention to move forward nonetheless.[60] Blunk ordered Cayley to retract this information.[61] However, given that the Pre-Trial Chamber was split on this matter along international versus national lines, Cayley was eventually not bound to do so.

Judge Blunk's own staff resorted to contacting the UN secretary-general to share their concerns over the judges' decision to close the investigation in Case 003, as well as Blunk's mismanagement of his office. Blunk subsequently threatened to take disciplinary action for "disloyalty" (Gillison 2011). In the absence of a reaction from the UN secretariat, six international staff of the co-investigating judges' office resigned. One of them, US scholar Stephen Heder, explained that the office had become "professionally dysfunctional" (Gillison 2011). In October 2011, an investigation[62] concluded that Blunk and You Bunleng had both been involved in obstructions of justice and procedural irregularities in closing the investigation in Case 003. Judge Blunk finally resigned.

This controversial episode was followed by what was to become the most virulent public display of a national-international divide on Cases 003 and 004. Reserve co-investigating judge Laurent Kasper-Ansermet from Switzerland was set to replace Blunk. However, Hun Sen opposed Kasper-Ansermet's appointment (Coughlan, Ghouse, and Smith 2012). The Cambodian Supreme Council of Magistracy subsequently refused to appoint him, arguing that the comments Kasper-Ansermet had made on Twitter violated provisions of the Code of Criminal Procedure, the Internal Rules, and the Code of Judicial Ethics. In his tweets, Kasper-Ansermet had shared information on Case 003 already accessible in the public domain, criticisms of co-investigating judges You Bunleng and Blunk, and his intention to reopen Case 003. The UN, however, concluded that the concerns raised about Kasper-Ansermet's social media activity were unfounded.

During his short tenure, Kasper-Ansermet would meet systematic opposition across the Court's national side: from the national co-investigating judges' office to the national Pre-Trial Chamber judges and the administrative offices. You Bunleng systematically denied to recognize his authority and refused all communications (see Kasper-Ansermet 2012; Wallace 2012). Both judges publicized their dispute through frequent press releases between December 2011 and February 2012 (OSJI 2012, 9). Kasper-Ansermet issued an order to reopen the investigation in Case 003. However, he met sustained resistance from the national side. This included the refusal of officers in the Court's Management Section to place any documents he filed on the case file and the refusal of national staff members to accept summons during an internal investigation he had initiated, reportedly under orders not only from the national co-investigating judge but also from the acting director of administration (Kasper-Ansermet 2012; Ciorciari and Heindel 2014, 183). Kasper-Ansermet was also refused drivers and transcribers for investigating missions and most symbolically denied access to the seal of his office. In light of this, international trial monitor Clair Duffy concluded: "This is the government's publicly expressed will being put into action at every level of the court by every Cambodian that has touched the files throughout the substance of the investigation" (quoted in Di Certo 2012). The Pre-Trial Chamber, seized with the matter of Kasper-Ansermet's authority to act, was unsurprisingly split, once again, along national-international lines.

The UN secretariat, uncharacteristically direct, insisted that the decision of the Supreme Council of the Magistracy not to appoint Kasper-Ansermet was a breach of the Framework Agreement, as he was clearly entitled to carry out the responsibilities of his office (Etcheson 2019). The UN secretary-general further noted with concern that You Bunleng and Chea Leang were both members of the Cambodian Supreme Council of the Magistracy, who had refused to appoint Kasper-Ansermet at the ECCC (UN Secretary-General 2012, §22). The secretary-general's office indicated that this decision constituted sufficient legal grounds for the UN to withdraw its assistance to the ECCC. Article 28 of the UN-Cambodia Agreement foresaw such an option: "Should the Royal Government of Cambodia change the structure or organization of the Extraordinary Chambers or otherwise cause them to function in a manner that does not conform with the terms of the present Agreement, the UN reserves the right to cease to provide assistance, financial or otherwise, pursuant to the present Agreement."

Analysts, however, perceived this move by the UN as "less a negotiation gambit than an attempt to regain some credibility with disheartened NGOs and victims' advocates" after the UN's handling of the controversies around Blunk (Giry 2012). Ultimately, UN officials did not reach any political agreement with the Cambodian government regarding Kasper-Ansermet's situation. Monitors of the Cambodian program of the Open Society Justice Initiative (OSJI) observed that the extent of public disagreements between the co-investigating judges and the increasing controversies around Kasper-Ansermet's work had "grated on many within the UN and among the court's donors" (OSJI 2012, 11). Frustrated, Judge Kasper-Ansermet resigned in March 2012.

Two international co-investigating judges would follow: American judge Mark Harmon (October 2012 to July 2015) and German judge Michael Bohlander (as of July 2015). They would pursue the investigations in Cases 003 and 004. Although several confidential disagreements were filed between the co-investigating judges, the judges did not bring any of these before the Pre-Trial Chamber.[63] This suggests, perhaps, an agreement by You Bunleng to allow the international judge's investigations to proceed as far as possible.[64]

In June 2013, Sou Met, suspect in Case 003, died. Four suspects remained in Cases 003 and 004. In August 2014, Harmon issued summons for Im Chaem and Meas Muth to appear at the ECCC, which they ignored. Harmon proceeded to issue arrest warrants. In Cases 001 and 002, the judicial police's co-operation with the ECCC had been noticed, as it stood in stark contrast with the domestic context, where it acts in constant confrontation with domestic courts (Un and Ledgerwood 2010). In the government's opposed cases concerning Im Chaem and Meas Muth, the judicial police, however, refused to execute Harmon's arrest warrants. The Ministry of Interior spokesman declared in March 2015: "We will not arrest them. It's impossible—we don't serve any order that may come from the ECCC. There are two investigating judges—one foreign, and one Khmer—and there needs to be a consensus agreement for full prosecution to take place. The Cambodian investigating judge supports the prime minister's view on the courts: The Cambodian judge cannot pursue the arrest of any more charged by the ECCC" (Lee and Nov 2015).

The judicial police's refusal marked once again a breach of the Cambodian government's obligations under the UN-Cambodia Framework Agreement. The UN engaged in discussions with the Cambodian government, yet the arrest warrants were never executed (Ryan and McGrew 2016, 28; see also OSJI 2015). Harmon proceeded to charge the accused in absentia. By December 2015, Harmon, and later his successor, Bohlander, had finally succeeded to inform all suspects in Cases 003 and 004 of their charges, thereby allowing the case file to finally be accessed by the defense lawyers. None of the cases, however, would ever move to trial.

The case against Im Chaem, severed into Case 004/1, would first come to conclusion. It ended with an unexpected agreement of both international and national co-investigating judges that she did not fall under the ECCC's personal jurisdiction. In February 2017, Bohlander and You Bunleng jointly issued a dismissal order. The judges confirmed the international co-prosecutor's analysis that Im Chaem had held formal positions in the Northwest Zone, including that of district secretary, and found that she "was responsible for a number of atrocious crimes," including an estimated 18,100 murders.[65] However, they concluded that this was not enough for her to fall within the Court's personal jurisdiction. The international co-prosecutor, the civil party lawyers, and the defense appealed the dismissal order. In June 2018, the Pre-Trial Chamber judges did not reach the required supermajority on whether Im Chaem fell under the ECCC's personal jurisdiction.[66] Based on an analysis of over a hundred pages, the international judges agreed with the international co-prosecutor that Im Chaem clearly fell under the category of "most responsible." They concluded that the co-investigating judges had "failed to take into account the full magnitude of the gravity of the crimes alleged or charged against Im Chaem, and of her full role and responsibilities" under Democratic Kampuchea.[67] In a drastically shorter opinion of two and a half pages, the Cambodian judges merely repeated their opposition to further trials, without providing any factual or legal analysis. Given the lack of a supermajority, the order dismissing Im Chaem's case stood, as per the foreseen procedural rules. The dismissal of her case was widely criticized by commentators and trial monitors (see, e.g., DeFalco 2018).

In the remaining cases—Case 003 against Meas Muth, Case 004 against Yim Tith and Case 004/2 against Ao An—the long-standing disagreements between nationals and internationals would persist. Between August 2018 and June 2019, after almost ten years of judicial investigation, the co-investigating judges issued two contradictory closing orders in each case. The Internal Rules did not foresee such a scenario: when unable to reach a consensus and to issue a joint closing order, the co-investigating judges should notify the Pre-Trial Chamber of their disagreement. In his closing order, Bohlander concluded that the three suspects fell within the ECCC's personal jurisdiction as "most responsible"—though not as senior leaders, as the international co-prosecutor had argued—and that the cases should move to trial. You Bunleng concluded that the charges should be dismissed. He further contended that in the negotiations between the Cambodian government and the UN the phrase "most responsible" only ever referred to Duch. He further referred to debates at the National Assembly, during which Sok An allegedly provided assurances that the suspects would be limited to senior leaders only. The national co-prosecutor and national Pre-Trial Chamber judges made similar arguments, including the references to Sok An's alleged comments at the National Assembly that the ECCC was only to prosecute five suspects. However, the publicly available minutes of the National Assembly debates and documentation of the negotiations between the Cambodian government and the UN clearly contradict the national judges' and prosecutor's versions. Ultimately, all three cases were terminated by a unanimous decision of the Supreme Court Chamber, who ruled that the "judicial limbo" the Cases found themselves in had to be ended.[68]

Case 004/2 against Ao An ended first. In December 2019, following appeals by Ao An's defense lawyers and the co-prosecutors of the contradictory closing orders, the Pre-Trial Chamber judges issued their considerations.[69] They starkly criticized the issuance of two split closing orders and unanimously concluded that this was a grave violation of the ECCC's legal framework. The judges, however, diverged along national-international lines when assessing the closing orders. The national judges argued that dismissing Case 004/2 was in accordance with the Cambodia-UN Agreement and ECCC law; yet they did not review any evidence on the suspect's alleged crimes. The two international judges found only the indictment to be valid. They argued that the default provisions within the ECCC legal framework consisted in the principle of continuation of judicial investigation: in the absence of a supermajority vote dismissing the indictment, it should be issued as proposed. Reviewing the law and the international co-investigating judge's assessment of evidence, they further concluded that Ao An fell within the Court's personal jurisdiction.

The split Pre-Trial Chamber's decision led to procedural deadlock, as nationals and internationals took opposite views on whether Case 004/2 should move to trial. The international Pre-Trial Chamber judges requested the Record and

Archives Unit of the Office of Administration to formally notify the Trial Chamber of the Pre-Trial Chamber's decision. Their national colleagues instead requested the unit to archive the case file. The international co-prosecutor and the civil parties' lawyers considered the Trial Chamber to be legally seized with the case. Unsurprisingly, the defense was of the opposite view. The Trial Chamber judges also split along international-national lines. The international judges agreed that their Chamber could have the "inherent authority" to address preliminary issues raised by the parties, while the national judges contended that the case was closed before the Pre-Trial Chamber.[70] Leaving no doubt on their position, the national judges asserted: "There will not be a trial of Ao An now or in the future."[71]

Brenda Hollis, the ECCC's international co-prosecutor since September 2019, refused to accept this "judicial and administrative stalemating" and appealed the Trial Chamber's failure to act on the indictment.[72] In August 2020, the Supreme Court Chamber finally ended Case 004/2 with a unanimous dismissal.[73] The judges argued that, given the unanimous decision by the Pre-Trial Chamber that the conflicting closing orders were unlawful and illegal, the case could not proceed to trial by the default position. They further criticized the Pre-Trial Chamber for not providing an actual final ruling through issuing its own valid closing order, although recognizing the extreme difficulty it found itself in.

Cases 003 and 004 faced a similar showdown. Following Hollis's appeals, the Supreme Court Chamber terminated the cases in the absence of a definitive and enforceable indictment. The bench blatantly explained that "judicial purgatory is not an option in any legal system."[74] Judge Maureen Clark, who had joined the bench in August 2019, issued dissenting opinions in both cases. She agreed with terminating the cases, but in her view, this was justified for reasons beyond the mere absence of a valid indictment, as her colleagues had argued. She reviewed the reasons put forward by the national co-prosecutor, national co-investigating judge, and national Pre-Trial Chamber judges in their opposition to Cases 003, 004 and 004/2, noticing "an extraordinary degree of repetition" in their reasoning.[75] In particular, she found two of their core arguments to be "based on a factual foundation which is shaky in fact and unsupported by law": the arguments that the international co-prosecutor's original investigation was unilateral and therefore illegal, and that Sok An had promised to the National Assembly that the ECCC would only ever charge five suspects.[76] She therefore argued that the opposition from the national co-prosecutor and judges did not make sense "unless one accepts that it was general and inflexible government policy to stop all trials after Cases 001 and 002."[77] In light of the irreconcilable differences between the Court's national and international sides in a context in which "realpolitik operates," she concluded that it would be both unconscionable and futile to proceed any further with these cases despite the alleged crimes' gravity.

A Hybrid Tribunal: Between Neo-patrimonialism and Pragmatism

The previous section shows that the CPP government successfully resisted attempts by international ECCC officials to call high-ranking CPP officials as witnesses to the Court, and to try suspects beyond the five in Cases 001 and 002. What does this resistance tell us about power structures within the hybrid setting of the ECCC? This section argues that the CPP's successful resistance shows that the ECCC's national side was subject to similar practices of control and constraints as Cambodia's domestic judiciary—but also that the key international actors invested and investing in the ECCC consistently compromised with this situation.

Domestic Political Control of the ECCC: Patronage, Loyalty, and Coercion

Cambodia's judicial system is characterized by a lack of judicial independence (Un 2009, 75). The distinction between the state's three main organs remains blurred in practice, with the executive dominating the judiciary. Interventions by the ruling party, including the prime minister, are common prior to, during or after trials. Key judicial bodies tasked with upholding judicial independence (the Supreme Council of Magistracy) and safeguarding the constitutionality of legislation (the Constitutional Council) are subordinated to the ruling party (Lao 2006; Soy and Hing 2019). The CPP further controls access to the profession of lawyers and the 1995-established Bar Association (Dunlap 2014). In 2007, the Cambodian League for the Promotion and Defense of Human Rights (LICADHO) observed that despite UNTAC's efforts and fifteen years of aid for legal and judicial reform, the primary functions of the courts continued to be to "persecute political opponents and other critics of the government; perpetuate impunity for state actors and their associates [, and] protect the economic interests of the rich and powerful" (LICADHO 2007, 1).

During the ECCC's lifetime, this situation even worsened. Civil society, UN representatives, and donors had long lobbied for the adoption of legislation and the establishment of judicial bodies—the Constitutional Council and the Supreme Council of Magistracy—as key for the judiciary's independence. The situation, however, did not change following the 2014 adoption of the three long-awaited judicial laws on the status of judges and prosecutors and on the organization and functioning of the Courts and of the Supreme Council of Magistracy. Their adoption instead reinforced executive control over domestic courts (Subedi 2014; FIDH, LICADHO, and ADHOC 2015). Moreover, the CPP's turn to an overt use of authoritarian practices relied upon an increasingly sophisticated instrumentalization of the judiciary, which civil society actors have experienced as a "weaponization" of law.[78] As Un (2019) has argued, this instrumentalization amounts to a form of "rule by law"—that is, the selective application of law for the suppression of the ruling party's opponents. Since the early 2000s, there has been a surge of lawsuits against members of opposition parties, journalists, and NGO leaders (Un and So 2012). In November 2020, "mass trials" were initiated against 138 members of the dissolved opposition party, which led to the conviction of 71 opposition politicians and activists in March and June 2022 (Muntarbhorn 2021; Human Rights Watch 2022). In such cases, courts can rely upon broad and ambiguous laws.[79]

Decades of colonial and repressive rule, war, and foreign occupation certainly played a role in shaping Cambodia's judiciary. A formal legislative and judicial system was first introduced under French colonial rule. However, the French minimally invested in legal education; the distinction between the executive and the judiciary remained blurred; and the newly established court structure bureaucratized, rather than eradicated, patronage relations (Low 2023). The judicial system was further embedded within colonial and racist aspirations of domination and repression (Low 2023). Following independence, the civil law system was modernized under Sihanouk's rule (1954–70) and maintained under the Lon Nol regime (1970–75). However, the judiciary's main use remained that of suppressing dissent. Under the Khmer Rouge, the judicial and legal order was annihilated, as was the traditional conciliation system. Judges and lawyers were systematically targeted and executed; only a few jurists survived.[80] Following the fall of the Khmer Rouge regime, the PRK re-established a formal judicial system. Authorities filled judicial positions by hiring individuals with high-school certificates, usually former schoolteachers and literate Cambodians without connection to former regimes (Gottesman 2004, 244). Under the Soviet-oriented regime, the party used the law and the justice system as political instruments to serve its interests (Etcheson 2019). The party viewed the courts with suspicion and government officials regularly interfered in judicial processes. After the 1989 withdrawal of Vietnamese troops, the subordination of the judiciary to the party persisted (Un and So 2012).

To explain the continued absence of judicial independence, scholars and rights activists point to the judiciary's embeddedness in neo-patrimonial structures of power. Practices of patronage and corruption allow for CPP control. Judges are members of the ruling party, and promotions and appointments are based on patronage rather than merit. This ensures that those in deciding positions are loyal to the CPP. Judges, prosecutors, court clerks further pay for their positions. Once appointed, they have to "recoup their investment" by "squeeze[ing] money out of those who come into contact with the judicial system" (Un 2006, 231–32). This makes the justice system inaccessible and unjust for the poor, since decisions are often rendered according to "the 'thinness' or 'thickness' of the stack of bribe money" (Un 2009, 89). Corruption, however, is not merely a financial transaction, as it is often conceived of in the West. It has not been solved by raising the inadequately low salaries of judges, prosecutors, and court officials. Judges and legal practitioners have to maintain "a personal relationship and ongoing backing from higher authorities" to secure their professional tenure and livelihood, if not their physical safety (Un and Ledgerwood 2010, 6). They thus accommodate high-ranking government officials or other powerful actors, out of affection—an essential aspect of patron-client relationships—or fear. If they do not protect the interests of powerful patrons in their work, they can face threats, physical attacks, removals, or reassignments to remote provinces (Un 2009; Morris 2017). This shapes the decision-making process of judges and legal practitioners even in the absence of direct and clear instructions: judges will render decisions according to their assessments of the political environment and the ruling party's interests, self-censor or remain inert while awaiting instructions (West 2019).

At the ECCC, the CPP's political control seems to have been asserted through similar neo-patrimonial practices. This can be seen in appointment and recruitment practices according to patronage networks and political reliability, as well as in the allegations of corruption that emerged early on. In such a context, the outcome in cases of political sensitivity is ensured through the loyalty and affection that characterizes patronage relations but also through coercion.

All ECCC Cambodian judges were to be appointed by the Supreme Council of Magistracy, though decisions were reportedly taken at the top by the prime minister (Ciorciari and Heindel 2014; Etcheson 2019). According to Etcheson (2019, 156), the different lists of candidates leaked during the noticeably long decision process suggests an intense "factional pulling and hauling" to accommodate the CPP's "byzantine web of interests and factions." The selected candidates for senior ECCC positions arguably included some of the best among Cambodian jurists. However, some of the appointed judges had dire records in judicial independence and were seen to lack professional credentials (LICADHO 2007; Etcheson 2019). This included most prominently Judge Ney Thol, president of the Military Court since 1987 and a member of the CPP Central Committee, appointed as ECCC Pre-Trial Chamber judge (see, e.g., US Embassy 2006).[81] He had presided over what was widely deemed to be a "sham trial" of opposition parliamentarian Cheam Channy in 2008 (Human Rights Watch 2005), and over the 1998 trial of then-exiled Prince Norodom Ranariddh and his subordinates following the 1997 coup (Kimsan 1998). Another judge, ECCC Trial Chamber reserve judge Thou Mony, had acquitted Hun Sen's nephew of alleged manslaughter in 2004. He also ruled twice against the later-acquitted suspects in the murder of trade unionist Chea Vichea (LICADHO 2007).

Having retained their positions in the national judiciary, some of the senior ECCC judicial officials would also be involved in widely criticized rulings during their ECCC tenure. The most controversial incident took place in November 2017, when the Supreme Court Chamber dissolved the main opposition party and banned 118 of its senior officials from participating in politics for five years. The Supreme Court Chamber judges included Kong Srim, president of the ECCC Supreme Court Chamber, and You Ottara, ECCC trial chamber judge, while the ECCC's national co-prosecutor Chea Leang served as its chief prosecutor (*Phnom Penh Post* 2017).

Beyond senior positions, the recruitment of ECCC national staff also often favored candidates close to the ruling party and the well-connected (Bates 2010).[82] This reflected most prominently *khsae* (ខ្សែ) or networks linked to Sok An, the most visible example being that of Chea Leang, his niece by marriage.[83] With time it seems that staff members appointed at the ECCC also brought along, or established, their own small patronage networks within the institution.[84]

As early as October 2006, OSJI (2006) raised the first concerns of a lack of transparency regarding the hiring practices on the Cambodian side. The UN Development Program (UNDP) requested an external audit of the Court's administration national side, which was completed in June 2007. It concluded that almost half of the twenty-nine personnel files reviewed "did not meet the minimum requirements in the vacancy announcements in terms of either academic qualifications or working experience" and that "recruitment was not performed in a transparent, competitive and objective manner" (UN Development Programme 2007, 12, 4). The report therefore recommended to nullify all recruitments made on the national side and to organize a new recruitment process under the UNDP's "close supervision" (5). The Cambodian government responded that recruitment and management of the national staff was not merely a technical matter: it was an issue of sovereign authority, as recognized in the Framework Agreement (Ciorciari and Heindel 2014, 85). In the end, UN officials declared themselves to be satisfied by the remedial steps taken, (for example, the adoption of a code of conduct), suggesting that the UN did not want to jeopardize the ECCC's work (Ciorciari and Heindel 2014). Irregularities seem to have persisted afterward.[85]

In addition to these irregularities in recruitment procedures, allegations of corruption at the ECCC also suggest that the CPP controlled the ECCC's national staff through neo-patrimonial practices of power. In 2007, "the most salient corruption allegations" to ever be seen at an internationalized court emerged at the ECCC (Ciorciari and Heindel 2014, 87–88). OSJI reported that Cambodian staff had informed them of having to pay a portion of their monthly salaries to their superiors to secure their positions. Some sources suggested this amounted to a third of their salary (Hall 2009). According to Etcheson (2019), rather than kickbacks, the financial transactions in fact consisted of CPP membership fees, which staff members were required to pay from their income. The issue only became public when the chief of protocol appointed by the director of administration Sean Visoth attempted to collect these fees from all national staff, rather than only CPP members. It is from the small group of non-CPP members working on the national side that court monitors learned of this, despite the absence of whistle-blower protections (Etcheson 2019). Rather than merely monetary transactions, the collection of such fees organized throughout the ECCC's hierarchy is central to ensuring loyalty and political control. A human rights researcher observed that with such practices, common in Cambodia's national administration, the message sent to staff is not that "you have to give me [for example, 30 percent] of your salary," but on the contrary that "you are allowed to keep [70 percent] of your salary."[86]

When OSJI reported on these allegations publicly, some donor countries threatened to withhold their funding. Australia, Japan, and France, however, continued to fund the Court. The UN reacted only after intense media coverage (Ryan and McGrew 2016, 66). In July 2008, the UN set up an anticorruption scheme for the international side of the court while UNDP froze the funds it administered to the national side (Ciorciari and Heindel 2014, 88–89). The Cambodian government strongly denied the allegations, refused an independent UN investigation or reporting process, and threatened to ban OSJI from Cambodia (OSJI 2007). In August 2008, the UN's Office of Investigation and Oversight Services started a confidential review to pressure the Cambodian government to respond to the allegations. In November 2008, Sean Visoth, the ECCC director of administration, was put under extended sick leave (Bates 2010). Key donors including Japan and Australia released funds to the Court's national side, amid concerns that Case 001 proceedings would be blocked, as trial hearings were scheduled to start in February 2009. Finally, in August 2009, the UN and the Cambodian government, with support from core donors, agreed on a model featuring a single, national counsellor to receive all complaints (Ciorciari and Heindel 2014, 90). Uth Chhorn, Cambodia's auditor-general, was appointed as national counsellor to receive complaints from staff. However, ECCC staff members did not have faith in his independence (Ryan and McGrew 2016, 67). The National Audit Authority he was heading had yet to make its reports public after seven years of operation (Ear 2009). Since his appointment at the ECCC, his report has not been released, nor have new public allegations of corruption been made. However, there are indications that similar practices persisted, the main difference being that the government became "more successful in keeping staffers from going public" (Ciorciari and Heindel 2014, 317n155).

Besides the continued payment of CPP membership fees out of monthly salaries,[87] national staff reportedly also continued to pay visits to the acting director of administration during yearly celebrations (e.g., international and Khmer New Year) to make "expensive gifts" so that "the boss sees them and knows that they're there."[88] While not always considered a form of corruption in my interviews,[89] this practice suggests the expectation of a pecuniary demonstration of loyalty. This becomes even more important given the ECCC's funding crisis, when securing one's job became increasingly uncertain. Those who did not have patrons (ខ្នង, *khnâng*) at the Court, who were not CPP members, who did not abide with such expectations and explicitly refused to be involved, were reportedly less likely to be kept as staffers when personnel cuts needed to be made.[90]

These observations suggest that the ECCC constituted an additional institutional platform for the CPP to entertain patronage networks, reward loyalty through access to well-paid positions and the status benefits or "prestige" of working at the ECCC,[91] and groom a new generation of CPP members working toward "strengthening the party."[92] The CPP government was thereby able to recoup important sums of donor money, at least until it changed its approach to ECCC funding in 2014.[93] For some of the national officers I interviewed, the CPP's political control and instrumentalization of the ECCC highjacked the quality of justice at the expense of victims.[94] Seeing that the preoccupation for money had taken precedence over questions of accountability and justice for victims, a former national ECCC officer, for instance, bitterly criticized the ECCC for ultimately "cheat[ing] the spirits of the Khmer Rouge victims," as the CPP was "making benefits over the dead" (ធ្វើអាជីវកម្មលើខ្មោច, *tvoe achivokâm loe kmaoch*).[95]

These observations of patronage and corruption at the ECCC help to analyze how the CPP's control of the Court's national side has taken place. While displaying the formal aspects of a legal and rational bureaucratic apparatus, power in the ECCC's national side truly lied in the patronage relations that structured its offices. This is not to say that all ECCC national officers were recruited through CPP patronage networks, that those recruited in this way necessarily lacked qualifications or a genuine motivation to pursue justice for victims of the Khmer Rouge regime. But those who came to the ECCC with a civil society background and without CPP backing had less power to achieve their work.[96] When it came to politically sensitive issues, the margin of maneuver was also limited for those wanting to work independently. At the ECCC, as in the national judiciary, deviating from the expectations or instructions of CPP patrons constituted a risk for judicial and administrative officials reliant on patronage networks (DeFalco 2018). Their own professional and social advancement would be at stake, as well as that of relatives working outside the ECCC who similarly depended on CPP patrons.[97] Speaking one's mind and not accounting for CPP interests would mean running the risk of being labeled as being part of the opposition party.[98] Self-censorship,[99] and avoidance or inertia when international colleagues raised politically sensitive issues,[100] thus constituted strategies of professional survival in the judicial field, and illustrated the CPP's political control at the ECCC (see, e.g., West 2019).

Early on, Un and Ledgerwood (2010, 8) observed that the ECCC's national judicial staff had to bear the Khmer saying in mind: "When the boat departs, the dock stays behind" (ទូកទៅកំពង់នៅ, *touk tov kompong nov*). If the tribunal could be a "temporary safe enclave for Cambodian judges and prosecutors to exercise international standards of justice," they could not ignore the realities of the national judicial system (8). OSJI (2010, 3) monitors similarly observed: "There are clearly members of the Cambodian legal profession working in the court who are deeply committed to seeing the ECCC act independently but who also see their options to effectuate that within the current system as extremely restricted. [. . .] In the end, the ability of individual Cambodian actors to resist interference by senior political figures and still maintain a position within the Cambodian legal system is limited."

Kent (2013, 320) also found that ECCC national officers "have come to be framed by very different concerns and considerations from those of their international colleagues, particularly in domains relating to security"—security having to be understood broadly here, as "social survival through protection, opportunity or even privilege." Marcel Lemonde (2013, 51) also described how early on in his tenure at the ECCC a Cambodian colleague warned him: "The judge added that I needed to mistrust *all* Cambodian judges: either they lived in fear of the ruling power, or they were close to it, but in any case, none of them was trustworthy or independent."

In an interview in 2014, an international judge also observed that the national judges worked in a "very different judicial and legal environment":

> We are sure that they do not receive any orders, it is not as crass as that, but equally we think that they know what they should be doing, how they should be reacting. That's not in the day-to-day work, I don't mean how to make a particular decision or anything as minor as that, but the direction. And [. . .] the national judges are very much put under pressure by their domestic colleagues in the domestic courts who constantly ask them why they're doing this, why they're doing that . . . So, they have a lot more pressure than we do. [. . .] [And] it's easy for us. We walk away at the end of it [. . .] [while] never having been in any sort of danger, emotionally, physically, psychologically.[101]

The coercion experienced by ECCC national staff members seems to have been exacerbated as the CPP government turned to increasingly overt authoritarian practices. In an interview in early 2014, for instance, an ECCC officer observed that some of the national civil party lawyers were particularly hesitant, at that time at least, to represent civil parties in Cases 003 and 004, given the CPP's strong opposition to these cases: "Some lawyers do not want to because first, there is no budget. Second, there is [. . .] a professional risk. [. . .]. To find work here, you need to be either pro-government, or absent. That's it! [. . .]"[102] He further explained that to be considered pro-government, one needed to be explicitly following the government's positions. In the highly polarized context of the Cambodian judicial and political system, "remaining quiet" became increasingly equated with being supportive of the political opposition.[103] This was even more the case for lawyers who needed to think ahead of how to secure their professional survival after ending their work at the ECCC. Access to less dangerous and more lucrative fields of law, such as business law, required them to abandon their commitment to human rights lawyering, and the hopes they had formed for a career in human rights when they first started to work at the ECCC.

There were, however, possible strategies to remedy the limited margin of maneuver available for national staff at the ECCC through task sharing with their international counterparts. An international defense lawyer, for instance, explained that while his national colleague agreed on raising political interference as a defense strategy, his colleague never engaged himself in writing on these positions: "They [the national defense lawyers] are independent, but, well, fearful of possible consequences. So, a lot of findings in relation to political interference he [a national co-lawyer] never co-signed. [. . .] But you know, I'm not Cambodian. So, it is easier for me to criticize."[104]

The UN, Donor Countries, and UN Staff: Particularizing the "Internationals"

This analysis of CPP resistance at the ECCC thus shows the CPP's control of national staff through neo-patrimonialism. But it also shows the compromise and pragmatism of some of the international actors invested and investing in the ECCC. This includes the UN and core donors, as well as UN appointed staff at the ECCC.

As discussed earlier in this chapter, when facing CPP resistance in Cases 003 and 004, the UN did not react strongly nor withdraw in the instances widely seen as breaches of the Agreement with the Cambodian government. The UN's weak position regarding Cases 003 and 004 has been lamented by national ECCC officers, who have felt left alone with the "fight for justice" (Ryan and McGrew 2016, 64). The UN's position was arguably the result of a weak mandate with the Court's split administrative structure, as well as of a lack of leadership and ownership, as commentators, UN appointed staff, and national officers at the ECCC have argued (Ciorciari and Heindel 2014; Ryan and McGrew 2016).[105] A former international judicial official, for instance, observed:

> What I find problematic is when one mistakes the target when saying that the tribunal is not functioning. We had absolutely no surprise from the Cambodian government, while on the contrary the UN has not risen to the challenge. [. . .] We are not naïve anymore. I agree that it is scandalous, but the government always said it. [. . .]. I am not saying that it is a good thing, but the prerequisites were laid since the beginning during the ten years of negotiations, and we knew with whom we were dealing, and that the national staff is entirely under instructions, that this is clear, it's in plain view of everyone, so to be surprised is a bit to play the card of hypocrisy. [. . .] The UN did not handle this situation well, certainly because of its initial biases on the impossibility of this tribunal to complete an impartial trial and [also it] did not invest the necessary human and strategic resources [. . .] for this tribunal to truly function.[106]

Other UN-appointed officials similarly noted a general reluctance from the UN to deal with the ECCC, frightened that it would be a failure.[107] After having been forced by the UN General Assembly to establish the Court, the UN Office of Legal Affairs, which was responsible for overseeing the implementation of the Cambodia-UN Agreement on the ECCC, was perceived as not really wanting to be involved. At the same time, the UN's investment of funds, personnel, and its reputation led to the necessity of declaring the ECCC's legitimacy and success (Ciorciari and Heindel 2014, 197–200).[108] The international co-investigating judge Siegfrid Blunk's puzzling attempts to close Case 003 without having conducted a proper investigation, for instance, led to speculations that he was acting under directions from the UN Office of Legal Affairs who wanted an end to the cases that were troubling the ECCC's reputation (97–98).

Besides the UN, core donors have also played a significant role in how the CPP was able to control the ECCC (see, e.g., Ciorciari and Heindel 2014, 79–82). Donors have not held a unified position at the ECCC, reflecting more generally donors' positionings in Cambodia (Un 2019, 26–29). As discussed above, donors such as Australia, Japan, and France also prioritized the ECCC's existence amid stark allegations of corruption and political interference. Heather Ryan, who monitored the ECCC for OSJI from 2006 to 2020, observed: "I've had conversations with representatives of donor states who have said to me, 'Look, this is Cambodia! We expect corruption, we expect political interference! [. . .] Don't be naïve and say that we have to do something about this, this is what we signed up for when we came here.' And there seems to be a feeling [. . .] that no one expected at the beginning that this Court would [. . .] follow the things that are articulated in its founding documents."[109]

At the ECCC, as in other fields of international intervention in Cambodia, prioritizing the preservation of bilateral relationships has shaped the behavior of key donors. Japan's "off-hands diplomatic" approach at the ECCC has, for instance, been interpreted in relation to Japan's concerns over the Cambodian government's increasing reliance on China (Ciorciari and Heindel 2014, 82).[110] Japan has been the ECCC's main donor, including during its formative years. It has also taken a different approach from other donors, as it has only funded transitional justice initiatives of the Cambodian state—such as the Legal Documentation Center—rather than local NGOs (Kum 2019).

In light of repeated funding crises, many donors—though not all[111]—also did not show much appetite to push for further trials beyond Cases 001 and 002.[112] This became particularly blatant in 2017, when both co-investigating judges Michael Bohlander and You Bunleng explained considering ending Cases 003, 004 and 004/2 due to a lack of funding in a document that was leaked to the press.[113] The situation subsequently improved, with, e.g., Japan stepping in. The request nonetheless confirmed concerns over the influence of donor fatigue and completion deadlines on the ECCC's work. In their request, the judges criticized donors' "expressions of discontent with the pace of the investigations" and the resulting "level of intended intrusion into judicial case management and decision-making."[114] But they also questioned the use of "results-based budgeting or 'milestones' as a measure of success and/or progress to judicial decision-making processes," which in their view is "incompatible with judicial independence."[115] These observations speak to contemporary critiques of donor's justice, of the commodification or marketization of global justice, and of the resulting introduction of neoliberal, managerial rationalities in the field of international criminal justice (Kendall 2011; Schwöbel-Patel 2021).

Finally, it is important to note that the issue of political interference has been widely litigated, given the defense lawyers' combative approach in Case 002. The ECCC judicial panels repeatedly ruled against defense motions on allegations of political interference. In concurrence with the jurisprudence of other international criminal tribunals, they set a high standard for disproving the presumption of independence and impartiality. Legal analysts found that defense applications were taken seriously, that the Chambers offered properly reasoned and often unanimous decisions (Jørgensen 2018, 178–90). Perhaps, in the absence of concrete evidence to prove that their national counterparts were controlled by the CPP,[116] and based on positive experiences of collaborations on Cases 001 and 002, UN-appointed staff members preferred to "tacitly accept that their colleagues face difficult moral choices and question them no further" (Staggs Kelsall 2009, 168). However, more critical accounts of these decisions question whether the judges were thereby not "shielding themselves from criticism directed toward their integrity and [. . .] protecting the Court from similar scrutiny," especially since some of the judges had spoken critically on political interference in their private capacity (Torrens 2016, 70; see also Orentlicher 2020).

In some instances, however, some of the UN-appointed staff members drew the line for themselves. As discussed above, staff members of the Office of Co-investigating Judges resigned after Blunk's attempts to close Case 003 and after the UN did not respond to their concerns. Moreover, in December 2017, after high-level national ECCC officials were involved in Cambodia's Supreme Court Chamber's decision to dissolve the opposition party and ban 118 opposition lawmakers from holding political office for five years, 22 (out of the approximately 150) international staff members submitted a statement of concern to the ECCC Office of Administration.[117] The UN High Commissioner for Human Rights had condemned Cambodia's Supreme Court Chamber's decision, but no connection was made with involved ECCC officials. Trial Chamber legal officer Harshan Athureliya, who led the initiative, explained that the petition was not about taking a political position or getting involved in domestic politics but about asking the UN for guidance on how to address this serious ethical and professional issue that cast the ECCC's integrity into doubt.[118]

The UN Ethics Office acknowledged the difficult nature of the situation, yet found it was for the administration to reply to the staff concerns. In the end, staff members were left to face this dilemma individually. Harshan Athureliya resigned. While respecting his colleagues' decision not to abandon their work at the ECCC, he found it intolerable to be working as an international civil servant for an institution that was designed to deliver justice and to promote the rule of law but turned a blind eye when several high-level ECCC officials effectively "signed the death sentence on democracy" in Cambodia.[119] While the UN would never withdraw from the process this late, one solution could have been that the involved national officials recuse themselves, he argued. In effectively not handling this situation, the UN was sending a poor message to Cambodian staff at the ECCC, some of whom had supported their international colleagues' initiative, and jeopardized the Court's legacy.[120] In their 2016 analysis of the ECCC's performance, Heather Ryan and Laura McGrew (2016, 67) had similarly warned that the Court may have "a negative impact, not solely because Cambodians are not allowed to operate with proper judicial independence, but also because the internationals—while articulating a commitment to oppose political interference—collude in diminishing hope for a judicial system that protects against the abuse of power."

While the roles of the UN, donors, and international staff at the ECCC certainly warrant further analysis, which goes beyond this chapter's aim, these reactions to CPP control of the ECCC point to frictions among the various international actors involved at, and monitoring, the ECCC. These frictions reflect long-standing divides between pragmatists and legalists that have shaped the ECCC's establishment, as discussed in chapter 1. On the one hand, pragmatists prioritized the establishment of the Court and later of trials in Cases 001 and 002, finding that a Khmer Rouge tribunal, trial sentences against suspects in Cases 001 and 002 were better than none. From this standpoint, although the suspects in Cases 003 and 004 were not tried, the record of the investigations of their alleged crimes, and in most cases the suspects' indictment, is an achievement. On the other hand, legalists refused to accept a Court which they saw from the start or over time as not being independent from the Cambodian government.

Over the years, scholars, commentators, and ECCC staff members have analyzed these polarized views of the ECCC from various angles. Lemonde (2013, 217), for instance, explained this divide using Max Weber's concepts of ethics of responsibility versus ethics of conviction. Etcheson (2019) has argued that this cleavage among international actors reflects a confrontation between conflicting ideologies on how law and politics relate.[121] On the one hand, international actors (e.g., senior officials in the UN Office of Legal Affairs or representatives of Human Rights Watch or Amnesty International) adopted a position of classical legalism. This view not only posits law and politics as separate spheres but also condemns any intrusion of politics into the field of law as a form of "pollution." On the other hand, international actors such as US diplomat David Scheffer and donor countries' representatives took a position of strategic legalism, using law for strategic policy goals. Finally, Alexander Hinton (2022) has identified these tensions as being tensions among legal purists, progressivists—who associate retributive justice with broader promises of transitional justice—and pragmatists.

These divergences subsequently shaped measures of success of the transitional justice process in Cambodia. As John Ciorciari and Anne Heindel (2014, 168–69) observed, some "see the exercise of judicial independence as a key barometer of the Court's success or failure" while "[o]thers, including people who have spent years seeking justice for victims, regret that the effort to prosecute more than five has overtly politicized the entire process, put the centerpiece Case 002 in jeopardy, and threatens to eclipse the Court's potentially positive legacy for Cambodia." More generally, these divergences reflect long-standing polarizations in assessments of the relevance and effectiveness of international aid and interventions in Cambodia ever since it became an experiment for liberal interventionism in the early 1990s. As Un (2013a, 284) has noted, "Diverse assessments of Cambodia's political and economic trajectory" have existed ever since, "varying from the image of a glass half-full to half-empty."

Accounting for these frictions is essential: they provide a more adequate understanding of the politics of international(ized) tribunals and a more complex picture of the international and national actors involved. They can help to particularize the international actors involved in hybrid settings, when too often international actors are merely neutralized and decontextualized as "experts." As Elizabeth Bruch (2010, 35–36) has argued in her analysis of hybrid courts: "The international becomes stripped of personal and national affiliations, neutralized as expert, while the national is overly personalized and nationalized. Moreover, this oversimplification is also writ large. The international community as a whole is often absolved from any complicity or misconduct in the intervention or in the conditions that may have fostered or exacerbated the conflict; the locus for responsibility remains solely with the national."

In this context, Rachel Hughes (2015, 724) reminds us that media portrayals of the ECCC as a "show trial" are reminiscent of media coverage of the

1979 People's Revolutionary Tribunal. They entertain an imaginary of Cambodia as a homogenous space, "not simply 'behind' the developed world and mired in a traumatic and violent past, but thirsting for justice and unlikely to get it." By doing so, such reports ignore that "complex impasses of law, conflict and social memory" occur everywhere; they also downplay the complicity of the UN and foreign powers in the violence that occurred prior to, during, and after Democratic Kampuchea (724). This perspective speaks to critiques of transitional justice as a neocolonial or neoimperialistic project that produces dehistoricized and depoliticized transitional justice narratives in complete disconnection from colonial legacies or the roles of Western countries and corporations in the crimes that are being investigated (see, e.g., Hinton 2011b; Kagoro 2012; An-Na'im 2013; Path 2017).

Conclusion

This chapter's analysis of CPP's resistance of a far-ranging criminal accountability process shows how the ECCC has intersected with domestic politics and has done so at a time of considerable contestation and consolidation of CPP power. First, the CPP's discursive resistance to the ECCC has reflected efforts to develop a narrative that glorifies the prime minister as sole guarantor of peace in the past, present, and future of Cambodia. The claims that the ECCC could lead to civil war if going too far with its investigations thus not only served to reaffirm the CPP's role as savior of the nation but also emphasized the personal role played by Hun Sen in achieving and defending peace in Cambodia. As Norén-Nilsson (2021) has argued, this peace narrative has paved the way for Hun Sen's "regal turn to authoritarianism," following the 2017 dismantling of the opposition and transition to a de facto one-party state (see also Ngoun 2022). It serves to assert the prime minister's claims for legitimacy and power both internally (against political rivals), and externally (against international actors such as the UN or Western powers) and their self-portrayal as apolitical and moral agents. This shows how claims for legitimacy continue to play a central role in the CPP's exercise of power, in a context in which raising the involvement of senior CPP officials in human rights violations during the Khmer Rouge regime and beyond, including through the combative use of legal avenues abroad, has been a central feature of political strategies of the political opposition.

Second, the analysis of CPP resistance at the ECCC has revealed how the ECCC's national side has been embedded within the neo-patrimonial structures of power that shape the domestic judiciary. The CPP's resistance at the

ECCC has been selective rather than obstructive of all proceedings. It has mainly come into play to block the appearance of senior CPP officials as witnesses at the ECCC and to limit the list of suspects beyond those in Cases 001 and 002. Yet its success has relied upon asserting political control over the ECCC's national side from the start of the ECCC's operations, through practices of both patronage and coercion. The CPP political elite has thereby used the ECCC as a platform for the distribution of positions and salaries, the rewarding of loyalty, and the recouping of important sums of donor money. If national staff members joined the ECCC with the aspiration to work independently, they were able to do so only within the limits set by the ruling party. They faced similar practices of coercion as their peers in the national judiciary, including through pressure to secure their professional existence after the end of their time at the ECCC. These practices unfolded during a period of considerable political uncertainty, and a turn to overly authoritarian practices that relied on an increasing instrumentalization of the domestic judiciary. These developments disappointed those who had invested their hopes in the UN's promise that the ECCC would bring justice to the Cambodian people through an independent judicial process and thereby contribute to the rule of law in Cambodia—including Khmer Rouge survivors, Cambodian lawyers, judicial officials, or civil society actors.

Finally, the story of CPP resistance at the ECCC is also the story of the pragmatism adopted by the international actors invested and investing in this project of transitional justice. If we analyze the ruling party's resistance to transitional justice in more depth, the notion of "political interference" will therefore quickly appear inadequate. This notion reflects a legalistic approach that locates politics at the ECCC with only one actor: the ruling political elite. This conceals the ways in which the CPP's resistance at the ECCC is not about a clash between law versus politics but of a competition between different political ideologies. Limiting politics at the ECCC to the influence of the CPP government conceals the key roles played by the UN, donor countries, and UN-appointed staff in shaping the ECCC, its continued existence, and its outcomes. Such a view further reifies the local versus the international as distinct rather than mutually constitutive spatial categories and attaches to each a single set of agency and normative values, which belies the heterogeneity of the involved actors.[122] It is a missed opportunity to understand how divergences among the involved international actors at the ECCC reflect more broadly inherent anxieties and unresolved tensions of the field of international criminal justice, which was established on the claim that it transcends politics only to grapple with repeated "crises" of legitimacy associated with the lived—and necessarily political—trajectories of its institutions (Mégret 2016).

3

Victim Participation

From the Village to the Courtroom, through Urban Spaces of Protest

Over the years, victim participation at the ECCC has brought Cambodians together to participate in the state-led process of transitional justice. The ECCC defines a victim as a "person or legal entity" who has "suffered harm as a result of the commission of any crime within the jurisdiction of the ECCC."[1] Victims can participate in the legal proceedings as witnesses, complainants, or civil parties. Of these options, civil party participation is the most progressive, visible, and direct form of participation. When admitted as civil parties, victims are represented by a civil party lawyer and gain access to the legal proceedings, outreach activities for civil parties, and reparation projects. Civil party participation at the ECCC, at least in its early years, was unprecedented in the field of international criminal justice.[2] It results from the ECCC's hybrid nature and Cambodia's civil law system, a legacy of French colonial rule.

In Cases 001 and 002, the ECCC received 94 and 4,128 civil party applications respectively. Of these, 76 applicants were admitted in Case 001, and 3,869 in Case 002.[3] Additionally, the ECCC received over 2,000 civil party applications in Cases 003 and 004.[4] Considering how many would qualify as Khmer Rouge victims under the ECCC's definition, this is a very small number. Nonetheless, civil party participation brought together Cambodians from different socioeconomic backgrounds, provinces—mostly from rural environments but also from urban areas—and diaspora communities, granting them a formal, legal status to participate in the legal proceedings in the capital city.

Civil parties' experiences of participation were not homogeneous. Given the scope of Case 001, which consisted of charges against a single defendant and one major crime site, the smaller number of civil party applicants in Case 001 allowed for their repeated attendance of Court hearings and NGO outreach activities. Represented by four legal teams, they could meet their lawyers regularly. Some of them, however, had a difficult experience in Case 001 due to the late rejection of their civil party applications at the end of the trial (see Stover, Balthazard, and Koenig 2011).[5] Civil parties in Case 002 had a much less intense experience of participation, given the Case's wide scope and decreasing donor support for NGO activities. They were also much more numerous and did not participate as individual parties anymore but as part of a consolidated group represented in Court by the lead co-lawyers. Finally, civil party applicants in Cases 003 and 004 had limited to no opportunities to participate in ECCC outreach events and trial proceedings, as the cases never reached trial.

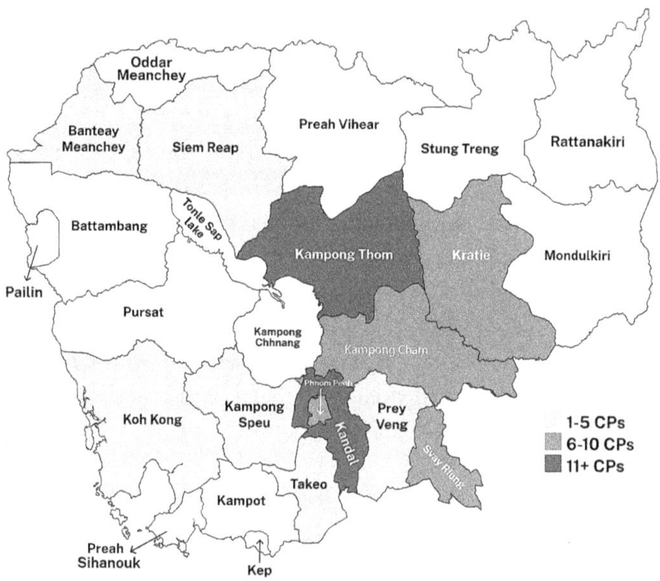

Banteay Meanchey	1	Kandal	12	Prey Veng	1
Kampong Cham	9	Koh Kong	1	Siem Reap	1
Kampong Speu	1	Kratie	6	Svay Rieng	7
Kampong Thom	11	Phnom Penh	9	Takeo	2

CP applicants = 90
Admitted CPs = 76 (including 15 overseas) ♂ 29 ♀ 47

Map 1. Civil parties per province (Case 001)

Civil parties were also offered different opportunities for participation. Some were invited to testify,[6] to participate in reparation projects, or to act as civil party representatives or focal points. The system of civil party representatives was introduced by the human rights NGO ADHOC to support the participation of the numerous civil parties in Case 002 (see Kirchenbauer et al. 2013). With this program, ADHOC offered trainings to a select number of Case 002 civil parties so that they could act as intermediaries between the ECCC, the lawyers, and the civil parties. This group thereby enjoyed greater access to information and outreach events. While the program ceased to operate in late 2015 for lack of funding, some of the civil party representatives later continued to work directly with the ECCC's Victims Support Section (VSS). To facilitate communication with civil parties across the country, the VSS also worked with "focal points" who are non-civil parties and often figures of

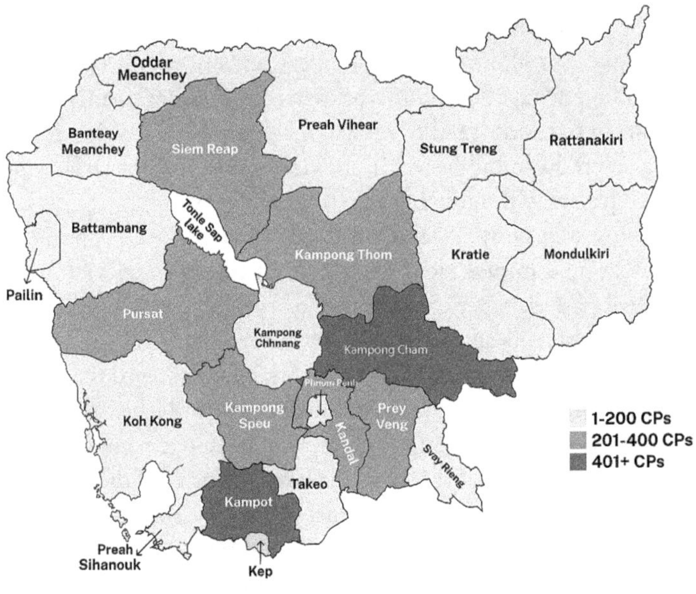

Banteay Meanchey	137	Kep	9	Preah Vihear	60
Battambang	62	Koh Kong	62	Prey Veng	205
Kampong Cham	464	Kratie	97	Pursat	265
Kampong Chhnang	158	Mondulkiri	57	Rattanakiri	33
Kampong Speu	307	Oddar Meanchey	16	Siem Reap	221
Kampong Thom	212	Pailin	14	Stung Treng	65
Kampot	520	Phnom Penh	127	Svay Rieng	149
Kandal	318	Preah Sihanouk	103	Takeo	81

CP applicants = 4128
Admitted CPs = 3867 (including 125 overseas) ♂ 1497 ♀ 2370

Map 2. Civil parties per province (Case 002)

authority within rural communities, such as commune chiefs, village chiefs, or teachers.

Civil party participation was also particularly affected by difficulties to secure funding. Since the Court's framework documents did not anticipate civil party participation, the Victims Unit, later renamed VSS, was only established in 2007 (Jarvis 2014). Concerns about financial and administrative costs, and a lack of understanding of legal aid,[7] also led to a lack of support from UN-appointed administrators at the ECCC (Ciorciari and Heindel 2014, 205–10). As a result, the Victims Unit (and later VSS)—initially led by a Cambodian head and UN-appointed deputy—became increasingly nationalized (207–10). Over the years, the ECCC would therefore heavily rely on NGOs who acted as vital intermediaries between the ECCC and civil parties, before they also faced decreasing donor funding (Sperfeldt and Oeung 2019). In the last few years, the COVID-19 pandemic, as well as the rejection by the ECCC administration of funding requests for human resources and for civil party outreach, contributed to a breakdown of communication between civil parties and their lawyers. In June 2022, a few months prior to the pronouncement of the ECCC's final verdict in Case 002/02, the international lead co-lawyer Megan Hirst therefore resigned as she found herself in the "untenable position" of having to represent civil parties without being able to meet them.[8]

By now, a rich body of scholarship has discussed victim participation at the ECCC. Some studies focus on whether Khmer Rouge victims, and specifically civil parties, experienced justice or even reconciliation. In the survey I conducted with colleagues in 2018,[9] we found that 68.8 percent of the 255 civil parties we met affirmed that "justice has been achieved for the victims of the Khmer Rouge regime" today, and 66 percent indicated that "the ECCC has brought justice for the victims of the Khmer Rouge regime and their families" (Williams et al. 2018). Moreover, a large majority of the civil parties surveyed were either satisfied (65.9 percent) or very satisfied (26.8 percent) with their experiences as civil parties. However, the follow-up qualitative research added much more nuanced insights to these findings regarding the limitations, disappointments, and frustrations that civil parties also experienced in their quest for justice at the ECCC.

The existing scholarship also examines the changes made to the civil party participation regime over time. Initially, civil parties were granted participation rights as equal parties to the proceedings. Along the way, however, significant changes were made concerning civil party eligibility and rights granted to civil parties, such as the right to speak in person in the Court and to select legal representation (see, e.g., Studzinsky 2009; Werner and Rudy 2010; Ciorciari and Heindel 2014; Killean 2018a). Most importantly, before the start of trial proceedings in Case 002, the judges amended the Internal Rules to streamline legal representation, introducing a system of two civil party lead co-lawyers. The new international and national lead co-lawyers were tasked with the strategy, advocacy, and representation of civil parties in Court.[10] These changes have been the subject of much controversy. Scholars and practitioners have, for instance, questioned the meaning of participation when individual civil parties are grouped in larger collectives, or when victim participation becomes framed as a trial-management issue (see, e.g., Mohan 2009; Elander 2012).

In this chapter, while drawing from this important body of scholarship, I take a different approach. I ask: How does civil party participation take place in the specific political context of Cambodia? How has it been shaped by preexisting power relations, and how has it (re)shaped power relations?

This approach requires us to locate where transitional justice has taken *place* for civil parties. While the participation of civil parties from the Cambodian diaspora has significantly expanded the geographies of justice at play at the ECCC, this chapter focuses on civil parties living in Cambodia. Here, civil party participation is defined by experiences in and movement across various places: from civil parties' homes to regional forums and the Courtroom in the capital city. If we draw from understandings of space embedded in the spatial turn (Soja 1989; Lefebvre 2009) according to which space, as a result of social interactions, both enables and limits agency, we can see that this movement is also a process of navigation between different sets of power relations—thereby offering different options for resistance and contestations.

Here, it is useful to differentiate between what political geographer Alex Jeffrey (2011) called "invited" and "invented" spaces of transitional justice. "Invited" spaces are spaces that are highly regulated by predefined sets of rules and procedures regarding how state-led and/or legal transitional justice processes are defined and meant to occur. The ECCC's Courtroom is clearly such an "invited space," where civil parties are "molded into" the preexisting procedures that strictly regulate it (Destrooper 2018b, 119). Only a few civil parties were granted access to this space, either to testify or to watch the hearings from the limited number of seats allocated to civil parties. The Courtroom, which is located on a stage, is separated from the public gallery by a glass wall. Over the years, many civil parties were also invited to follow the trial hearings from the public gallery. The ECCC's public gallery can accommodate almost five hundred persons.[11] From there, civil parties were allowed to attend public trial hearings, which were varyingly exciting or understandable depending on whether they consisted of technical, legal deliberations; civil party and witness testimonies of witnesses; or comments from the accused. Although civil parties were invited to attend these hearings in the public gallery based on their civil party status, they were nonetheless relegated to a role of "outsiders" there (see also Elander 2018a, 108–16; A. Kent 2022). Sitting alongside the public, they were equally expected to remain silent during the hearings and were exposed to similar security measures.

Despite such restrictions, accessing these "invited spaces" still provided various opportunities for (in)formal interactions with diverse actors. During important hearings, such as the opening or closing of a trial, many Cambodian and international journalists or researchers would, for instance, attend the trial, interview civil parties, and give them a platform to voice their claims, grievances, and views. When at the ECCC, civil parties would also be able to meet their lawyer, access psychosocial support when testifying, or receive other support from the VSS. However, as Leang Sok and Toshihiro Abe (2019) also observed, the social and political pressure to abide by expected norms of social behavior in the formal settings of these "invited spaces," given also the presence of authoritative figures, limited possibilities to publicly express dissent and contention.

Besides accessing such "invited spaces," civil parties also accessed spaces of transitional justice that were more of an "invented" nature. Jeffrey (2011) speaks of "invented spaces" to refer to spaces that are less formal and more open to critical deliberation about transitional justice. We can think of the various outreach activities or trainings organized by NGOs—for instance, for civil party representatives, or the reparation projects implemented by NGO staff members—in which some civil parties participated. The civil party forums organized by the VSS in various provincial capitals can also be analyzed from this perspective, especially as they became more interactive with time. These events usually included a morning session during which several members of the Court—including the co-lead civil party lawyers, as well as officials from the Public Affairs section or officials from judicial offices—provided an update on ongoing ECCC proceedings. In the second part of the forum, civil parties were able to meet their lawyers in groups and discuss various issues (e.g., reparation projects). At these forums, especially during the afternoon meetings with lawyers, or coffee and lunch breaks, civil parties could raise more contentious issues and question what they saw as fundamental limitations of the transitional justice process.

Jeffrey's (2011) analytical distinction of "invited" versus "invented" spaces is thus useful to analyze where civil party participation *takes place* and how civil parties, when participating, become confronted not only with how the transitional justice process is set to be but also expectations of how they are to be when participating. But it is also important to keep in mind that with many civil parties coming from rural areas, rural-urban divides also shaped civil parties' agency and their possibilities to voice dissent. In Cambodia, rural environments are characterized by hierarchical social structures and are often subject to higher social and political control than urban areas, including stricter surveillance by the ruling party (see, e.g., C. Hughes 2003, 198; CAS and World Bank 2006, 198). As a result, the capital city—and specific places within—have long played a particular role in the public expression of grievances. In fact, while public protests were still allowed, urbanized protesters[12]—citizens from rural areas protesting in the capital city based on grievances resulting from their rural experiences—were an important figure in the landscape of contentious politics in Cambodia. A significant aspect of civil party participation is thus that it offered access to the capital city. While not everyone could make use of the capital city in the same way—travelling to Phnom Penh for the first time could be a disorienting and confusing experience[13]—civil parties could thereby access places in which they could feel more comfortable to publicly voice dissent than in their home communities. Moreover, civil parties who in their home villages were isolated for not supporting the ruling party were able to meet like-minded civil parties.

Besides the political significance of movement across urban-rural spaces, it is also necessary to locate civil party participation in the context of neo-patrimonialism and the turn to hegemonic authoritarianism. This is not about making "routine references to top-down, traditional authoritarianism or mono-structural patronage relations as an all-explanatory device" in the Cambodian, specifically rural, context, as Öjendal and Kim (2006) warn us of making. Civil party participation has taken place over a significant length of time, during which many changes at the national, regional, and local levels affected the political climate in rural areas. As we have seen in chapter 1, patronage relations are also dynamic and reinvented by those who hold power, rather than being static and homogenous. In fact, the transitional justice process at the ECCC is part of such adaptations, and if we are to understand its political nature, we need to pay attention to how these aspects affect the experiences and agency of civil parties participating in the process.

This chapter comprises three sections. The first section starts the analysis of civil party participation with civil parties' initial encounters with the ECCC in rural areas. This takes us back in time to early outreach activities for civil party participation, between 2007 and 2010, and brings our attention away from the Courtroom in the capital city to rural areas. The chapter then turns to two cases of civil party resistance during the later stages of civil party participation: the protests against the ECCC's limited approach to reparations (section 2) and the discursive resistance of some civil parties against the ECCC's limited focus on the Khmer Rouge past (section 3).

The Early Days of Civil Party Participation

First Encounters with the ECCC: Views from the Villages

Most civil parties come from rural areas: it is there that their first encounters with the ECCC took place during the application process for civil party participation. Most of the first interactions regarding the ECCC were, however, not directly with ECCC officers but NGO representatives. Given the lack of funding for victim participation at the ECCC, NGOs conducted most of the outreach for civil party participation, making use of their existing networks across the country (Sperfeldt and Oeung 2019). In Case 002 for instance, 82 percent of the applications were filed through intermediary NGOs.[14]

In rural contexts, preexisting social and power relations mediated perceptions of information sharing and outreach for civil party participation. In the qualitative research that I conducted in rural areas between November 2013 and June 2018, I saw several examples of how initial outreach activities disturbed the existing information economy. Some of the civil parties I met shared how considerable misunderstandings emerged, which at times remain until today. Those who disseminated information on the possibility of victims' participation were at times faced with skepticism: fellow community members perceived them to be mainly motivated by personal or political aims.[15] For example, some respondents initially thought that the villager advocating for filing civil party applications was doing that merely for personal gains: it was seen as an act of "partyism" or "familyism."[16]

Thinking back about the early days of the ECCC, many civil parties moreover shared having experienced fear when deciding to apply for civil party participation.[17] This is not to say that everyone was afraid: some civil parties I met explained they had not been worried and could not think of any reasons why they should have been.[18] However, many civil parties I interviewed recalled not only how they were afraid when submitting civil party applications but also how many in their immediate surroundings had been too afraid to submit civil party applications.[19] This suggests that fear constituted a widespread experience.

The survey I jointly conducted with colleagues in 2018 corroborates these observations. Almost a third of the 255 civil parties and civil party applicants surveyed (30.4 percent)—yet considerably fewer of the 55 complainants surveyed (17.6 percent)—mentioned that they were worried when submitting their application (Williams et al. 2018, 73). Most importantly, this includes 16.7 percent of the 29 civil party applicants in Cases 003 and 004 surveyed (76). This is significant since applicants for civil party participation in Cases 003 and 004 did so years after the first trial had taken place at the ECCC. Concerns thus persisted even after the ECCC's work and civil party participation had become more visible and established. Other studies on victim participation show similar findings (Killean 2018b). This includes an earlier survey conducted by Stammel et al. (2010, 51) between October 2008 and May 2009 with 247 civil party applicants in 19 provinces. Respondents were asked whether they were concerned about their personal safety because of their civil party application. While 46 percent answered not being concerned at all, and only a few respondents reported having had actual negative experiences as a direct result of their application, 17.3 percent did answer being "very concerned," and 29.6 percent "a little bit concerned."[20]

These fears seem to be linked to different temporalities and experiences of political violence. In my research, most of the respondents mentioned being afraid that former Khmer Rouge cadres would try to prevent civil parties from accusing them and revealing their involvement in crimes under the Khmer Rouge. Civil parties were concerned that if they applied, former Khmer Rouge cadres, whom they still feared, would take revenge against them, harm, kill or disappear them. One civil party from Pursat province, for instance, explained: "I was afraid [because] I exposed myself. I was afraid [that] it would happen again. And when I was called to go [to the ECCC], I was afraid even more. I was afraid of Pol Pot. [. . .] I was scared when I was interviewed [by lawyers / ECCC staff members]. I was really scared. I was thinking 'are they going to take me to kill?' [*laughing*]."[21]

Another civil party applicant from Takeo province recalled how she used to leave her house and hide at the market whenever members of the Documentation Center of Cambodia (DC-Cam) came to conduct outreach on the ECCC:

> I was afraid [when I heard about the Court] and thought, Why did they come here? Where did they come from? [. . .] Because I heard [what] the elder people said. [. . .] And we ran, and they interviewed [villagers] whose siblings or parents died, and I didn't want to meet them and went somewhere else, like to the market. [. . .] [I was afraid] because I had fear since the Pol Pot regime. [. . .] And everyone said when you filed the complaint if the Khmer Rouge came here again, you would die, and they would kill everyone [. . .]. I thought that they would kill everyone in my family, and I was afraid. Later, DC-Cam went to the village chief and let the commune chief invite the people. Then he called me to join, and I asked why they called me to go there, because I was afraid, and I cannot talk, and I fear them. And he said they did not do anything to you. They just invited us to join.[22]

It is only with the persistence of the outreach team, and because many fellow villagers applied for civil party participation, that this respondent finally changed her mind. In other cases, many did not apply because they still suffered from the psychological consequences of the Khmer Rouge regime. A civil party from Kandal province, for instance, explained to me:

> It's because of their *broken courage* from the Khmer Rouge regime and at that time they didn't trust and they're still afraid of [the] Khmer Rouge. They're afraid that the Khmer Rouge would come to spy on them. If we filed complaints like that, they would have grudges against us and take revenge [. . .]. For Cambodian people, they didn't even trust their own spouses or children because under Pol Pot, they didn't dare to speak anything. If we trusted someone [. . .], they reported that to the chief then we would be taken to be killed right away. If we did something wrong, they would take us to be killed—those small little kids called us, and we disappeared. [. . .] At that time, they had *broken courage* and they didn't dare to do it.[23]

Broken courage (*baksbat*, បាក់ស្បាត) is, in Khmer, a common idiom of distress that is culturally more significant than post-traumatic stress disorder to describe the psychological suffering experienced through exposure to traumatic events, in particular under the Khmer Rouge (S. Chhim 2013).

The fear described by this civil party can be very intimate. A civil party applicant in Case 003 and 004 from Kampot province, for instance, explained that although she was not really afraid, she still applied "quietly" and "secretly."[24] She made sure not to talk about her application with anyone, including her relatives, so that her direct neighbor—a former Khmer Rouge unit chief whom she knows killed people—would not learn about it. This example shows that survivors were probably even more careful or afraid when they continued to live alongside former Khmer Rouge cadres. While most cadres fled to the northwestern provinces in December 1978 or early 1979 during the invasion of the Vietnamese army, McGrew's (2011) research has shown that former Khmer Rouge cadres and victims who continued to live alongside each other did so in forms of "surface" or "shallow" coexistence rather than deep reconciliation. When victims continued to live next to larger communities of former cadres, they continued to experience significant levels of anxiety (McGrew 2011, 515).

The findings from our 2018 large-scale survey confirmed that the fear of former Khmer Rouge was a prevalent concern for civil parties during the application process (Williams et al. 2018, 73). The majority of respondents who indicated in our survey that they had been worried when applying explained that they were "afraid of facing pressure or revenge from the Khmer Rouge leaders,"—that is, from the accused or their families (41.3 percent). Civil parties also mentioned the fear of being threatened by former Khmer Rouge still in government today (7.9 percent) and by low-level former Khmer Rouge cadres (4.8 percent). A minority mentioned being afraid because the accused "are government officials" (3.2 percent).

The fear civil parties experienced when first submitting their applications was also linked to the absence of clear ruptures between past and present power relations. A civil party from Siem Reap province, for instance, observed in 2014: "I was afraid to apply to become a civil party. I was afraid of some people, the powerful and rich people, that they would get angry with me and the others who became civil parties in order to discuss who was responsible for the killings. I was afraid, but then I dared to do it, because everyone was applying."[25] Another civil party added: "I know that ADHOC always helped and supported the victims. So, I always tried to help people to apply. But many people are afraid. Because some of the Khmer Rouge are still leaders today, for example, the governor, or those in the military. They are officials, in the entire country, and they are now still working as governors. So, some are afraid, while others dare to ask for justice."[26]

This interconnection between past and present positions of power apparently even led low-level government officials to be wary about applying for civil party status. The civil parties from Siem Reap province further explained that although the official government position is to support the ECCC, filing a civil party application tended to be perceived as controversial, delicate, or compromising for low-level government officials: "Even village chiefs are afraid to become civil parties. For village chiefs, or, for example, those who work at the Provincial Hall, they are afraid because the governor of the province used to be a Khmer Rouge general."[27]

As discussed in chapter 2, the ruling party's position toward the ECCC has been ambiguous, fluctuating between both engagement and resistance. This also explains the lack of engagement from local authorities affiliated to the ruling party, as a civil party representative from Siem Reap province explained to me in 2018:

> [I]t was strange, in Siem Reap city, the local authorities, like the [commune] and village chiefs who [still] have anger toward the Khmer Rouge, they still didn't file a complaint [. . .]. I was the one who told them to file a complaint, but they didn't. It's like they follow the order from the top people. They will file a complaint only if the provincial chief would file a complaint. [. . .] But during that time, the government didn't seem to bother about the Khmer Rouge tribunal at all. They only find ways to prevent it from having any progress. If there is also participation from the

> government, there would be so many civil parties participating. Not just thousands, maybe it would have reached millions.[28]

In 2014, a village chief from Kandal Province also explained that he was cautious in his position on the ECCC, which by then had existed for a decade: "Myself, I just follow the news, but I don't share anything. I'm afraid that I could make a mistake because I'm an authority, so I just listen to others."[29]

Another concern of civil parties when engaging with the ECCC was that local authorities would perceive them as being involved in opposition politics or human rights activities.[30] A civil party from Siem Reap province explained:

> At first, I was also afraid. Because [of the political situation] at that time [. . .] when I was called to come once [to the ECCC], I didn't dare to go. [. . .] I was afraid that if I went, the people in the village will have trouble with me, that I joined any political parties [. . .]. The next time, I decided to go. When I came back, I told the village [authorities] that I'm not [involved] in any politics; I am at the side of the Khmer Rouge tribunal. After that, I went often. [. . .] At that time [the one] who came to register us [as civil parties] was also on the opposition party. [. . .] That's why [. . .] they're afraid we were with another party [. . .]. This is why I was afraid to go. [. . .]. [When I came back,] the village chief, he said: "Where have you been, you were at the opposition party, right? That's why you went." I [. . .] explained the reasons I went, that I didn't take any sides, this was neutral. The tribunal talked only about the Khmer Rouge's story; it didn't affect the political.[31]

In this case, local authorities were suspicious because the person conducting outreach was directly linked to the political opposition.[32] In other cases, suspicion was possibly linked to the fact that NGOs promoting human rights and democracy were the ones being most active in disseminating information and assisting with filing applications. NGOs, and in particular human rights NGOs such as ADHOC, are often scrutinized by local authorities. As Un (2019, 36) explains, the CPP does not consider them as "good NGOs" who "advance people's material needs" and lead to economic improvement, which the CPP could then take credit for, but as "bad NGOs" who are only undermining their rule. Although not the case everywhere,[33] such a suspicious stance from local authorities possibly impeded outreach efforts in rural areas for civil party participation. In 2018, a civil party from Takeo Province, for instance, recalled the difficulties he faced a decade earlier when he tried to share information on victim participation at the ECCC, as part of his grassroots association:

> If I had known this from the beginning, I would not have caused troubles for myself. Do you know this? My association was assigned to share

> information [about civil party participation] in [the] province. I submitted documents [to the local authorities for permission to conduct outreach] and did not hear anything for one month. They did not sign for me as they were strict back then. If we disseminated the information, they would say that we were associated with politics by leading people to join other political parties. But our principle was totally different. We wanted people who suffered during the Khmer Rouge regime to understand about the ECCC, which was created to find justice for their relatives who died in the regime. [. . .] They suspected me that I might belong to the other [political] parties. [. . .] When the ECCC was first created, the officials did not understand clearly about it. They were afraid that there would be movement to join other parties. So [. . .] even [when] there was gathering like at my house, there would be people watching us; what we were talking about; what the complaint was about. [. . .] At that time, it [. . .] was not easy to gather or help filing complaints like now. [. . .] Whenever we had a session to share information to the people, there would be a village chief and police watching what we talked about, but since we had the documents, we would just follow the documents.[34]

It is only after ECCC representatives contacted the local authorities that he was finally able to conduct outreach on civil party participation. In our 2018 survey, similar challenges related to the political situation were also raised, although to a lesser extent. Smaller percentages of the 255 civil parties and civil party applicants surveyed mentioned having been afraid of being accused of disinformation (11.1 percent) or political involvement (9.5 percent) when applying for civil party status. Some also mentioned being afraid because they were involved in opposition politics (6.3 percent) or human rights activities (1.6 percent). It is possible that this phenomenon was underreported since we conducted our survey only a few months ahead of the national elections of July 2018.

Concerns related to the contemporary political situation were not necessarily disconnected from fears of the "Khmer Rouge," which also challenged initial engagement of civil parties. For a civil party from Kandal province in 2014, for instance, past and present experiences of political violence intertwined and exacerbated her fear when applying for civil party status. She explained having been afraid at first because she thought that the Khmer Rouge "regime could happen again."[35] Although she was eventually able to overcome that fear, she still worried that in Cambodia today, since the judicial system was not independent, "the police can arrest anyone without evidence, anytime." When we met in March 2014, the arrests and violent crackdown on protesters that had taken place in Phnom Penh in January 2014 were still very present in her mind. Her fear, however, also coalesced with previous experiences of repressive policies and continued impunity, most notably the forcible conscription and forced labor of Cambodians under the People Republic of Kampuchea in the 1980s, a policy known as "K5": "I am afraid since even before 1993. They also forced people to become soldiers back then [*lowers her voice to a whisper*] under the K5 plan. I had a brother who was forcibly recruited for K5."

This case shows that, for civil parties, the time of focus at the ECCC—the Khmer Rouge regime—is not entirely past. Moreover, Khmer Rouge experiences are connected to other experiences of political violence, repression, and fear, leading to a sense of ontological insecurity (see also Öjendal and Kim 2006).

Applying for Civil Party Status in the Context of Fear

For those civil parties who did experience fear, applying for civil party participation thus amounts to an act of personal courage. A civil party representative from Takeo Province observed: "Sometimes the authority did not allow them to file complaints, but they secretly went to file complaints. How many civil parties are there in the whole country? There are only about four thousand people. We were seriously afraid at that time; *those four thousand people were the ones who dared.* There are more cowards than ones who dared."[36]

While some civil parties mentioned having overcome their initial fears thanks to encouragement and reassurance from NGOs or ECCC staff members,[37] others explained that they applied firmly believing that they would face imminent danger. A female civil party from Kampong Chhnang, for instance, recalled: "I thought [. . .] that if I were to die [because of the Khmer Rouge after applying], that's ok."[38]

The decision to bear witness and to speak out on the Khmer Rouge regime is also significant considering widespread experiences of *baksbat*, or broken courage, among survivors. Through the act of speaking out, survivors may transform their experiences of victimhood. They redefine themselves from silenced victims to actors assisting in the investigations and prosecutions of crimes. This decision transforms them into agents who refuse to give in to fear and demand justice for the harms they experienced. This analysis speaks to the work of feminist scholars Linda Alcoff and Laura Gray (1993, 260), who argued that bearing witness can constitute an act of resistance that "in and of itself transforms power relations and subjectivities, or the very way in which [survivors] experience and define" themselves. The decision to speak and bear witness in the aftermath of the Khmer Rouge regime is even more powerful when one considers the extreme isolation that shaped individual experiences under the Khmer Rouge regime, as well as the secrecy[39] and dissonance between language and action that characterized this totalitarian regime (see, e.g., Etcheson 1984, 159; Bernath 2011).

The Khmer expression used colloquially to refer to "filing a civil party application" illustrates this aspect of civil party participation. While the formal legal term would be *dak peak bândoeng* (ដាក់ពាក្យបណ្ដឹង), many transitional justice professionals and civil parties used the expression "to give one's name" (ដាក់ឈ្មោះ, *dak chmah*). This is an expression that is also indifferently used to refer to the act of signing a petition, or to applying to become a complainant at the ECCC. Referring to the decision to apply for civil party status as "giving one's name" equates it with the act of publicly and visibly standing for something or joining a cause. It reflects a willingness to bear the risk of being personally identified or targeted for the decision to come forward for civil party participation. Applying for civil party status in rural areas and sharing information on this indeed signaled a certain readiness to take the risk of compromising one's reputation. Research in Cambodian villages has shown how practices of "rumor," "gossip," or "ostracism" constitute a significant form of social control as they shape one's symbolic capital, which is all the more important if one is disadvantaged according to class and gender (C. Hughes 2001, 7–8). In such a context, maintaining a "good reputation for hard work, loyalty and honesty is essential to safeguard opportunities for employment and patronage" (13).

Sometimes, the courage to join the ECCC as a civil party was equated with the act of holding on to "anger." A woman from Kampong Cham Province, herself not a civil party, observed that those victims participating in the ECCC were those still having anger: "I think that, well, they still have anger, it's good for them. Their anger. Their stories, they still have anger, that's why they participate in the Khmer Rouge tribunal. [. . .] I already do the merit at the pagoda, so my anger is released bit by bit. But for those who do not do the merit at the pagoda yet, they will be satisfied too [. . .] [when participating in the tribunal]."[40]

Many of the respondents interviewed during our 2018 large-scale study on victim participation also explicitly associated the meaning of justice with either seeking revenge for those who had died or with expressing anger toward the former Khmer Rouge.[41] Such observations on the motivations underlying civil party participation assign a certain aggressive dimension to it. This resonates with Kali Tal's (1996, 7) work on "bearing witness," which she defines as "an aggressive act [. . .] born out of a refusal to bow to outside pressure to revise or repress experiences, a decision to embrace conflict rather than conformity

[. . .]. Its goal is change." These findings indeed highlight civil parties' refusal to let go of the conflictive past. It showcases their insistence that justice needs to be sought now, in this secular world, rather than later during the cycle of birth and rebirth, which in Buddhist beliefs functions as an instance of punishment for wrongdoings (Jacobsen 2005).

Some respondents, however, shared negative views of the anger that functioned as a driving force for civil party participation. A civil party from Kratie who participated in early outreach efforts for the NGO Khmer Institute for Democracy, for instance, observed that some villagers rejected civil party participation because they thought it represented a form of "blood revenge"—although they would later come to regret their decision.[42] A village chief from Kandal province, whom I met in 2014, also equated civil party participation with taking revenge, and thus contradicting Buddhist values: "In this community, nobody filed an application. Most of the villagers don't want to take revenge, they're following the [Buddhist] religion, they are old and most of them focus on their faith, so they don't think about taking revenge anymore, unlike others. So that's why nobody filed applications here, they don't want to have any bad effect from doing something."[43]

The perception that civil party participation was an act of revenge may have played into the decision of some victims to apply for the status of complainant instead. Vann Nath, a painter and one of the few survivors of S-21, explained that he had chosen to participate in Case 001 as a complainant because he was not interested in revenge. However, there was a lot of confusion regarding the differences between the legal categories of civil party versus complainant (Williams et al. 2018, 71–72). The view that civil party participation constituted a form of revenge may thus only have played a minor role in delimiting civil parties from complainants. In our 2018 study, only 3.3 percent of the 59 complainants surveyed explained having chosen to participate as complainants because civil party participation does not reflect their Buddhist values, and 3.3 percent because participating as a civil party is about taking revenge (72).

Civil Party Applications from Former Low-Level "Khmer Rouge Cadres"

If we analyze the early stages of civil party participation, it is important to consider a specific subcategory of civil party applicants—low-level former Khmer Rouge cadres—for which applying for civil party status at the ECCC was imbued with additional meanings.

Under the ECCC's rules, those not falling under the purview of the ECCC's personal jurisdiction—senior leaders and those most responsible for crimes committed under the Khmer Rouge regime—can qualify as a direct or indirect victim of the Khmer Rouge regime. As an international civil party lawyer at the ECCC explained, being a victim is ultimately about "what you have endured and not what you have done."[44] Many former low-level Khmer Rouge cadres and soldiers submitted civil party applications. It is difficult to have any definite number, but national civil party lawyers have estimated they represented approximately 10 percent of the civil parties in Cases 001 and 002.[45] This includes the more visible group of 118 civil parties admitted in Case 002 for having been victims of the internal CPK purges,[46] some of whom powerfully described the betrayal they felt from the CPK in their testimonies.[47] Civil parties at the ECCC have thus constituted a "subversive group of civil parties" that challenges binary, "naïve ideas on victims and perpetrators."[48]

What is the meaning of civil party participation, then, for former low-level Khmer Rouge cadres? It seems that when deciding to apply for civil party status, they claim for themselves the identity of "victims" of the Khmer Rouge regime, thereby rejecting the ascribed identity of a "perpetrator." Through participating in the state-sanctioned process of transitional justice in the capital city, they possibly aim at transforming their personal experiences and the stigma they face in their own, most often rural, communities.

Negative stigmas of former Khmer Rouge cadres indeed persist until today (Sirik 2020).[49] Research has shown that there is a "wholesale condemnation of those involved in the Khmer Rouge regime" (K. Chhim 2012, 54). In our 2018 survey, 29.1 percent of the 439 respondents agreed with the statement that "former Khmer Rouge" were being treated differently by their neighbors in their communities, and only 37.3 percent disagreed (Williams et al. 2018, 55). More strikingly, around two-thirds of our respondents (64.5 percent) indicated that they would be uncomfortable if one of their children would marry into the family of a former Khmer Rouge, and only 4.5 percent said they would feel comfortable with this. These findings display a considerably more negative perception of former Khmer Rouge than previous surveys.[50] In our 2018 survey, three-quarters of respondents moreover reported having feelings of hatred toward those Khmer Rouge responsible for violence (75.6 percent). On this issue, past surveys report comparably high findings.[51] These negative stigmas can hamper the public acknowledgments of having been "part of the Khmer Rouge," even if this means having joined the Khmer Rouge cause as a child, following the call of the late King Sihanouk, or having been a Khmer Rouge soldier.[52]

Interestingly, these stigmas exist in parallel to a discourse of generalized, passive victimhood (Manning 2012b; Emde 2014; Williams 2019). This discourse serves the political function of legitimizing the ruling party in a way that does not address CPP officials' own problematic past under the Khmer Rouge regime.[53] But this discourse is also embraced at a more general level by the population. There is a certain understanding that everyone was a victim under the Khmer Rouge regime, and many Cambodians acknowledge that the internal purges led to "perpetrators" being victimized and that, in turn, the repression and terror of the regime explains why many were complicit or committed crimes (Niem, Keo, and Sin 2011). Many Khmer Rouge cadres who were responsible for crimes committed against the civilian population became the target of the regime's increased paranoia and cycles of internal purges (see, e.g., Chandler 2002). Moreover, many Cambodians were forced to participate in the system of oppression and political violence as low-level cadres to survive.

In the qualitative interviews I conducted over the years, many respondents, including Cambodian judges at the ECCC, felt that everyone is a victim of the Khmer Rouge regime.[54] The Victims Association of Democratic Kampuchea, called Ksaem Ksan and established in 2009 as one of the few associations of victims of the Khmer Rouge regime, also explicitly adopted a broad definition of victims, accepting as a member "anyone who considers him-/herself as a victim" of the Khmer Rouge.[55] In our 2018 survey, we also found that former low-level Khmer Rouge cadres are widely perceived as being less responsible for the violence of the regime than their superiors, and are even seen as victims (see Williams et al. 2018, 56). Over half of our 439 respondents agreed with the statement that "low-level former Khmer Rouge were just following orders and are also victims of Angkar" (53.7 percent, of which 16.8 percent agreed completely). Only 17.3 percent of respondents disagreed (of which 6.2 percent disagreed completely) with this statement.

There is thus a certain contradiction between, on the one hand, a widespread understanding that almost everyone was a victim under the Khmer Rouge and, on the other hand, the persistence of a negative stigma for former Khmer Rouge cadres. This is something that I could clearly observe during my qualitative research. Respondents displayed a recurrent discrepancy between their acceptance at a general, impersonal level that former cadres also suffered and were victimized, and their refusal to acknowledge and accept this in relation to those whom they personally identified as having directly harmed them or their loved ones (see also Manning 2017, 122–25).[56] For instance, many civil parties interviewed said they would accept that former lower-level Khmer Rouge cadres file civil party applications if they had been victimized. But when it came to the specific cases of former cadres whom they personally knew, reactions were different.[57] Respondents did not understand why these former cadres would want to file a civil party application, or why the ECCC would accept their applications. Civil parties whom I met in Kandal province were, for instance, deeply troubled by the civil party status of their two neighbors, a former chief of a kitchen unit and a former militiaman, while the applications of other villagers, classified as "new people" and not holding any position of power under the Khmer Rouge, had been rejected: "I still wonder why they became civil parties [. . .]. It wasn't the same as for us, they had enough to eat, enough rice porridge [. . .]. They did bad things [. . .]. They are maybe victims as well but just a little bit, not like us [. . .]. I don't understand why the ECCC decided this way [. . .]. I'm angry because the real victims who lost their family could not become civil parties. My neighbor, for example, suffered tremendously. [. . .] She lost all of her relatives and wasn't accepted!"[58]

A civil party from Kampot Province who used to be a Khmer Rouge soldier also told me how some of his neighbors, including the village and commune chiefs, did not understand him at first: "Actually, I was a Khmer Rouge soldier so when I filed a civil party application, I faced all other civil parties and people that I am a Khmer Rouge soldier. At first, they asked 'You were a Khmer Rouge, why do you want to file a complaint against the Khmer Rouge?' [. . .] Some understood about my history, but some did not know me well, for example, the village or commune chief. [. . .] They think that I'm a Khmer Rouge, so why shall I file a complaint as a civil party?"[59]

Another civil party from Kampot Province explained that in a neighboring village, a former Khmer Rouge militiaman, after initially considering filing a civil party application, decided not to do so in the end: "If you are forced to kill someone, you are a victim. But maybe you would not feel comfortable to file a complaint or a civil party application in that situation. For example, in [the neighboring village], one villager was forced to kill his own father, otherwise he would have been killed himself. He knows for himself that he is a victim, but other people don't know that he was forced to kill his father, so they don't accept that he files a civil party application. So, in the end, he was afraid to file an application or a complaint and did not do it."[60]

I could not confirm this information about the former militiaman through data triangulation, nor did I raise this issue when I met him later. Yet as Lee Ann Fujii (2010) has argued in her interpretation of testimonies of war and violence in Rwanda, the relevance of such stories is not tied to questions of their veracity or truthfulness. This story highlights a sociopolitical landscape in which former cadres are denied the legitimacy to file civil party applications and to thereby claim the identity of victim, especially when they are seen as having been involved in direct killings.

These perceptions of a lack of legitimacy for former Khmer Rouge cadres to claim civil party status were echoed in the observations of an international civil party lawyer in Case 001. She observed how civil parties who were not former Khmer Rouge cadres—those whom she called "victims' victims"—felt uncomfortable after being grouped alongside "former Khmer Rouge."[61] While divisions among civil parties along such lines may not have been very visible at the beginning of civil party participation, they entered the public realm with the controversy around the memorial project for S-21 victims (see, e.g., McPherson 2014). Civil parties in Case 001 had requested the establishment of a memorial listing the names of those who had died at Tuol Sleng and Choeung Ek as a reparation measure. The request was rejected by the Trial Chamber. The victim association Ksaem Ksan continued to lobby for the establishment of this memorial at S-21.[62] In the end, a memorial was built with funding from the German government. Inaugurated in March 2015, it displays the names of 12,273 prisoners.[63] Most of the prisoners killed at S-21 and the related Choeung Ek execution site were in fact Khmer Rouge cadres targeted in internal purges. As Thierry Cruvellier (2010) observed, some of the victims of S-21 "would have been among the accused before the ECCC had they not been destroyed by the very machinery of death they had served or helped to create." The plan to inscribe the names of S-21 victims on the memorial was therefore criticized for placing the name of former Khmer Rouge cadres alongside victims who had not participated in Khmer Rouge violence, most prominently by Youk Chhang, head of the Documentation Center of Cambodia. The names were inscribed following final consultations with civil parties (Jarvis 2015).

This event shows how survivors and victims of the Khmer Rouge regime still differentiate between experiences of victimization according to whether one held any position of power during that time. It further demonstrates the existence of a dominant victim subject position based on the criteria of innocence. There seems to be an expectation of innocence tied to the notion of who counts as a legitimate victim and can formally participate as such in the transitional justice process. During my research, I also found that some of the NGO representatives and ECCC officers drew upon binary identities of (innocent) victims and (guilty) perpetrators, at least at the early stages of civil party participation in Cases 001 and 002 (see Bernath 2016). These findings echo the work of other scholars who observed that transitional justice processes, if not more broadly the peacebuilding field, often implicitly equate victims with innocence (e.g., Bouris 2007; Baines 2009; Drumbl 2012; Wilke 2013).

In this context, the possibility of applying for civil party participation offered low-level cadres the opportunity to use a state-led transitional justice process to question the negative perceptions they were facing in their home communities. This can be seen with the case of a civil party from Prey Veng Province whom I met in 2014 and 2018. Her main motivation to participate as a civil party seemed to be that of challenging the social stigma of being a "former

Khmer Rouge." In Case 001, she testified on her husband's arrest and death at the security center S-21, and on her baby's death while she was consigned to hard labor at the re-education center S-24. During her testimony, which was broadcast live on national television, she acknowledged having voluntarily joined the "ranks of the Khmer Rouge revolution" as early as 1971, before reaching the rank of a company chief. She further declared that she had wanted to become a civil party precisely to demonstrate that she was not a "member of the Khmer Rouge": "When I had the possibility, I submitted a civil party application in order to be able to speak in the name of the members of my family who were victims of the regime so that I could *prove that I am not a member of the Khmer Rouge* and that I am responsible and loyal to the nation and that I have felt betrayed by this group."[64] Former low-level Khmer Rouge cadres who had joined the revolution in the early days and were later on victims of the party's internal purges also powerfully testified, in Case 002, on the sentiment of betrayal they had felt from the leadership.[65]

When I interviewed this civil party from Prey Veng province in 2014, almost five years after her testimony, she told me feeling that since then, the way her relatives and neighbors perceive her has improved: "Before I didn't want to tell anyone, because I was afraid of my own security [. . .] People don't like the Khmer Rouge, because they lost their relatives [. . .]. But when the ECCC was established, I didn't want to hide it anymore [. . .]. After I testified, they were not angry with me anymore, they were happy that I shared my story [. . .]. They stopped being angry with me because they understood my experience [. . .]. Also, they pity me since."[66]

This example shows the significance of movement across various places gained through civil party participation. This civil party was indeed able to use the transitional justice process taking place nationally, and her participation in the Courtroom in the capital city, to challenge the stigma and discrimination she faced in her home community (see also Elander 2018a, 137–38). Applying for civil party status can thus potentially constitute a form of "identity-based resistance"—that is, resistance against "the resister's expected or attributed identity" (Hollander and Einwohner 2004, 537). As Erica Bouris (2007, 125) has argued, in the case of complex political victims, this is much more than "saying no"; it involves the "positive construction of a different self with different relations." While this constitutes an "inward-looking practice of the self," it also represents "a process performed in the social" that refutes and questions "dominant modes of subjectivation" (124).

However, this case also shows that the civil party participation of former low-level cadres cannot necessarily constitute a transformative experience. Instead of publicly displaying a complex identity of both victim and former low-level cadre, it seems that she detached herself from the "Khmer Rouge" label during her testimony to exclusively claim a victim identity. Instead of challenging expectations that victims must necessarily be innocent, such testimonies may then reinforce binary understandings of victims versus perpetrators. In another case of a former Khmer Rouge cadre who testified as a civil party in Case 002, it is the defense who questioned his victim status.[67] These examples illustrate the challenges in overcoming expectations of the "ideal" victim in a Courtroom setting.[68]

After the analysis of these early experiences of civil participation, and of how these were mediated by preexisting power relations in rural areas, the next section turns our attention to the later stages of participation. Once being granted civil party status, civil parties were able to access the various invited and invented spaces of transitional justice. This provided civil parties with access to knowledge on the ongoing process, whereby they came to know what it could offer them and how this possibly diverged from their own views, needs, and priorities.[69] Over the years, civil parties raised many questions on the ECCC's limitations (see, e.g., L. Sok and Abe 2019, 203–4; Manning 2017). Civil parties mobilized over several issues of contention, thereby challenging assumptions on (Cambodian) victims being passive. Especially in Case 001, groups of civil parties resorted to boycotting the trial proceedings whenever they were dissatisfied with decisions or the curtailment of their rights. This includes the boycott of 28 civil parties when the Trial Chamber ruled that civil party lawyers were not allowed to question character witnesses (Saliba 2009). Civil parties also refused to attend hearings when the Trial Chamber sentenced Duch to thirty-five years of imprisonment instead of the life sentence they had asked for.[70] Civil parties also boycotted Case 001 trial hearings in solidarity to those who saw their civil party status rejected by the Trial Chamber.[71] In the remainder of this chapter, I focus in more detail on two issues of contention for civil parties: the ECCC's limited reparations mandate and their limited temporal focus.

Civil Party Protests for Individual, Financial Reparations

At the ECCC, one of the few internationalized tribunals to hold a specific reparations mandate, the ECCC can be granted "collective and moral" reparations.[72] The category of "moral" reparations, which is unprecedented in international or domestic legal frameworks, has been clarified by the ECCC Supreme Court Chamber as referring to "the aim of repairing moral damages rather than material ones."[73] As for the category of "collective reparations," it was used so as to affirm "the unavailability of individual financial awards."[74] With this exclusion of individual, monetary reparations, the ECCC deviates from civil claims under domestic law in Cambodia.[75] The Trial Chamber judges justified this as follows: "Such departures from national law were considered necessary in view of the large number of Civil Parties expected before the ECCC and the inevitable difficulties of quantifying the full extent of the losses suffered by an indeterminate class of victims. Reparations before the ECCC were therefore intended to be essentially symbolic (aimed at conferring official recognition upon victims, and assisting to restore dignity and preserve the collective memory) rather than compensatory."[76]

Initially, the Internal Rules only allowed for reparations "awarded against, and [. . .] borne by convicted persons."[77] In Case 001, the Trial Chamber judges found the accused to be indigent. In a decision later confirmed by the Supreme Court Chamber, they only awarded two out of the five civil party reparations requests: the compilation and publication of statements of apology made by the accused during the trial, and the inclusion in the judgment of civil parties' names and those of immediate victims. The other requests—access to free psychological and physical health care, funding of educational programs on S-21 crimes, the establishment of memorials and pagodas at S-21 and in civil parties' communities—were rejected for exceeding the scope of available reparations. This decision on reparations was widely criticized as "really the most minimal, most conservative, and perhaps it's fair to say unimaginative that could have been ordered."[78]

In anticipation of the second trial, the judges significantly amended the Internal Rules, having realized the failure of the original reparations framework in delivering meaningful reparations to civil parties. First, they expanded the VSS mandate to develop and implement, together with external governmental and nongovernmental partners, "non-judicial measures addressing the broader interests of victims."[79] While this expanded the ECCC's reparation mandate beyond the scope of civil parties, only two main initiatives were implemented by VSS as non-judicial measures.[80] Second, the Trial Chamber was granted the authority to recognize reparation projects designed by civil party lawyers, together with the VSS, when they had secured external funding.[81] This introduced a new funding avenue for reparations beyond the conviction-borne form of reparations, which was effectively a dead end at the ECCC. In Case 002, the work of civil parties' lawyers, VSS, and NGOs would focus on this form of reparations.

The suspects in Case 002 were indeed also declared to be indigent. This was most controversial in the case of Ieng Sary and Ieng Thirith, who were known to have accumulated significant wealth. After striking an amnesty deal with then co–prime minister Hun Sen in 1996, they enjoyed "an elite lifestyle in Phnom Penh" (Fawthrop 2013; see also Caswell 2014, 143). Civil party lawyers repeatedly requested investigations into the properties owned by defendants and asked for measures to preserve their assets for reparations, yet to no avail. The new avenue for externally funded reparations would, however, allow for reparation requests disconnected from the defendants' financial situation. In Case 002/01, the co-lead civil party lawyers, civil party lawyers, VSS staff, and Cambodian NGOs jointly developed reparations requests, in consultations with civil parties in and outside of Cambodia.[82] In August 2014, the Trial Chamber judgment in Case 002/01 granted eleven out of the thirteen reparations measures submitted. This included the designation of May 20 as a national Remembrance Day, mobile exhibitions, and psychosocial support in the form of testimonial therapy. In its November 2018 judgment in Case 002/02, the Trial Chamber endorsed twelve of the fourteen reparation projects submitted by the civil party lead co-lawyers. This included education projects about the Khmer Rouge history, the documentation of specific experiences of civil parties such as the Vietnamese and Cham minorities, the commemoration of civil parties' suffering, and mental health support.

Studies have shown that civil parties and Cambodian citizens consistently displayed a preference for individual, monetary compensation. In a study conducted between October 2008 and May 2009 with 247 civil party applicants in nineteen provinces, more than one third of the respondents (38.9 percent) preferred individual over collective reparations, while 30.3 percent stated wanting individual monetary compensation (Stammel et al. 2010, 35–36).[83] In our 2018 study, 44.8 percent of the 255 civil parties and civil party applicants surveyed explained having expected the ECCC to provide individual, financial reparations when they first applied (Williams et al. 2018, 114). Moreover, 64.7 percent of the overall 439 respondents still saw individual, financial reparations as the most helpful measure to deal with the Khmer Rouge past at the time of the survey—that is, fifteen years after the ECCC's establishment (Williams et al. 2018, 118). While the respondents' economic situation was not the only determining factor in seeking for individual financial reparations, we found that those who did not earn enough to make a living were statistically significantly more likely to ask for financial reparations than those who indicated earning enough for a living or for some savings (111).

Repertoires of Civil Party Resistance

Over time, different forms of civil party resistance emerged on the issue of reparations. Civil parties first used discursive forms of resistance to resist the transitional justice process from within, yet against the terms set by policymakers. They made use of the different "invented" spaces of transitional justice—civil parties' forums, thematic conferences, press conferences, meetings with their lawyers, interviews with researchers and journalists—even though it was made clear to them that their demands exceeded the realm of possibilities.

Interventions from civil parties at conferences and civil parties' forums in 2008 and 2013 illustrate this discursive resistance:[84]

> Even though I survived, I am dead. [. . .] I lost my husband at S-21. I want [financial/individual] reparations for all victims, especially widows like me who have suffered the most [. . .] because we had to combine so many roles in our life after the Khmer Rouge.[85]

> I am interested in the benefits of civil parties. I observe only two types of interests: collective reparations and building *stupas*,[86] but no individual interests. But what can we do to fight for the individual interests for civil parties?
>
> There is no financial or individual reparation to improve the living standards of the civil parties. [. . .] I am an orphan; I lost my family, my house . . . My wife also is an orphan. I agree that we want *stupas* for the young generation to see, but we also need [financial] reparations to improve our living standards. [. . .] Millions have been spent already and it takes so long.[87]

During a forum organized by the VSS in Kampong Cham in February 2018, which gathered 162 civil parties from neighboring provinces, a civil party underlined the tragic urgency of these claims: "I am fifty-two, fifty-three years old now. I used to be forty-one or forty-two when I applied [for civil party participation] eleven years ago! Many [civil parties] have died, we need support from the Court. In my village, eight [civil parties] have died. In his village, approximately three, maybe thirty in Prey Veng province. I will be next to go [*laughs*]."[88]

In these "invented" spaces, civil parties formulated their claims in a way that reflected the ECCC's typology of reparations. In our 2018 study, too, we found that those civil parties who actively participated would formulate their visions of justice or reconciliation within the frames introduced by the ECCC and extensively draw from the ECCC's terminology to voice their demands and grievances (Williams et al. 2018). For example, civil parties would specifically frame their claim for financial support as a claim for "individual, financial reparations." This contrasted with other respondents not closely involved in the transitional justice process, who also asked for financial support. This shows that participating provided not only access to knowledge on the ECCC proceedings but also exposure to the discourses of transitional justice actors, which civil parties could use to make their claims heard.

In addition to this discursive resistance, civil parties also resisted through a public protest on 17 October 2014. With the opening of the evidentiary hearings in Case 002/02 scheduled for that day, there was a lot of attention on the ECCC from journalists, researchers, civil society actors and donors. From 150 to 200 civil parties coming from various areas across the country staged a demonstration in front of the ECCC gates, holding signs in Khmer and English reading "We are the civil parties. We need individual reparations" (Kuch 2014b; White 2014). They claimed to represent 1,780 civil parties (Killean 2018a, 24). For this protest, they received the help of a Cambodian human rights NGO whose staff felt that although their demands were clearly exceeding the ECCC's mandate, civil parties still deserved to be heard. Civil parties prepared a petition signed by a significant number of civil parties from across the country. Threatening to retrieve their civil party applications if their claims were not heard, they attempted to enter the ECCC compound to submit their petition. Security officers prevented them from doing so and, in the end, the Cambodian co-lead lawyer met them at the gate. In their petition, they asked for a compensation of US$13,500 for each family member lost during the Khmer Rouge regime.

The protesting civil parties chose this specific amount in relation to figures put forward for compensations for the relatives of the victims of the Koh Pich (Diamond Island) stampede during the Khmer Water Festival celebrations on 22 November 2010. While it is unclear whether the relatives of the 353 victims[89] who died in the incident ever received any compensation—and if they did, how much—several public figures, organizations and institutions were fast in making public donation pledges after the incident (CCHR 2011c, 78–79). A few days after the incident, the prime minister even described the stampede as "the biggest tragedy in more than 31 years since the Pol Pot regime" (Mydans 2010b). He announced that no one would be prosecuted or punished but that the families of the victims "would each be given at least USD 12,000" (Cheang 2010). These promises for compensation were seen by civil society members as an attempt to pacify victims' relatives and to contain criticism of the Koh Pich urban development plans, as authorities refused to address claims for accountability and blatantly circumvented the judiciary.[90]

In claiming for this amount in their petition, the civil parties thus questioned their differential treatment in comparison to victims in the Koh Pich case. One civil party observed: "At Koh Pich, the victims are given lots of money, they just went for a walk [there when the stampede happened]. We on the other hand have lost everything [under the Khmer Rouge and don't receive any financial individual compensation]."[91]

This public and collective form of resistance illustrates the fluidity of forms of resistance across different sites of resistance. Submitting petitions and organizing a public protest in the capital city of Phnom Penh, often with third-party support from NGOs (see, e.g., Blot 2015), constitutes a common form of resistance.[92] It is often used to voice collective grievances related to land and local governance (see, e.g., CAS and World Bank 2006; Subedi 2010, para. 42).

During this civil party protest, the use of law remained marginal, without being entirely irrelevant. Civil parties did not claim for monetary reparations through legal means, with their civil party lawyers. Rather, they addressed a petition to the ECCC judges. After their protest at the ECCC, they "marched the petition"[93]—as a participating civil party explained—to submit it to the foreign embassies who were the ECCC's key donors, in a rally across Phnom Penh. Civil parties also submitted their petition to the Council of Ministers—referred to as "the place of Hun Sen," in the words of a civil party.[94]

This strategy might reflect the resignation of civil parties' lawyers, who are more than aware that legal avenues are not available to make their clients' claims heard at the ECCC, given the existing framework for reparations. It may also reflect common strategies used in the context of neo-patrimonial structures of power: rather than making use of explicit rules or official institutional channels, which is not where power lies, this form of resistance addresses those individuals who are seen as de facto holding power (CAS and World Bank 2006, 29–32). In this context, addressing grievances to not only national but also international actors such as embassies is a common protest strategy. This case thus shows not only "how people make claims" across different sites of resistance but also "what they know about making claims and the reception by targets of their claims" (Tarrow 2013, 2).

The Response of Transitional Justice Professionals

What were the reactions to these various forms of civil party resistance? ECCC staff members recognized early on that financial, individual reparations were not an option given the sheer number of victims, as well as because such measures would benefit only those formally participating as civil parties. Helen Jarvis, former head of the ECCC Victims Unit and advisor to the Cambodian Task Force on Khmer Rouge Trials explained in a 2018 interview: "Some people would of course like to get financial compensation, but I think most people realize there are two big reasons mitigating against it. One is that everybody, almost everybody, can be seen as a victim in one way, probably everybody. And secondly, if you allowed [. . .] individual financial reparations for those who are civil parties, then what about people who suffered just as greatly but didn't have the opportunity to become a civil party. I think that could create a great deal of jealousy and feelings of unfairness. [. . .] So I think the idea of modeling collective reparations was a sound approach, even if some were disappointed."[95]

Moreover, negotiating the issue of financial reparations would problematically open a "Pandora's box" of uneasy questions, including that of quantification. A national VSS officer argued that it was thus better to focus on "national reconciliation": "We try to manage their expectations that they are going to receive only collective and moral, rather than individual, reparations, and this is leading to national reconciliation. It is difficult to determine any individual compensation! Because then people would say 'I'm handicapped, I have a problem with my leg, I want to get US$1,000.' The people who have problems with their ears would say 'Ok, I need US$1,000 too.' And then others would ask, 'Why do those with problems with their ear get compensation, while I have problems with my eyes?' It's a mess, you know, it's a mess."[96]

Many lawyers and NGO actors are also deeply aware that, in any given context, victims will have numerous and high expectations that transitional justice processes cannot meet.[97] An international civil party lawyer, for instance, observed: "You always have to deal with the expectations of victims, which are always enormous and will go far beyond what will be possible. [. . .] And so, at some point in time, you have to make them understand that we will enter into a [judicial] framework [that] [. . .] cannot answer to everything. [. . .] It's all the finesse of a civil party lawyer."[98]

For many of those closely working with civil parties, claims for monetary reparations, which clearly expand the ECCC's realm of the possible, were therefore essentially to be dealt with in terms of adequate communication and expectation management. It is a matter of avoiding harm through raising expectations that cannot be met. This, however, was not an easy task. The Khmer term commonly used to refer to reparations to civil parties, *somnâng* (សំណង), inherently implies some form of monetary payment: it literally means "compensation." Moreover, civil claims under domestic law foresee individual, financial compensation.[99] It is also common for perpetrators to offer financial compensation to victims or their families in attempts to avoid criminal prosecution (Rudi 2022). In this context, asking civil party applicants what reparations they expected, as part of filling the Victim Information Form, was seen as problematically contributing to raising expectations for monetary reparations.[100] An initial lack of clarity as to what the categories of "moral" and "collective" reparations actually meant in the early years of the ECCC further complicated outreach efforts and made it difficult for NGO intermediaries to explain the Court's mandate to civil party applicants (Sperfeldt 2022).

A tension also exists between expectation management and empowerment, between communicating to and disciplining victims (Sperfeldt 2022). For instance, some of those closely working with civil parties took a proactive approach in supporting civil parties even if this meant amplifying their criticisms of the Court's limited reparations mandate. They would, however, be accused of stirring up civil parties' expectations. During the civil party protest for financial reparations in October 2014, some ECCC staff members also reacted with fatigue, if not exasperation. The protesting civil parties were seen as those victims who "always want more" and clearly do not understand the Court's mandate.[101] Over time, however, some came to realize that providing space for dissenting claims is an important aspect of participation that allows for empowerment.[102]

Civil Party Expectations and Protests in the Context of Neo-patrimonialism

The civil party demands for financial reparations can also be seen in the context of neo-patrimonialism, as an expression of civil parties' expectations for ECCC officers to act as patrons. Such expectations were possibly triggered by the ways in which money has been a constant feature of public discussions regarding the ECCC ever since its establishment.[103] Given the ECCC's voluntary funding scheme, media coverage of the Court indeed regularly mentioned important sums of money either pledged by donor countries or still to be secured.

Moreover, the encounters of the rural population with ECCC staff were often shaped by the—possibly inadvertent—display of wealth and power. An international civil party lawyer, for instance, argued that ECCC officers conducting outreach in rural communities created unrealistic expectations: "I think the biggest problem was created in 2007 [. . .] when people in United Nations cars arrived in the villages and said that now there would be a tribunal. . . . Civil parties come, reparations! They did not explain exactly what we would have. This has made our work much more difficult."[104]

This is reminiscent of experiences made by the rural population in encounters with members of the UN peacekeeping forces in the early 1990s. In her analysis of UNTAC as a "new patron," Frieson (1996, 232), for example, recalled: "At the time of the arrival of UNTAC, many Cambodians had high expectations of these UNTACs who drove around in large white cars and spent money freely." Beyond the case of Cambodia, these experiences also speak more generally to how the material practices of the humanitarian world, with its omnipresent "hybrid form of the [white] Land Rover/aid worker," has come to embody the material assets and associated powers of aid organizations such as the UN (Smirl 2015).

Although it was not necessarily the main motivation for civil party participation at the ECCC (Williams et al. 2018, 71), it is therefore not surprising that in this context, survivors would have some hope to somehow benefit from the large sums of money to be spent on the ECCC. With many civil parties being of rural and poor socioeconomic background, their relationship with ECCC staff members can further be seen from the perspective of patronage relationships: essentially instrumental relationships between people of unequal wealth and power, or access to resources and power (see chapter 1).

Civil parties also received some material benefits through per diems or travel opportunities to the capital city. Although these benefits do not constitute individual financial reparations, civil parties emphasized them in interviews as important aspects of their participation (see Williams et al. 2018, 79). Some perceived them as a form of "paying attention to the victims," and therefore as a gesture which makes civil parties feel "safe" that justice is being sought for them.[105] These perceptions highlight the importance of procedural justice for civil parties, as Rachel Killean (2018b) has argued. But it also suggests that civil parties can perceive the ECCC as a patron not only in terms of providing minimal forms of material benefits but also in terms of providing important services such as a sense of protection or security.

Over time, however, it became painfully obvious for civil parties that the large sums of money dedicated to finding justice were not distributed to them as victims but instead spent on ECCC salaries. In June 2018, a civil party from Kandal province observed the resulting frustrations among fellow civil parties: "They said that the staff members at the tribunal were using the victims like us to earn money, like for buying a car [or a house] or something like that. [. . .] They said we went there like that just for those people to earn money, and we didn't get any money, just for those people who got the money."[106] Speaking to a journalist of the *Phnom Penh Post* during the October 2014 protest in front of the ECCC, a female civil party also questioned the disconnect between civil parties' material benefits and the millions spent on the Court: "They said that NGOs help. Help, help, help, but [we] don't see. [We] people know nothing. I heard that America helps. And others help, help, help, but we don't see any money. Help, but we do not get any of the money, so where does all the money go? Is that not for victims? Victims [who] lost husbands, children, relatives. All of us want that funding to release our minds, we don't want to be stressed. It's been already eight years that we've held on. Now they said it's finished [there's a] judgment. If they have finished, it means it's the end of the story, what else?" (White 2014).

Reflecting upon the reparation projects in Case 002, a civil party representative from Kandal province argued that the Court or indeed the donors were biased toward supporting NGOs, since NGOs were the ones who in the end received funds rather than victims:

> All Cambodians, civil parties, they focused on the individual reparations. This means financial reparations. [. . .] When I made a made a petition to the tribunal, there were thousands of thumbprints. [. . .] We just want a financial reparation [. . .] to make a religious ceremony to dedicate to our parents and relatives that died. Not wanting that money to be rich. But the tribunal said that there would never be an individual reparation. However, all the proposals that we requested, there wasn't anything that the tribunal provided. Instead, there was only a reparation that was a project of one organization. If that organization requested for any reparation, the tribunal agreed to that. [. . .] If one organization shows them any project plans, they would agree to that. [. . .] I want to meet the donors and tell them to reconsider, again, before they gave any donation to any organization, what is their intention to do so? There should be some benefits for the civil parties. If there aren't any benefits for the civil parties, there wouldn't be any justice.[107]

Christoph Sperfeldt and Rachel Hughes (2020) draw similar conclusions in their analysis of the "projectification" of reparations in Case 002. While the Court's new reparation framework extended the number and types of actors involved and the ways of knowing about the Khmer Rouge past, it also led to the exclusion of civil parties from decision-making processes and funding streams as they were merely framed as project beneficiaries. This civil party representative's observations further speak to Paul Gready and Simon Robins's (2017) critique that transitional justice interventions often prioritize established NGOs located in the capital city and marginalize grassroots social movements.

The civil party representative from Kandal further observed that the absence of financial reparations for civil parties felt particularly unfair considering the treatment of the accused: "I am very disappointed. Why am I disappointed? The accused, whenever they are sick, there is an ambulance to take them to the hospitals. But the civil parties with me already passed away."[108]

In this context, a civil party representative from Siem Reap Province argued that only one civil party—Chum Mey—had truly benefited from participating in the transitional justice process. As one of the few survivors from S-21 and a prominent civil party in Case 001, Chum Mey was able to publish his story with the support of the Documentation Center of Cambodia and to sell his book at the Tuol Sleng Genocide Museum (see also Caswell 2014, 136–45). Compared to Chum Mey,[109] everyone else was asked too much from the Court, this civil party representative argued:

> Nowadays, the one who got justice at a 100 percent is only Chum Mey. He gets quite a lot of benefits from the ECCC. [. . .] Because he's taking Tuol Sleng Genocide Museum as a place where he does his own business, thus he got justice in this way. Others, there are some civil parties who suffered until death, they didn't even have enough money to buy a coffin. They didn't get any benefits from the tribunal. [. . .] Chum Mey, alone, can feel calm now, but the other civil parties don't get anything to make them feel calm. For example, during the Khmer Rouge regime, their families got killed and their wealth has been destroyed, thus we sue because we want to find justice, to ask the tribunal to help us. Like the [national] court these days, when we know who is guilty, we can ask them to compensate us. But in our case, when we sue [at the ECCC], the tribunal told us to reconcile and stop holding any grudges. This is impossible because we don't get anything in return. This is what the civil parties believe.[110]

Chum Mey long tried to make ends meet through offering his services as a guide for tourists at the museum (Cruvellier 2011, 209–10). In our conversations over the years, he expressed his awareness of having over time acquired a privileged position among civil parties.[111] Some civil parties I met also observed his solidarity and efforts to share his newly acquired wealth with fellow civil parties.[112] The perception of his exceptional financial position, however, still shows that the ECCC simply did not meet the material expectations of many civil parties.

When the ECCC staff members do not deliver the goods and services civil parties expect, some of them may then turn away from the ECCC as a patron, especially in the context of decreasing outreach activities. The civil party representative in Siem Reap who commented on Chum Mey, for instance, concluded: "Now, we all forget about it because we don't know anything anymore about the progress of the Khmer Rouge tribunal."[113] This speaks to how patronage relationships are "constantly in a state of flux" and to how patrons "may rise or fall depending on whether or not they can really provide the goods and services that their clients need" (Ledgerwood 1992, 4).

If some of the relationships between civil parties and ECCC representatives such as civil party lawyers or VSS officers can be seen from the perspective of patron-client relationships, there is also another side to the equation. Civil parties, in return for protection and financial benefits, are expected to display their loyalty, deference, and friendship to their patrons (see, e.g., Jacobsen and Stuart-Fox 2013). A lawyer, for instance, observed how some national civil party lawyers displayed a "paternalistic approach" to their clients, as if to them, "civil parties are there for the lawyers, rather than the other way around, as it is supposed to be."[114] A paternalistic or instrumentalist approach to civil parties could also be observed with some of the international civil party lawyers in Case 001 who only traveled to Cambodia for the major trial hearings that attracted a lot of international media attention and visibility, and seemed to mainly use their appearance in Court as a steppingstone for their own careers (see, e.g., Cruvellier 2011, 323–27).

In a patron-client relationship, if civil parties come to transgress expectations, they may fear that this would question their patron's benevolence toward them. As already mentioned in this book's introduction, I observed how some of the civil parties who had signed the petition for financial reparations had such concerns. For instance, a civil party from Kampot, after sharing his support for the petition, asked me: "But you won't tell my lawyer that I said this, right? Otherwise, I won't be invited anymore [to the ECCC and to civil party forums]."[115]

This example here underlines how research interviews can constitute important spaces of everyday resistance, even more so in contexts where citizens may not be "afforded the luxury" of engaging in public forms of dissent (Scott 1985, xv). In research interviews, respondents can contest aspects of the transitional justice process, even if publicly they opt for "the public language of conformity"—or what Scott (1985, 289–90) has analyzed as the "public transcript." Regardless of whether the civil party lawyer would really have stopped inviting him to the ECCC or to outreach activities, this example further shows that, in a neo-patrimonial context, participation in a legal transitional justice process such as the ECCC is not always necessarily experienced as a matter of *rights* to which civil parties are formally entitled to. It becomes a matter of *favors* generously granted by patrons, who may operate as gatekeepers for participation, in exchange for their client's loyalty.

This is not to imply that all relationships between civil parties and their lawyers or other ECCC staff members are necessarily of a patron-client nature and that, even if they are, they are primarily shaped by fear. In fact, scholars emphasize that an essential characteristic of a patron-client relationship is its affectionate dimension (Pak et al. 2007; see also Scott 1972, 94). This is also something that I could observe in some interviews, such as with the civil party from Kampot province mentioned above. After asking me to refrain from sharing his support of the protests for financial reparations, he explained that his lawyer deeply "liked" his group of civil parties. It is through this prism of affection that he was even making sense of the fact that his international lawyer would only represent Cham civil parties in his village—when this was a result of the ECCC's categorization of this specific civil party group as distinct victims of the crime of genocide. He explained: "[The national lawyer] only takes civil parties who are Cham because the French lawyer told him so. I don't understand why . . . [but I think it might be] [b]ecause he *likes us*. He *likes* the Cham people. [. . .] It's like *an affection*, when you like someone, you go with him. Everybody likes [the national civil party lawyer]."[116]

Moreover, the patrons acting as gatekeepers for opportunities to participate at the ECCC may not necessarily be ECCC officers involved in outreach or victim participation in rural areas but patrons to whom civil parties already had preexisting relationships. In 2014, a civil party from Kandal Province, for instance, observed how access to information on opportunities for victim participation was regulated by preexisting patronage networks in his area: "We don't know any reason why they file a civil party application, but their networks or leaders know about filing a civil party application, so they tell them."[117]

Once the ECCC granted villagers civil party status, local figures of authorities may further act as gatekeepers in deciding who would be invited to ECCC activities. This includes the so-called focal points—that is, village chiefs, commune chiefs, or teachers chosen by the VSS to act as intermediaries between the ECCC and civil parties, after ADHOC's scheme of civil party representatives was discontinued for lack of funding. We could see this in our 2018 study. Most of the civil parties we surveyed observed that civil party representatives and focal points were inviting civil parties to participate in outreach events or ECCC hearings according to a fair rotation system. Four respondents, however, qualified the selection for participation as clearly unfair (Williams et al. 2018, 81). One civil party, for instance, explained that it is only "those who have network" with the village chief who are chosen to attend an ECCC hearing. Another observed that, when they are invited to the Court, civil parties must pay some money to the focal point from the per diems received. ECCC officers working with civil parties had also observed such cases.[118] Interestingly, in our survey, two of the respondents reporting an unfair rotation system for civil party participation were in fact rejected civil party applicants. They were unaware that the Court had declared their application to be inadmissible. Their experience of a lack of opportunities to participate in ECCC-related activities, in comparison to other civil parties in their village, was thus possibly a result of the Court's rejection of their civil party applications rather than necessarily a lack of access to relevant patronage networks. Regardless of the reasons for their marginalization, their case still shows that experiences of patronage and of how such unequal power relations usually play out for the marginalized are used as an explanatory prism to make sense of their experiences of civil party participation (or the lack thereof).

Kent (2022) has also argued that outreach activities have become increasingly embedded in CPP patronage networks, as intermediary actors stepped in when the ECCC and NGOs decreased their outreach activities for lack of funding. She observed how two formerly marginalized villagers, empowered by new relations with CPP patrons, organized outreach tours to the ECCC. While the ECCC outreach tours organized by NGOs and the ECCC had been initially free of charge, these villagers would take a small contribution from participants. Moreover, the tours would increasingly feature a different route, with a stop at the prime minister's Win-Win Monument in Phnom Penh instead of the Choeung Ek killing fields.

The Complicated Ethics of Claiming for ("Blood") Money

Civil party resistance for individual, financial reparations also reveals that when claiming for monetary compensation, civil parties are not only requesting a measure explicitly excluded from the ECCC's mandate. They also make claims of a nature often perceived to be unethical, especially when asked for the loss of life rather than the loss of assets. As Claire Moon (2012, 195) has argued in her research on Argentine's Madres de la Plaza de Mayo, financial reparations perform "a strange transubstantiation in which money granted in recompense for the dead makes their bodies exchangeable for, or "turns them into," other commodities."

In Cambodia, unease with claims for monetary compensation already emerged in the early days of civil party participation—for instance, at a November 2008 conference on "Reparations for the Victims of the Khmer Rouge Regime" organized by the Cambodian Human Rights Action Committee (CHRAC) and the ECCC Victims Unit in Phnom Penh. During the conference, a Buddhist monk invited to give an input on "the Buddhist perspective on reparations," asked civil parties requesting financial reparations: "Does it match the loss of lives of the beloved ones? What has money to do with feelings of the heart?"[119]

Many civil parties were acutely aware of this challenge. Bou Meng, one of the civil parties who took the floor at the 2008 conference, for instance, acknowledged the impossibility of quantifying the loss of life—his wife's—yet he precisely used this impossibility to argue that the amount he asked for was in fact very reasonable: "I want a compensation of US$50,000 for my wife's death. [Duch] executed my wife. If it happened to the judges' wives, how would they feel? Would US$50,000 be enough?"[120]

In interviews, civil parties who had signed the petition for individual, financial reparations also consistently avoided mentioning any specific amount. Instead, they repeatedly highlighted how they would use this money to pay respect to their loved ones through religious ceremonies and the building of stupas.[121] For many civil parties, this was often a genuine motivation for demanding financial reparations. A Case 002 civil party from Phnom Penh, for example, explained:

> Reparations [compensations] are very necessary. In a liberal market economy, victims need money for what? To continue their living after [escaping] death. Second, they use that money to practice religious ceremonies according to their religious belief. Some follow Buddhism, Islam,or Christianity. In all liberal market economies, we cannot eliminate money. We have to provide it to them so that they can . . . feel released. [. . .] I mean we cannot make them feel completely satisfied since we cannot exchange people with money. But if there is no money, the ECCC creates another issue to make people more hurt in addition to the [experiences of the] Pol Pot regime. [. . .] Our tradition is that the one who is alive always performs religious ceremony for the deceased. Thus . . . money is very important. We cannot perform religious ceremony without the money. When we [. . .] [ask for financial reparations], it seems like it is all about money, money, money. It does not mean that I want that money to be rich. I just want to pay respect for the deceased, for them to feel at ease.[122]

This quote is illustrative of how victims who come forward to claim for individual, financial reparations are confronted with the expectations of how a "good victim" should be, regardless of the purported use of the compensation money. As Moon (2006, 273–74) has argued, it is in those moments where there is a "discrepancy between those who conform and those who do not" that we can most clearly see such expectations.

The Political Economy of Transitional Justice

Civil parties' resistance for individual, financial reparations also raises important questions regarding the setting of priorities when large amounts of money are spent in contexts of poverty, and of a "brutal and predatory" transformation from command economy to free market capitalism (C. Hughes 2015b). This can be illustrated with the two population-based, quantitative surveys on the ECCC conducted by Pham et al. (2009 2011). In 2008, the overall priority mentioned by the large majority of respondents (83 percent) was that of "economy, jobs and poverty," followed by services to meet basic needs such as health (20 percent) and food (17 percent) (Pham et al. 2009, 34–35). In 2010, the number of respondents naming "economy, jobs and poverty" as their overall priority even increased to 98 percent (Pham et al. 2011, 19–20). The two surveys also included a question on whether respondents would have preferred that the money spent on the ECCC be spent on "something else": 52.6 percent of respondents mentioned their preference for the ECCC's budget being spent on something else in 2008; even more so did in 2010 (63 percent).

Through their protests, civil parties thus "'speak back to' the analytical categories" that structure transitional justice discourse and practice (Moon 2012, 190–91). Their protests point to the "invisibility of economics" in transitional justice as a field of knowledge, practice, and policymaking, as well as the marginalization of claims for socioeconomic justice (Miller 2008; Franzki and Olarte 2014; Lai 2020).

Scholars have analyzed how the marginalization of violations of economic, cultural, and social rights in the field of international criminal justice has shaped the ECCC and ECCC-related work of human rights NGOs (DeFalco 2011; Schmid 2015, 109–10; Destrooper 2018a). What these civil party protests show us here is another dimension of the "invisibility of economics" in transitional justice. The protests are not about the contestation of a prioritization of violations of civil and political rights over economic, cultural, and social rights in prosecutorial strategies or judgments at the ECCC. Instead, they question the marginalization of understandings of justice as *socioeconomic* justice, be it for victims' experiences of violations of economic, social, and cultural rights or for violations of their civil and political rights. If we take these protests seriously, we can see that they are about civil parties demanding to have a stake in Cambodia's political and economic order, and to have their claims for socioeconomic justice heard in response to the harm they suffered from under the Khmer Rouge regime.

Over the years, besides demands for individual and financial reparations, civil parties have also repeatedly requested medical-related services; schools; infrastructure such as roads, bridges, or irrigation systems; or housing as forms of collective and moral reparations (see, e.g., Ly 2011; Sperfeldt 2022). In our 2018 survey, more than one-third of the respondents we met for qualitative, follow-up interviews—which included 21 noncivil parties and 6 rejected civil party applicants—explicitly defined justice in terms of addressing livelihood needs and providing socioeconomic support. They equated the provision of justice with money for religious ceremonies as well as with support for the elderly, mental health support, infrastructure and schools, development, enough food, and adequate and equal salaries (see Williams et al. 2018, 41–42).

While the ECCC's reparation mandate from the start clearly excluded reparations for material harms—for example, the destruction or loss of property—the reparations that were in the end provided for "moral" harms also denied most claims for socioeconomic justice. Most of the reparations awarded in Case 002/01 and 002/02 indeed focused on recognizing harm or raising awareness of victims' suffering through intergenerational, artistic, and educational activities. Only four reparation projects focused on rehabilitative mental health services. In Case 002/02, the Trial Chamber judges rejected the component of a project proposed by HelpAge Cambodia, which envisioned the distribution of loans for income-generating activities to increase income security of elderly civil parties. In the judges' view, these activities would effectively consist of individual, monetary payments and therefore exceeded the scope of the ECCC's reparations framework.[123]

Civil party requests for hospitals, schools, or infrastructure were excluded even earlier in the process, as they did not feature in the final list of reparation projects submitted to the Trial Chamber. Such requests were often considered not only to exceed the ECCC's scope but also to constitute an entirely separate form of "needs" related to development. When civil parties were consulted by NGO intermediaries and lawyers between October 2010 and May 2011 regarding their reparation claims in Case 002, requests that were seen as not permissible or feasible were effectively filtered out (Sperfeldt 2022). According to Sperfeldt (2022, 136), the civil party consultations, although conducted with the best intentions, thereby confused "what the Court had to offer with what the civil parties actually desired."

In debates on reparation as a transitional justice measure, differentiating between transitional justice versus development claims is linked to concerns that equating reparations and development dilutes governmental responsibilities to address mass atrocity (see, e.g., Roht-Arriaza 2004). Nonetheless, as Zinaida Miller (2008, 286) has shown, such a "separation of development from the transitional [justice] mechanisms increases the sense that economic equality has no role to play in the conception of justice." Moreover, it leads to narrowing down the larger discussion on economic redistribution and claims for socioeconomic livelihoods to the technicalities of reparation mandates.

Civil Party Participation and the ECCC's Limited Focus on 1975–1979

Another important issue of contention for civil parties participating in the ECCC proceedings has been its temporal jurisdiction. The ECCC can only investigate crimes committed from 17 April 1975 to 6 January 1979—that is, the period during which the Communist Party of Kampuchea held formal power over the entire country. As we have seen in chapter 1, the limitation to this period was a result of the protracted, political negotiations that led to the establishment of the ECCC.

Discursive Strategies of Resistance and the Metaphor of the "Crocodile"

Here again, civil parties used the multiple "invented" spaces of the transitional justice process, which they could access, to voice their criticism of the Court's limited temporal focus. This includes regional civil parties' forums organized by the VSS and the ECCC's Public Affairs Section, thematic conferences that brought together different stakeholders working on the ECCC, press conferences at the tribunal, and bilateral meetings with their lawyers, as well as interviews with researchers such as myself.[124] In these spaces, civil parties repeatedly raised the issue of temporal jurisdiction and broader questions of responsibility, demanding explanations from ECCC representatives. In 2014, a national civil party lawyer described to me how he was repeatedly facing such questions from his clients:

> [Civil parties] still want to add more [to the trial], the facts out of the scope of investigations or beyond the limitation of the period to the Khmer Rouge regime. [. . .] They want to know more about the destruction and war crimes committed from 1970 until 1975 during the civil war between the Khmer Rouge and the Lon Nol regime [. . .]. Because they all say that this is also the responsibility of the Khmer Rouge [. . .]! And some civil parties want to confront Vietnam, China, America . . . all of the countries related to supporting the Lon Nol regime and the Khmer Rouge regime and responsible for the war in Cambodia which destroyed the country. But I tell them that we cannot [do this] because this Court limits the temporal and personal scope of the trial.[125]

In raising these questions, civil parties thus demand that the larger context in which the Khmer Rouge regime took place be examined and that the regime's root causes be addressed (see also Manning 2012a). To some civil parties, this limitation of the ECCC's personal jurisdiction affects its ability to deliver "justice" and to find the "truth." A civil party in Case 002 from Siem Reap province, for instance, argued during an interview in 2014 that the ECCC cannot find justice since it does not account for the long-term implications of the conflicts that led to, and followed, the Khmer Rouge regime: "The Court [. . .] only looks at 17 April 1975 to 7 January 1979, only this, it doesn't talk about before and after! But to have justice, we need to know [everything], from the beginning until the end! We cannot only look at the middle, at one part of it only. This is not justice!"[126]

Allegations of political interference from the CPP government seemed to fuel civil parties' criticism that the Court only looks at a truncated portion of the past. Many civil parties whom I interviewed closely followed the refusal of high government officials to testify as witnesses at the tribunal (see also Ryan and McGrew 2016, 72). In doing so, they also scrutinized the role of international actors in the transitional justice process. A Cambodian civil party lawyer, for instance, told me:

> Some want the witnesses working in the Cambodian government who were summoned by the Court to testify and to be accused. [. . .] They know that these government officials refused to do so and so they ask, "Why doesn't the Court dare to call them?" This is one of the questions which is really difficult to answer . . . [. . .] The civil parties, they know that some or most of the high-ranking officials in the government right now are former Khmer Rouge. If this Court tried to summon them, maybe there would be problems, even if I cannot say war . . . [. . .] But civil parties ask why did the UN, with UNTAC, come to Cambodia and dare to do everything for peace in Cambodia, and right now, when it's about finding justice for the people, why don't they dare the same way as before? I always explain that we cannot push the UN. [. . .] The UN cannot bring troops of soldiers to come to Cambodia again, so the UN lets the Court find justice and use their power to guarantee the proceedings of the Court.[127]

Many civil parties I met also tried to monitor whether Cases 003 and 004 were moving forward or not.[128] In 2014, a civil party from Kampot province, for instance, was wondering whether these Cases would come to trial after the visit of the UN Secretary-General, Ban Ki Moon, to the ECCC:

> The government shall not prevent cases. Cases 001 and 002 are already being tried, but they were only policymakers, so the killers [those who killed directly] are in Cases 003 and 004. [. . .] I still ask myself why the government protects them, because they are people who committed crimes. For example, [. . .] in Svay Rieng, Chou Bundeth is free. He shot at a few workers during the demonstrations around 1–2 years ago, he still lives in impunity. I don't want that to happen, I don't want that people who commit crimes are still free. For Cases 003 and 004, they are the killers, not the top leaders![129]

He further argued that the position of the ruling CPP on Cases 003 and 004 may have played a role in the 2013 general elections: "The CPP lost voices during the last elections, because the prime minister was against Cases 003 and 004, so he lost popularity."

When I met this civil party in Kampot province again in 2018, he had by then helped several of his fellow villagers to apply for civil party participation in Cases 003 and 004. In our 2018 survey, respondents displayed strong support for Cases 003 and 004 to move forward. In fact, 80.2 percent of our 439 respondents (including civil parties, civil party applicants, complainants, non-participants, and participants in NGO projects) indicated that they wanted the ECCC to address these Cases (see Williams et al. 2018, 62–63). Asked why, they explained that Cases 003 and 004 moving to trial would provide them with a sense of justice (26.4 percent), bring justice to the victims (25.1 percent) or to Cambodia (19 percent)—but also that it would show that the ECCC is independent (14.3 percent).

When questioning the ECCC's limited temporal jurisdiction, some civil parties interestingly adopted the very terms used by Nuon Chea in public hearings. During his opening statements in Case 002/01 in November 2011, Nuon Chea paternalistically addressed his "beloved Cambodian people" and "Khmer children" and used the metaphor of the "crocodile" to criticize the ECCC's limited temporal jurisdiction, in line with his defense team's strategy of rupture:

> I, Nuon Chea, have been given an opportunity today which I have been waiting for so long. That is, to explain to my beloved Cambodian people and the Khmer children the facts [that] occurred in Cambodian history. As I clarified, if my health is fine, I will try to explain and to provide resolutions to all the problems in order [to explain] our history, which is a proper history, [and] not for the purpose of serving any particular tendency. I am of the opinion that this Court is unfair to me since the beginning because only certain facts are to be adjudicated by this Court. I must say *only the body of the crocodile is to be discussed [at this Court], not its head or the tail.* [. . .] The root causes and [their] consequences are those that happened pre-1975 and post-1979 [but they] are ignored by this Court.[130]

Subsequently, in interviews, civil parties mobilized this metaphor of the crocodile when criticizing the ECCC's limited temporal jurisdiction. For instance, in November 2014, three years after Nuon Chea's statement, two civil parties from Siem Reap province argued:

> This Court is only looking at one piece. As Nuon Chea mentioned, there are three pieces of a crocodile, but they only look at one piece only. It's injustice already. But I want to know about the Khmer Rouge; this is why I became a civil party. First, I want to know who created the Khmer Rouge.

> And then, from 1975 to 1979, why did they kill people when they had already defeated the Lon Nol regime? And then, after 1979, until 1990, a communist regime was established. Why didn't they introduce a democracy at that time when the war was already finished?[131]

> I cannot say that Nuon Chea wasn't responsible, but I think there were also other persons who were responsible, including our leaders today in Cambodia. [. . .] I've attended a Case 002 hearing in Phnom Penh at the ECCC, and I saw Nuon Chea himself asking why did we cut the crocodile into pieces, and why do we only examine his body, and not his head or his tail? [. . .] When you try something in front of a Court, it has to be the full story, but I don't think that this tribunal speaks of the true story, it is not correct.[132]

The civil parties here sided with the accused and former Khmer Rouge leader Nuon Chea to question the ECCC's limited temporal jurisdiction, debunking expectations that they would necessarily stand in direct opposition with the accused in the judicial proceedings. This may be linked to how Nuon Chea's intervention made sense to civil parties, because he spoke directly in Khmer, unfiltered by translation, but also because he mobilized a local cultural idiom. As Maurice Eisenbruch (2018, 831–33) has shown, the crocodile metaphor connects to various popular expressions, including the idea that Cambodians have historically been "caught between the Thai tiger to the West and the Vietnamese crocodile to the east."

As can be seen in their quotes, these civil parties, however, do not necessarily deflect attention away from Nuon Chea's responsibilities—as his defense team aims to do with such questioning of the ECCC's temporal jurisdiction. But they similarly demand a broadening of the scope of discussions to better comprehend "why Khmers killed Khmers," given the involvement of foreign actors in the conflict. Perhaps they use the arguments provided publicly and repeatedly by another formal party in the Court proceedings, even if it is from the accused and his team, to give more authority to their arguments.

Resisting Discourses on the Past and the Depoliticization of Civil Party Participation

These discursive strategies of resistance are significant for several reasons. First, they challenge the official discourses on the Khmer Rouge past sanctioned by the CPP government (see chapter 2). Rather than being satisfied with the sole focus on the "three years, eight months and twenty days" of the Khmer Rouge regime, civil parties demand a broader discussion of what happened before, during, and after. They thereby move beyond the narratives on the past introduced by the memory politics of the various governments that came after the Khmer Rouge regime, which until today serve the purpose of legitimizing the ruling party's narrative as "savior of the nation."

Second, in raising these political questions about the past, these civil parties question the relegation of their participation to the orchestrated expression of their suffering under the Khmer Rouge regime. Focusing on one's own, personal experiences of the Khmer Rouge regime is a common and "comfortable" behavior for civil parties, as a national officer at the VSS observed:

> Civil parties, when they are asked to say A, they generally don't say [A], they just want to elaborate their stories. [. . .] If you want to ask them: "Please say something about your own experience in the Courtroom, how do you feel?" Then, consistently, they just say a few words and they jump to their own story: "When I lived under the Khmer Rouge, it was hard, it was difficult . . ." [. . .] Why? Because their mentality has been fixed to the hardships, to the difficulties, to the problems . . . [. . .] because . . . that is their experience. Or maybe it is comfortable to say this, rather than [to speak of] a new experience in the Court [. . .]. They are too nervous to say something new, it is comfortable to say something that they know fluently. [. . .] It's easier, they have a lot of information to produce from that.[133]

Over the years, I also observed how repeating personal stories of suffering and harm, at times with the same words and public display of emotions, has become a routine for some of the civil parties regularly invited at public events (see also Kochanski 2021).[134] These observations speak to Aafke Sanders's (2006) anthropological research on how survivors remember the Khmer Rouge regime. Struck by the collective aspect of narratives, Sanders identified the standardization of stories into "catastrophe tales" through the narrative construction around a few key themes—food, forced labor, the repressive regime of *Angkar*—and processes of both remembrance and forgetting. She observed that this standardization serves the purpose of soothing both the audience and the narrator. It establishes safe narratives that engage only with the narrator's ordinary memory (*mémoire ordinaire*) and not with their deep memory (*mémoire profonde*). As such, it constitutes a psychological coping strategy when narrating the Khmer Rouge regime, Sanders (2006) concluded.

When publicly speaking in the "invented" or "invited" spaces of transitional justice, resorting to such standardized ways of speaking of the past is also a safe way to stay within the realm of the officially sanctioned narratives on the past, and within the scope of what is expected of civil parties. A civil party I met twice in 2014 in Siem Reap, for instance, told me that he thought he was no longer invited to join civil party forums organized by the VSS precisely because he raised controversial questions about the Khmer Rouge past. He was more interested in discussing the nature and factions of the Khmer Rouge movement, or the role of foreign countries, than in narrating his experience of suffering:

> When I participate in a [forum], for instance, the one in Kratie . . . I've protested and some [of the ECCC administrators] were not happy. . . . I went to [the forum] in Kampong Cham, I've always protested, saying that it's not the Khmers who executed the Khmers, the Khmers are intelligent too, they didn't kill the Khmers just on their own like that, it is [also] because of external parties. [. . .] But the ECCC administrators stopped me. They only want us to say who was killed amongst our family by the Khmer Rouge, that we are victims, how our life was as victims . . . [*shrugs his shoulders, raises his hands halfway up, his palms facing the ceiling*] They forced me not to speak of anything concerning Indochina, and so on. . . . They only want me to speak of how I was tortured, who harmed me, that there wasn't enough food [*laughs*].[135]

When civil parties raise larger questions on the past, including on the root causes of the Khmer Rouge regime and a longer list of suspects responsible for the crimes committed, they thus also question the "enunciative modalities" produced at the ECCC—that is, the processes through which certain subjects of discourse are granted the authority to speak. With such discursive strategies of resistance, civil parties, become "subversive speakers" (Alcoff and Gray 1993).[136] As survivors of violence, they claim for themselves the roles not only of witness but also of expert; not only of reporter but also of theorist of these experiences.

This civil party also explained that although he was not interested in monetary compensation, he had still signed the petition for financial reparations out of solidarity. Notwithstanding the specific performance of resistance (signing a petition) or its visible, public aim (claiming for financial reparations) civil party resistance thus also takes meaning in relation to the official victim subject positions that civil parties must engage with and negotiate when they participate in transitional justice processes.

In 2018, another civil party also reflected on the type of behavior he felt was expected of civil parties at the ECCC: "Even if I am someone who does not really understand well about laws, I am brave enough to express my thoughts and ask questions, not like the elderly people [the other civil parties] who are between seventy and eighty years old. They don't really know anything. They just follow the order of the others. For me, I will never accept that. I have to know clearly about this kind of stuff. [. . .] But the elderly people, [. . .], they always follow the order of the others. These are the types of people that they really want, those who listen to them. [. . .] Those who ask a lot, they will be hated. Those who don't ask a lot of questions, the court will like them. This is very difficult."[137]

Another civil party from Prey Veng Province similarly observed that many civil parties were quite old: "Other civil parties—I know from the meetings I joined—I saw that most or many of them don't know how to read and write because under the Khmer Rouge, they did not learn, they are not educated. Maybe 60 percent [of them]. They are also very old now, when they go to the meetings, they feel sleepy and only a few can understand."[138]

In fact, these characteristics of civil parties may also be the result of the hidden costs of civil party participation, of how it requires time to participate and the capacity to travel frequently (see also chapter 4). This is something that we could clearly see in various findings of our 2018 survey. In our sample, we included 28 civil parties whom we had categorized as "marginalized" for attending significantly less hearings or civil party forums than others. We wanted to understand the reasons for the lower levels of their participation. We found that some of them had to turn down invitations from the Court because they were unable to travel, being either too old or too busy (see Williams et al. 2018, 81–82). A number of the 59 complainants we surveyed raised similar issues. Some 33.3 percent of those who indicated that they would not have preferred to apply for civil party status explained that this was because civil party participation required too much time. Ten percent explained it required too much travel (Williams et al. 2018, 92). Finally, 28 percent of the 125 respondents surveyed as "non-participants" in the ECCC mentioned not having applied for civil party participation because they had no time, believing it would be too time-consuming or expensive (Williams et al. 2018, 95).[139]

In 2018, an international civil party lawyer similarly concluded that the civil parties constituted quite a specific category of the general population: "I think that we do have a pool of civil parties that is specific. It is older people, people who are not busy, people who need money. It is people who are happy to go for strolls—except when they are in bad health. [. . .] Civil party participation allows them to travel around, it allows them to have a small per diem."[140]

There may thus have been a self-reinforcing dynamic at play, which led to this lack of active and dissenting engagement with core questions on the past, and on who is responsible, which the civil parties quoted above regretted. Those who could have participated more actively in such debates may not have taken part as civil parties or may not have been able to attend many outreach activities because of the hidden costs of participation. Those who joined the invited and invented spaces of transitional justice and were interested in these deeper and more difficult discussions felt restricted and disciplined. These instances of civil party resistance against the ECCC's limited temporal jurisdiction thus show us that civil party participation constitutes an ambiguous space of participation, which both enables and restricts civil party agency. This even more so in the increasingly overt authoritarian context.

Civil Party Participation in the Context of Authoritarianism

Civil party participation at the ECCC also needs to be seen in the context of a country "embarked on an openly authoritarian path" in which "expanding political participation through state-sponsored avenues serves to constrain contestation" (Norén-Nilsson and Bourdier 2019, 3).

First, it seems that the increasingly open authoritarian context has over time led to an increased exposure of the ECCC's civil party participation scheme to the ruling party's agenda. For instance, two months prior to the July 2018 general elections, a civil party noticed that he was no longer invited to VSS civil party forums. He believed that this was not only because he had been part of, or indeed had led, the protests for financial reparations a few years earlier and always asked many questions in civil party forums. He felt it was also because he was affiliated with the Cambodia National Rescue Party (CNRP), the political opposition party that had just been banned.[141] With the 2018 elections, this reach of party politics into civil party participation also took place quite overtly in some meetings between civil party lawyers and civil parties in rural areas facilitated by local authority figures, in which the village chief would close the meeting with a call to civil parties to vote for the CPP.[142] A former ECCC officer regretted that "there was no sense of responsibility" during election periods, as outreach activities would be used to mobilize support for the ruling party.[143] This would, however, even occur beyond election periods, because the VSS never had any capacity or independence to organize events across the country without the support of local authorities, mostly affiliated with the CPP.

Second, rather than being encouraged or celebrated as a form of emancipation, civil party mobilization has also been cast as a political threat[144] in a context in which the ruling party views any grassroots mobilization that could turn into a large social movement with suspicion. This emerged in the case of Ksaem Ksan—one of the very few victims' associations in "a country of victims without victims' associations" already mentioned earlier.[145] This association brought together civil parties from various socioeconomic, geographical, and educational backgrounds. It emerged in the specific context of Case 001, which, given its scope, allowed for more intense experiences of participation. The association was established out of contestation against the increasing restrictions of civil parties' rights. In August 2009, 28 civil parties in Case 001 protested against the Trial Chamber's decision that civil parties lawyers would have no right to question character witnesses.[146] On 13 September 2009, 33 civil parties in Cases 001 and 002 founded Ksaem Ksan to voice civil party claims beyond the trial proceedings.[147] After its establishment, Ksaem Ksan continued to amplify civil party voices and their critiques of ECCC decisions, such as the Trial Chamber's limited decision on reparations in Case 001.[148] Its aim was to support its members to participate in the ECCC proceedings but also to provide both spiritual and material support to its members (see, e.g., Agger 2015).

Even if it is possible that an important number of Ksaem Ksan members had a personal preference for the opposition, the association aimed to remain neutral and nonpartisan: "The vision of our association is neutral, not on the government side or the NGO side" (Chum 2012, 49). Ksaem Ksan members would not publicly mention their political affiliation in outreach activities for civil parties. The focus of Ksaem Ksan was never about political opposition to the ruling party but about advocacy for civil parties' rights. A respondent who had supported the association's work observed: "They never say anything [at the ECCC] about them being in the opposition, or the Sam Rainsy Party or the Human Rights Party. They only speak of the right, the right of victims, the right to justice. [. . .] When Ksaem Ksan members talk about the association of Ksaem Ksan, the vision is to claim for rights. It's always about the right to justice, the right to reparations."[149]

Nonetheless, when Ksaem Ksan members were asked to speak as civil party representatives during civil party forums, they were not necessarily allowed to speak of Ksaem Ksan and had to focus on updates on the trial proceedings and give their perspective as an "exemplary victim."[150] Some civil parties who were part of Ksaem Ksan were also apparently not reinvited to the regular regional forums organized by the VSS, at least up to 2014, perhaps because they were perceived to be affiliated with the opposition.[151]

Moreover, Ksaem Ksan members faced difficulties from provincial authorities when they wanted to organize regional forums for their members, because they were suspected of being "a group from the opposition." Beyond the individual political affiliation of some of its members, it is the grassroots nature of Ksaem Ksan and its potential important mobilization basis across Cambodia that appeared threatening to local or provincial authorities. This is to be seen in the context of the history of one of the two opposition parties that joined the opposition coalition CNRP, the Human Rights Party, which was established in 2007 by the prominent civil society figure Kem Sokha, founder of the Cambodian Center for Human Rights (CCHR): "They [the authorities] are afraid [. . .] because there is the experience of someone like Khem Sokha, who used to head the Centre for Human Rights. He organized a public forum and then changed it to a political party, the Human Rights Party. And so Ksaem Ksan is an association, and when they organize such a forum, they [fear that they] might later on turn to the Ksaem Ksan Party."[152]

Another explanation given was that if Ksaem Ksan was to become successful in attracting donor funding for activities for victims of the Khmer Rouge regime, it was competing with aspirations of CPP officials to establish the VSS as a perennial institution and tap into donor funding in the name of victims.[153]

Ksaem Ksan's efforts to grow as a victims' association would come to a standstill following the prime minister's push for the adoption of the "genocide denial law" in early June 2013. Just weeks ahead of the 2013 national elections, the prime minister accused Kem Sokha—by then acting president of the newly founded CNRP—of denying the existence of the Khmer Rouge security prison S-21, in a clear attempt to inhibit popular support for the opposition. These allegations relied on an audio excerpt of comments made by Kem Sokha, which was never released despite demands from the CNRP. Kem Sokha denied these allegations and argued that his comment was taken out of context. The prime minister framed Kem Sokha's alleged comments as violating the dignity and suffering of victims and survivors of the Khmer Rouge regime. In his speech on 27 May 2013, the prime minister argued:

> This statement not only hurts grandfather Chum Mey and grandfather Bou Meng, but also the spirits of those who died at Tuol Sleng and elsewhere in the country under the execution of the Khmer Rouge. It also hurts the regime's living survivors across Cambodia. [. . .] I don't understand why only for the purpose of defeating me [. . .] and the Cambodian People's Party, they disdain the spirits of millions of victims in total and hundreds of thousands at Tuol Sleng alone. Honorable novices, imagine how painful it was when the survivors like grandfather Chum Mey, grandfather Bou Meng were tortured? How painful it was when our relatives were killed. [. . .] You [*pronoun referring to an unknown third person*] have crossed the line. For a political gain over the Cambodian People's Party, you dare to disrespect the spirits of the victims and the survivors.[154]

As we can see, the prime minister called out both Chum Mey and Bou Meng in his speech. Both were not only S-21 survivors and prominent civil parties in Case 001 at the time; they were also co-heading Ksaem Ksan as president and vice president, respectively.

It is not to be underestimated that Kem Sokha's alleged comment that S-21 had not existed was painful to hear for civil parties, in particular for S-21 survivors, especially since this took place after the pronouncement of the appeal judgment in Case 001.[155] Even before the prime minister singled them out in his public speech, Chum Mey and Bou Meng had both threatened to file a lawsuit against Kem Sokha if he did not apologize for his remarks. Chum Mey had further pledged to organize a demonstration of 20,000 persons and gave Kem Sokha an ultimatum of ten days to apologize (Heng 2013).

However, the fact that the prime minister called them out by their names in a public speech clearly put intense pressure on them. A person closely involved with Ksaem Ksan observed: "[In such a context,] [i]f you want to stay neutral, that is, if you don't want to explicitly join the CPP or the CPP's position, well then you are perceived as an enemy immediately. It is like under the Khmer Rouge: if you are not a friend, you're automatically an enemy, even if in fact you haven't joined or adhered to the opposition!"[156]

On 9 June 2013, it was in the end only Chum Mey who led a demonstration against Kem Sokha. Two days before, the National Assembly swiftly adopted the Genocide Denial Law in an extraordinary session (Article 19 2013). Only 86 parliamentarians, including 84 CPP members, were present after the opposition parliamentarians of the Sam Rainsy and Human Rights Parties had been stripped of their parliamentary status and salaries. After the law's adoption, the 9 June protest gathered an estimated 10,000 people in Phnom Penh. Human rights organizations also observed smaller protests in other parts of the country, estimating a total of 12,500 to 30,000 protesters across Cambodia (S. Vong and Worrel 2013). A few days after the protest, Chum Mey also filed a lawsuit against Kem Sokha for defamation and denial of Khmer Rouge crimes (Kong 2013).

Although Chum Mey repeatedly insisted that he was acting as a private citizen and denied having received government support for his protest, journalists identified several indications of government involvement (see, e.g., Kong 2013). First, the prime minister himself urged Cambodians to join the protest, and protesters were able to exercise their freedom of expression and assembly "without pressure" (Chhorn 2013). Moreover, some protesters were apparently paid to take part in the demonstrations, and security guards were seen telling protesters how to hold signs (Chhorn 2013). In addition, local government authorities supplied drinking water and transportation for protesters, as well as material and food. Opposition lawmaker Mu Sochua finally observed that when representatives went to the CNRP headquarters in Tuol Kork to deliver a petition after the demonstration, they were escorted by the Phnom Penh municipal police chief (Chhorn 2013). During my fieldwork, I also received indications of the government involvement in these protests, although Chum Mey, whom I had met several times since 2011, vehemently denied having received such support.[157] In particular, it seems that the government involvement included that of Chum Sokha, advisor to the prime minister and TV presenter, as well as then–ECCC public affairs chief Dim Sovannarom. The latter took care of the translation at the protest's press conference.[158] After the 2013 elections, he was granted the title of "His Excellency" by the CPP government.

It is possible that the pressure on Chum Mey was also exercised in economic terms. Chum Mey's income was then mainly based on the selling of his memoirs at the Tuol Sleng Genocide Museum, which had been an institution close to the CPP government after its creation (Chhim 2012, 48). If he did not play his part in the protest, he could possibly face difficulties in selling his book at Tuol Sleng.[159] Others argued that Chum Mey had fallen prey to the usual CPP strategy of constraint and corruption, and that he was rewarded financially for his political support.[160] A member of the association whom I met in Kampong Cham in 2014, for instance, considered that Chum Mey had "sold himself": "I don't think his action was right. [. . .] He demonstrated against Kem Sokha, and Sokha is the one who is working to find justice for the people [as opposition leader]. The CPP gave him money, that is why he demonstrated, and, also, they hired people from provinces to join the demonstration."[161]

Ultimately, Chum Mey's role in leading the protest led to a significant crisis within the otherwise rather united Ksaem Ksan association. Senior members of Ksaem Ksan, including Bou Meng, had already distanced themselves ahead of the protests, although some members did participate in the 9 June demonstration.[162] Ksaem Ksan members then attempted to oust Chum Mey from his role of president for politicizing the association and thereby threatening its unity. However, because of a lack of funds to hold a General Assembly to elect a new president (Kuch 2013a; 2013b), Chum Mey remained president "by default." Ksaem Ksan members whom I met in 2014 thus referred to him as the "president who keeps the house" (ប្រធានចាំផ្ទះ, *brothean cham phteah*) yet lacks any support from the membership base.[163] Since this incident, the association has lost its potential as an avenue for civil party grassroots mobilization in Cambodia.

Conclusion

If we turn our attention to the places in which civil parties experience the transitional justice process, we can see the various ways in which they both engage in, and resist, this process. This analysis challenges essentialist, monolithic and static approaches to Cambodian culture as characterized by unquestioned obedience to authoritarian rule, docility, excessive deference, and conservatism. It also questions more generally assumptions on passive victims in the aftermath of mass atrocity, and of "actors in war-torn regions as powerless, passive beneficiaries" (MacGinty 2011, 85). However, civil party participation also emerges as an ambiguous space of participation, which both enables and limits civil party agency in various ways.

This speaks to several scholarly critiques of transitional justice interventions, while adding new insights from the context of Cambodia. First, the ambiguous nature of civil party participation shows that victims, when participating in such processes, must navigate the many expectations toward them. Scholars have shown how these expectations are shaped by imaginaries of the "ideal victim" as an innocent victim who is reasonable in their claims and use of emotions (Lefranc, Mathieu, and Siméant 2008) and is able to ultimately "let go of the past" and move on (Hamber and Wilson 2002; Mueller-Hirth 2017). Such assumptions are rooted in problematic, binary understandings of victim-perpetrators (Bouris 2007). But they also result from normative views that transitional justice processes are quintessentially good and will therefore necessarily be beneficial for victims (Rubli 2012, 10). These imaginaries are also produced through the reliance of international criminal justice institutions on a particular imagination of "victims" as necessarily searching for retributive justice (Fletcher 2015). Second, this chapter's analysis confirms observations that a set of experts—those whom Tshepo Madlingozi (2010) calls "transitional justice entrepreneurs" but also researchers such as myself—will come to speak on behalf of victims, including in ways that take their agency and voices away. We have seen that in Cambodia these experts may also perform or be perceived as patrons. The expectations that victims face in a transitional justice process may therefore also be linked to obligations of displaying loyalty, deference, and affection in patron-client relationships. Third, this chapter has shown how transitional justice interventions often prioritize established NGOs located in the capital city and thereby marginalize grassroots social movements. We have seen that such a limitation of spaces for grassroots mobilization also needs to be analyzed in relation to authoritarian practices in contexts such as Cambodia. Finally, this chapter's analysis speaks to critical scholarship that uncovers how transitional justice—as a field of practice, policymaking, and research—marginalizes claims for socioeconomic understandings of justice. The marginalization of such justice claims is perhaps experienced even more vividly in neo-patrimonial contexts where national or international staff members of transitional justice institutions are seen as enriching themselves in the name of victims.

For civil parties, the transitional justice process thus constituted a key site of contestation over the nature and direction of the multiple transitions that Cambodia has undergone. This included contestations over the nature and extent of the transition from war to (negative) peace. Civil parties had to overcome persisting fears of the Khmer Rouge and an ontological sense of insecurity fueled by the layering of past and present experiences of political violence when deciding to participate. The transitional justice process also featured contestations over the nature and extent of the transition away from authoritarianism. Civil parties needed to assess the space available to them for voicing dissent in public settings; for having open, contentious discussions about the past, or for engaging in grassroots social movements and collective actions of public protest. Finally, yet as importantly, their contestations featured struggles over who is benefiting from the country's aggressive transformation from command economy to free market capitalism, and from the money-loaded international interventions that are taking place in this context.

4

Nonparticipation

Transitional Justice in the Context of Political Violence

The ECCC proceedings unfolded in the context of a turn to openly repressive authoritarian practices following the 2013 contestation of CPP rule and the 2017 effective outlawing of electoral competition. This turn has been accompanied by political violence, consisting of the suppression of political opposition; of environmental, human rights, or trade union activism; and of dissent against the privatization of natural resources and against land disputes. These political developments stand in sharp contrast to teleological approaches of transitional justice, which locate transitional justice processes as part of linear transitions from authoritarianism to liberal democracy (Hinton 2018). They further question claims that transitional justice processes—hybrid tribunals in particular—are not only intrinsically valuable for providing justice and addressing impunity but also instrumentally significant for the goods they supposedly deliver: deterrence and peace, democracy, and the rule of law (see, e.g., McAuliffe 2011; Ainley 2014).

This chapter asks: How has the domestic political context affected the relevance of the state-sanctioned transitional justice process in Cambodia? To analyze this, I turn to the transitional justice perspectives of citizens who have been affected by political violence in contemporary Cambodia, and who have been engaged in contestation of the ruling party's co-optation of political and economic power. This significantly broadens the focus laid in the previous two chapters, which examined how the political context has affected the ECCC's proceedings, as well as victim participation as a formal site of engagement with, participation in, and resistance to transitional justice. This chapter instead brings into focus contemporary human rights violations, which fall outside of the scope of the ECCC's mandate and are of a different nature and scale than the Khmer Rouge regime. It further engages with the perspectives of Cambodians not participating in the transitional justice process. This chapter is thereby an exercise of epistemological disruption and decentering of the study of transitional justice. It offers empirical insights on the perceptions of the ECCC of Cambodians who have generally remained at the margins of, if not entirely absent from, assessments and studies of transitional justice in Cambodia.[1]

This chapter comprises four sections. The first provides an overview of the three case studies of political violence in contemporary Cambodia that lie at the heart of this chapter's analysis. The second section turns to these respondents' relationship to the transitional justice process at the ECCC, which is characterized by nonparticipation. It discusses the multiple reasons for this nonparticipation: from a lack of access to knowledge on the Court, to political economies of survival and activism and an absent interest in the Court's work. The remainder of the chapter then turns to instances of nonparticipation that can be read as forms of resistance to transitional justice. Drawing from sociolegal approaches, the third section shows that nonparticipation at the ECCC results from everyday experiences of the law. Cambodians who experience the national judiciary as an agent of injustice question the ECCC's independence. Perceiving the Court to be embedded in the political status quo, they take the principled decision *not* to participate. Finally, the fourth section discusses nonparticipation as a form of temporal resistance. Opting out from participation in transitional justice is a way of rejecting the construction of the present in absolute opposition to the Khmer Rouge past—a teleological temporality that lies at the heart of CPP's claims for legitimacy and is also reflective of the transitional justice imaginary.

Political Violence in Contemporary Cambodia: Three Case Studies

The analysis in this chapter draws from qualitative interviews conducted with three groups of respondents who experienced political violence and human rights violations in contemporary Cambodia and are engaged in current political struggles. The first two groups of respondents were selected for being affected by displacement and land conflicts in urban and rural areas. Struggles for land access and control have played a central role in the country's social and political life. Land conflicts are inherently connected to the Khmer Rouge past, processes of state formation, and elite capture in postwar reconstruction. The third group consists of respondents who participated in the unprecedented protests following the contested 2013 elections that saw the ruling party's previous electoral success questioned, as citizens rallied over claims for social justice and substantial reforms to address inequalities, corruption, and land conflicts. The protests led to what Cambodian human rights NGO LICADHO (2015, 2) then qualified as the "worst state violence" in over a decade, as the CPP government proceeded with a crackdown on protesters and supporters of the opposition coalition CNRP.

Land Conflicts in Cambodia: Case Studies from Urban and Rural Areas

Ever since French colonial rule, large-scale land acquisition has played a key role in processes of consolidating centralized state control over territory and natural resources, while the extraction of natural resources has been at the heart of strategies for political control (Diepart and Schoenberger 2016). Under the Khmer Rouge regime, the country underwent "one of the twentieth century's most fundamental upheavals in socialization of landholding," as the Communist Party of Kampuchea enforced its total collectivization policy (Scurrah and Hirsch 2015, 2). Private property rights, introduced under the French Protectorate (1863–1953), were abolished; land ownership records were destroyed; and all land tenure systems erased (Un and So 2011). After the fall of the Khmer Rouge regime in 1979, the Vietnamese-installed People's Republic of Kampuchea (PRK) adopted a more moderate land collectivization policy, the implementation of which occurred under considerable flexibility. As many villagers returned to the villages they lived in prior to 1975, the collective system of farming introduced by the PRK was soon abandoned and replaced by private household farming (Scurrah and Hirsch 2015). However, the possibility to claim rights to land for residential purposes was based on occupancy, and the PRK did not recognize pre-1975 tenure claims (Un and So 2011). The 1980s also saw an increasing depletion of natural resources by political and military actors. The 1970–75 civil war and the Khmer Rouge's focus on agricultural development had ironically preserved the country's forests from the destruction associated with Southeast Asia's rapid natural resource–led development (Le Billon 2002). After 1979, however, logging became an essential strategy for Khmer Rouge factions to finance their war against the PRK, while the PRK government itself controlled logging in eastern Cambodia (Diepart and Schoenberger 2016).

With the reintroduction of private land ownership and economic liberalization in 1989, land tenure conflicts soon emerged, and further escalated in the 1990s and 2000s. The first land law introduced in 1992 recognized ownership rights, through formal documents, as well as temporary possession rights, based on use of the land. It further allowed for the conversion of possession rights into ownership if the land was still unregistered and had been held for five consecutive years (Un and So 2011). However, only a small percentage of the applications received in the land titling program resulted in occupancy certificates (Biddulph 2014). Moreover, this new law and the privatization reform led to land grabbing and power abuses, including in the capital city, though with fluctuations along elections cycles (Un and So 2011; Beban, So, and Un 2017).

Most land conflicts are concentrated in areas of poor urban settlements, along seasonal lakes, and in forest lands (S. So 2010). A forest concession system, first introduced under colonial rule, was reestablished in the 1990s, promoted by the World Bank and other international donors (Scurrah and Hirsch 2015; Diepart and Schoenberger 2016). Its aim was to launch a transparent system under central government control that could provide revenues for post-war reconstruction efforts and put an end to illegal logging. However, the resulting commodification of forests played into the struggles between the political factions of the 1993-established government coalition. Forest and land concessions were used in the competition for control through the reconstruction of patronage networks (Le Billon 2002; Diepart and Schoenberger 2016).

The case studies selected for this chapter include land conflicts in poor urban settlements and forest areas—or rather, former forest areas. These conflicts emerged in the context of the 2001 land law introduced by the CPP government after international pressure (Neef, Touch, and Chiengthong 2013). The 2001 land law provided a legal framework for land tenure and administration and introduced significant reforms. These included the extension of "ownership" rights to residential and agricultural land and the introduction of a new categorization system for land ownership, which differentiates between state-public land, state-private land, private-individual land, and indigenous/communal land. The law also formalized a land concessions system granted on state-private land, which substituted the granting of Economic and Social Land Concessions to the previous forest concessions system.

Formally, Economic Land Concessions (ELCs) were introduced to foster agroindustrial activities and employment in rural communities in so-called degraded or underutilized land, through the injection of private capital investments in the context of ASEAN integration (Neef, Touch, and Chiengthong 2013; Diepart and Schoenberger 2016). Instead, it became a central tool for the CPP's assertion of power, the intensification of its control over land, and its extraction of natural resources (Diepart and Schoenberger 2016; Loughlin and Milne 2020). It further led to a worsening of land conflicts and evictions, and negatively impacted human rights (Subedi 2012). In 2012, the CPP declared a moratorium on ELCs, as an attempt to curb social unrest ahead of the upcoming commune and legislative elections. By then, a total of 2.6 million hectares had been allocated under ELCs, representing more than 10 percent of the country and more than half of its arable land (Loughlin and Milne 2020). Five powerful tycoons and CPP senators owned 20 percent of this land (Global Witness 2013). Almost one million people—approximately 6 percent of the population—had been adversely affected by land grabbing (ADHOC 2014).

In addition to ELCs, the 2001 Land Law introduced Social Land Concessions (SLCs) to tackle landlessness and offer land security at the periphery of ELCs. The implementation of SLCs took place with the support of international actors such as the World Bank and the German development assistance. However, only limited numbers of Cambodians ultimately benefited from SLCs.[2] Moreover, the impact of SLCs on rural livelihoods was limited and mitigated by poor living conditions (OHCHR 2018). The implementation of SLCs further ignored previous land claims, with some villagers pressured into abandoning their claims for potential recognition under the SLC scheme, while others had their land taken away for SLCs (Loughlin and Milne 2020). Researchers also argue that the CPP has mainly used SLCs to strengthen the distribution of concessions to tycoons through ELCs, while curbing villagers' claims to possession rights on public land (Neef, Touch, and Chiengthong 2013). According to LICADHO (2009, 11), SLCs have been used as a strategy to "displace the poor from their existing land" through forced evictions and "turn [their land] over to private companies for 'lucrative' development projects."

Land Conflicts in the Capital City (I): Respondents from Boeung Kak

It is in this context that I conducted interviews with selected groups of respondents affected by land conflicts and evictions taking place in both urban and rural areas. The first group of respondents were three women from the Boeung Kak community, affected by land evictions in the capital city. They were born respectively in 1940, 1965, and 1986. I conducted semistructured interviews and life-story interviews in March 2013 and repeat interviews in January 2016 and February 2018.

Boeung Kak (Lake Kak) was one of seven lakes located in the center of Phnom Penh. In February 2007, the 133 hectares of the lake and its surroundings were leased as an ELC for ninety-nine years to Shukaku Inc., a company owned by CPP senator Oknha Lao Meng Khin,[3] for US$79 million (Chan 2014). To secure the legitimacy of this lease, the Council of Ministers issued a subdecree on 7 August 2008 that transferred the area from "State Public land" to "State Private land."[4] As of August 2009, residents started to receive eviction notices. They were given one week to accept one of the compensation options, none of which met the requirements of international law (Biddulph 2014). Many of the approximately 4,200 families living on or around the lake, some since the 1980s, had valid claims for legal ownership of their homes under the 2001 Land Law, but these were rejected. Boeung Kak residents protested the subsequent filling of the lake with sand that started on 26 August 2008—to no avail. Facing increased flooding, mud, and mosquitoes, 500 families finally agreed to move to a relocation site (Kry 2014, 19). In September 2009, with the support of the Geneva-based Centre on Housing Rights and Evictions (COHRE), the Boeung Kak families threatened with eviction filed a request for inspection regarding violations of land rights to the World Bank. The World Bank had funded the Cambodian government's Land Management and Administration Project,[5] in the context of which the Boeung Kạk development was taking place (Biddulph 2014). In November 2010, the World Bank Inspection Panel concluded that Boeung Kak residents had been "denied access to a due process of adjudication of their property claims." However, the Cambodian government had by then already cancelled the World Bank loan and the situation for Boeung Kak residents continued to deteriorate. Residents repeatedly conducted protests, with women at the forefront (Hennings 2019), yet these only resulted in further arrests and injuries (Kry 2014, 20–21). They also faced threats, harassment, and intimidation so that they would accept an inadequate compensation or relocate to a remote resettlement site (CCHR 2011a). In August 2011, the World Bank publicly announced a moratorium on loans to the Cambodian government pending an adequate compensation for the 774 families still living in the area—that is, a remaining 20 percent of the initial residents (CCHR 2011a). Shortly thereafter, the government granted 12.44 hectares to these residents. However, about 10 percent of the remaining families were excluded from the grant for allegedly being located outside of the land grant zone. Despite the issuance of land titles to those households living in the granted land area, and progress in issuance of land titles for some of the remaining families, the dispute has not been entirely resolved, and Boeung Kak activists have faced repeated arrests for continuing to stage protests.

Land Conflicts in the Capital City (II): Respondents from Borei Keila

Besides respondents from Boeung Kak, I also conducted life-story and semistructured interviews in January 2016 with three women from Borei Keila, born respectively in 1947, 1948, and 1971.[6] Borei Keila constitutes another site of land conflict in the capital city. The urban poor community living in the vicinity of the national Olympic stadium has a history of resistance to eviction dating back to the 1990s and early 2000s (Rabé 2010). In early 2003, the government designated this area as an SLC for residential development and declared Borei Keila as the site for a "land sharing" project. This land sharing project, a new mechanism of land conflict resolution, was adopted by the Council of Ministers in May 2003 after successful lobbying from a coalition of national and regional housing rights activists (Rabé 2021). The site was intended to be divided among a private developer; the Ministry of Education, Youth and Sport; and residents. Instead of resorting to the usual practice of forcible relocation of the urban poor, without fair compensation, the project foresaw the accommodation of urban commercial development, whereby the urban poor were promised secure tenure and access to new housing on new plots on site. However, the claims of the original residents of Borei Keila were systematically marginalized throughout the implementation of the project, while those who protested it faced violent repression.[7]

For this slum-redevelopment project, the government accepted a proposal of Phanimex Company without any bidding process (Rabé 2021), in the context of the CPP's politicoeconomic patronage networks. Phanimex Company is a private developer owned by businesswoman Suy Sophan, known to have close links to the prime minister, his wife, and Chinese investors (Human Rights Watch 2014). The Borei Keila agreement granted 2.6 hectares of the land to Phanimex for commercial development, in exchange of which it was to build ten multistory apartment buildings on 2 hectares of land to rehouse the 1,776 residents. The remaining 9.52 hectares were to be returned to the Ministry of Education, Youth and Sport but instead were later also sold to the private developer (Rabé 2010, 10).

The residents, who had possession rights according to the 2001 Land Law, were not properly consulted on the nature of this agreement. Moreover, after constructing only eight out of the ten promised buildings, Phanimex Company claimed bankruptcy in 2010 (Khouth 2012), leaving approximately 384 families in temporary shelters on site, without access to proper housing. After years of limbo, in 2012, these families were forcibly evicted to make way for commercial development (Rabé 2021). In January 2012, more than 200 mixed forces (police officials, military police, company employees, and security guards), equipped with fire trucks and bulldozers, demolished their temporary shelters and moved residents to two remote resettlement sites, where they faced a humanitarian crisis (ADHOC 2012; CCHR 2012; Subedi 2012, §142). More than hundred families refused to relocate and continued to live at or around

Borei Keila in highly precarious conditions (CCHR 2012; Talocci and Boano 2017). The women I interviewed were part of this group of residents; they had been involved in years of protests. In November 2015, the authorities offered onsite housing to 34 of the 154 families who had continued to protest, which they completed by January 2016. The protests slowly dwindled as the last groups resorted to accepting, under pressure, final compensation offers (US$3,000 to 5,000) and/or relocation to poor-quality housing in a remote district (Khouth 2016; Rabé 2021).

Land Conflicts at Cambodia's Margins: Respondents from Rattanakiri

The third group I met for this research consisted of community representatives from Rattanakiri, a remote province in northeastern Cambodia affected by land conflicts. I conducted interviews with six respondents in February 2014 during their visit to Phnom Penh for a workshop organized by the NGO Equitable Cambodia. In contrast to respondents from Boeung Kak and Borei Keila, these respondents were only men, respectively born in 1936, 1954, 1962, 1963, and 1988. All were community representatives from different villages and different ethnic minorities (Kachok, Krung, and Tampuan).

Rattanakiri hosts eight ethnic minority highlander groups, and 64 percent of Cambodia's indigenous communities (Smith 2017, §35). Forests are crucial for the communities' livelihoods as well as their sociocultural practices and spiritual belief systems. However, land and forests in Rattanakiri are experiencing high pressure. Population growth, ever greater numbers of nonindigenous settlers, and rapidly expanding market penetration has fueled an illegal land market (Fox and Poffenberger 2013, 103). The livelihoods and identities of indigenous communities are threatened by illegal logging of protected trees for the luxury wood trade in the context of CPP-driven patronage. Moreover, ELCs have encroached over indigenous people's territory and led to the conversion of forests into commercial crops and monoculture plantations for the production of commodities, predominantly rubber (Bugalski and Ratha 2014; Global Witness 2015; CCHR 2016). In this context, reserved cultivation lands, as well as burial grounds and spirit forests, have been confiscated and destroyed (Bugalski and Ratha 2014). The introduction of individual titling also had reverse effects on community land practices and the social fabric (Park and Maffii 2015). The illiteracy of many indigenous people in the national Khmer language, weak governance, and a lack of transparency have hampered participation in decision-making processes relating to land disputes. The indigenous communities, a particularly vulnerable group among Cambodia's rural poor (Ghai 2010, 40), thereby experience these transformations "not only in the form of rapid land loss, but also as processes of political and economic marginalization" (Padwe 2017).

Contestation of CPP Power: A Case Study of (Urbanized) Protesters at Freedom Park

In addition to these groups affected by land conflicts in urban and rural settings, I also interviewed respondents engaged in the protests of unprecedented scale that followed the 2013 legislative elections. As discussed in chapter 1, the CPP's long hold over electoral votes was contested by a sharp rise of electoral support for the newly established opposition coalition party, the Cambodia National Rescue Party (CNRP). The electoral outcome took many analysts by surprise—including the CPP. It rendered visible the "seismic changes" and deep social, economic, and generational transformations that had taken place in the country in the context of growing discontent over issues of corruption, land grabbing, deforestation, inequalities, and increased access to information through internet and social media networks (McCargo 2014, 73).

The CNRP leaders, however, rejected the election results and boycotted the National Assembly. They claimed that they had won the elections but that voter fraud prevented their victory. On 15 September 2013, the CNRP initiated its first multiday demonstration, calling for either a recount of the votes or a reelection (LICADHO 2014). The second multiday rally called by the CNRP in October 2013 garnered about one hundred thousand protesters. From mid-December 2013, protesters camped out in Freedom Park over several weeks, turning this central location and government-sanctioned protest zone in central Phnom Penh into the epicenter of unprecedented protests.[8]

These protests saw the conglomeration of different grievances, beyond that of electoral fraud. These included labor wages, land disputes, a sense of rising inequalities between the rich and the poor, lack of government services, and government corruption. They coalesced into a "broader movement for social change" (Strangio 2014a, 47). While building on previous urban protest movements, these protests were of a new scale,[9] and led to unprecedented, personalized calls for regime change. The gradual move of the protest's slogans from *Dau!*, "Change!" (ដូរ), to *Hun Sen oey, chhoh chhenh tov!*, "Hun Sen, get out!" (ហ៊ុន សែន អើយ ចុះចេញទៅ),[10] illustrates a significant erosion of public deference toward the prime minister.[11] The protests displayed a more complex social fabric, featuring economically and marginalized groups but also the support in terms of funding and logistics of elite members of the political opposition and members of the diaspora communities in the US or France.[12] Garment workers, asking for an increase in the minimum wage, nonetheless often remained at the forefront of demonstrations (Lawreniuk 2020). The protests were also largely fueled by rural discontent: many Cambodians came from rural areas to join the demonstrations in the capital city, sometimes camping in Freedom Park for several days or even weeks at end. Drawing from McCargo (2014), I propose the term of "urbanized protesters" to capture, on the one hand, their rural lives and the rural embeddedness of their grievances and, on the other hand, the significance of the urban environment for the expression of their discontent, at least until 2018.[13]

While no representative survey was conducted of the 2013 Freedom Park protesters, Norén-Nilsson (2015) has sketched the profile of a typical pro-CNRP demonstrator based on sixty-four in-depth interviews of CNRP supporters from December 2013. She describes the typical CNRP protester as a "land-owning middle-aged farmer who considers him/herself to be of average economic standing, but is indebted, who has access to radio, but not to social media" (267). In her study, demonstrators explained their allegiance to the CNRP for its leadership's ability to understand general living conditions and respect ordinary people; its political agenda of improving living conditions, most importantly its promise of salary rises, pensions, or free education; its democratic principles and rights-based agenda; and finally, its patriotism. Land concessions and land rights, difficult living conditions, and worker rights further ranked highest among a list of reasons respondents were asked to choose from to explain their support for the CNRP.

This chapter draws on semi-structured interviews conducted with six protesters on 3 and 4 January 2014, three of whom constituted "urbanized protesters," as they joined the protests from their rural communities. On 3 January 2014, I interviewed an elder woman and an elder man from Kampong Cham Province, a traditionally CPP-dominated province in which the CNRP had made strong gains in the 2013 elections. They had been camping out in Freedom Park since mid-December when they had traveled to Phnom Penh with fellow villagers to join the protests. The next day, 4 January 2014, marked the end of the unprecedented, wide-scale protests. Civilian "thugs," paid by the CPP, were given weapons such as electric batons, slingshots, and sticks to brutally disperse protests, while security force personnel stood by or joined the violence (LICADHO 2014, 8–9). Mixed forces of police and military police also used live ammunition, indiscriminately firing into the crowds of protesters, residents, and bystanders, leading to the death of at least seven men and injuries of forty-eight persons. Journalists covering the protests were also targeted, while several waves of arrests of protesters were carried out (Subedi 2014, §13; FIDH, LICADHO, and ADHOC 2015, 14). After this violent crackdown on Freedom Park, I interviewed an elder man who had joined the protests for several weeks from his village in rural Cambodia, as well as two men and one woman, aged twenty-nine, twenty-eight, and twenty-one, from Kampong Cham Province, who worked at a garment factory in Phnom Penh. All four of them were waiting near Wat Phnom to see how the situation would unfold, while trying to remain out of sight of the security forces. After the interview, they decided to spend the night at Wat Samaki Rainsey in Stung Meanchey, a pagoda then known to be one of the few pagodas—if not the only one—outside of CPP control in Phnom Penh, offering shelter to dissident monks, land dispute victims, and marginalized communities (see, e.g., Saut Sok 2019).

The Multidimensionality of Nonparticipation at the ECCC

How did these groups of respondents, affected by violence in contemporary Cambodia, relate to and perceive the ECCC? Most of the respondents from Boeung Kak, Borei Keila, Rattanakiri, and Freedom Park identified themselves as Khmer Rouge victims, and would also qualify as such according to the ECCC's legal definition. None of them, however, were formally participating as a civil party, witness, or complainant in the ECCC proceedings. How can we explain their nonparticipation in Cambodia's transitional justice process?

Drawing from MacGinty's (2012) typology of nonparticipation in liberal peace interventions, we can mainly distinguish between two types of nonparticipation: involuntary versus voluntary nonparticipation. Some did not participate in the ECCC proceedings due to a lack of access to knowledge and information or an incapacity to participate. Others explained that their nonparticipation was voluntary: they were simply not interested in the ECCC.

These insights are indicative of the larger context of nonparticipation in the transitional justice process on the Khmer Rouge regime in Cambodia. They reflect the findings of the mixed-methods study that I conducted together with colleagues (Williams et al. 2018).[14] For the quantitative part of the study, we surveyed a total of 439 respondents across the country from January to April 2018, including 125 respondents who had not participated as complainants or civil parties at the ECCC. This included 58 respondents who never attended any NGO projects related to the ECCC or the Khmer Rouge regime, and 67 respondents who joined such NGO activities.[15] The qualitative part of the study included qualitative in-depth follow-up interviews in May and June 2018 with 15 of the 125 respondents sampled as "nonparticipants" in our survey. In this study, the 125 "nonparticipants" also explained their nonparticipation at the ECCC because of a lack of access to knowledge and information, an incapacity to participate, and a general absence of interest in the ECCC.[16]

Lack of Access to Knowledge and Information: More than Technical Impediments

For some respondents from Boeung Kak, Borei Keila, Rattanakiri, and Freedom Park, nonparticipation resulted from their limited access to information and explanations on the ECCC. This was the case, for instance, for a woman from Kampong Cham province born in 1947, whom I met in January 2014 in Freedom Park during the CNRP demonstrations. She explained: "In total, two of my brothers died under the Khmer Rouge regime. [. . .] I want justice, but I don't know where to find it. [. . .] I haven't heard about the Khmer Rouge tribunal. I heard that there was a tribunal that is trying the Khmer Rouge leaders. [. . .] I heard that there is a trial but in fact I am not sure whether it is going on or not."[17]

In our 2018 survey, we also found that nonparticipation for the 125 respondents had been mostly involuntary and resulted from a lack of information on the ECCC and the possibilities for participation (Williams et al. 2018). We asked this group of respondents why they had not applied to participate as either a civil party or complainant, framing this as an open question, with the possibility of providing multiple answers. More than one-third replied that they did not know how to apply (36.4 percent). Almost one-quarter indicated that they had learned of the possibility too late and missed the ECCC's deadlines for submitting the necessary victim information form (24.4 percent), and one-quarter explained that they had been unsure whether they qualified for applying as a civil party or complainant (24.3 percent). Finally, one-sixth of the respondents explained that they simply did not know that they could apply (16.7 percent).

Several other surveys had revealed the limited levels of knowledge of, and awareness about, the ECCC among the general population. A research team of the Documentation Centre of Cambodia, for instance, found in February 2009 that 17.3 percent of 1,110 urban residents of district towns—that is, a population group with arguably higher access to information—had never heard of the tribunal, and 44.2 percent said they had heard "a little" about the tribunal (Chy 2009). Phuong Pham et al. (2009) from the Human Rights

Centre at Berkeley University found that 39 percent of respondents of its population-based survey conducted in 2008 had no knowledge of the ECCC, while 46 percent only had limited knowledge thereof. In their follow-up population-based survey in 2011, Pham et al. (2011) observed that both awareness of and knowledge about the ECCC had increased. However, 38 percent of their respondents still stated that they felt little informed, and 39 percent moderately informed. Several years later, in our 2018 survey, 42.5 percent of our 439 respondents expressed that they had little knowledge of the ECCC, while 13.9 percent identified themselves as having no knowledge at all (Williams et al. 2018).

NGOs and the ECCC certainly faced numerous challenges in their attempts to address this lack of awareness and knowledge and to inform the public about opportunities for victim participation. Challenges included the difficulty to reach the majority of the population, which lives in rural areas, given a lack of information structure and low rates of literacy (Ciorciari and Heindel 2014). With NGOs taking the essential role of intermediaries between survivors and the Court, civil parties were highly concentrated in those areas where the NGOs had preexisting networks. Access to civil party status was thus significantly shaped by access to NGO outreach. Donor "fatigue" to fund outreach activities also significantly hampered outreach efforts since at least 2010 (Ciorciari and Heindel 2014; Sperfeldt and Oeung 2019) and increasingly since 2014–15 (Kum 2019).

Unawareness of the Court's existence as a barrier to participation is, however, not merely a technical problem. A seventy-eight-year-old community representative from a village in the northeastern province of Rattanakiri, for instance, explained not understanding what a tribunal means: "I know the tribunal, but only from hearsay. I don't understand much what the tribunal is. . . . When offences are committed amongst us, which we cannot resolve between us, we go to 'the tribunal.' But I don't understand much what this means."[18] This was surprising to me, since I had learned that his neighbor was a civil party and had traveled all the way to Phnom Penh to testify in a public hearing. I had thus assumed that he must have had easier access to information on the Court, and many occasions to discuss the ongoing proceedings with his neighbor, with whom he was on good speaking terms. This case illustrates that distance to the Court goes beyond mere physical or geographical remoteness. It reflects the disconnect between traditional and common forms of dispute resolution and the Western-oriented judicial process at the ECCC (Urs 2007). Introduced under French colonial rule, the Western judicial system in Cambodia did not displace local dispute resolution methods (Luco

2002). In such a context, many of those living in rural areas are "unfamiliar with the formal proceedings and the law" (Yrigoyen Fajardo, Kong, and Phan 2005, 11).

The Incapacity to Participate and the Political Economies of Survival and Activism

In addition to a lack of information, a lack of time and resources also characterized the involuntary nonparticipation of those I interviewed in Boeung Kak, Borei Keila, Rattanakiri, and Freedom Park. Respondents explained that they carried the task of caring for others and thus lacked the time to engage with the ECCC in an active and sustained way. In his typology of nonparticipation, Roger MacGinty (2012) speaks of this as an "incapacity" to participate based on the necessity of "simply getting on with life" and the political economy of survival (MacGinty 2011, 87–88). In our 2018 survey, we also found that more than a quarter (28 percent) of the 125 respondents who had not formally participated in the ECCC explained that they had had no time for applying or believed that participating as a civil party or complainant would simply be too time-consuming and/or expensive.

For citizens experiencing human rights violations, this lack of time is not only linked to the need of securing one's livelihood. It can also be tied to the decision to protest. A fifty-one-year-old woman from the urban community of Boeung Kak, for instance, explained what it meant to be an "activist,"[19] especially when one is struggling to sustain one's livelihoods: "And because I am busy with taking part in the demonstrations, I cannot take care of my house or family. [. . .] Until today, I remain poor. I have so many problems in my life, and I don't have any free time. I am on my own to [. . .] support my own life and my family."[20]

A community representative from Rattanakiri also shared his feeling of incapacity in following the ECCC. He framed this in terms of "weakness" and in relation to the unresolved disappearance of his relatives: "I lost my uncles and the family of my wife under the Khmer Rouge. They were Khmer Rouge soldiers, but they disappeared, and I don't know where. I would like to claim for justice [at the ECCC] for them, but I am too weak, and I don't know the reason of their disappearance."[21] This feeling of powerlessness illustrates the extreme unequal access to justice for the poor. Without access to the necessary financial resources and patronage networks that would provide guidance in how to behave, including what monetary transactions to make, securing access to "justice" feels out of reach for this respondent. As Un (2009, 89) has noted regarding the national judiciary, cases are more often than not judged "based upon the 'thinness' or 'thickness' of the stack of bribe money," rather than upon the law. Moreover, cases involving only poor defendants and plaintiffs often remain unprocessed, since the poor are "metaphorically seen by court officials as bony, less juicy, low price fish that can be overlooked" (89).

The Unimaginable for Transitional Justice Advocates: An Absent Interest in the ECCC

Finally, respondents from Boeung Kak, Borei Keila, Rattanakiri, and Freedom Park also shared their voluntary nonparticipation in the ongoing transitional justice process. Some respondents explained having never been interested in following the news of the ECCC, while others said they had listened sporadically to the news on the ECCC proceedings on either radio or TV. One respondent mentioned that although she was previously keen on listening to news about the ECCC on the radio, she later became disinterested and did not follow the proceedings anymore.[22] Some of the respondents joined an outreach tour and thus had the possibility to visit the ECCC in Phnom Penh and attend a public hearing. For instance, a young community representative of Rattanakiri Province aged twenty-six had joined a trip that consisted of a standard outreach tour of the capital city, including stops at the Tuol Sleng prison, the Choeung Ek memorial and the ECCC, in 2012: "Before, I had never heard of the Khmer Rouge regime [and the ECCC]. But in 2012, I was able to visit the Khmer Rouge tribunal in Phnom Penh. I was invited to see a hearing at the place of the big tribunal. At the end, they gave us documents. We were maybe fifty, forty persons from our village who went to see the tribunal. Before, nobody knew. When we returned to the village, we discussed among us the judgment of the leaders of the Khmer Rouge."[23] However, after the trip, the Court did not remain a prominent topic of discussion or reflection in his home village for very long, as he returned to his everyday life.

In our 2018 survey, we also asked the 125 respondents who had not participated in the ECCC proceedings whether they are generally interested in the ECCC. More than one-third replied not being interested (38.8 percent). As we conducted our survey in 2018, this finding perhaps also speaks to a faded public interest toward the ECCC at that time, twelve years after the ECCC started its operations.[24] Yet more importantly, one-third of those who had never considered applying as either civil parties or complainants explained that this was because they were not interested in the ECCC (30.3 percent).

Taken together, these findings from interviews with citizens facing political violence in contemporary Cambodia and from our survey with respondents not formally participating at the ECCC highlight the multidimensionality of nonparticipation. They remind us that we cannot readily equate nonparticipation with resistance to transitional justice. This would misattribute "forms of consciousness and politics that are not part of [the] experience" (Abu-Lughod 1990, 47). However, a closer examination of the perspectives of those affected by contemporary political violence reveals that for some, nonparticipation constituted forms of resistance to transitional justice. It is to these instances of resistance that I turn to in the remainder of the chapter.

Everyday Experiences of the Law and Resistance to Transitional Justice

The nonparticipation of citizens facing political violence in contemporary Cambodia also reveals their everyday experiences of the law. Here, I draw from Sally Engle Merry (1985, 1990) and Patricia Ewick and Susan Silbey's (1998) seminal work on legal consciousness in sociolegal studies. This approach invites us to focus on routine experiences and perceptions of law in the everyday to reveal the presence and consequences of law in social relations, not only through research on "how and by whom the law is used, but also when and by whom it is not used" (34).

Analyzing the nonparticipation of citizens facing political violence in contemporary Cambodia illuminates experiences and perceptions of the law and the justice system as agents of injustice and of repressive state power. This emerges from both interviews and the observation of their nonparticipation at the ECCC. As Ewick and Silbey (1998, 46) argue, legal consciousness is "revealed in what people do, as well as what they say." We can thereby see that nonparticipation constitutes an act of resistance to a transitional justice process that takes place in a context in which citizens continue to experience law and the judiciary as a tool for political violence.

Their nonparticipation contains political claims that need to be heard from within the field of transitional justice: claims for structural reforms for an independent judiciary and the nonrepetition of political violence. Even though such claims have become side-lined in how transitional justice has come to be implemented in Cambodia, in fact they echo central aspirations of transitional justice as it is conceptualized by the UN and other policymakers. They speak to the idea of guarantees of nonrecurrence, which is conceptualized by the UN as one of the core pillars of transitional justice.

Perceptions of the ECCC's Lack of Independence

Many respondents from Boeung Kak, Borei Keila, Rattanikiri, and Freedom Park did not trust the ECCC because of their experiences of the national judiciary. One elderly man whom I met after the crackdown on the CNRP demonstration at Freedom Park on 4 January 2014 explained that it is the ECCC's lack of independence that had informed his principled decision not to participate as a civil party. He argued: "I find it unjust because in the Chambers, there are three Cambodians and two foreigners. And if the Cambodian side has a specific tendency, they can then influence the tribunal. [. . .] The role of civil parties, I leave that to others. The tribunal has spent a lot of time, the proceedings are very long. Some accused have died in detention. I find that this tribunal cannot be successful in its work, so I am not interested in it."[25]

While explaining that he was generally not interested in the ECCC, throughout our discussion, he in fact shared his detailed and updated knowledge of the ECCC's complicated legal proceedings. In his view, the ECCC is not separate from the national judicial system but instead deeply embedded in it. His nonparticipation stems from his questioning of the legitimacy of the Cambodian judges at the ECCC, whom he does not trust, and whose presence therefore jeopardizes in his view the legitimacy of the entire institution.

Such a lack of trust in the national ECCC judges was certainly not an isolated case in my discussions with the respondents from Borei Keila, Boeung Kak, Rattanakiri, and Freedom Park. On the contrary, most of them had also invested a lot of hope, at the beginning of the ECCC at least, in the participation and involvement of international actors, whom they considered to be impartial. One respondent from Boeung Kak, born in 1986, explained that, after having initially closely followed the ECCC's proceedings, she was soon disappointed. Because of what she sees as the ECCC's failure to secure independence from governmental interference, the money spent on the ECCC was wasted and should rather have been used to alleviate hardships faced in the context of land evictions:

> I used to follow the news on the ECCC, but after a while I didn't want to listen anymore. I do appreciate that the international side has come in, but the internationals can't do anything for this Court. [. . .] Everything is in the hands of the government. [. . .] It is a waste of money and has no meaning for the people . . . [. . .] You can see the suffering we are going through now, the Khmer Rouge do not have any meaning anymore, because it's already past, it's already gone. And they [the defendants] are

> very old. Why don't you just use the money to deal with the actual things which you can see are happening with us right now, rather than waste the money for the ECCC?[26]

According to Venerable Luon Sovath, it is this association of the ECCC with the lack of independence and impartiality of the national justice system that explains the sense of hopelessness he observed among Cambodians when it comes to the ECCC. Venerable Luon Sovath is a monk activist from Chi Kreng commune in Siem Reap, who has become known for his support of various communities' struggles for human rights (see, e.g., CCHR 2011a) before having to flee the country in 2021. In February 2016, I met him at the Samaki Rainsy Pagoda in Stung Meanchey, located at the capital city's outskirts. He explained:

> Before, we Cambodian people hoped that the Khmer Rouge Court can find justice for history. [. . .] We had hope. . . . But after the Court started, from year to year, people became hopeless. Why are they hopeless? Me too I became hopeless . . . Because the Khmer Rouge Court in Cambodia is not independent, it does not have full power to conduct its work. It starts with one case, two cases, and always, the government threatens the Court. And then the Court, [. . .] they can only [investigate] within Cambodia [. . .]. The Khmer Rouge regime was [. . .] not only Khmers who killed Khmers! It was about politics, because of the communist involvements from China, or Vietnam. But when they defined who are responsible for the crimes committed under the Khmer Rouge regime, they only identified Khmer people! [. . .] And then only one or two persons! Now Pol Pot has already died, Nuon Chea is old. . . . But the powerful officials within the Khmer Rouge regime, right now they still have power, in the government. Prime Minister Hun Sen also is a Khmer Rouge! [*laughs*] [Foreign Minister] Hor Nam Horng also is a Khmer Rouge! Many, many ministers used to be officials under the Khmer Rouge regime. But why do they accuse only one or two persons? [. . .] We need an international court. [. . .] We complained, we protested! But the government refuses, no, no, no, no, wanting a joint tribunal.[27]

This lack of trust toward the ECCC was also reflected in the larger context of my empirical research over the years. The majority of the forty civil parties whom I met between 2013 and 2016 during my PhD research in Phnom Penh and Siem Reap and across seven provinces (Kandal, Takeo, Kampot, Prey Veng, Svay Rieng, Kratie and Kampong Cham) also shared a deep sense of suspicion toward the Cambodian judges at the ECCC. Most of them said that they do not trust them, perceiving them to be corrupt and partial. Many even explained that they would not have participated as civil parties had the ECCC not received international assistance. The few respondents who claimed to fully trust the national judges were often CPP village chiefs or self-identified supporters of the CPP government.

This mistrust of the ECCC's national staff was also reflected in the 65 qualitative interviews conducted with colleagues a few years later, in 2018, as part of our mixed methods study. Following our quantitative survey with 439 respondents, we met 65 civil parties, civil party representatives, rejected civil party applicants, and complainants, as well as 15 respondents who had not participated in the ECCC proceedings. Nearly half of the interviewees across all categories expressed that they trusted international staff at the ECCC either more than, or equally as, national staff. Only very few interviewees shared feelings of trust in the national staff. Many interviewees were disappointed by what they saw as their lack of professionalism, legal qualifications, or commitment in finding justice. In contrast, they perceived the ECCC's international staff to be more professional and committed.

Interestingly, these findings from our qualitative follow-up interviews stood in rather stark contrast with the results of our quantitative survey, in which national staff gained the most trust. In the survey, 54 percent of the 439 respondents said they fully believed the ECCC to be independent; 22 percent a little; with only 16 percent not really and 8 percent not at all. Sixty percent of the respondents further affirmed trusting the ECCC fully; 30 percent a little. Only a few said they would not really (3 percent) or not at all (7 percent) trust the ECCC. Moreover, among the survey respondents, the national staff earned more trust than the international staff.[28] Based on my long-term empirical research, as well as on observations of other researchers and practitioners of a "pervasive sense of mistrust" toward the domestic judiciary and the ECCC's national judges (L. Sok and Abe 2019, 201; see also Sreang 2006; Killean 2018b), I believe that this discrepancy between quantitative and qualitative findings can to a large extent be explained by the fact that our study took place in the tense political context preceding the legislative elections of July 2018. Some respondents may have been afraid to express their dissatisfaction of the national ECCC staff during the quantitative data collection, while they may have felt more at ease to share their thoughts in the qualitative interview, which was also their second encounter with our study team.[29]

Everyday Experiences of Struggling "Against the Law"

Coming back to the case of citizens from Boeung Kak, Borei Keila, Rattanakiri, or Freedom Park, the lack of trust toward the national judiciary is connected to intimate experiences of the law in their everyday life. We can see this with Nget Khun from Boeung Kak, also known under the nickname of "Yey Mummy." Nget Khun, born in 1940, has relentlessly participated in protests as a land rights activist since 2007, despite her advanced age, and also after having personally received a land title in 2015 (Baliga and Chakrya 2017). In 2016, during one of our several encounters, she explained not trusting the ECCC because of her own experience with the national judiciary. She observed: "Cambodia is difficult in terms of rights. I don't know if Nuon Chea is guilty. Maybe, it is just like in my case, I am innocent, but I was put in jail. I don't know."[30]

At that time, Nget Khun had already been arrested and detained several times. In May 2012, she was among thirteen women activists arrested during a peaceful gathering and press conference aimed at marking the boundaries of the demolished homes of eighteen families in Boeung Kak. In a trial criticized by human rights organizations for "not meeting the most rudimentary fair trial standards," the activists were convicted and sentenced to two and a half years imprisonment and a fine of US$500 on the charges of alleged obstruction of a public official with aggravating circumstances and illegal occupation of public property (Forum-Asia et al. 2012). In June 2012, following domestic and international pressure, Nget Khun and the other detained activists were released after thirty-four days of imprisonment with a suspended prison sentence. One of the detained activists described her experience of detention for a Human Rights Watch report (2015, 75): "I wanted to commit suicide. . . . The way the guards at prison talked to me was very horrible, like I am not a human being. . . . An inmate warned me that if I reported anything, I would be dead."

In November 2014, Nget Khun was again arrested alongside six other women activists from Boeung Kak. They had organized protests in front of the city hall in Phnom Penh after the filling of the lake by the company Shukaku Inc. and the subsequent flooding of their houses (Mech 2014). Each woman was charged and convicted of obstructing public traffic. They were sentenced to the maximum penalty of one year in prison and fined US$500. In April 2015, Nget Khun and her fellow activists from Boeung Kak were released from Prey Sar prison, following a royal pardon. In the increasingly open authoritarian context following the 2018 national elections, and the crackdown on journalists, human rights defenders and political commentators, Nget Khun explained, at the age of seventy-nine, that she was now particularly cautious with her decisions to make use of her right to protest: "I really want to go out and protest, but we can't do it. I'm scared they'll beat me if I go out. We talked about it together and we are all scared of arrest" (Mech and Wright 2018).

Because of her experiences of the law, Nget Khun thus questioned whether Nuon Chea, a former senior Khmer Rouge leader accused at the ECCC, was truly guilty. She preferred giving the benefit of doubt to Nuon Chea, rather than to trust that the ECCC proceedings were impartial and independent. Her view here stands out in a context in which ECCC defense lawyers regularly deplored that, in reporting or public discussions of the trials, the presumption of innocence of the accused was not being upheld. In Nget Khun's perspective, the ECCC is thus clearly embedded within the political status quo. Her nonparticipation in the transitional justice process results from how she has experienced the national judiciary as an agent of injustice. Drawing upon Ewick and Silbey's (1998) typology of legal consciousness, her relationship to law is not about standing "*before the law*"—that is, experiencing legal procedures as objective and remote from everyday life, and therefore as appropriate and just. Nor is it one of engaging "*with the law*"—that is, accepting the law to strategically use it for one's own purposes. Instead, her relationship to law can be described as one of being "*against the law.*" Her encounters and experiences with the state and the law in her everyday life have been something against which she struggles, precisely because her experiences of law depart from her strong sense of justice, her ideal of law and of an independent judicial system that would protect rather than threaten her, and her beliefs about what she is rightly entitled to as a citizen.

This position of not wanting to engage with the ECCC, based on one's everyday experiences of the law, was also shared by an "urbanized protester" from Kampong Cham Province. When I met him during the January 2014 protests in Freedom Park, he explained that he could not "listen to the Khmer Rouge tribunal" anymore because it was merely providing a platform for the senior leaders of Democratic Kampuchea to deny their responsibilities for the crimes committed. To him, this denial is a painful experience, precisely because it echoes contemporary narratives of denial from the prime minister:

> I don't want to listen to the Khmer Rouge tribunal, or the Khmer Rouge leaders. When they speak, they refuse to acknowledge their guilt, their responsibility toward the Cambodian people. It is terrible for me. It is exactly the same as Mister Hun Sen is doing now. It is the same as Pol Pot, as Khieu Samphan, Ieng Sary, or Nuon Chea. They answer that they didn't know that three million people died in Cambodia! It is not different from Hun Sen, these two communisms[31] of Pol Pot and Hun Sen are the same! We need to change Mister Hun Sen to have a real democracy for Cambodia. [. . .] I think that it is not different. One example, people were killed in Koh Pich and related to the land grabbing issues. And Hun Sen never took responsibility for that, he says that he doesn't know. It is not different than the Khmer Rouge, they say that they didn't know.[32]

His refusal to engage with the ECCC can thus be read as an individual act of resistance, which establishes "unreachable spaces of personal identity and integrity" (Sarat 1990) in the context of impunity and a lack of accountability in contemporary Cambodia.

Not Going Far Enough: Unfulfilled Claims for an Independent Judiciary and Guarantees of Nonrecurrence

Other respondents who refused to participate in the ECCC and generally displayed a negative perception of the ECCC did not deny that it nonetheless retained some significance. Their disappointments and disengagement resulted from what they saw as the ECCC's inability to induce the deeper transformation processes they had hoped for. More specifically, in their eyes, the ECCC was not able to guarantee the nonrecurrence of human rights violations from which they suffer.

One of the respondents who participated in the CNRP demonstrations in Freedom Park, for instance, underlined the importance of the ECCC, especially if it were to proceed with trials in Cases 003 and 004 and overcome the government's opposition to these cases: "I think that it is [most] important to reflect on what is going on currently. But I also wish that the Khmer Rouge tribunal continues its work until the end, even if it won't try all the cases of the Khmer Rouge, it should continue until the end."[33]

Another respondent at Freedom Park, from Kampong Cham Province, saw the importance of the ECCC in terms of warning current government leaders that they too can be held accountable: "I think that the Khmer Rouge tribunal is important. But how? Because it is about the leaders [. . .]. The role of the Court is of course only for the Khmer Rouge leaders, but I believe that this is the best way to inform the current leaders of the Cambodian government to pay attention to it, and this is the best way to warn them that if they too do bad things, they will be held responsible for their actions. [. . .] I am appealing to the Court that it should finish all the [Khmer Rouge-related] cases but then also continue from now on, with what is still here happening in Cambodia."[34]

Nget Khun from Boeung Kak also argued: "If the Khmer Rouge tribunal could find justice, maybe the government or the powerful persons would respect the law more."[35] A representative from a community in Rattanakiri facing deforestation and land conflicts also concluded: "The tribunal is important, yes, to rearrange the direction of the country."[36]

These perspectives remind us of an essential and fundamental aspect of transitional justice frameworks: structural reforms, including for an independent judiciary, as part of guarantees of nonrecurrence. Such disappointments that the ECCC does not go far enough echo critiques voiced by scholars and practitioners on the lack of transformation of transitional justice interventions and speak to scholarship examining how guarantees of nonrecurrence could help address this lack without yet again overloading the field (Roht-Arriaza 2016; Mayer-Rieckh 2017; McEvoy 2018).

Nonparticipation as a Form of Temporal Resistance

In addition to everyday experiences of the law, another theme that stood out in interviews with respondents from Boeung Kak, Borei Keila, Rattanakiri, and Freedom Park was the mismatch between their experiences of contemporary violence and the teleological discourses on the past, present, and future produced at the ECCC and by the ruling party. Drawing from Natascha Mueller-Hirth's (2017, 188) work, we can understand this mismatch as a temporal conflict—"differences in experiences, constructions, and uses of time"—between the ruling party and the ECCC's transitional justice process, on the one hand, and citizens experiencing political violence in contemporary Cambodia, on the other. While the notion of temporality—that is, the subjective or constructed experience of time—has recently gained traction as an object of enquiry in the study of transitional justice and peacebuilding (Mueller-Hirth and Rios Oyola 2018), including in the study of the ECCC (Hinton 2014), it has not been examined in relation to experiences of contemporary political violence in Cambodia.

This chapter's last section analyses the teleological temporality produced by the CPP: an idealized and linear trajectory through time from death, violence, and destruction under the Khmer Rouge, to peace, economic progress, and development. This temporality is to some extent echoed at the ECCC and in related discourses on transitional justice in Cambodia. I argue that the CPP's construction of the present in absolute opposition to the Khmer Rouge past, which is reflected in the transitional justice process, leads to the socio-temporal marginalization of experiences of contemporary political violence. It renders anachronistic experiences of human rights violations that took place after the Khmer Rouge regime. In this context, for citizens affected by human rights violations, nonparticipation in transitional justice constitutes a strategy of temporal resistance to the CPP's political construction of the country's allegedly successful transitions from war to peace, from genocidal rule to democracy, and from absolute deprivation to economic prosperity.

The CPP's Teleology: From Genocidal Darkness to a Time of Peace, Development, and Economic Prosperity

Ever since the 1979 ousting of the Khmer Rouge from central power, the official historiography of the ruling party has based its legitimacy on its role as "liberator" of the country from the grip of the murderous Khmer Rouge, while silencing its own involvement in that very same regime, as well as in violations that took place after the end of Democratic Kampuchea (see chapter 2). As Un (2011, 555) has observed, this "moral claim to be the party that liberated Cambodians from the murderous Khmer Rouge regime" has featured in the CPP electoral campaigns ever since the UN-sponsored 1993 election. In the run-up to the 2013 elections, the CPP "again campaigned on the memory of the Khmer Rouge, using the brutal regime as a yardstick for its own achievements" (Un 2013b), making use of novel technologies (Norén-Nilsson 2016, 182–83). Not only does the CPP's self-legitimation strategy draw from a "narrative of rescue" (Ainley 2013), but it also relies on a specific teleological temporality, which contrasts the darkness of the catastrophic genocidal past of the Khmer Rouge regime with the reconstruction of the country and the attainment of peace, development, and economic prosperity.

The CPP's teleological temporality and its portrayal as savior of the Cambodian nation has been performed annually in two specific events: the celebration of May 20, held in remembrance of the victims of the Khmer Rouge regime; and the celebration of January 7, commemorating the removal of the Khmer Rouge from power following the Vietnamese army's entry in Phnom Penh on 7 January 1979.

The May 20 celebration was initiated in 1983 as a national holiday for a "day of anger" (*tivea chăng komhoeng*, ទិវាចងកំហឹង). Its purpose was to legitimize the Vietnamese-backed People's Republic of Kampuchea (highlighting its role in ousting the Khmer Rouge) and to mobilize the population as the fighting against Khmer Rouge forces persisted along the Thai-Cambodian border (R. Hughes 2006). Throughout the 1980s, formal visits to the Tuol Sleng Genocide Museum, Choeung Ek, and other killing fields across Cambodia were scheduled for schoolchildren, teachers, and Buddhist monks on this day (Chandler 2008, 362). Put on hold under the UN administration, it was revived after the 1993 national elections and renamed "Day of Remembrance" in 2001 (K. Chhim 2012, 27). Ceremonies were held at sites of atrocity and mass graves, under the supervision of local CPP authorities. The most important ceremony, however, took place at the memorial of Choeung Ek, the execution site of security center S-21 (Tuol Sleng) located fifteen kilometers from downtown Phnom Penh. This event brought together CPP officials, Buddhist monks, young students, and survivors of the Khmer Rouge regime for a program of official speeches and Buddhist prayers and rituals for the dead, as well as a theatrical enactment of the CPP narrative of rescue by a group of young Cambodians (Emde 2014, 299–301; Manning 2017, 151–55). This performance focused on the representation of scenes of Khmer Rouge terror, including mainly brutal killings, executions, and torture. The young actors playing the Khmer Rouge were all dressed in black and armed with clubs and wooden arms. Those playing their victims, screaming and crying as they or their loved ones die in the play, were dressed in rags. Watching this dramatic performance, many members of the public cried in an unusual public display of emotions (Khouth 2009; Emde 2014). These emotional scenes of brutality end with the life- and nation-saving arrival of actors playing soldiers of the Kampuchean United Front for National Salvation and the Vietnamese army and swinging the CPP and the Cambodian national flag, alongside pictures of Hun Sen.[37] In this context, opposition parties reject the legitimacy of May 20 for commemorating Khmer Rouge atrocities.

In August 2014, the ECCC Trial Chamber adopted the reparation request to turn May 20 into a National Remembrance Day in its Case 002/01 judgment. This was confirmed in the appeal judgment in November 2016. Civil parties had requested the adoption of an official, government-recognized National Remembrance Day to honor the victims of the Khmer Rouge regime and acknowledge the crimes that occurred as a form of reparation. Civil parties had proposed several dates. April 17 was, for instance, considered by many civil parties as more meaningful for representing "the true start of the suffering and trauma."[38] Some civil parties felt uncomfortable with the choosing of May 20, given its politicized nature. The CPP government, however, only agreed to schedule this on May 20. This was perceived as an indication of political interference, if not an attempt for politically harnessing the ECCC's reparation measure.[39] However, it is only in February 2018 that the CPP government finally issued a subdecree to declare May 20 a national holiday (*Phnom Penh Post* 2018). In 2020, the government even canceled the holiday, allegedly in order to increase workdays (K. Sok 2020), ignoring its previous commitment to recognize this ECCC-endorsed reparation measure for Khmer Rouge survivors. Efforts to follow up with the government were stalled for being considered too sensitive, yet civil parties have continued to request the government's reendorsement of this national holiday as well as their participation in memorialization activities on May 20 (see, e.g., Cohen, Mattes, and Yogendran 2022).

In contrast, the annual celebration of January 7 has consistently played a fundamental role for the CPP's ritualized performance of its savior discourse. According to Norén-Nilsson (2016, 15), this day even constitutes "the defining national moment" for the ruling party. It is considered to be the most "meaningful and valuable day for the CPP" (K. Chhim 2012, 28). After having been halted during the coalition CPP-FUNCINPEC government in the early 1990s, 7 January has been revived as a public holiday. It is officially celebrated as the "Day of Victory" or "Victory over Genocide Day" (ទិវាជ័យជំនះលើរបបប្រល័យពូជសាសន៍), usually at the national and regional CPP headquarters (K. Chhim 2012; Emde 2014).

During my research, I attended and observed the CPP celebrations of the thirty-fifth anniversary of the end of the Khmer Rouge rule on 7 January 2014. The ceremony took place at Koh Pich (Diamond Island) in Phnom Penh and staged the then-triumvirate of the ruling party: the prime minister and CPP vice president Hun Sen, the late CPP and senate president Chea Sim, and the honorary president of the CPP and National Assembly president Heng Samrin. The political choreography of this event included crowds of students and members of CPP-aligned youth groups cheering and waving flags, traditional music and dances, the release of balloons and doves, and the presence of foreign diplomats from countries such as Vietnam, Myanmar, Cuba, North Korea, China, and Russia (S. Vong 2014). At this celebration, CPP officials made their first public remarks after the violent repression of protests in Phnom Penh on 3 and 4 January 2014. The atmosphere was tense, with noticeable strong surveillance and monitoring of the event by security forces (Ponniah and Vong 2014). My presence as a foreigner trying to talk to attendants was monitored by a security staff member in civilian clothes.

The speech given by Heng Samrin on that day echoes the speeches usually delivered by the prime minister, which from one year to the next show striking similarities in terms of structure, themes, and terminology.[40] The following excerpt from Heng Samrin's speech neatly summarizes many of the CPP's tropes that inform the party's self-idealization as the nation's rescuer:

> My fellow compatriots, today, we are thriving in the light of peace, development, and achievements, but all of us cannot forget the darkest period that ever existed in the history of our nation. It is Democratic Kampuchea that inhumanly exercised its genocidal policies toward its people. In the period of three years, eight months and twenty days after coming to power on 17 April 1975, Pol Potists effectively destroyed all of Cambodia's ailing infrastructures that had already greatly suffered in the previous five years. People had their rights stripped and had been tortured and more than three million were killed, while others who survived were living in the wall-less

> prison awaiting to be killed. It is undeniable that Cambodian people would drown to the bottom of a sea of blood and would have vanished entirely if there was no life-saving liberation in a timely manner. In such critical time, only the CPP stood up to fight against Pol Pot's regime [. . .]. The 7th January Victory liberated the lives of Cambodian people in time, ended the darkest period in Cambodia, and opened the new page of an era whereby people earned their freedom, honor, and dignity and took their future in their own hands. [. . .] Our fellow citizens consider 7 January Victory as their second birthday, and without this day, we do not have everything we have today.[41]

This excerpt illustrates the purposeful rhetorical marking of the period during which the Khmer Rouge held control over the entire country ("three years, eight months and twenty days") and the personification of those responsible as committed to a specific leader and his agenda ("the Pol Potists"). Both rhetorical elements have become pivotal in shaping national discourse about the past. This emphasis on a clearly delineated time frame and specific perpetrators with specific allegiances hermetically isolates the Khmer Rouge regime from the complex conflict dynamics and the multitude of actors who hold responsibility for crimes committed prior, during, and after the Khmer Rouge rule.

As we can see in this excerpt, the CPP's narrative of rescue also relies upon a discursive construction of the present in an entire antithesis to the "darkest period in Cambodia," the Khmer Rouge rule. This produces a linear and teleological temporality: January 7, 1979, is the "second birthday" of Cambodia and its people. In contrast to the Khmer Rouge past, today thereby becomes a time of stability and peace, as well as development and modernization,[42] with all achievements ultimately being measured against the Khmer Rouge regime. In his 7 January 2014 speech, Heng Samrin continued:

> In the past thirty-five years, stemming from 7 January 1979, the Kingdom of Cambodia has enjoyed uncountable positive changes in all fields and been appreciated and applauded by people from all over the world. From being the nation left in ash, with the traces of war and genocide, Cambodia has transformed to a dynamic developing nation with hope it firmly holds. Cambodia that has gone through chronic war, violence, and broken social fabric and has become a peaceful, united, stable, and democratic nation. Meanwhile, Cambodia that used to be regarded as backward has earned its rank as other nations in the world. [*Motivating the crowd*:] Long live the spirit of 7th January Victory Day!

On 7 January 2020, during the celebration of the fortieth anniversary of the end of the Khmer Rouge regime, Prime Minister Hun Sen similarly drew an absolute contrast between the Khmer Rouge past and contemporary Cambodia:

> In conclusion, for the past forty years, stemming from the 7 January victory, Cambodia has realized its changing image beyond anyone's expectation. From a country oppressed and destroyed by protracted wars, national and territorial divisions, and insecurity, Cambodia has become a country in full peace, national reconciliation and territorial unity, strong security, and has become one of the regional's and world's most attractive tourist destinations, where people live in peace harmoniously as a family, in a community, and in the whole nation. From once a killing field, ruled by power of dictatorship, and atrocious crimes of the genocide, Cambodia has now become a land of freedom steadfastly respect[ing the] principle of liberal pluralist democracy through regular elections organized in a free, fair, and just manner, and a rule of law state in which everyone is equal before the law. From being insulted, embargoed and isolated, politically and economically, Cambodia has now become an independent state with full sovereignty and territorial integrity, and is making active integration into regional and world structures and architectures, fulfilling its role actively, with equal right and footing in all regional and world affairs. Once a country receiving UN peacekeeping force, Cambodia has now become a country that sends its troops to serve under the UN peacekeeping missions in many countries. Once a backward country economically, plagued by poverty and food shortages, Cambodia has now become a country that exports rice, guarantees firmly food security, and is among countries with high and rapid economic growth in the world.[43]

As discussed in chapter 2, the repeated emphasis on peace is a central rhetorical element in Hun Sen's and the CPP's legitimacy claims. A few days prior to the 7 January 2020 celebration, the CPP government had initiated its "Thank You Peace" campaign. CPP officials started to display this slogan across social media, urging state institutions and schools to promote it as well. Analysts and civil society actors criticized this as a deflection away from social inequality and the country's overt turn to authoritarianism (Chak 2020; RFA 2020). In his speech on 7 January 2020, Hun Sen emphasized once again that peace is not only the CPP's most precious achievement; it is also the foundation for all other achievements: "Where there is peace, there would be a sustainable development and peaceful and prosperous life. Where there is peace, there would be a lasting guarantee and progress of democracy and rights and freedom. Success of development process and firm democracy would have repercussions on guaranteed sustainability of peace. Once we lose peace, we lose everything."[44]

As discussed in chapter 2, tied to this rhetorical trope of peace is the portrayal of the CPP—and Hun Sen—as the sole guarantor of peace and stability. Any alternative to Hun Sen's and the CPP rule is painted as a return to civil war, instability, chaos, and suffering (see also Future Forum 2017). This is an argument that CPP officials often used during the campaign toward the 2013 election (see, e.g., LICADHO 2014, 4; McCargo 2014, 73). In his 7 January 2019 speech, following the 2018 elections, Hun Sen also attacked the CNRP and proponents of the "color revolution"—an expression used to refer to any activities or statements perceived to be critical of the CPP—as those who will destroy any positive achievement reached since the end of the Khmer Rouge regime.

In these celebrations of January 7, we can thus see how the CPP performs a temporality that presumes an idealistic, linear trajectory through time—from death, violence, destruction, to peace, economic progress, and development.

The Teleology of Transition at the ECCC

The teleological and linear temporality at the heart of the CPP's self-legitimation discourses is, to some extent, echoed in the temporality of transitional justice. Scholarly work has highlighted how transitional justice builds upon a "transitions paradigm" (Arthur 2009) and a liberal vision of history as progress (Hazan 2010), which nourishes a normative "before-and-after narrative of change" and implies that "'before' was worse, and 'after' will lead to better" (Theidon 2009, 295; see also Mueller-Hirth and Rios Oyola 2018). As Hinton (2011a, 7) has argued, this "transitional justice time" reduces complex, protracted and multilayered conflicts into a shrunken, "immediate past," which stands in opposition to the delimitation of "future horizons" through the "promised end of the transition, an idyllic state of civilized democracies." Implicitly, this "transitional justice time" then "parses societies into a pre-state of conflict and a post-state of liberal democracy, along with a related set of binaries (violent/peaceful, chaotic/orderly, barbarism/civilization, primitive/sophisticated, irrational/rational, traumatic/healthy, and so forth)" (Hinton 2014, 13). Even though in recent years the field has increasingly moved away from the notion that the pursuit of transitional justice necessarily presupposes a political transition, it continues to frame the relationship between time and justice as linear, teleological, or ruptural (Miller 2021).

In the Cambodian context, scholars have questioned the "transitional justice time" produced at the ECCC. Reflecting upon the ECCC's slogan "moving forward through justice," Peter Manning (2017, 10) has, for instance, questioned the framing of the ECCC as an institution that enables a "progressive linear sequence from a state of disorder to a state of correction." He argues that this does not capture the complex relationships that Cambodian communities have with memories of political violence, even more so as these exceed the ECCC's temporal jurisdiction. Hinton (2014) has further examined how linear and teleological "transitional justice time" stands in disconnect to "vernacular time" —that is, people's local temporal practices of remembrance and dealing with the Khmer Rouge time, which are informed by Buddhist cyclical conceptions of time.

My argument here is that "transitional justice time" also needs to be examined in relation to experiences of human rights violations and political violence in contemporary Cambodia. Not only does the ECCC's focus on the Khmer Rouge regime deny the experiences of those whose experiences of human rights violations and political violence are located in a different past (e.g., crimes committed by the Khmer Rouge prior to 17 April 1975 or after 6 January 1979, the US bombings prior to the Khmer Rouge regime, or violations that took place in the 1980s). It can also silence the experiences of human rights violations located in the present. This is done through not only the delimitation of the ECCC's temporal jurisdiction but also the adoption of overly celebratory language by advocates of the ECCC. In August 2014, for instance, David Scheffer, the UN Secretary-General's Special Expert on UN Assistance to the ECCC, argued: "The winds of international justice swept through the fields, forests, and towns of Cambodia where millions perished" (Saling 2014). He spoke after the Trial Chamber handed down its verdict in Case 002/01 against Nuon Chea and Khieu Samphan—yet this was also a context of impunity regarding human rights violations related to land conflicts and the crackdown of the demonstrations following the 2013 contested elections.

At times it seems that transitional justice professionals also implied a hierarchy of crimes that sets aside contemporary experiences of political violence in comparison to Khmer Rouge crimes. In December 2013, for instance, I attended a civil party forum organized by the ECCC in Phnom Penh. The forum brought together approximately two hundred civil parties from diverse provinces, including Battambang, Pailin, Kampong Thom, Kampong Cham, Pursat, Kampong Chhnang, Kratie, and Phnom Penh. The forum took place amid the contestations of the government's handling of the July 2013 elections and a context of uncertainty, if not fear, as to how the political situation would unfold. At that time, for instance, friends of mine, including former colleagues at the ECCC, asked whether they could count on my support, among others for helping them to secure a visa and to bring their family abroad if the political situation was to further deteriorate. A few of them, born after the end of the Khmer Rouge regime, considered civil war to be a realistic scenario, out of fears that

Hun Sen would violently defend his power. In this context, at the December 2013 civil party forum, Nicholas Koumjian, then–international co-prosecutor, briefly addressed the contemporary political situation. His reference to the ongoing events, however, only reinforced a hierarchy on the top of which the Khmer Rouge regime was placed as the only issue of utmost importance: "We all have issues with families, with work, concerns with the elections if you look at the newspapers today. But in a hundred years, no one will remember these issues, because the Khmer Rouge are the important issue. It is your history, and your grandchildren will ask you what happened under the Khmer Rouge."[45]

Such observations speak to the work of Helen Mack and Mónica Leonardo (2012) in the context of Guatemala. They argued that the narrow focus on the past of transitional justice scholars and policymakers leads to a failure to account for the meaning of crime in the daily experience of Guatemalans. Not only does it obscure the high levels of "ordinary" crime taking place today; it also disregards the links between the crimes committed during the civil war and the current high crime rate and introduces a problematic hierarchy of crimes (Mack and Leonardo 2012).

Resisting Political Violence as a Time That Is Past

In this context, citizens facing political violence in contemporary Cambodia engage in temporal resistance against the temporalities produced by the ruling party and the ECCC. Their claims that they are suffering from violence today disrupt the linear teleological discourse of the CPP political elite, which dismisses any contemporary grievance as minor and irrelevant when compared to the Khmer Rouge genocide. Their emphasis on contemporary human rights violations also stands in conflict with the ECCC's teleological temporality.

This temporal resistance emerges discursively, when respondents from Boeung Kak, Borei Keila, Rattanakiri, or Freedom Park challenge notions of a clear break between the Khmer Rouge past and the present (see also A. Kent 2016). In a striking reversal of the CPP's teleology, they, for instance, use the Khmer Rouge past to highlight the destitution of the present rather than to celebrate its achievements. Many respondents have repeatedly described the CPP regime as "a second Pol Pot [regime]" (ប៉ុលពតទីពីរ, *Pol Pot ti pi*). Moreover, those affected by land conflicts foregrounded a prolongation of the Khmer Rouge past into the present, emphasizing how they continue to experience fear in the everyday since the Khmer Rouge regime.

Respondents from Boeung Kak and Borei Keila, for instance, portrayed the threat of sudden eviction, of losing one's home and being relocated to empty stretches of land outside of the city, as a repetition of the forced transfer of urban populations they experienced under Khmer Rouge rule. In 2013, while facing the imminent threat of eviction as well as police harassment and intimidation, Nget Khun told me: "Now, whenever the police are coming, in uniform or in civilian clothes, or other government officials, we are terrified and under shock . . . [. . .] Even at night I sleep in fear. [. . .] Although I didn't do anything wrong, I spent an entire month in jail, more than a month."[46]

As feminist approaches to political violence in the everyday have shown, subjective experiences of fear are not necessarily sustained through visible, exceptional, large-scale events of physical violence but through small, repeated acts of harassment or violence in the everyday (Das 2007). In their work on land grabbing in Cambodia, Schoenberger and Beban (2018) have also shown how the vividness of such experiences of fear in the everyday emerge from pervasive threats and intimidation performed by a complex and shifting set of state and nonstate actors.

For the respondents from rural communities in Rattanakiri, the experienced continuity between the Khmer Rouge regime and their current situation lies in the perpetuation of a ruptured relationship between the land or forests and their livelihoods. One community representative from Rattanakiri, for instance, observed that the abolition of private property and the prohibition of individual harvest of the forest under the Khmer Rouge had been replaced today by the destruction of natural resources and land grabbing: "The difficulties I face today and those I faced under the Khmer Rouge are the same. Before, one could benefit from the forest, the animals, but we had no right to do so. [. . .] Now we have the rights, but we have no more forests, no more animals, no more land."[47]

Another community representative highlighted the significance of land grabbing in the context of the livelihoods of ethnic minorities:

> If I compare the Khmer Rouge regime to the current situation, before they were killing people, but now, it is as if they were [killing life itself], because we can't do anything. The ethnic groups live from rice cultivation and the fruits of the forests, and because we don't have these rights anymore, life is very hard to live. [. . .] Land is precious and expensive, as much as the life of a person is. Land is the same as life. When you have land, you can cultivate rice, do some trading, many things . . . But when you don't have land anymore, it is as if you have no life anymore.[48]

A twenty-six-year-old community representative from Rattanakiri emphasized that land and forests are resources for future generations (see also Poffenberger 2013, xiv). They are crucial not only for upland rice cultivation and harvest but also in terms of identity and cultural and spiritual practices: "I have the impression that my future, that of the new generation, [is gone] if the land is confiscated. There will be no more land for the new generation. [. . .] It is not only the forest which has been confiscated but also the land of our ancestors. And that is a much-respected place [. . .], and respect is very important because, for instance, when there is no more rain, we make offerings, we offer chicken or cows, and we pray to the ancestors to bring us rain again."[49] He further underlined how land disputes disrupt cycles of life and death in his village, since the land confiscated also included parts of the forest that holds ancestral tombs, as well as those parts of land kept for the tombs of the future generations.

Some respondents went further than comparing the present with the Khmer Rouge past: they argued that the current situation was even worse than what they experienced under the Khmer Rouge regime. Respondents from the urban communities of Boeung Kak and Borei Keila especially voiced this perspective. They grounded these claims in comparisons between past and present evacuation practices. Whereas the Khmer Rouge displaced entire urban and rural communities, today, the respondents complained, only "the poor" are singled out for such practices of political violence.[50] The comparison with the Khmer Rouge past served to express their deep sense of injustice.

This was, for instance, the position of Nget Khun from Boeung Kak. Under the Khmer Rouge regime, she and her family were categorized as part of the "new people" or "April 17 people"—that is, the population who was evacuated from urban areas in April 1975 and became relegated to the bottom of the newly imposed social hierarchy. At that time a mother of four, Nget Khun lost two of her children: one child disappeared, and another died from hard labor and malnutrition. In 2013, when I first met her, she was still under the threat of eviction. She then argued: "When the Khmer Rouge evacuated the people from the cities, everybody had to leave, no matter whether you were rich or poor. But for what's happening now, it is not the same. Only the poor people are evacuated, are transferred out of the city. [. . .] It's even worse than then because the rights of the people are not the same, between the rich and the poor."[51]

Another activist from Boeung Kak was aged ten when the Khmer Rouge seized power. She lost one relative under that regime. She similarly emphasized a sense of profound injustice in the targeting of the poor in contemporary Cambodia:

> Under Pol Pot, of course terrible things happened. People were killed and we had nothing to eat. But I liked the idea of being equal, of having no rich and no poor. Today, there are rich people, and then there are the poor

> who just wait to die, and the rich can just transfer them to somewhere else, beat them up . . . [. . .] After the Pol Pot time, I thought that my life would be better than before. But unfortunately, this was not the case, I do not have any happiness in my life. I have problems with my land, with the government . . . I really regret this a lot because I cannot find happiness in my life like the others.[52]

A married couple from Borei Keila made similar comments. The wife explained: "Today is no different. My life is even more difficult than before. Under the Khmer Rouge regime, they killed people. Everyone lived under the control of Angkar. There were no rich, no poor. If Pol Pot killed a person, this person was dead, it was the end . . . [. . .] Now, they don't kill people, but it is worse than under the Khmer Rouge regime. Now it is only the poor who suffer. We cannot earn our living; we cannot live easily. The powerful people (អ្នកធំ, *neak thum*) make the poor people's lives so difficult. For instance, I have to live without a place to stay, without rights, without justice." Her husband added: "Before, under the Khmer Rouge, they were targeting everyone, now they are targeting only one group, [the poor]."[53]

Finally, a respondent participating in the CNRP demonstrations in early 2014 at Freedom Park also voiced the stance that the situation today was worse than under the Khmer Rouge:

> It is even worse now than during the Khmer Rouge time. The land grabbing issues . . . people are pushed away; the land is sold to the companies. The Khmer Rouge did not do that to me. Now all the poor were evacuated, and they sold the land to the company. [. . .] I learned about the evacuations from the cities under the Khmer Rouge, but it is worse now because, before, everybody had to leave. [. . .] Everyone was affected, not only one group. [. . .] But right now, it is only the poor who suffer from the land grabbing issue. [. . .] The Khmer Rouge, when they took power, of course they killed the people. But all the forest and the motherland stayed the same, the territory . . . But Hun Sen destroyed everything while in power, the natural resources . . . Hun Sen killed the people and then sold the territory. He evacuates the people from their homeland and sells the land to the companies.
>
> [*A fellow demonstrator, sitting next to the respondent, nods and adds*:] Under the Khmer Rouge, we did not have enough food, we lost our lives . . . But today, we are losing our Khmer earth and water,[54] and this concerns all of Cambodia, and every Cambodian.[55]

While this respondent admitted that she had "worked with the Khmer Rouge" for three years from 1970 until 1973, thereby indicating her voluntary affiliation with the Khmer Rouge movement before its access to central power, she also stressed that once "the Khmer Rouge started to kill people," she had asked to be transferred back to her hometown and distanced herself from the movement.

The presence and widespread use of such counternarratives to the portrayal of the Khmer Rouge rule as the worst period of political violence does not mean that these citizens facing contemporary political violence did not suffer under the Khmer Rouge. The method of life-story interviews, adopted whenever possible for this chapter's empirical research, clearly showed that the Khmer Rouge rule constituted a time of exceptional suffering and significant disruptions. Respondents narrated the Khmer Rouge regime through the themes of loss of life and loved ones, of displacement and uprootedness, of loss of livelihoods and properties. They displayed strong emotions and deep sorrow more than thirty years later. Portraying the present as worse than the Khmer Rouge regime and decades of war therefore needs to be seen as a discursive strategy that relies upon the crucial hindsight of having, in the end, survived this difficult past and moved on. One respondent, who participated in the CNRP protests in Phnom Penh at the end of 2013 and early 2014, for instance, told me: "Under the Khmer Rouge regime, I lost my brother, who was a former cadre. They took him to be killed. That was in 1975. In total, two brothers of mine died under the Khmer Rouge regime. [. . .] [But] the current situation is the biggest issue. My brothers already died; they passed away a long time ago . . . The current situation is the main issue today."[56]

Certainly, the discursive strategy of drawing parallels between the situation today and the Khmer Rouge regime also impresses upon a foreign researcher the degree of injustice they are currently subjected to. It demonstrates the salience, until today, of references to the Khmer Rouge regime as a basis for claims-making for victims of human rights violations in Cambodia. For these respondents, it has not remained unnoticed that after international actors such as the UN and Western countries sidelined demands for accountability for Khmer Rouge crimes for a long time, they did finally intervene and establish, albeit belatedly, expensive, extraordinary legal proceedings.

In addition to discursively resisting the CPPs' teleological temporalities, respondents also underscored their temporal resistance with active and visible protests. Some respondents, in fact, explained their decision to protest precisely through their previous experiences of the Khmer Rouge. While the "complex interplay and layering of the [Khmer Rouge] past" can contribute to disciplining Cambodians, leading to self-censorship and decisions not to protest, the cumulative effect of experiences of fear and political violence over time and space can also play into decisions to join demonstrations or social movements (Schoenberger and Beban 2018, 10). Rather than their current suffering disqualifying their past experiences, the elder respondents I met explained that they had decided to take action because they had already experienced suffering under the Khmer Rouge. Nget Khun from Boeung Kak, for instance, explained her activism: "I used to experience an evacuation already during the Khmer Rouge regime. [. . .] It's more than enough. Now I am old. [. . .] I don't want to experience that anymore, I try to stay here and ask for my rights, which I have, no matter if I'm poor or rich. [. . .] It's the same thing happening again today, it's repetitive [of the Khmer Rouge time]. But I don't want to take it anymore. Under Pol Pot, I also had no choice, but right now I'm much older, I need to try, I don't want to take it anymore. It is enough, during the Khmer Rouge and this time now . . . I should be able to receive a better life."[57]

Another respondent who participated in the CNRP protests at Democracy square before the police crackdown in early January 2014 similarly explained his decision to demonstrate: "I have huge regrets from the time of the Khmer Rouge. [. . .] From 1970 until 1975, it was the Lon Nol regime, but in fact the Khmer Rouge already "liberated" the area where I was living in 1971. Many people then died in my family. My brother died, my cousins . . . My father committed suicide after the death of his relatives because he was afraid. [. . .] I cannot count how many of my relatives died. [. . .] This is why I am not afraid today [. . .], because of the experience of that time. [. . .] I was traumatized from that time, [. . .] and the country has since never been peaceful, and it would be lost. So finally, I decided that I am not afraid anymore, I have to show up and participate in these demonstrations to liberate the country."[58]

Significantly, the term this protester used to underline his decision to demonstrate, "*chenh mok*" (ចេញមុខ), translated above as "to show up," literally means to "bring out one's face." This signalizes a move from subtle, everyday forms of resistance to public, confrontational, visible forms of resistance and increased risk-taking—in this case, from discursive to embodied performances of temporal resistance.

Resisting the Present as a Time of Democracy, Development, and Peace

The temporal resistance of those affected by political violence in contemporary Cambodia does not only consist of resisting the notion that political violence is a time that is past. It is also a resistance of the ruling party's discursive construction of the present as a time of democracy, development, and peace. This resistance consists in emphasizing that all these elements remain unfulfilled promises until today.

Many respondents first questioned the CPP's claim that a linear and successful transition from authoritarianism to democracy had taken place. Some respondents identified the current government's nature as "communist," arguing that it does not respect "the people." An "urbanized protester" participating in the CNRP demonstrations in early January 2014, for instance, argued:

> Before, under the Khmer Rouge, it was even more totalitarian. [. . .] But since 1979 and even after the 1993 elections, the regime retained its communist tendency. [. . .] This means that there is no democracy, that the power is totalitarian and does not take into account the people's views, it is only the leaders who have power. [. . .] But I want a truly democratic society. Nobody should be above the law, everybody should be controlled by the law, even the leaders. [. . .] With democracy, I mean that the importance should be given to the people, and that the people should be those making the decisions, that's democracy."[59]

The respondent associated the term "communism" with absolute power or authoritarian rule, or a one-party state, not with a particular form of economic organization. This is a recurrent assertion my interview partners made and explains why they used this term to characterize the practices of a regime based on a capitalistic market economy. It reflects the opposition party CNRP's frequent use of "communism" in its critique of the CPP government.[60]

Another respondent participating in the same demonstrations likewise stressed the continuity of "communist" rule to reject linear narratives of successful political progress toward democracy:

> Hun Sen is a communist, he is implementing a communist idea. But I would like to have democracy here in Cambodia. [. . .] I can see that there is communism here in Cambodia since Lon Nol was ousted from power [in 1975], since the Pol Pot regime. Now, it is also about absolute power, like in the Pol Pot time. [. . .] I can see that every day, the rule of Hun Sen is the same as Pol Pot. The only difference is the driver. It is a little bit different [. . .] [since] there are two branches of communism, the Vietnamese-oriented one [as today] and the Chinese-oriented one [as under Pol Pot]. But it remains communist, the leader is communist. What do I mean by that? That he doesn't respect the law. [. . .] Hun Sen continues to act as if he is above the Cambodian people, the same as Pol Pot. I don't want that to happen again.[61]

A community representative from Rattanakiri also criticized the discrepancy between the government's rhetorical promises "to the organization of the UN" and its actions, which he claims contradict the very meaning of democracy:

> The government presented to the organization of the UN that we are a democracy in Cambodia, but there is a big gap between the poor and the rich; the poor become more and more poor and there is no equality. To the UN organization, the government promised to respect human rights, to

> respect other interests of the poor, but in fact they don't respect as they promised. They promised to eliminate corruption, to reduce poverty, and to respect human rights, but it is only a theory, in practice it is the contrary which is happening. Currently, the authorities both at national and local level do not respect the people, and this benefits the rich people who gain all the time. [. . .] Democracy means a regime in which the people are taken into consideration as being more important than the authorities. The authorities are only representatives of the people, so the people are the most important. But in fact, currently, the authorities do not help the people but the companies.[62]

Importantly, as we can see here, social equality and an equal access to and fair distribution of economic resources are defined as central components of democracy. In this regard, a second theme—that of development—also emerged in the respondents' criticism of the discrepancy between the current state of Cambodia and the ruling party's discourse. Several respondents took direct aim at the CPP's discourse of development, arguing that even though today "people live under the government's mantra of development,"[63] this clearly does not reflect their everyday experiences. A respondent from Borei Keila, for instance, explained:

> The period now, it's the "period of human rights." [. . .] But these are really only for the powerful people [អ្នកធំ, *neak thum*]. For instance, here in Borei Keila or in some provinces, they take our land away. If a powerful person wants a place, they just get it for themselves. They cut the trees who belong to everyone, as they wish. [. . .] They call this "development." But [. . .] [t]he rich get richer, and the poor get poorer. [. . .] The objective of development, it's supposed to be for the poor. But in reality, it's a development only for the rich, who continue to become even richer. For instance, the objective of "developing" Borei Keila here was [supposedly] for the poor. But then we quickly saw that it was only the rich who got richer; the poor had to leave to go to places like Andong village or Phnom Bat village. [. . .] The powerful people [អ្នកធំ, *neak thum*] say that people like me, or like those who live here in Borei Keila, we can't discuss this problem with them, because we don't have enough knowledge. Even in tribunals, too, powerful people are always right, and the poor don't have rights. They give money to the judges so that they keep silent. Even me, I was jailed for three months and twenty days, but I didn't commit any mistake . . . The powerful people always are right.[64]

Respondents from Rattanakiri province similarly argued: "I don't trust the government. [. . .] First of all, because the government has said that the country needs to be developed to reduce poverty. But on the contrary, what is happening is that the country is developing but poverty increases, as does the gap between the rich and the poor."[65]

Central to this critique of the CPP's assertion that development is in full swing in Cambodia is the refutation that the Khmer Rouge regime can continue to serve as an eternal reference point for measuring the country's achievements, since such a comparison only serves to deny the real challenges faced. Venerable Luon Sovath explained the obsolescence of the CPP's never-ending comparison to the Khmer Rouge rule:

> The rich families, those in power, [. . .] [t]hey say "Oh, Cambodia right now is a modern country, it is an achievement country! A developed country!" [*laughs*] They always compare it to the Khmer Rouge regime: "The Khmer Rouge didn't have phones, smartphones, or anything . . ." [. . .] But how can we draw such comparisons? The world is moving! The world is not as before. And why does Cambodia still compare to the past? "Oh, before, there weren't motorbikes, there weren't cars, right now it is a modern, developed country!" But, in reality, a developed country is not like this. For example, the factory workers, right now they [. . .] have very bad living conditions. Their salary is minimal [. . .]. The labor law is not respected by companies. When factory workers stand up to demand an increase of their salary, the government starts to use violence. They shoot at the people, some people died, some were arrested, some were injured and are disabled until today. [. . .] There are many problems in Cambodia. We can't compare to before [and say,] "Oh, today it isn't like that anymore, it is better." No! If we were better, Cambodia should be able to produce many things on its own! But what is the country producing right now? Before there were gold mines, iron mines, and forests—over 70 percent of land in Cambodia was forests. And the wildlife, and nature, Cambodia had it all before. But the government says that the country is developing right now. But how? Developing and destroying forests? [. . .] If we compare to the old times, it is always different and seemingly better.[66]

A respondent from Rattanakiri similarly questioned the CPP's self-legitimation and narrative of rescue and its focus on the symbolic date of January 7: "Yes, it is correct. The 7 January has liberated the country and saved all lives. But these past few years, recently, it is not like the CPP's theory because this country's development affects the lives of the villagers, of the population, and it is not helping them but aggravating things. And before, the CPP was right, they constructed hospitals, schools . . . except these past few years. The CPP does not respect the people anymore, the villagers but rather helps companies."[67]

Finally, peace also emerged as a consistent theme in the criticism of the CPP's ruling party discursive portrayal of the current state of affairs. Respondents questioned that peace had ever truly been achieved. A respondent at Freedom Park, for instance, argued that peace remained absent until today, emphasizing the discrepancy between rhetoric and reality: "Since UNTAC arrived and until today, I don't see true peace. Peace has the meaning of mental harmony. But until now, it is only a picture that aims to show that the job was implemented, that elections were organized in the country, but the democracy has not really been practiced. It is only on paper, but not for the people. [. . .] The leaders [since the first election in 1993] are only eager for power."[68]

In the context of the 2020 CPP "Thank You Peace" campaign, Chak Sopheap, director of the Cambodian Center for Human Rights (CCHR), similarly criticized the nature of peace that had been secured. She foregrounds a positive understanding of peace, which goes beyond the end of physical violence and the silence of arms and that requires validation through the population's subjective experiences (Chak 2020):

> By focusing only on the country's stability and the absence of widespread conflict, this simplistic slogan suggesting that peace has been achieved overlooks—either willfully or ignorantly—the realities on the ground. Severe social injustices, high levels of corruption and a lack of political representation leading to the disenfranchisement of a huge portion of the Cambodian population continue to plague Cambodia and stand in the way of a truly peaceful state. Peace cannot simply be declared; it only exists if and to the extent that it is felt by the population. The people of Cambodia's appreciation of whether peace has been achieved or not is the only one that matters. A people-oriented approach, rooted in democracy and respect for human rights, is therefore direly needed if true peace is ever to become a reality.

Conclusion

Turning our attention to the perspectives of those who experience political violence and human rights violations in contemporary Cambodia highlights the ways in which the ECCC is embedded in the political context. Such an analysis is an essential endeavor of epistemological disruption, of decentering the study of transitional justice, as it can tell us about the meanings with which the state-sanctioned transitional justice process is endowed for citizens who, for multiple reasons, are not formally participating in the ECCC proceedings. It brings our attention back to the broader and longer-term social and political struggles, which initially called for transitional justice to be included on the political agenda.

These struggles can be uncovered through a focus on nonparticipation. Not all forms of nonparticipation, as we have seen in this chapter, can be read as resistance to the state-sanctioned transitional justice process. Citizens facing human rights violations in Cambodia today may have chosen to actively make use of possibilities for formal victim participation at the ECCC had they had better access to information or had access to the necessary time and resources. Certain instances of nonparticipation, however, do constitute forms of resistance to the state-sanctioned transitional justice process. They emerge from everyday experiences of the judiciary as an agent of injustice and repression. These experiences directly inform perceptions of the ECCC. Even though it is an internationalized institution, the ECCC is deeply mistrusted for being embedded in the political status quo. Over time, this lack of trust can turn to disappointments that the ECCC is not able to act independently and to go far enough to induce transformative changes, in terms of an independent justice system that could prevent the repetition of human rights violations.

Finally, nonparticipation also takes place in the context of temporal conflicts. The CPP's teleological narrative of a linear transition from genocide, war, and economic deprivation to peace, development, and democracy, which is to some extent echoed in the transitional justice process, renders anachronistic contemporary experiences of political violence. The temporal resistance of citizens struggling with human rights violations today, however, is not only a critique of the CPP and of its subversion of Cambodia's political and economic transformations since the early 1990s. It is not only about political claims regarding the situation in the country and about how and by whom it should be governed. This temporal resistance is also about claims that need to be heard from within the field of transitional justice. Although not framed in the language of transitional justice, these claims are ultimately about guarantees of nonrecurrence, about the structural reforms that are needed to prevent the recurrence of violence and human rights violations. They are also claims about socioeconomic equality, an aspect that has been systematically neglected in the field of transitional justice (Lai 2020).

Conclusion

This book has analyzed the politics of transitional justice in the specific political context of Cambodia, through an empirical focus on resistances. It has thereby traced how the Khmer Rouge tribunal has shaped, and has been shaped by, longer-term contestations over imaginaries of justice, peace, and the political order. For some readers, focusing on resistances to transitional justice may appear to be merely a distraction from weighing the ECCC's successes and failures as a transitional justice process. The book is indeed not an analysis of how the ECCC has scored in terms of investigating the individual, criminal accountability of the senior leaders and those most responsible for crimes committed between 1975 and 1979—or an assessment of what it has achieved considering the multiple expectations that it has itself raised, or that have been projected onto it over the years. Instead, the book has focused on the selective resistance of the Cambodian ruling party against a far-reaching criminal justice process at the ECCC, zooming into highly contested cases rather than examining the legal proceedings that unfolded more smoothly. The book has engaged with civil party protests, which put forward demands that clearly exceed the Court's mandate. It has analyzed the transitional justice perceptions of a group of citizens who do not formally participate in the process and voiced demands of justice in relation to contemporary, rather than past, experiences of violations. Rather than being sideshows that distract us from the implementation of the ECCC's mandate, I hope to have shown that researching these instances of contestations and resistance can help us to better understand the politics of transitional justice in the specific political context in which it unfolds.

With this analysis, I do not intend to imply that efforts to providing accountability for the crimes committed under the Khmer Rouge regime have been meaningless. Having met many survivors who shared with me that they had experienced some form of justice at the ECCC, I personally do not subscribe to all-encompassing critiques of the ECCC. I have also explored elsewhere with colleagues whether, and how, the ECCC has been able to achieve justice and reconciliation from the perspectives of survivors of the Khmer Rouge regime (Williams et al. 2018). Nonetheless, I believe that it remains important to understand how and why the transitional justice process in Cambodia is resisted and contested.

The ECCC at the Intersections of Transitional Justice Politics and Domestic Politics

A focus on resistances can help us understand how the ECCC constitutes a site in which individuals navigate and make claims that relate to a complex range of contemporary power relations in Cambodia. Such an analysis further highlights the ways in which the transitional justice process at the ECCC, instead of being a neutral, technical exercise, constitutes a central site of struggles over the meanings and directions of the country's social, economic, and political transformations.

First, the analysis of the ruling party's resistance to a far-reaching process of criminal accountability has shown how the ECCC has been shaped by its efforts to preserve and consolidate its power in a dynamic political context. During the ECCC's years of operation, the CPP has faced significant contestation both at the polls and in the streets, indicating perhaps an erosion of its long-rehearsed discourse of savior of the nation, especially toward the youth, who have not lived under Khmer Rouge rule or experienced the country's decades of war. However, the CPP has continued to rely upon this self-legitimation discourse, and its discursive resistance to Cases 003 and 004, portrayed as a threat to the CPP's hard-won peace, is part of these repeated claims to power and legitimacy. The discursive opposition to Cases 003 and 004 has also been part, more recently, of the prime minister's increasingly personalized peace narrative that has accompanied the country's transition to hegemonic authoritarianism. Furthermore, the ruling party's control of the national side of the court has successfully shielded senior CPP officials from appearing as witnesses at the ECCC and blocked further trials in Cases 003 and 004. The CPP has thereby prevented the further exposure of the Khmer Rouge past of senior CPP officials or of its co-optation of former Khmer Rouge leaders and cadres into its patronage networks that contributed to its consolidation of power in the 1990s. This successful control of the ECCC's national side has been asserted through neo-patrimonial practices of patronage, and coercion.

The ruling party has thereby made use of the ECCC as a platform for the distribution of positions and salaries, the rewarding of loyalty, or the grooming of a new generation of administrators and judicial officials committed to strengthening the party. This control of the ECCC's national side has taken place in parallel to the increasingly sophisticated instrumentalization of the domestic judiciary that has accompanied the country's transition to hegemonic authoritarianism.

The CPP's successful, selective resistance at the ECCC also reveals the pragmatism of those invested and investing in transitional justice in Cambodia. The UN and donor countries have prioritized a limited number of trials over an independent and far-reaching transitional justice process on the Khmer Rouge past. This has disappointed those Cambodian and foreign lawyers, judicial officials, civil society actors and Khmer Rouge survivors who initially subscribed to the UN's discourse of "bringing justice to the Cambodian people" through an independent judicial process, while frustrating their hopes that the ECCC could thereby also contribute to improving the rule of law. The analysis of this first site of resistance thereby challenges normative assumptions on resistance in the field of transitional justice, if we think of the trope of spoilerism, which reduces actors' positionalities to a simple "pro-" or "anti-" transitional justice stance. This analysis also questions simplistic binaries of national versus international actors, which attach a single set of agency and normative values to heterogenous groups of actors. In their discursive resistance to a far-reaching transitional justice process, the CPP can certainly put forward a convincing argument that after the problematic roles the UN and Western powers played in the context of the Khmer Rouge regime and decades of conflict in Cambodia, they cannot easily claim a high moral ground for intervening as neutral, apolitical agents for justice.

Second, the analysis of civil party participation as a site of resistance has shown how participation in transitional justice was mediated by power relations at different levels, from the village to the Courtroom in the capital city. Navigating through different places has both enabled and limited the agency of civil parties, and offered various options for mobilizing, resisting, and voicing their grievances. Through formal participation, civil parties accessed "invented spaces" that are more open to critical deliberations, such as meetings with trusted lawyers or NGO forums. They have also traveled to urban spaces in which they could publicly express their dissent in the capital city along like-minded peers and outside of more narrowly monitored village environments. Civil parties thereby publicly protested various aspects of the transitional justice process—most prominently, as we have seen, the ECCC's reparations mandate—as well as its narrow temporal jurisdiction. Through their various forms of resistance, civil parties have challenged problematic, static approaches to Cambodian culture as essentially one of unquestioned obedience, docility, excessive deference, and conservatism. Civil parties have also challenged the depoliticization of their participation. They indeed demanded to move beyond a truncated focus on 1975–79, which isolates the Khmer Rouge crimes from the broader context in which they were committed and silences the participation of international actors and the political elite in the decades of war and violence that preceded and followed it.

At the same time, through their participation, civil parties have become exposed to expectations of how they are supposed to be and to behave within the transitional justice process and in Cambodia's political context. Here the intersections of domestic politics with the ontological, epistemological, and methodological biases of transitional justice interventions were particularly restrictive for civil parties' agency. This could be seen with the prioritization of formally established NGOs over grassroots movements and the exclusion of civil parties from decision-making processes and funding streams, which took place alongside the CPP's instrumentalization of the victims' association Ksaem Ksan ahead of the 2013 national elections that effectively put an end to Ksaem Ksan's mobilization of Khmer Rouge survivors across socioeconomic and geographic divides.

Third, the analysis of the nonparticipation of citizens experiencing contemporary political violence has brought to the fore perceptions that the ECCC is embedded in the political status quo. Not all forms of nonparticipation in transitional justice can be read as resistance. In interviews, respondents who did not formally participate in the ECCC proceedings explained how this resulted from a lack of knowledge on the ECCC and possibilities for formal participation, a lack of the necessary resources to participate, or, simply, an absence of interest in the ECCC. However, nonparticipation also stemmed from everyday experiences of the law. Citizens who are subject to human rights violations and participate in public dissent of the CPP rule have come to experience the judiciary as an agent of injustice and repression. These experiences directly informed their mistrust of the ECCC and their principled decision not to participate as civil parties or complainants in a judicial process that is not independent. Nonparticipation is thus also about the disappointment that the transitional justice process is not going far enough, as it remains unable to address claims for the nonrepetition of human rights violations and for structural reforms of the judiciary. Moreover, nonparticipation also becomes a form of resistance to transitional justice when it is about a rejection of the CPP's and the ECCC's teleological temporalities, which both posit a rupture with a time of political violence, relegated to the Khmer Rouge past.

These insights highlight the intersections of the ECCC's and the Cambodian ruling party's temporal governance—that is, their relationship between time and justice (Miller 2021). The CPP's and the ECCC's focus on the narrow timeframe of 1975–79 herewith renders anachronistic continued and contemporary experiences of political violence, such as, for example, repression in the context of land struggles in both urban and rural areas. But it also conceals the ways in which contemporary political violence is part of the political elite's co-optation of the country's economic transformation at the expense of the poor. Claims for socioeconomic justice have thereby not only been dismissed by the ruling party in its necessarily flattering comparison of the current situation to "year zero" at the end of the Khmer Rouge regime. Such claims have also not been heard from within the field of transitional justice in Cambodia.[1]

Taken together, the analysis of these three sites of resistance broadens the realm of politics of the Khmer Rouge tribunal beyond the political negotiations that led to its establishment and the allegations of political interference from the ruling political elite. First, this analysis highlights the politics of transitional justice, in terms of the ontological, epistemological, and methodological biases that have shaped the ECCC as an institution imbued by the "transitional justice imaginary" (Hinton 2018). Second, it highlights how the ECCC has been shaped by domestic politics and structures of power at the national and subnational levels.

While this analysis can help to locate the marginalization of a number of claims for justice in Cambodia at the intersection of transitional justice politics and domestic politics, it also speaks to scholarly works that have cautioned against calls for quick remedies. More "local" transitional justice, more victim participation, or more attention to socioeconomic forms of justice will not in itself transcend preexisting power structures. Addressing the limits of transitional justice interventions will require not only understanding how the "transitional justice imaginary" narrows down imaginaries of justice in specific ways. It will also require accounting for the political agency of domestic and foreign political actors and moving beyond assumptions of a "malleability" of the political and socioeconomic structures in which transitional justice institutions operate (McAuliffe 2017b; Kochanski 2018).

What Cambodia Post-ECCC?

On 22 September 2022, the ECCC's final trial ended with the pronouncement of the appeal judgment against former head of state Khieu

Samphan. At the public hearing, the frailty of the accused, aged ninety-one, as well as of the participating civil parties, was a vivid reminder that the ECCC, established twenty-five years after the fall of the Khmer Rouge regime, had always been a race against time. Khieu Samphan was the last one alive out of the initial four suspects in Case 002. The precise number of civil parties who have died since the start of Case 002 remains unknown, given a breakdown of communication between civil parties and their lawyers in recent years.[2] For many civil parties, however, the ECCC's last verdict came too late.

This unforgiving pressure of time perhaps added to the zealous assessments of the ECCC's efficiency, independence, and legacies, which have accompanied the ECCC ever since it came into existence. With allegations of "political interference" and corruption emerging early on, assessments of the ECCC in the media have often been very negative. This media coverage has been underpinned by vigorous critiques from human rights organizations, who saw in the unfolding of Cases 003 and 004 the confirmation of their concerns that the ECCC had never been equipped with sufficient safeguards against political interference from the Cambodian government. For analysts and practitioners familiar with the domestic judiciary in Cambodia, the promises of positive legacies of a hybrid tribunal in terms of spillover contributions to the rule of law certainly seemed naïve from the start (see, e.g., Urs 2007; L. Sok and Abe 2019). It appeared even more so in recent years, given the country's transition to hegemonic authoritarianism, which relied upon an increasingly sophisticated instrumentalization of the judiciary. At the same time, advocates of the ECCC have reminded critics that holding on to the idea of a perfect tribunal only played into the interests of former Khmer Rouge leaders for impunity, as the alternative to the ECCC was not a perfect tribunal but no trials at all (Fawthrop and Jarvis 2004; Fawthrop 2017). Scholars also cautioned that broad critiques of the ECCC were reminiscent of earlier pathologizing portrayals of Cambodia; and that the situation was much more complex than merely a dichotomy between international liberalism and local authoritarianism (Ainley 2013; R. Hughes 2015). Researchers further highlighted the unpredictability of the ECCC as a cultural and political event, and the creativity resulting from local encounters with global justice (R. Hughes 2015; Hinton 2018)—even though the optimism for the potential for more open-ended, "combusting" encounters in the "inventive spaces" of transitional justice has in recent years given way to concerns over the crackdown of civil society and the increased political reappropriation of outreach activities (R. Hughes 2018; A. Kent 2022). As Orentlicher (2020, 629) has noted, any swift attempt to declare the ECCC as either a success or a failure has been necessarily fraught: "How to assess a deeply flawed institution that nonetheless rendered historic justice presents challenges for which there are no generally accepted metrics. Yet this is precisely the paradox presented by the ECCC's record."

As it is winding down, the ECCC will continue to weave and consolidate its own narrative of legacy as a hybrid institution during its residual functions. Perhaps this will come with a downsizing of measures of success that has been characteristic of international(ized) criminal tribunals in their completion phase (Mégret 2016). The political interests of the CPP government to declare that justice has been, once again, achieved for Khmer Rouge victims, and to thereby foreclose any further discussions on the Khmer Rouge past—or for that matter, any other past—may converge with the necessity for the UN to declare the ECCC a success. It remains to be seen whether and how civil parties and Khmer Rouge survivors—the declared beneficiaries of the transitional justice process—and Cambodia's new generations will be able to take part in these debates on the ECCC's legacies, and to continue to raise broader questions over the country's political, social, and economic transformations since the fall of the Khmer Rouge regime.

Notes

Introduction

1. See photo of the protests on the book cover. Journalists gave different accounts of the number of civil parties present during the protest. See, e.g., White (2014) and Naren (2014a).

2. See Kent (2016) for a similar approach.

3. In Case 001, the Trial Chamber and Supreme Court Chamber found that at least 12,272 victims had been executed at S-21. By the end of Case 002/2, the co-prosecutors consolidated a list of 18,133 prisoners. See Co-prosecutors, 2 October 2017, Co-prosecutors' Amended Closing Brief in Case 002/02, ECCC Document E457/6/1/1, §651–54.

4. Cambodian naming conventions list names in a reverse order when compared to Western naming conventions (here, for instance, Ieng is the family name and Thirith the given name, so in the West she would be referred to as Thirith Ieng). I have followed the Cambodian way for Cambodian names throughout the text, with the exception of references to Cambodian scholars.

5. Eighty-six of these interviews were conducted in 2018 either with or by colleagues, as part of the mixed methods study discussed below (Williams et al. 2018).

6. See "Cambodia—Rural Population," World Bank, accessed 1 February 2023, https://data.worldbank.org/indicator/SP.RUR.TOTL.ZS?locations=KH&most_recent_year_desc=true.

7. See "Labor Force, Total—Cambodia," World Bank, accessed 1 February 2023, https://data.worldbank.org/indicator/SL.TLF.TOTL.IN?locations=KH.

8. This project was carried out from November 2017 until December 2018 with a core team, including Dr. Timothy Williams, Boravin Tann, and Somaly Kum. The project consisted of a collaboration among the Center for Conflict Studies of the University of Marburg, swisspeace, and the Center for the Study of Humanitarian Law at the Royal University of Law and Economics in Phnom Penh. The project was funded by the German Federal Ministry for Economic Cooperation and Development. See

Williams et al. (2018, 19–30) for more details on the study's methodology and a demographical overview of the respondents.

9. ADHOC is the French acronym of the Cambodian Human Rights and Development Association. Founded in 1991, it is one of the main human rights organizations in Cambodia.

10. I observed the forums organized by the Victims Support Section (VSS) of the ECCC in Phnom Penh (23 December 2013 and 26 January 2018), Kampot (29 November 2013), and Kampong Cham (13 February 2018). I also conducted participant observation of the public forums on "Justice and National Reconciliation" organized by the Center for Social Development, in Pailin (24 October 2008) and Stung Treng (10 April 2009).

11. This includes, most recently, online observation of the Workshop on "Victims and Dissemination of the Advisory Report on Victim-Related Activities of the ECCC during the Residual Phase" organized by the ECCC in Phnom Penh on 3–5 May 2022.

12. While resistance studies is not understood by all scholars as a coherent academic field of its own, it is a label widely used by scholars engaged in the study of resistance (see, e.g., Lilja and Vinthagen 2006; Seymour 2006).

Chapter 1. Transitional Justice, Politics, and Resistance in Cambodia

1. ECCC Trial Chamber, 7 August 2014, Case 002/01 Judgement, ECCC Document E313, §157.

2. All transliterations are based on Franklin E. Huffman's Franco-Khmer transcription system, as reproduced in Heder and Ledgerwood (1996b, xvii). Exceptions were made for words whose transcription in English differs but has become established in scholarship on Cambodia.

3. ECCC Trial Chamber, 7 August 2014, Case 002/01 Judgement, ECCC Document E313, §219.

4. These remain contested terms in Cambodia. Their use locates sides of the political divide: those close to the ruling party celebrate the 1979 "liberation," while those close to the opposition speak of an "invasion" by Vietnam. See, e.g., Sisovann and Welsh (2007) or Future Forum (2017).

5. As of 1982, they shared this seat with their allies of the Coalition Government of Democratic Kampuchea (Ciorciari 2009).

6. The ECCC considered that the 1979 judgment against Ieng Sary did not have any legal effect because of the deficiency of the proceedings.

7. Literally, the day of "holding onto anger" (*tivea châng komhoeng*, ទិវាចងកំហឹង).

8. May 20 was chosen in remembrance of the day in 1976 the CPK had ordered the total collectivization of life.

9. See Preamble and article 15.2 of the Agreement on a Comprehensive Political Settlement of the Cambodia Conflict, www.usip.org/sites/default/files/file/resources/collections/peace_agreements/agree_comppol_10231991.pdf.

10. See Royal Decree, 14 September 1996, NS/RKT/0996/72, https://www.eccc.gov.kh/en/documents/legal/amnestypardon-leng-sary.

11. For more detailed accounts, see Hammarberg (2001); Fawthrop and Jarvis (2004); Heder (2011); Scheffer (2012); Ciorciari and Heindel (2014); Etcheson (2019); Gidley (2019).

12. See Fawthrop and Jarvis (2004), Bird (2015), or Etcheson (2019) for more details on accountability efforts in the US.

13. Letter from the First and Second Prime Ministers of Cambodia addressed to the Secretary-General, 21 June 1997, UN Document A/51/930 S/1997/488.

14. See UN General Assembly Resolution 52/135, 12 December 1997, UN Document A/RES/52/135.

15. See Article 14(1), new ECCC Law; Rule 77(13), ECCC Internal Rules.

16. Law on the Establishment of the ECCC for the Prosecution of Crimes Committed during the Period of Democratic Kampuchea, https://www.eccc.gov.kh/en/document/legal/law-on-eccc.

17. Information calculated based on the ECCC revised budget documents from 2008 until 2022, https://www.eccc.gov.kh/en/about-eccc/finances.

18. See ECCC Law, article 1.

19. See "Internal Rules and Regulations," ECCC, accessed 1 February 2023, https://www.eccc.gov.kh/en/document/legal/internal-rules.

20. The co-prosecutors could expand their introductory submission through supplementary submissions—e.g., following civil parties' requests.

21. US$2,995,000 per year, for three years. See UN General Assembly, ECCC—residual functions: Report of the Secretary-General, 19 March 2021, A/75/809. See also UN General Assembly Resolution, ECCC—residual functions, 12 July 2021, A/RES/75/257 B.

22. Interview, Helen Jarvis, then-head of the ECCC Public Affairs section, Phnom Penh, 4 April 2008.

23. See ECCC Law, article 44 (1) new.

24. By 31 October 2022, the Cambodian government provided a total of US$21.5 million in in-kind contributions (ECCC 2022b).

25. DK minister of defense Son Sen was executed with his wife, Yun Yat, under orders from Pol Pot in mid-1997; Pol Pot died in April 1998 under unclarified circumstances; and Kae Pok, member of the CPK Central Committee, died a few days after the UN withdrew from the negotiations in 2002.

26. Initially, the office of co-prosecutors identified a total of sixteen "persons of interest" (Etcheson 2019). The first introductory submission included the five suspects later covered in Cases 001 and 002. Investigators excluded three other suspects, concluding that their alleged crimes were not particularly heinous, or that not enough inculpatory evidence was available. Three suspects died: Ta Mok in 2006, Di Thin in late 2007, Van Rith in 2008. Di Thin was an ethnic Tampuon and allegedly secretary of Sector 101 under DK.

27. A total of 108,425 persons attended the trial and appeal hearings in Case 002/1, and 84,279 in Case 002/2. Attendance was significantly lower for Case 002/2 appeal hearings, given the COVID-19 pandemic. See ECCC (2022a).

28. The TV shows produced by the Asian International Justice Initiative and Khmer Mekong Films are available at https://krtmonitor.org/tv-show/.

29. See CCHR, "The Duch Trial: A Good Example for Cambodian Courts," 26 July 2010, https://www.opensocietyfoundations.org/newsroom/duch-trial-good-example-cambodian-courts.

30. See chapter 3 for more details on reparations at the ECCC.

31. Trial Chamber, 2 November 2011, Decision on Ieng Sary's Rule 89 Preliminary Objections (Ne Bis in Idem and Amnesty and Pardon), ECCC Document E51/15.

32. Trial Chamber, 22 September 2011, Severance Order Pursuant to Internal Rule 89ter, ECCC Document E124.

33. DeFalco and Sirik (2022), however, argue that Case 002 problematically sidelined less visible forms of everyday atrocities.

34. See Co-lawyers for Civil Parties, 4 February 2010, Sixth Investigative Request of Co-lawyers for Civil Parties concerning the Charge of Genocide against the Khmer Nationals, Case 002, ECCC Document D349.

35. Although not reaching a conclusion on the facts, Cambodian Trial Chamber judge You Ottara issued a dissenting opinion on this matter in the Case 002/2 judgment, criticizing the Chamber's narrow approach.

36. ECCC Trial Chamber, 16 November 2018, Case 002/02 Judgement, ECCC Document E465, §4517. See also Jarvis (2016, 27–28).

37. In Case 001, Duch was found guilty for one single case of rape as an act of torture, despite attempts of civil party lawyers to broaden the counts of sexual violence (see Oosterveld and Viseur Sellers 2016; E. Palmer and Williams 2017). In Case 002/1, except for the recognition of the specific harms experienced by women regarding pregnancy and childbirth (under the crime against humanity of "other inhumane acts"), the Court produced a gender-neutral narrative of the forced population movements (see Sankey 2016).

38. See International Co-prosecutor, 24 April 2014, Co-prosecutors Supplementary Submission regarding Forced Marriage and Sexual or Gender Based Violence, Case File 004, ECCC Document D191.

39. For the purpose of simplicity, in this book, I generally refer to Case 004 as encompassing the cases against all three suspects.

40. Supreme Court Chamber, 28 December 2021, Decision on international Co Prosecutor's appeal of the Pre-Trial Chamber's Failure to Send Case 004 to Trial as Required by the ECCC Legal Framework, ECCC Document 2/1/1/1, §30.

41. UN General Assembly, 7 July 2021, ECCC—residual functions, Resolution A/RES/75/257 B, accessed 3 December 2021, https://www.un.org/en/ga/75/resolutions.shtml.

42. See chapter 4 for more details on the 2013 protests.

43. See chapter 2 for more details on the judiciary.

44. In its 2016 report, Global Witness (2016) has shown how Hun Sen's immediate family has systematically captured the most profitable sectors of Cambodia's economy such as trading, tourism, energy, media, construction, and real estate and thereby

registered business holdings with a total listed share capital of more than US$200 million.

45. I am grateful to reviewer 2 for this information.

Chapter 2. The Khmer Rouge Tribunal

1. Interview, Heather Ryan, trial monitor for the Open Society Justice Initiative (OSJI), 19 March 2014, Phnom Penh. See also Staggs Kelsall (2009).

2. Interview, international human rights researcher at LICADHO, 19 December 2013, Phnom Penh.

3. The analysis relies on speeches published in *Cambodia New Vision*, the official online newsletter of the Cambodian Cabinet (available at http://cnv.org.kh/speech/). Given its curated nature, this section also relies on media reports of the speeches and the full transcript of three key speeches (on file with author).

4. Hun Sen, "Presentation of MoP's Final Population Census," Phnom Penh, 7 September 2009. Speech on file with author. The version published in *Cambodia New Vision* does not mention the "200,000 to 300,000 deaths."

5. Hun Sen, "Selected Impromptu Comments at the Opening of the International Conference on Responsibility to Protect (R2P), Challenges and Opportunity in Asia and the Pacific," *Cambodia New Vision*, 26 February 2015.

6. Hun Sen, "Selected Comments at the Graduation of Batches of Judges," *Cambodia New Vision*, 11 May 2006.

7. Interviews in Phnom Penh: Long Panhavuth, legal consultant for OSJI, 30 January 2014; senior international ECCC officer, 3 February 2014; former international ECCC officer, 17 February 2014. See also Ainley (2013).

8. In 2005, for instance, Sam Rainsy filed a lawsuit under the Alien Tort Claims Act and the Torture Victims Protection Act in the US regarding the 1997 grenade attack (LICADHO 2007). In 2008, Sam Rainsy accused Hor Nam Hong, deputy prime minister since 2004 and former foreign minister of the CPP government, of directing the Khmer Rouge prison of Boeung Trabek under Democratic Kampuchea. Hor Nam Hong subsequently filed a defamation lawsuit against him and the journalist who had reported on his comments. The case was shelved while Hor Nam Hong exported the resolution of the legal dispute to France, where Sam Rainsy's first autobiography in French contained further allegations against Hor Nam Hong. It was reopened in Cambodia in 2011, and Sam Rainsy, then in exile, was sentenced to two years of imprisonment (and a total of fourteen years in relation to other charges). Pardoned by the king days before the 2013 elections, Sam Rainsy returned to Cambodia. In 2015, following the removal of his lawmaker status and immunity, he faced the revival of the two-years sentence. He refused a deal with the CPP that reportedly included sending a public letter to Hor Nam Hong in which he would apologize for accusing him of collaborating with the Khmer Rouge and recognize "the Cambodian People's Party of Hun Sen as the national liberator from the Khmer Rouge." Facing additional charges in relation to claims he made on the alleged Vietnamese encroachment of Cambodian territory,

Sam Rainsy has chosen to remain in exile ever since. See Giry (2012); Meas and Vong (2015). In 2017, Sam Rainsy threatened to file a complaint with the International Criminal Court regarding Hun Sen's involvement in the K5 military plan in the 1980s and submitted a request to a court in the US to subpoena the multinational energy company Chevron to release surveillance video footage of the July 2016 murder of Kem Ley in a Chevron-operated Caltex gas station in Phnom Penh (Hutt 2017).

9. Hun Sen, "Presentation of MoP's Final Population Census," Phnom Penh, *Cambodia New Vision*, 7 September 2009 (emphasis added).

10. Hun Sen, "Excerpt from the Off-the-Cuff Speech of Samdech Techo Hun Sen at the Inauguration of Hyatt Regency Hotel Phnom Penh" (unofficial translation), *Cambodia New Vision*, 15 December 2021 (emphasis added).

11. Interview, H.E. Khieu Kanharith, 1 March 2014, Phnom Penh.

12. Interview, Long Panhavuth, 30 January 2014, Phnom Penh.

13. Interview, Long Panhavuth, 30 January 2014, Phnom Penh. See also Peou (2017).

14. Interview, international ECCC officer, 20 January 2014, Phnom Penh.

15. Informal discussion, international ECCC officer, 21 January 2016, Phnom Penh.

16. Interview, national ECCC officer, 26 January 2016, Phnom Penh.

17. Hun Sen, "Selected Comments at the Dissemination Workshop on 'Cambodia Trade Integration Strategy 2007—Responding to Opportunities and Challenges,'" *Cambodia New Vision*, 5 December 2007.

18. Hun Sen, "Selected Comments at the Graduation at the Human Resources University," *Cambodia New Vision*, 24 February 2009 (emphasis added).

19. Hun Sen, "Excerpt of Speech Delivered at the Opening Ceremony of Bak Kheng Water Treatment Plant and Inauguration of Chamkarmon Water Treatment Plant" (unofficial translation), *Cambodia New Vision*, 1 February 2021.

20. Interview, secretary of state, ministry of land, 30 January 2014, Phnom Penh.

21. Interview, secretary of state, ministry of land.

22. Hun Sen, "Selected Comments at the Inauguration of the Water Reservoir of Tamouk in the District of Punnhealoeu, Kandal Province," *Cambodia New Vision*, 8 January 2005 (emphasis added).

23. Hun Sen, "Selected Comments and Press Briefing during the Extraordinary Session of the Fifth Legislative National Assembly" (unofficial translation), *Cambodia New Vision*, 8 August 2014 (emphasis added).

24. See, e.g., Remarks by His Excellency Dr. Bin Chhin, on the delivery of the Trial Judgement in Case 002/02 against Nuon Chea and Khieu Samphan, 16 November 2018, available at https://pressocm.gov.kh/en/archives/38798.

25. Lemonde also acted alone in requesting an interview of King Father Sihanouk but ultimately did not follow up on this.

26. Interview, senior ECCC officer, 28 January 2016, Phnom Penh.

27. Interview, former ECCC officer, 19 March 2014, Phnom Penh.

28. Interviews in Phnom Penh: former ECCC officer, 19 March 2014; Dim Sovannarom, head of ECCC Public Affairs section, 7 February 2014.

29. Pre-Trial Chamber, 8 June 2010, Decision on NUON Chea's and IENG Sary's Appeal Against OCIJ Order on Requests to Summons Witnesses; as quoted in Ciorciari and Heindel (2013, 28).

30. See Pre-Trial Chamber, 9 September 2010, Second Decision on Nuon Chea's and Ieng Sary's Appeal against OCIJ Order on Request to Summons Witnesses, ECCC Document D314/1/12.

31. Pre-Trial Chamber, Second Decision, p. 26.

32. Nuon Chea, 22 July 2013, Nuon Chea's Sixth Request to Summon Heng Samrin, ECCC Doc. E236/5/1/1.

33. In Case 002/2, Nuon Chea also requested to call as witnesses CPP senator Ouk Bunchhoen (former DK Eastern Zone leader) and Pol Saroeun, Cambodia's current supreme commander of the Royal Cambodian Armed Forces (former DK vice-chairperson of the East Zone General staff).

34. See Trial Chamber, 7 August 2014, Final Decision on Witnesses, Experts and Civil Parties to be Heard in Case 002/01, ECCC Document E312, §86–111; 18 July 2017, Decision on Witnesses, Civil Parties and Experts Proposed to be Heard during Case 002/02, ECCC Document E459, §195–275.

35. Nuon Chea, 29 December 2014, Nuon Chea's Appeal against the Judgment in Case 002/1, ECCC Document F16, §74.

36. Supreme Court Chamber, 23 November 2016, Case 002/1 Appeal Judgment, ECCC Document F36, §134–55.

37. In Case 002/2, however, the international co-prosecutor did not have any objections to summoning Heng Samrin and others as witnesses, while the national prosecutor disagreed. See ECCC Trial Chamber, 18 July 2017, Decision on Witnesses, Civil Parties and Experts Proposed to Be Heard during Case 002/02, ECCC Document E459, §199.

38. Supreme Court Chamber, 23 November 2016, Case 002/1 Appeal Judgment, ECCC Document F36, §123.

39. Interview, international ECCC officer, 1 February 2018, Phnom Penh.

40. See, e.g., Nuon Chea Defense team, 22 February 2012, Application for Summary Action against Hun Sen pursuant to Rule 35, ECCC Document E176; 25 April 2012, Application for Immediate Action Pursuant to Rule 35, ECCC Document E189.

41. Restrictions imposed on the defense by the Trial Chamber president were read as necessary trial management efforts or, more critically, as attempts to protect Heng Samrin from public scrutiny (Manning 2017, 86–88; Gidley 2019, 134).

42. Nuon Chea, 29 December 2014, Nuon Chea's Appeal against the Judgment in Case 002/1, ECCC Document F16, §62.

43. In January 2009, they had also filed a complaint in the Municipal Court claiming that their client was not given a fair trial, following the allegations of corruption at the ECCC.

44. Opposition politicians have, however, used legal avenues outside of Cambodia to file lawsuits against the prime minister and the CPP elite. In 2005, Sam Rainsy filed a lawsuit under the Alien Tort Claims Act and the Torture Victims Protection Act in

the US regarding the 1997 grenade attack, although he dropped the lawsuit in 2006 (see, e.g., LICADHO 2007, 6). In 2014, international human rights organizations (featuring international defense lawyers who worked at the ECCC) filed a communication under article 15 of the Rome Statute to the Prosecutor of the International Criminal Court, on behalf of victims, alleging that land grabbing and mass forced evictions that had taken place in Cambodia since 2002 amounted to crimes against humanity under international law (Global Diligence 2014).

45. International Co-prosecutor, 14 June 2019, International Co-prosecutor's Response to the National Co-prosecutor's Appeal of the Case 003 Indictment, ECCC Document D267/9, §35.

46. Supreme Court Chamber, 17 December 2021, Decision on International Co Prosecutor's Appeal of the Pre-Trial Chamber's Failure to Send Case 003 to Trial as Required by the ECCC Legal Framework, ECCC Document 3/1/1/1, §195, dissenting opinion of Judge Clark, §109.

47. In Etcheson's (2019) view, delaying tactics did not only affect Cases 003 and 004. He argues, for instance, that in January 2007, the national judges' stalling of the drafting of the Internal Rules was linked to concerns of the CPP government that the international co-prosecutor would expand the list of suspects to be prosecuted.

48. All quotes from Pre-Trial Chamber, 18 August 2009, Annex I: Public Redacted Version, Considerations of the Pre-Trial Chamber regarding the Disagreement between the Co-prosecutors Pursuant to Internal Rule 71, ECCC Document, §31–36.

49. Online interview, Craig Etcheson, 7 October 2022.

50. Pre-Trial Chamber, 18 August 2009, Annex I: Public Redacted Version, Considerations of the Pre-Trial Chamber regarding the Disagreement between the Co-prosecutors Pursuant to Internal Rule 71, ECCC Document, §31.

51. ECCC Internal Rules, original version, preamble, p. 4.

52. Translated from French into English by the author.

53. Interview, international judge, 29 January 2014, Phnom Penh. Another international judge similarly contested Lemonde's account in an interview (31 January 2014, Phnom Penh).

54. Reportedly, Robert Petit had even provided Chea Leang with the assistance of one of his staff to help her draft her response to his filing of the disagreement before the Pre-Trial Chamber. Online interview, Craig Etcheson, 7 October 2022.

55. Pre-Trial Chamber, 18 August 2009, Annex I: Public Redacted Version, Considerations of the Pre-Trial Chamber regarding the Disagreement Between the Co-prosecutors Pursuant to Internal Rule 71, ECCC Document.

56. Interview, Heather Ryan, trial monitor for the Open Society Justice Initiative, 19 March 2014, Phnom Penh. (See also Lemonde 2013.)

57. Informal discussion, international ECCC officer, 19 January 2016, Phnom Penh.

58. See Statements and Memorandum from the Co-investigating Judges, dated 2, 8, and 9 June 2010, available at http://www.eccc.gov.kh/sites/default/files/media/PROCIJ%28JUne2010.pdf.

59. Pre-Trial Chamber, 10 September 2010, Decision on Application for Disqualification of Judge You Bunleng, ECCC Document 8.

60. Interview, international prosecutor, 3 February 2014, Phnom Penh.

61. International Co-investigating Judge, 18 May 2011, Order on International Co-prosecutor's Public Statement regarding Case File 003, ECCC Document D14.

62. The co-investigating judges had initiated the investigation after reports of unusual behavior by alleged ECCC staff seemed to suggest attempts to influence witnesses. Instead, the international investigator mandated for this investigation launched an investigation into Judge Blunk (Etcheson 2019).

63. See Supreme Court Chamber, 28 December 2021, Decision on International Co Prosecutor's Appeal of the Pre-Trial Chamber's Failure to Send Case 004 to Trial as Required by the ECCC Legal Framework, ECCC Document 2/1/1/1, p. 13.

64. Online interview, Heather Ryan, former OSJI trial monitor in Cambodia, 22 September 2022.

65. Co-investigating Judges, 10 July 2017, Closing Order (Reasons): Redacted, Im Chaem (Case 004/1), ECCC Document D308/3.

66. Pre-Trial Chamber, 28 June 2018, Considerations on the International Co-prosecutor's Appeal of Closing Order (Reasons), ECCC Document D308/3/1/20.

67. Pre-Trial Chamber, Considerations, §339.

68. Supreme Court Chamber, 10 August 2020, Decision on International Co Prosecutor's Immediate Appeal of the Trial Chamber's Effective Termination of 004/2, ECCC Document E004/2/1/1/2, §60.

69. Pre-Trial Chamber, 19 December 2019, Considerations on Appeals against Closing Orders (Case 004/2). ECCC Document D359/24 & D360/33.

70. See President of the Trial Chamber, 3 April 2020, Statement of the Judges of the Trial Chamber of the ECCC Regarding Case 004/2 Involving Ao An, available at https://www.eccc.gov.kh/en/articles/statement-judges-trial-chamber-eccc-regarding-case-0042-involving-ao (last accessed 01.09.2022).

71. President of the Trial Chamber, Statement.

72. International Co-prosecutor, 4 May 2020, International Co-prosecutor's Immediate Appeal of the Trial Chamber's Effective Termination of Case 004/2, ECCC Document E004/2/1, §24.

73. Supreme Court Chamber, 10 August 2020, ECCC Document E004/2/1/1/2.

74. Supreme Court Chamber, 28 December 2021, Decision on International Co Prosecutor's Appeal of the Pre-Trial Chamber's Failure to Send Case 004 to Trial as Required by the ECCC Legal Framework, ECCC Document 2/1/1/1, §30.

75. Supreme Court Chamber, 17 December 2021, Decision on International Co Prosecutor's Appeal of the Pre-Trial Chamber's Failure to Send Case 003 to Trial as Required by the ECCC Legal Framework, ECCC Document 3/1/1/1, §195.

76. Supreme Court Chamber, Decision, §109.

77. Supreme Court Chamber, 28 December 2021, ECCC Document 2/1/1/1, §48.

78. Interview, Venerable Luon Sovath, 6 June 2022, Péry, Switzerland.

79. This includes the Law on Associations and Non-governmental Organisations, the Defamation Law, the Anti-Corruption Law, the Laws on Political Parties and on the Election of Members of the National Assembly and the Genocide Denial Law (Anstis 2012; Un 2019). More recently, concerns have been raised regarding the State of Emergency Law adopted in the context of the COVID-19 pandemic (Muntarbhorn 2021), adopted or envisaged legislation on the regulation of internet access (see, e.g., Beban, Schoenberger, and Lamb 2020), and the lèse-majesté legislation (Norén-Nilsson 2021).

80. There are different accounts of the number of legal professionals who survived DK. Gottesman (2004, 4) mentions eight.

81. In Case 001, Judge Ney Thol, however, recused himself from participating in the decision on Duch's appeal against his provisional detention, and in the co-prosecutors' appeal of the Closing Order, perhaps concerned about the appearance of bias given his previous role at the Military Court, where Duch had been detained.

82. An example given in interviews was that of the only three funded positions for national civil party lawyers. Interviews in Phnom Penh: former national ECCC officer, 21 January 2016; civil party lawyers, 17 January 2014 and 30 January 2014.

83. Further examples mentioned included You Bunleng, national co-investigating judge; Dim Sovannarom, head of the Public Affairs Section after 2011; or Sok An's nephew, national counsellor to the Office of the Co-prosecutors. Interviews, Phnom Penh: international human rights researcher at LICADHO, 19 December 2013; international ECCC officer, 20 January 2014; national ECCC officer, 20 January 2014.

84. Examples shared in interviews included the recruitment of two nieces of Chea Leang as assistants in the Office of the Co-prosecutors, or of several nephews of co-investigating judge You Bunleng in the Office of the Co-investigating Judges.

85. An example shared with me was the editing of applications and CVs of candidates preselected by the administration, so that they would appear as the best candidates in the recruitment process involving international members.

86. Interview, international researcher at LICADHO, 19 December 2013, Phnom Penh.

87. Online interview, Craig Etcheson, 7 October 2022.

88. Interview, former national ECCC officer, 28 January 2016, Phnom Penh; informal conversation, national ECCC officer, 23 January 2016, Phnom Penh.

89. See, e.g., interview, former national ECCC officer, 21 January 2016, Phnom Penh.

90. I received indications of two such cases in 2016.

91. A national ECCC officer observed that judicial positions at the ECCC were coveted for the prestige of working at an internationalized court, with state-of-the-art equipment, dedicated to investigating a devastating period in the country's modern history that deeply affected every Cambodian. Interview, national judicial official, 12 February 2014, Phnom Penh. See also Kent (2013).

92. Some ECCC national officers recently received the title of Excellency and moved on to important positions outside of the ECCC. The former head of Public

Affairs, Dim Sovannarom, has, for instance, become a member of the National Election Committee in 2017.

93. Interview, former national defense lawyer at the ECCC, 20 March 2014, Phnom Penh.

94. Online interview, former national ECCC officer, 2 September 2022.

95. Interview, former national ECCC officer, 21 January 2016, Phnom Penh.

96. Online interview, former ECCC officer, 7 September 2022. See also Ciorciari and Heindel (2014, 374–75n34)

97. Online, informal conversation, Cambodian civil society member, 7 October 2022.

98. Online interview, former national ECCC officer, 2 September 2022.

99. Interview, international ECCC officer, 20 January 2014, Phnom Penh.

100. Online interview, former ECCC officer, 7 September 2022.

101. Interview, international ECCC judge, 29 January 2014, Phnom Penh.

102. Interview, ECCC officer, 17 January 2014, Phnom Penh.

103. Interview, ECCC officer.

104. Interview, international defense lawyer at the ECCC, 7 February 2014, Phnom Penh.

105. For example, interviews in Phnom Penh: international ECCC officer, 20 January 2014; international ECCC judge, 29 January 2014. Also, an online interview, Megan Hirst, former international lead co-lawyer, 7 September 2022. An international judge criticized that, in early years, the UN ran the Court "like a road project." Interview, 31 January 2014, Phnom Penh.

106. Skype interview, former international ECCC judicial official, 19 December 2014.

107. Interviews in Phnom Penh: international judge, 31 January 2014; international ECCC officer, 20 January 2014.

108. Interview, Heather Ryan, OSJI trial monitor in Cambodia, 19 March 2014, Phnom Penh.

109. Interview, Heather Ryan.

110. See, e.g., US Embassy, Cambodia (2006).

111. In its 2017 budget proposal, the US Senate considered limiting funds to Case 003. The suspect in Case 003, Meas Muth, had allegedly been implicated in the 1975 seizure of the US container ship SS *Mayaguez*. This conditionality for ECCC funds was later withdrawn; however, it problematically implied that funding was only justified when acts had been committed against US interests (see, e.g., Etcheson 2019).

112. Interview, international ECCC officer, 20 January 2014, Phnom Penh. (See also Ciorciari and Heindel 2014, 198.)

113. Co-investigating Judges, 11 August 2017, Combined Decision on the Impact of the Budgetary Situation on Cases 003, 004, and 004/2 and Related Submissions by the Defence for Yim Tith, ECCC Document D349/6.

114. Co-investigating judges, Combined Decision, §55.

115. Co-investigating judges, Combined Decision, §35.

116. An international judge, for instance, insisted that international judges would leave the ECCC if they knew their national colleagues to be taking instructions from the government. Interview, 31 January 2014, Phnom Penh.

117. According to the ECCC's 2017 revised budget provision, the ECCC had a total of 158 UN-appointed staff in 2017.

118. Online interview, Harshan Athureliya, 28 September 2022.

119. Interview, Athureliya. In contrast, an international ECCC officer who did not sign the petition at that time commented that it was out of less idealistic views of what the ECCC could achieve—that is, seeing the ECCC not as invested with the mission to contribute to the rule of law in Cambodia but as giving Cambodian judges more independence at the ECCC than they had in domestic courts.

120. Interview, Athureliya.

121. See Staggs Kelsall (2009) for a similar argument.

122. See Arnould (2016) for a similar argument in her analysis of contestations in transitional justice policymaking in the Democratic Republic of Congo.

Chapter 3. Victim Participation

1. ECCC Internal Rule 23 bis, Revision 9, available at https://www.eccc.gov.kh/en/document/legal/internal-rules.

2. The Extraordinary African Chambers and the Special Criminal Court in Central African Republic established in 2012 and 2015, respectively, also provide for civil party participation.

3. Two civil party applicants withdrew before the start of the Case 002/2 trial. Some civil parties were admitted in more than one case. My thanks go to Hang Vannak and Kaing Monida from the ECCC Victim Support Section for kindly providing me with the breakdown of civil parties per province that I used for the maps included in this chapter.

4. According to numbers provided by the ECCC Victims Support Section in September 2022, 647 civil party applications were received for Case 003, 2014 in Case 004 (the section did not divide applicants into Case 004, 004/1, and 004/2).

5. At the end of the trial, the Trial Chamber rejected the application of 23 civil party applicants, unaware of the provisional nature of their status. The Supreme Court Chamber later restored the status of 10 applicants.

6. There were 22 civil parties in Case 001; 31 in Case 002/01; and 63 in Case 002/02.

7. Online interview, Megan Hirst, former international lead co-lawyer, 7 September 2022.

8. Letter of resignation of Megan Hirst, 16 June 2022, https://www.voanews.com/a/6650130.html.

9. See this book's introduction for more details on the survey's methodology.

10. ECCC Internal Rule 12 ter, Revision 9.

11. According to the ECCC (2022a), by September 2022, a total of 244,668 persons had attended public hearings.

12. With this term, I draw from McCargo (2014, 74), who speaks of "urbanized villagers" in Thailand and Cambodia to describe both the rural embeddedness of most voters and the significance of their urban experiences in their voting behavior. See chapter 4.

13. Interviews with a civil party representative in Prey Veng Province (12 May 2018) and with a Case 001 civil party in Kampong Thom Province (20 May 2018).

14. ECCC Office of the Co-investigating Judges, 15 September 2010, Case 002 Closing Order, ECCC Document D427.

15. E.g., interviews, civil party in Case 002 (and applicant in Cases 003 and 004) (male, age 61) and civil party in Cases 001 and 002 (female, age 61), Kampot province, 20 and 21 February 2014.

16. Field notes on file with author, March 2014.

17. E.g., 2014 interviews (Case 001 civil party, 13 March 2014, Kandal province; group of civil parties, 28 November 2014, Siem Reap; Case 001 and 002 civil party, 29 November 2014, Siem Reap). See also individual interviews with 15 civil parties from the provinces of Pursat (20, 28, and 29 May 2018); Kampong Cham (10 May, 11 May, 5 June 2018); Kampot (18 May 2018; 6 June 2018), Kampong Chhnang (30 May 2018; 6 June 2018), Kandal (13 and 21 May 2018), and Takeo (17 and 18 May 2018). Members of the diaspora possibly also shared such fears. Nou Leakheana, Executive Director of the Applied Social Research Institute of Cambodia (ASRIC), explained that most of the civil parties in the US who participated with ASRIC's support felt afraid. Notes on file with author, civil party conference Opening of the Trial in ECCC / Case 002: Expectations of Victims, Sunway Hotel, 21 November 2011, Phnom Penh.

18. E.g., interviews with 5 civil parties from the provinces of Prey Veng (12 May 2018), Kampong Cham (12 May 2018), Kampot (18 May 2018), Siem Reap (21 May 2018), and Kandal (22 May 2018). See also interview with a rejected civil party applicant from Kandal Province (21 May 2018).

19. E.g., interview with a group of 5 civil parties, Siem Reap (28 November 2014); interview with 2 civil parties from Kandal (13 May 2018) and Kampong Cham Provinces (10 May 2018).

20. See also the 2006 pilot study assessing fears of potential witnesses in Takeo Province of the Documentation Center of Cambodia (Jansen 2006).

21. Interview with a civil party conducted by colleagues Timothy Williams and Tim Khuochsopheaktra, 28 May 2018, Pursat.

22. Interview, civil party, 17 May 2018, Takeo.

23. Interview, civil party, 13 May 2018, Kandal.

24. Interview conducted by colleagues (Timothy Williams and Somaly Kum), civil party applicant in Cases 003/004, 6 June 2018, Kampot.

25. Interview, civil party in Cases 001 and 002 (male, age 55), 29 November 2014, Siem Reap.

26. Interview, group of civil parties, 28 November 2014, Siem Reap.

27. Interview, group of civil parties.

28. Interview, civil party representative from Siem Reap, 21 May 2018.

29. Interview, village chief (male, age 72), 14 March 2014, Kandal Province.

30. Interview, civil party in Case 002 and applicant in Cases 003 and 004 (male, age 61), 20 February 2014, Kampot Province.

31. Interview, group of civil parties, 28 November 2014, Siem Reap.

32. See also Jansen (2006, 32), noting that members of the political opposition were in a vulnerable position to act as witnesses at the ECCC.

33. For instance, a civil party from Kratie Province who supported the outreach efforts of the NGO Khmer Institute for Democracy for victim participation as early as 2006 explained that she never faced any problems from local authorities. Interview, 5 March 2014, Kratie Province.

34. Interview, civil party representative, 18 May 2018, Takeo Province. See also interview, civil party and former Khmer Rouge soldier, 26 February 2014, Svay Rieng Province.

35. Interview, civil party in Case 001 (female, age 57), Kandal Province, 13 March 2014.

36. Interview, civil party representative, 18 May 2018, Takeo Province (emphasis added).

37. E.g., interview conducted by colleagues (Timothy Williams and Boravin Tann), civil party, 28 May 2018, Pursat Province.

38. E.g., interviews conducted by colleagues (Timothy Williams and Boravin Tann), with a civil party in Kampong Chhnang Province, 30 May 2018, and with a civil party in Pursat Province, 29 May 2018.

39. See, for instance, the testimony of David Chandler: ECCC Trial Chamber, Transcript of the public hearing of 6 August 2009, trial day 55, ECCC Document E1/59.1, pp. 10–11.

40. Interview, participant of NGO transitional justice activities, 20 May 2018, Kampong Cham. See also interview with a female civil party, 21 February 2014, Kampot Province.

41. This was mentioned by one-seventh of the 65 respondents of our survey whom we met for follow-up, qualitative interviews (Williams et al. 2018, 34). In our survey, "taking revenge" was, however, not mentioned widely as motivation for participation as a civil party or complainant: only 2.7 percent or 1.8 percent, respectively, mentioned this as their motivation (Williams et al. 2018, 71).

42. Interview, civil party (female, age 61), 5 March 2014, Kratie Province.

43. Interview, village chief (male, age 72), 14 March 2014, Kandal Province.

44. Interview, international civil party lawyer, 1 February 2018, Phnom Penh.

45. E.g., interview, national civil party lawyer, 5 February 2014.

46. See Civil Party Lead Co-lawyers, 2 October 2017, *Amended Closing Brief in Case 002/02*, ECCC Document E457/6/2/3.

47. Civil Party Lead Co-lawyers, *Amended Closing Brief in Case 002/02*, paras. 965–67.

48. Interview, international civil party lawyer, 1 February 2018, Phnom Penh.

49. Also, interviews with a former cooperative chief and with a local civil society trainer, 24 and 25 February 2014, Prey Veng Province.

50. In the nationwide population-based survey conducted in 2008 by Pham et al. (2009, 28), 49 percent answered that they would feel uncomfortable living in the same community as former Khmer Rouge cadres or if their children married children of former Khmer Rouge cadres, while 31 percent said they would feel uncomfortable attending the same pagoda.

51. In the population-based survey conducted in 2008 by Pham et al. (2009, 29) it was 82.9 percent, and it was 81 percent in the follow-up survey conducted in 2010 by Pham et al. (2011, 30).

52. Interview, international civil society member, 27 January 2011, Phnom Penh.

53. Interview, international civil society member.

54. Interviews, Cambodian judges at the ECCC, 7 and 10 February 2014, Phnom Penh.

55. Interview, Chum Sirath, then vice president of Ksaem Ksan and Case 001 civil party, 27 August 2010, Phnom Penh.

56. E.g., interview, civil party applicant, 25 February 2014, Kampot Province.

57. Also interview, national civil party lawyer, 20 November 2013, Phnom Penh.

58. Interview, civil parties, 13 March 2014, Kandal Province.

59. Interview, civil party (male, age 61), 20 February 2014, Kampot Province.

60. Interview, civil party in Cases 001 and 002 (male, age 58), 20 February 2014, Kampot Province.

61. Interview, international civil party lawyer, 27 January 2011, Phnom Penh.

62. See Sperfeldt (2022) for more details on this initiative, including a critique of how the memorial project was gradually disappropriated from Ksaem Ksan.

63. This is the number of detainees identified by the ECCC in Case 001. Some space was kept on the wall to allow for the inscription of additional names (communication with staff member of the Tuol Sleng Genocide Museum, 25 March 2020).

64. ECCC, 24 August 2009, Transcript of trial proceedings in Case 001, ECCC Document E1/67, pp. 46–47 (emphasis added).

65. Interview, international civil party lawyer, 1 February 2018, Phnom Penh.

66. Interview, civil party, 28 February 2014, Prey Veng Province.

67. Transcript of trial proceedings in Case 002/2, 29 August 2016, E1/465.1, pp. 90–92.

68. See Sirik (2020) and Williams (2019) for a discussion on whether, and how, former Khmer Rouge cadres are able to embrace more complex identities in civil society projects.

69. In our survey, we found a statistically significant impact of the degree of participation at the ECCC on knowledge: the more someone participated in the transitional justice process, the higher their knowledge on the ECCC tended to be (Williams et al. 2018, 61).

70. Interview, civil party representative, 12 May 2018, Prey Veng Province.

71. Interview, civil party in Case 001, 9 May 2018, Siem Reap Province.

72. ECCC Internal Rule 23 and 23 quinquies (revision 9).

73. Supreme Court Chamber, 3 February 2012, Appeal Judgment: Case of Kaing Guek Eav alias Duch, ECCC Document F28, §658–59.

74. Supreme Court Chamber, Appeal Judgment, §658–659.

75. This exclusion was explicitly formulated in the sixth revision of the Internal Rules, with Rule 23 quinquies (1) stating: "These benefits shall not take the form of monetary payments to civil parties."

76. Trial Chamber, 26 July 2010, Case 001 Judgment: Case of Kaing Guek Eav Alias Duch, ECCC Document E188, §661 n.1144.

77. Rule 23 (11), ECCC Internal Rules, Original Version.

78. Karim Kahn, civil party lawyer, ECCC Press Conference, 26 July 2010. Notes on file with author.

79. Rule 12 bis (4), ECCC Internal Rules, Rev. 9.

80. These measures were the memorial built in Tuol Sleng and a program for civil parties who had experienced conflict-related sexual violence funded by the UN Trust Fund.

81. Rule 23 quinquies (3.b), ECCC Internal Rules, Rev. 9.

82. See, e.g., Civil Party Lead Co-lawyers, 12 March 2012, Initial Specification of the Substance of the Awards That the Civil Party Lead Co-lawyers Intend to Seek—Hearing of 19 October 2011, ECCC Document E125/2.

83. See also Pham et al. (2009, 43–44; 2011, 35–37); Poluda, Siv, and Yim (2019); Rudi (2022); and Cohen, Mattes, and Yogendran (2022).

84. Conference on Reparations for Victims of the Khmer Rouge Regime organized jointly by the ECCC Victims Unit and the Cambodian Human Rights Action Committee on 26 November 2008 in Phnom Penh. Notes on file with author. See also quotes in Mohan (2009, 760).

85. Civil party from Phnom Penh, regional civil party forum, 23 December 2013, Phnom Penh (notes on file with author).

86. Traditionally, Cambodians of Buddhist faith use stupas to contain the cremated remains of their family members and pray for their spirits.

87. Civil party from Phnom Penh, regional civil party forum, 23 December 2013, Phnom Penh (notes on file with author).

88. Regional civil party forum, 13 February 2018, Kampong Cham (notes on file with author).

89. There were 353 deaths reported weeks after the incident; however, uncertainties over the total number remained. See CCHR (2011c, 19–20).

90. Interview, international civil society leader, 28 January 2011, Phnom Penh.

91. Interview, civil party representative (male, age 64), 31 January 2016, Kampot Province.

92. Interview, director of a leading Cambodian human rights organization, 7 February 2018, Phnom Penh.

93. Interview, civil party, 21 May 2018, Kandal Province.

94. Interview, civil party.

95. Interview, Helen Jarvis, former head of the ECCC Victims Unit, ECCC Public Affairs section, and advisor to the Cambodian government's Task Force on Khmer Rouge Trials, 5 February 2018, Phnom Penh.

96. Interview, national VSS officer, 3 February 2014, Phnom Penh.

97. E.g., interview, national lead co-lawyer for civil parties, 13 February 2018, Kampong Cham.

98. Interview, international civil party lawyers, 20 November 2013, Phnom Penh.

99. Interview, national civil party lawyer, 7 February 2018, Phnom Penh.

100. Interview, national co-investigating judge You Bunleng, 10 February 2014, Phnom Penh.

101. Field notes, informal discussion with assistant of civil party lawyers, November 2014, Phnom Penh.

102. E.g., interview, national civil party lawyer, 13 February 2018, Kampong Cham.

103. Interview, Helen Jarvis, then-head of the ECCC Public Affairs section, 4 April 2008, Phnom Penh.

104. Interview, international civil party lawyers, 20 November 2013, Phnom Penh.

105. Interview with two civil parties from Kampong Cham Province (10 and 11 May 2018). See also interview conducted by Timothy Williams and Boravin Tann, civil party from Kampong Chhnang Province, 6 June 2018.

106. Interview by Timothy Williams and Boravin Tann, civil party from Kandal Province, 7 June 2018.

107. Interview, civil party representative, 22 May 2018, Kandal Province.

108. Interview, civil party representative, 22 May 2018, Kandal Province.

109. See the section "Civil Party Participation and the ECCC's Limited Focus on 1975–1979" of this chapter for more on Chum Mey.

110. Interview, civil party representative, 21 May 2018, Kampong Thom. See also interview with group of civil parties, 28 November 2014, Siem Reap.

111. Interviews, Chum Mey, 8 February 2016 and 8 February 2014, Phnom Penh.

112. E.g., interview, civil party, 15 March 2014, Phnom Penh.

113. Interview, civil party representative, 21 May 2018, Kampong Thom.

114. Interview, international civil party lawyer, 29 January 2016 and 1 February 2018, Phnom Penh.

115. Interview, civil party representative (male, age 64), 31 January 2016, Kampot Province.

116. Interview, civil party representative (emphasis added).

117. Interview, civil party interviewed on 13 March 2014 (female, age 57), Kandal Province.

118. Informal conversations, national ECCC officers from the VSS and the Witness Support Section, Phnom Penh (notes on file with author).

119. Conference notes on file with author.

120. Conference notes on file with author.

121. Individual and group interviews with civil parties, 28 and 29 November 2014, Siem Reap.

122. Interview, civil party, 31 May 2018, Phnom Penh.

123. Trial Chamber, 16 November 2018, Case 002/02 Judgement, ECCC Document E465, §4464.

124. E.g., interview, civil party, 13 March 2014, Kandal Province.

125. Interview, national civil party lawyer, 30 January 2014, Phnom Penh.

126. Interview, civil party in Case 002 (male, age 57), 30 November 2014, Siem Reap.

127. Interview, national civil party lawyer, 30 January 2014, Phnom Penh.

128. E.g., interviews with a civil party and Buddhist monk, 29 November 2013, Kampot Province; and with a civil party, 13 March 2014, Kandal Province.

129. Interview, civil party, 20 February 2014, Kampot Province.

130. ECCC, 22 November 2011, Transcript of Trial Proceedings, Trial Day 2, Case 002/01, ECCC Document E1/14.1, p.77 (emphasis added).

131. Interview, civil party in Case 002 (male, age 57), 29 November 2014, Siem Reap.

132. Interview, civil party in Case 002 (male, age 61), 30 November 2014, Siem Reap.

133. Interview, national officer at the VSS, 3 February 2014, Phnom Penh.

134. Observations of interventions of civil parties, e.g., at the 2019 conference of the International Associations of Genocide Studies held in Phnom Penh, 17–19 July 2019.

135. Interview, civil party in Case 002 (male, age 57), 30 November 2014, Siem Reap.

136. This is Mohan's (2009, 752–58) analysis regarding Seng Theary, a civil party lawyer and civil party who asked to directly address the ECCC Chambers during the trial proceedings in Case 002, without a lawyer's mediation of a lawyer. Seng Theary withdrew her civil party application after this was refused.

137. Interview, civil party representative, 22 May 2018, Kandal Province.

138. Interview, civil party, 28 February 2014, Prey Veng Province.

139. See also, e.g., interview, village chief, 11 March 2014, Takeo Province.

140. Interview, international civil party lawyer, 1 February 2018, Phnom Penh.

141. Anonymized source, 22 May 2018.

142. Informal conversation with ECCC officer, January 2018, Phnom Penh.

143. Interview, ECCC officer, 2 September 2022.

144. During the drafting process of the ECCC Internal Rules, Cambodian judges also did "not favor victims coming forward as civil parties" (US Embassy, Cambodia 2007; see also Ciorciari and Heindel 2014, 207–10). This led to speculation that among others, their opposition reflected the CPP government's fear that civil party participation would encourage "people to submit new evidence" that could threaten its legitimacy (US Embassy, Cambodia 2007).

145. Interview, coordinator of the German civil peace service program in Cambodia, 13 August 2010, Phnom Penh.

146. See, e.g., Joint Press Release by ASRIC, CHRAC and Ksaem Ksan, 24 March 2013.

147. See, e.g., Porée (2009a, 2009b).

148. Ksaem Ksan Press release, February 24, 2012, "Convicted Person Duch's Apologies: A Trick to Avoid His Conviction by ECCC." A portion of this press release has been reproduced in Jarvis (2014).

149. Anonymized interview, 17 January 2014, Phnom Penh.

150. Personal observation, regional civil party forum, 23 December 2013, Phnom Penh, Cambodia (notes on file with author).

151. Anonymized interview, 17 January 2014, Phnom Penh.

152. Anonymized interview.

153. Anonymized interview.

154. Hun Sen, inauguration speech of achievements in Langka pagoda in Phnom Penh, Phnom Penh, 7 January 2014. Speech on file with author (translated into English by Hin Dilen).

155. E.g., interview, civil party in Case 001, 15 March 2014, Phnom Penh.

156. Anonymized interview, 17 January 2014, Phnom Penh.

157. Interview, civil party Chum Mey, 8 February 2016, 8 February 2014, Phnom Penh.

158. Anonymized source, 15 March 2014.

159. Anonymized source. This assumption was reinforced by the observation that Bou Meng, who did not participate in the protest, seemed to subsequently face increased difficulties in selling his book at Tuol Sleng.

160. Online interview, former Ksaem Ksan member, 9 November 2022.

161. Interview, Ksaem Ksan member, 5 March 2014, Kampong Cham.

162. Interview, civil party in Case 001 and Ksaem Ksan member, 15 March 2013, Phnom Penh.

163. Anonymized source, 15 March 2014.

Chapter 4. Nonparticipation

1. Kent (2016) is here an important exception.

2. According to Diepart and Schoenberger (2016), as of June 2014, only 12,374 families had benefited from the SLC scheme and were allocated a total of 113,167 hectares of land—i.e., only 4 percent of the total area granted as ELCs.

3. Along with his wife, Choeung Sopheap (alias Yeay Pu), Lao Meng Khin is also infamously known as director of Pheapimex. Pheapimex holds land concessions equivalent to 7.4 percent of the total land area in Cambodia. It is believed to be Cambodia's most powerful company and is accused of land grabbing and deforestation in Pursat Province (2007). Both Lao Meng Khin and Choeung Sopheap are close to Hun Sen and his wife, Bun Rany, with Pheapimex believed to be a major donor to the CPP (Un 2019; Hayman and Rith 2007). The lease awarded US$0.60 per square meter to the government, while market value around Boeung Kak lake was estimated to be US$700–1,000 per square meter (S. So 2010, 2).

4. See "Timeline Tracking the Development of Phnom Penh's Boeung Kak's Lake," *Phnom Penh Post*, 29 September 2008.

5. This project was launched in 2002 with the aim of economic development by improving land tenure security for the poor through land titling, with technical and financial support from the World Bank, Finland, and Germany.

6. The husband of one of the respondents from the Borei Keila eviction site was also present during the interview at their home, and at times joined our discussion.

7. Rabé (2021) notes that a sizeable number of Borei Keila residents also benefited from land speculation and abuse of the land sharing rules, such as from the buying and selling of community names and from their role as intermediaries of the developers.

8. The park is literally called "Freedom Park"; however, at the time of these protests it was referred to in Khmer as "Democracy Square," in a renewal of the "Democracy Square" movement that was initiated in the wake of the 1997 grenade attacks and the 1998 elections (see C. Hughes 2003, 196–204).

9. At least 131,500 persons are estimated to have participated in one of the main demonstrations on 21 December 2013 (Murray and Khouth 2014).

10. Field notes, observation of the protests in Phnom Penh, November 2013–4 January 2014.

11. Interview, international human rights researcher at LICADHO, 19 December 2013, Phnom Penh.

12. Field notes, observation of the protests. See also Strangio (2014a, 55).

13. McCargo (2014, 74) speaks of "urbanized villagers" in the context of Thailand and Cambodia to describe the rural embeddedness of most voters and the significance of their urban experiences in their voting behavior.

14. See the introduction for more details on the study's methodology.

15. The selection of these 67 was based on lists of participants provided by the following NGOs: ADHOC, Kdei Karuna, Youth for Peace (YfP) and Youth Resource Development Program (YRDP).

16. Our 2018 survey also showed other reasons for voluntary nonparticipation: the view that participation did not offer any material benefits (15.3 percent thought participating would not bring them any benefits, and 6.8 percent did not apply because they learned that civil parties cannot receive financial reparations) or a belief that the ECCC could not bring justice (9.5 percent). Regarding involuntary nonparticipation, different concerns related to a sense of insecurity also shaped the respondents' decisions not to apply for civil party / complainant participation (11.7 percent were afraid to "give their name," 9.3 percent were unsure whether the ECCC could be trusted, 8.5 percent did not apply because submitting a civil party application was associated with opposition politics, and 6.4 percent had been discouraged from applying by family or community members). See Williams et al (2018).

17. Interview, respondent at the CNRP demonstration (female, age 67), 3 January 2014, Phnom Penh.

18. Interview, community representative from Rattanakiri (male, age 78), 9 February 2014, Phnom Penh.

19. The term "activist" became a term translated into Khmer in the context of struggles of urban communities of Phnom Penh after the 2012 commune elections (Blot 2015).

20. Interview, respondent from Boeung Kak (female, age 51), 26 January 2016, Phnom Penh.

21. Interview, community representative from Rattanakiri (elder man, age unknown), 9 February 2014, Phnom Penh.

22. Interview, respondent from Boeung Kak (female, born in 1965), 22 March 2013, Phnom Penh.

23. Interview, community representative from Rattanakiri (male, age 26), 9 February 2014, Phnom Penh.

24. Interview, international civil party lawyer, 1 February 2018, Phnom Penh. See also Kent (2022).

25. Interview, respondent at the CNRP demonstration (elderly man, age unknown), 4 January 2014, Phnom Penh.

26. Interview, respondent from Boeung Kak (female, born in 1986), 22 March 2013, Phnom Penh.

27. Interview with Venerable Luon Sovath, 1 February 2016, Phnom Penh.

28. Lawyers earned the most trust (55.8 percent for Cambodian lawyers, 49.7 percent for international lawyers), followed by the judges (54.4 percent for Cambodian judges, 49 percent for international judges) and the prosecutors (52.8 percent for Cambodian prosecutors, 44.1 percent for international prosecutors), while the Victim Support Section—an office staffed and run by national staff—was slightly less trusted (44.2 percent). See Williams et al. (2018).

29. During the qualitative follow-up interviews, two respondents explicitly reported having felt insecure to provide their genuine answers during the earlier survey and explained that their answers in the follow-up interviews reflected their true opinions (i.e., that they trusted the international staff and not the national ECCC staff). Alternative explanations for the discrepancy in our findings included the passage of time, or the background of the interviewers. Since a foreign researcher was present for the qualitative interviews but not for the survey conducted by a Cambodian-only team, respondents might have wanted to present an answer that appeared more favorable to the foreign researcher—e.g., mentioning trusting the international side of the Court more—to please or not offend them when this may not have been reflecting their genuine views. Finally, there is also always the possibility that interviewees simply changed their mind between the survey and the in-depth interviews that were conducted a few months later.

30. Interview with Nget Khun, respondent from Boeung Kak, 25 January 2016, Phnom Penh.

31. See next section for further discussions on framing the Hun Sen regime as a communist regime.

32. Interview, respondent at the CNRP demonstration (elder man, age unknown), 3 January 2014, Phnom Penh.

33. Interview, respondent at the CNRP demonstration (male, age unknown), 4 January 2014, Phnom Penh.

34. Interview, respondent at the CNRP demonstration (male, age 60), 3 January 2014, Phnom Penh.

35. Interview, Nget Khun, 25 January 2016, Phnom Penh.

36. Interview, community representative from Rattanakiri (male, age 26), 9 February 2014, Phnom Penh.

37. Observation of the 20 May 2009 celebrations at the Choeung Ek memorial site (notes on file with author).

38. Comment by Katrina Natale, who worked as international consultant in the Lead Co-lawyer Section from 2010 to 2015, in Sok (2020).

39. Interview, civil party lawyers, 30 January 2014 and 1 February 2018, Phnom Penh. See also K. Sok (2020).

40. See, e.g., the translated and published 7 January speeches of Prime Minister Hun Sen, from 2017 to 2020, at https://pressocm.gov.kh/en/archives/category/documentary/speech/.

41. Heng Samrin, 7 January 2014, Cambodia Marks the 35th Anniversary of the January 7 Victory Day, Phnom Penh. Speech on file with author (translated into English by Hin Dilen).

42. In addition to this key feature of the CPP's self-legitimation discourses, scholars have noted the CPP use of selected rhetorical tropes, including those of modernity and development, which does not exclude the mobilization of contradictory rhetorical tropes such as that of reform and tradition. See C. Hughes (2013).

43. Hun Sen, 8 January 2019, Speech Samdech Techo Hun Sen to the Meeting in Commemoration of the 40th Anniversary of the 7 January Victory (7 January 1979–7 January 2019), available in English at https://pressocm.gov.kh/archives/46468.

44. Hun Sen, Speech.

45. Regional civil party forum, 23 December 2013, Phnom Penh (notes on file with author).

46. Interview with Nget Khun, 22 March 2013, Phnom Penh.

47. Interview, community representative from Rattanakiri (male, born 1936), 9 February 2014, Phnom Penh.

48. Interview, community representative from Rattanakiri (elder man, age unknown), 9 February 2014, Phnom Penh.

49. Interview, community representative from Rattanakiri (male, age 26), 9 February 2014, Phnom Penh.

50. In his research on geographies of violence in Cambodia, Springer (2013) has encountered similar analogies between the Khmer Rouge regime and contemporary political violence, including the observation that the difference with the Khmer Rouge regime mainly lies in the singling out of the poor in contemporary political violence. See also similar accounts made by female activists from Boeung Kak Lake in Brickell (2014).

51. Interview, Nget Khun, 22 March 2013, Phnom Penh.

52. Interview, respondent from Boeung Kak (female, born in 1965), 22 March 2013, Phnom Penh.

53. Interview, respondent from Borei Keila (female, born in 1971), 26 January 2016, Phnom Penh.

54. The affective expression *thoek dey khmaer* (ទឹកដីខ្មែរ) is often used to speak of the Cambodian national territory and has a patriotic connotation (Blot and Guillou 2016, 162).

55. Personal interview, respondent at CNRP demonstrations (female, born in 1947), 3 January 2014, Phnom Penh. During the conversation, this respondent also regretted the loss of territory to "the Vietnamese," thereby echoing the nationalism and anti-Vietnamese sentiments that featured centrally in the electoral rhetoric of the CNRP (Strangio 2014a).

56. Interview, respondent at CNRP demonstrations (female, born in 1947), 3 January 2014, Phnom Penh.

57. Interview with Nget Khun, 22 March 2013, Phnom Penh.

58. Interview, respondent at the CNRP demonstration (male, age 60), 3 January 2014, Phnom Penh.

59. Interview, respondent at the CNRP demonstration (elder man, age unknown), 4 January 2014, Phnom Penh.

60. Interview, Son Chhay (formerly Member of the National Assembly and Party Whip for the Sam Rainsy Party, at the time of interview Chief Party Whip and Member of the National Assembly for the CNRP), 20 March 2013, Phnom Penh.

61. Interview, respondent at the CNRP demonstration (male, age 60), 3 January 2014, Phnom Penh.

62. Interview, community representative from Rattanakiri (male, born 1962), 9 February 2014, Phnom Penh.

63. Interview, community representative from Boeung Kak (female, age 30), 29 January 2016, Phnom Penh.

64. Interview, respondent from Borei Keila (female, born 1947), 27 January 2016, Phnom Penh.

65. Interview, community representative from Rattanakiri (elder man, age unknown), 9 February 2014, Phnom Penh.

66. Interview, Venerable Luon Sovath, 1 February 2016, Phnom Penh.

67. Interview, community representative from Rattanakiri (male, age 51), 9 February 2014, Phnom Penh.

68. Interview, respondent at the CNRP demonstration (male, age 60), 3 January 2014, Phnom Penh.

Conclusion

1. At the time of writing, the response from the prosecutor of the International Criminal Court on the complaint related to crimes committed in the context of land grabbing in Cambodia since 2002 submitted by Richard Rogers of Global Diligence LLP, with the support of the International Federation for Human Rights (FIDH) and

Global Witness, is still pending. It remains to be seen whether pursuing the issue through this legal avenue will prove useful to the involved victims.

2. In January 2021, civil parties' lawyers, informally knew of a total of 312 civil parties out of the 3,869 civil parties in Case 002, although they estimated that real numbers were probably much higher. See Civil Party Lead Co-lawyers, 4 January 2021, Civil Party Lead Co-Lawyers' Response to Khieu Samphân's Appeal of the Case 002/02 Trial Judgement, ECCC Document F54/2.

Works Cited

Abe, Toshihiro, ed. 2019. *The Khmer Rouge Trials in Context.* Chiang Mai: Silkworm Books.

Abu-Lughod, Lila. 1990. "The Romance of Resistance." *American Ethnologist* 17 (1): 41–55.

ADHOC. 2012. "Residents at Borei Keila in Phnom Penh Forcibly Evicted." Cambodian Human Rights and Development Association, 6 January. https://www.adhoccambodia.org/force-evicted-the-people-in-borey-key-la-in-phnom-penh/.

———. 2014. "Report: Land Situation in Cambodia in 2013." Cambodian Human Rights and Development Association, 27 May. https://www.adhoccambodia.org/km/report-land-situation-in-cambodia-in-2013-2/.

Affonço, Denise. 2005. *La digue des veuves.* Paris: Presses de la Renaissance.

Agger, Inger. 2015. "Calming the Mind: Healing after Mass Atrocity in Cambodia." *Transcultural Psychiatry* 52 (4): 543–60.

Ainley, Kirsten. 2013. "Transitional Justice in Cambodia: The Coincidence of Power and Principle." In *Transitional Justice in the Asia Pacific*, edited by Renee Jeffery, 125–56. Cambridge: Cambridge University Press.

———. 2014. "Justifying Justice: Verdicts at the ECCC." *Justice in Conflict* (blog), 16 September. http://eprints.lse.ac.uk/60175/.

Akashi, Yasushi. 2012. "An Assessment of the United Nations Transitional Authority in Cambodia (UNTAC)." In *Cambodia: Progress and Challenges since 1991*, edited by Pou Sothirak, Geoff Wade, and Mark Hong, 153–65. Singapore: Institute of Southeast Asian Studies.

Alcoff, Linda, and Laura Gray. 1993. "Survivor Discourse: Transgression or Recuperation?" *Signs: Journal of Women in Culture and Society* 18 (2): 260–90.

Amnesty International. 2012. "Cambodia: "Khmer Rouge Judgment Welcome, but Raises Human Rights Concerns." Press release, 3 February. https://www.amnesty.org/en/latest/press-release/2012/02/cambodia-khmer-rouge-judgment-welcome-raises-human-rights-concerns-2012-02/.

An-Na'im, Abdullahi A. 2013. "Editorial Note." *International Journal of Transitional Justice* 7 (2): 197–204.

Anstis, Siena. 2012. "Using Law to Impair the Rights and Freedoms of Human Rights Defenders." *Journal of Human Rights Practice* 4 (3): 312–33.

Arnold, Dennis. 2017. "Civil Society, Political Society and Politics of Disorder in Cambodia." *Political Geography* 60 (September): 23–33.

Arnold, Dennis, and Dae-oup Chang. 2017. "Trade Unions and Labor Rights in Cambodia." In *Routledge Handbook of Contemporary Cambodia*, edited by Katherine Brickell and Simon Springer, 191–201. Abingdon: Routledge.

Arnould, Valerie. 2016. "Transitional Justice in Peacebuilding: Dynamics of Contestation in the DRC." *Journal of Intervention and Statebuilding* 10 (3): 321–38.

Arthur, Paige. 2009. "How 'Transitions' Reshaped Human Rights: A Conceptual History of Transitional Justice." *Human Rights Quarterly*, no. 31: 321–67.

Article 19. 2013. "Cambodia: Law against Non-recognition of the Crimes Committed during Democratic Kampuchea." June. http://www.article19.org/data/files/medialibrary/37127/13-06-27-cambodia-LA.pdf.

Aun, Chhengpor. 2016. "A Decade Later, Khmer Rouge Tribunal Leaving a Mixed Legacy." *Voice of America Cambodia*, 21 June. https://www.voacambodia.com/a/a-decade-later-khmer-rouge-tribunal-leaving-a-mixed-legacy/3384074.html.

Baaz, Mikael, and Mona Lilja. 2016. "Using International Criminal Law to Resist Transitional Justice: Legal Rupture in the ECCC." Edited by Briony Jones and Thomas Brudholm. *Conflict and Society: Advances in Research* 2 (1): 142–59.

———. 2017. "(Re)categorization as Resistance: Civil Society Mobilizations around the Preah Vihear Temple." *International Journal of Politics, Culture, and Society* 30:295–310.

Baines, Erin. 2009. "Complex Political Perpetrators: Reflections on Dominic Ongwen." *Journal of Modern African Studies* 47 (2): 163–91.

Baliga, Ananth, and Khouth Sophak Chakrya. 2017. "Boeung Kak: A Disastrous Decade." *Phnom Penh Post*, 3 February.

Bates, Alex. 2010. "Transitional Justice in Cambodia: Analytical Report." Atlas Project, October. https://www.yumpu.com/en/document/read/7421101/transitional-justice-in-cambodia-analytical-report-atlas.

Beban, Alice, Laura Schoenberger, and Vanessa Lamb. 2020. "Pockets of Liberal Media in Authoritarian Regimes: What the Crackdown on Emancipatory Spaces Means for Rural Social Movements in Cambodia." *Journal of Peasant Studies* 47 (1): 95–115.

Beban, Alice, Sokbunthoeun So, and Kheang Un. 2017. "From Force to Legitimation: Rethinking Land Grabs in Cambodia." *Development & Change* 48 (3): 590–612.

Becker, Elisabeth. 1989. *Les larmes du Cambodge.* Paris: France Loisirs.

Bell, Christine. 2009. "Transitional Justice, Interdisciplinarity and the State of the 'Field' or 'Non-Field.'" *International Journal of Transitional Justice* 3 (1): 5–27.

Bernath, Julie. 2011. "La justice pénale à l'épreuve du totalitarisme: Les Chambres Extraordinaires au sein des Tribunaux Cambodgiens." MA thesis, Institut d'Études Politiques de Paris.

———. 2016. "'Complex Political Victims' in the Aftermath of Mass Atrocity." *International Journal of Transitional Justice* 10 (1): 46–66.
———. 2018. "The Politics of Difference in Transitional Justice: Genocide and the Construction of Victimhood at the Khmer Rouge Tribunal." *Journal of Intervention and Statebuilding* 12 (3): 367–84.
Biddulph, Robin. 2014. "Cambodia's Land Management and Administration Project." 86th ed. WIDER Working Paper. Helsinki: World Institute for Development Economics Research, UN University. https://www.wider.unu.edu/sites/default/files/wp2014-086.pdf.
Bird, Annie R. 2015. *US Foreign Policy on Transitional Justice.* Oxford: Oxford University Press.
Blot, Julie. 2015. "A Social Geography Approach to Understanding the 'Right to the City' in Phnom Penh." Presented at the Human Sciences Encounters Phnom Penh Podcast, Phnom Penh, 30 September. https://shs-encounters-cambodia.ird.fr/content/view/full/213225.
Blot, Julie, and Anne Yvonne Guillou. 2016. "Cambodge." In *L'Asie du Sud-Est 2016: Bilan, enjeux et perspectives*, edited by Abigaël Pesses, 160–88. Bangkok: Irasec et Les Indes Savantes.
Bouris, Erica. 2007. *Complex Political Victims.* Bloomfield, CT: Kumarian Press.
Braaf, Rochelle. 2014. "Sexual Violence against Ethnic Minorities during the Khmer Rouge Regime." Cambodian Defenders Project, Phnom Penh, Cambodia, March. http://gbvkr.org/wp-content/uploads/2014/05/Research-Report.pdf.
Brickell, Katherine. 2014. "'The Whole World Is Watching': Intimate Geopolitics of Forced Eviction and Women's Activism in Cambodia." *Annals of the Association of American Geographers* 104 (6): 1256–72.
Brown, Michael. 1996. "On Resisting Resistance." *American Anthropologist* 98 (4): 729–35.
Bruch, Elizabeth. 2010. "Hybrid Courts: Examining Hybridity through a Post-colonial Lens." *Boston University International Law Journal* 28 (1): 1–38.
Buckley-Zistel, Susanne, and Anika Oettler. 2011. "Was Bedeutet: Transitional Justice?" In *Nach Krieg, Gewalt und Repression: Vom schwierigen Umgang mit der Vergangenheit*, edited by Susanne Buckley-Zistel and Thomas Kater, 21–38. Baden: Nomos Verlagsgesellschaft mbH & Co KG.
Bugalski, Nathalie, and Thuon Ratha. 2014. "A Human Rights Impact Assessment of Hoang Anh Gia Lai's Economic Land Concessions in Ratanakiri, Cambodia." Equitable Cambodia and Inclusive Development International. https://www.inclusivedevelopment.net/wp-content/uploads/2020/05/rubberhriawebfinalcompressed.pdf.
Bultmann, Daniel. 2019. *The Social Order of Postconflict Transformation in Cambodia: Insurgent Pathways to Peace.* Lanham, MD: Lexington Books.
———. 2020. "Wo sind all die roten Khmer geblieben?" *Blickwechsel, Stiftung Asienhaus*, May.

Carothers, Thomas. 2002. "The End of the Transition Paradigm." *Journal of Democracy* 13 (1): 5–21.

CAS and World Bank. 2006. *Justice for the Poor? An Exploratory Study of Collective Grievances over Land and Local Governance in Cambodia.* Phnom Penh: Center for Advanced Studies (CAS); Washington, DC: World Bank.

Caswell, Michelle. 2014. *Archiving the Unspeakable: Silence, Memory, and the Photographic Record in Cambodia.* Critical Human Rights. Madison: University of Wisconsin Press.

CCHR. 2011a. "Fact Sheet: Boeung Kak." October. CCHR Case Study Series. http://www.cchrcambodia.org/admin/media/factsheet/factsheet/english/CCHR%20Case%20Study%20Fact%20Sheet%20-%20Boeung%20Kak%20%28ENG%29.pdf.

———. 2011b. "Fact Sheet: Loun Sovath." July. CCHR Case Study Series. http://www.cchrcambodia.org/admin/media/factsheet/factsheet/english/CCHR_Case_Study_Factsheet_Loun_Sovath_en.pdf.

———. 2011c. "The Koh Pich Tragedy: One Year on, Questions Remain." https://cchrcambodia.org/admin/media/report/report/english/CCHR%20Report%20-%20The%20Koh%20Pich%20Tragedy.%20One%20Year%20on,%20Questions%20Remain%20(ENG).pdf.

———. 2012. "Fact Sheet: The Continuing Borei Keila Tragedy." May. CCHR Case Study Series. http://cchrcambodia.org/admin/media/factsheet/factsheet/english/2012_05_25_CCHR_Case_Study_Fact_Sheet_The_Continuing_Borei_Keila_Tragedy_ENG.pdf.

———. 2016. "Access to Collective Land Titles for Indigenous Communities in Cambodia." February. http://cchrcambodia.org/admin/media/report/report/english/2016_02_11_CCHR_Report_Access_to_Collective_Land_Titles_%28ENG%29.pdf.

Chak, Sopheap. 2020. "'An All-Time Low': Cambodia's Search for Peace and Democracy Continues." *Southeast Asia Globe*, 15 September. https://southeastasiaglobe.com/cambodias-peace-and-democracy/.

Chan, Muyhong. 2014. "Questions Raised over Land Sale at Lakeside." *Phnom Penh Post*, 24 June.

Chandler, David. 1991. *The Tragedy of Cambodian History.* New Haven, CT: Yale University Press.

———. 2000. "Will There Be a Trial for the Khmer Rouge?" *Ethics and International Affairs* 14 (1): 67–82.

———. 2002. *S-21, ou, Le crime impuni des Khmers rouges.* Paris: Editions Autrement.

———. 2008. "Cambodia Deals with Its Past: Collective Memory, Demonisation and Induced Amnesia." *Totalitarian Movements and Political Religions* 9 (2–3): 355–69.

———. 2018. *A History of Cambodia.* 4th ed. New York: Routledge.

Cheang, Sopheng. 2010. "Cambodian PM Says No Punishment for Fatal Stampede." *San Diego Union-Tribune*, 29 November.

Chhim, Kristina. 2012. "'Pacifying Vindictiveness by Not Being Vindictive': Do Memory Initiatives in Cambodia Have a Role in Addressing Questions of Impunity?" Impunity Watch. https://www.impunitywatch.org/publications/pacificying-vindic

tiveness-by-not-being-vindictive-do-memory-initiatives-in-cambodia-have-a-role-in-addressing-questions-of-impunity/.

Chhim, Sotheara. 2013. "Baksbat (Broken Courage): A Trauma-Based Cultural Syndrome in Cambodia." *Medical Anthropology* 32 (2): 160–73.

———. 2014. "A Place for Baksbat (Broken Courage) in Forensic Psychiatry at the ECCC." *Journal of Psychiatry, Psychology and the Law* 21 (2): 286–96.

Chhorn, Chansy. 2013. "Kem Sokha Summonsed over Tuol Sleng Comments." *Cambodia Daily*, 24 June.

Chigas, George. 2000. "The Politics of Defining Justice after the Cambodian Genocide." *Journal of Genocide Research* 2 (2): 245–65.

Christensen, Mikkel Jarle. 2019. "The Judiciary of International Criminal Law: Double Decline and Practical Turn." ICourts Working Paper Series 166.

Christensen, Mikkel Jarle, and Astrid Kjeldgaard-Pedersen. 2018. "Competing Perceptions of Hybrid Justice: International v. National in the ECCC." *International Criminal Law Review* 18 (1): 127–53.

Chum, Mey. 2012. *Survivor: The Triumph of an Ordinary Man in the Khmer Rouge Genocide.* Documentation Series no. 18. Phnom Penh: Documentation Center of Cambodia.

Chy, Terith. 2009. "A Thousand Voices." *Searching for the Truth*, March 5. Documentation Center of Cambodia. http://www.genocide-watch.com/images/Cambodia_09_03_05_A_Thousand_Voices.pdf.

Ciorciari, John D. 2009. "History and Politics behind the Khmer Rouge Trials." In *On Trial: The Khmer Rouge Accountability Process*, edited by John D. Ciorciari and Anne Heindel, 33–84. Phnom Penh: Documentation Center of Cambodia.

———. 2010. "The Duch Verdict." *Cambodia Tribunal Monitor*, 28 July. https://cambodiatribunal.org/2010/07/28/the-duch-verdict/.

Ciorciari, John D., and Anne Heindel. 2013. "Experiments in International Criminal Justice: Lessons from the Khmer Rouge Tribunal." *Michigan Journal of International Law* 35 (2): 369–442.

———. 2014. *Hybrid Justice.* Ann Arbor: University of Michigan Press.

Clark, Phil. 2018. *Distant Justice: The Impact of the International Criminal Court on African Politics.* Cambridge: Cambridge University Press.

Cohen, David, Melanie Hyde, and Penelope Van Tuyl. 2015. "A Well-Reasoned Opinion? Critical Analysis of the First Case against the Alleged Senior Leaders of the Khmer Rouge (Case 002/01)." Honolulu: East-West Center. https://www.eastwestcenter.org/publications/well-reasoned-opinion-critical-analysis-the-first-case-against-the-alleged-senior.

Cohen, David, Daniel Mattes, and Sangeetha Yogendran. 2022. "Report on the May 2022 Workshop on Victim-Related Activities during the Implementation of the ECCC's Residual Mandate." ECCC, 15 July. https://www.eccc.gov.kh/en/publication/report-may-2022-workshop-victim-related-activities-during-implementation-ecccs-residual.

Coughlan, John, Sana Ghouse, and Richard Smith. 2012. "The Legacy of the Khmer Rouge Tribunal: Maintaining the Status Quo of Cambodia's Legal and Judicial System." *Amsterdam Law Forum* 4 (2): 16–35.

CPK Party Centre. 1988. "The Party's Four-Year Plan to Build Socialism in All Fields, 1977–1980." In *Pol Pot Plans the Future: Confidential Leadership Documents from Democratic Kampuchea, 1976–1977*, translated and edited by David Chandler, Ben Kiernan, and Chanthou Boua, 36–118. New Haven, CT: Yale Center for International and Area Studies.

Crothers, Lauren. 2013. "KR Tribunal Stopped by Strike Over Salaries." *Cambodia Daily*, 6 March.

———. 2014. "Prosecutor Seeks Case 004 Rape Investigation." *Cambodia Daily*, 25 April.

Cruvellier, Thierry. 2010. "Cambodia: Reflections on the *Duch* Trial." *Crimes of War Project* (blog), 26 July. Archived website (US Library of Congress). https://www.loc.gov/item/lcwaN0021886/.

———. 2011. *Le maître des aveux.* Paris: Gallimard.

Das, Veena. 2007. *Life and Words: Violence and the Descent into the Ordinary.* Berkeley: University of California Press.

DeFalco, Randle. 2011. "Accounting for Famine at the ECCC: The Crimes against Humanity of Extermination, Inhumane Acts and Persecution." *International Journal of Transitional Justice* 5 (1): 142–58.

———. 2018. "The Uncertain Relationship between International Criminal Law Accountability and the Rule of Law in Post-atrocity States: Lessons from Cambodia." *Fordham International Law Journal* 42 (1): 1–60.

———. 2022. *Invisible Atrocities.* Cambridge: Cambridge University Press.

DeFalco, Randle, and Savina Sirik. 2022. "The Fluctuating Visibility of Everyday Violence in Khmer Rouge Era Cambodia." *Southern California Interdisciplinary Law Journal* 31:217–143.

De Langis, Theresa. 2014a. "A Missed Opportunity, a Last Hope? Prosecuting Sexual Crimes under the Khmer Rouge Regime." *Cambodia Law and Policy Journal* 2 (July): 39–43.

———. 2014b. "This Is Now the Most Important Trial in the World: A New Reading of Code #6, the Role against Immoral Offenses under the Khmer Rouge Regime." *Cambodia Law and Policy Journal* 3 (December): 61–78.

De Nike, Howard J., John Quigley, and Kenneth J. Robinson, eds. 2000. *Genocide in Cambodia: Documents from the Trial of Pol Pot and Ieng Sary.* Philadelphia: University of Pennsylvania Press.

Destrooper, Tine. 2018a. "Neglecting Social and Economic Rights Violations in Transitional Justice: Long-Term Effects on Accountability; Empirical Findings from the ECCC." *Journal of Current Southeast Asian Affairs* 37 (2): 95–124.

———. 2018b. "The Performance of Justice? Scenic Anthropology and the Role of Victims in Courtrooms." *International Journal for the Rule of Law, Courtroom Procedures, Judicial Linguistics and Legal English* 2 (1): 108–26.

De Vos, Christian, Sara Kendall, and Carsten Stahn, eds. 2015. *Contested Justice: The Politics and Practice of International Criminal Court Interventions.* Cambridge: Cambridge University Press.

Diamond, Larry. 2002. "Elections without Democracy: Thinking about Hybrid Regimes." *Journal of Democracy* 13 (2): 21–35.

Di Certo, Bridget. 2012. "Judge Decries 003, 004 'Sabotage.'" *Phnom Penh Post,* 22 March.

Dickinson, Laura A. 2003. "The Promise of Hybrid Courts." *American Journal of International Law* 97 (2): 295–310.

Diepart, Jean-Christophe, Chanrith Ngin, and Il Oeur. 2019. "Struggles for Life: Smallholder Farmers' Resistance and State Land Relations in Contemporary Cambodia." *Journal of Current Southeast Asian Affairs* 38 (1): 10–32.

Diepart, Jean-Christophe, and Laura Schoenberger. 2016. "Concessions in Cambodia: Governing Profits, Extending State Power and Enclosing Resources from the Colonial Era to the Present." In *The Handbook of Contemporary Cambodia,* edited by Katherine Brickell, Simon Springer, and Sok Udom Deth, 157–68. New York: Routledge.

Doyle, Michael W. 1995. *UN Peacekeeping in Cambodia.* Boulder, CO: Lynne Rienner.

Drumbl, Mark. 2012. "Die Überwindung der Opferrolle: Zum Bild des Kindersoldaten im internationalen Recht." *Zeitschrift für Friedens- und Konfliktforschung* 1 (2): 249–74.

Dunlap, Bridgette. 2014. "The Rule of Law without Lawyers: American Legal Reformers and the Cambodian Lawyer Shortage." *SSRN Electronic Journal.* https://papers.ssrn.com/sol3/papers.cfm?abstract_id=2424255.

Dy, Khamboly. 2007. *A History of Democratic Kampuchea (1975–1979).* Phnom Penh: Documentation Center of Cambodia.

Ear, Sophal. 2009. "Cambodian 'Justice.'" *Wall Street Journal,* 1 September.

ECCC. 2022a. "Quarterly Progress Report, 1 July–30 September 2022." 30 September. https://www.eccc.gov.kh/en/quarterly-progress-report-data-july-september-2022.

———. 2022b. "Summary of Contributions to Date by Donors as at 31 October 2022." 31 October. https://www.eccc.gov.kh/en/about-eccc/finances/summary-contributions-date-donors-31-october-2022.

Edwards, Penny. 2007. *Cambodge: The Cultivation of a Nation, 1860–1945.* Honolulu: University of Hawai'i Press.

Eisenbruch, Maurice. 2018. "The Cloak of Impunity in Cambodia II: Justice." *International Journal of Human Rights* 22 (6): 822–43.

Elander, Maria. 2012. "The Victim's Address: Expressivism and the Victim at the ECCC." *International Journal of Transitional Justice* 7 (1): 95–115.

———. 2018a. *Figuring Victims in International Criminal Justice: The Case of the Khmer Rouge Tribunal.* New York: Routledge.

———. 2018b. "Prosecuting the Khmer Rouge Marriages." *Australian Feminist Law Journal* 42 (1): 163–75.

Emde, Sina. 2014. "Emotion, Erinnerung und Gewalt in Kambodscha zwischen staatlicher Politik und lokaler Verarbeitung." In *Sprachen der Emotion: Kultur, Kunst, Gesellschaft*, edited by Gunter Gebauer and Markus Edler, 290–315. Frankfurt: Campus Verlag.

Escobar, Arturo. 1984. "Discourse and Power in Development." *Alternatives* 10 (3): 377–400.

Etcheson, Craig. 1984. *The Rise and Demise of Democratic Kampuchea.* London: Routledge.

———. 2004. "Politics of Genocide Justice in Cambodia." In *Internationalized Criminal Courts and Tribunals: Sierra Leone, East Timor, Kosovo and Cambodia*, edited by Cesare P. R. Romano, André Nollkaemper, and Jann K. Kleffner, 181–205. New York: Oxford University Press.

———. 2005. *After the Killing Fields: Lessons from the Cambodian Genocide.* Westport, CT: Praeger.

———. 2006. "A 'Fair and Public Trial.'" In "The Extraordinary Chambers," special issue, *Justice Initiatives* (Spring): 7–24.

———. 2019. *Extraordinary Justice: Law, Politics, and the Khmer Rouge Tribunals.* New York: Columbia University Press.

Ewick, Patricia, and Susan S. Silbey. 1998. *The Commonplace of Law: Stories from Everyday Life.* Language and Legal Discourse. Chicago: University of Chicago Press.

Fawthrop, Tom. 2013. "Khmer Rouge Leader Ieng Sary Had US$20m in Hong Kong Account." *South China Morning Post*, 31 March, sec. News.

———. 2017. "Cambodia's Khmer Rouge Tribunal: Mission Accomplished?" *Diplomat*, 17 July.

Fawthrop, Tom, and Helen Jarvis. 2004. *Getting Away with Genocide? Elusive Justice and the Khmer Rouge Tribunal.* London: Pluto Press.

FIDH, LICADHO, and ADHOC. 2015. "Shadow Report for the UN Human Rights Committee's Consideration of the Second Report of Cambodia." 17–18 March. http://www.licadho-cambodia.org/reports/files/204FIDH-LICADHO-ADHOC-ShadowReportICCPR2014-English.pdf.

Fletcher, Laurel E. 2015. "Refracted Justice: The Imagined Victim and the International Criminal Court." In *Contested Justice: The Politics and Practice of International Criminal Court Interventions*, edited by Christian De Vos, Sara Kendall, and Carsten Stahn, 302–25. Cambridge: Cambridge University Press.

Forum-Asia, Human Rights Watch, Witness, Amnesty International, Civil Rights Defenders, Southeast Asian Press Alliance, Freedom House, and Frontline Defenders. 2012. "Cambodia: Joint Letter Regarding Boeung Kak Lake Activists." 29 May. https://www.hrw.org/node/246438/printable/print.

Fox, Jefferson M., and Mark Poffenberger. 2013. "Land Use and Forest Change in Ratanakiri." In *Cambodia's Contested Forest Domain: The Role of Community Forestry in the New Millennium*, edited by Mark Poffenberger, 103–28. Honolulu: University of Hawai'i Press.

Franzki, Hannah, and Maria Carolina Olarte. 2014. "Understanding the Political Economy of Transitional Justice." In *Transitional Justice Theories*, edited by Susanne Buckley-Zistel, Teresa Koloma Beck, Christian Braun, and Friederike Mieth, 201–21. New York: Routledge.

Frieson, Kate. 1996. "The Politics of Getting the Vote in Cambodia." In *Politics, Propaganda and Violence in Cambodia: Democratic Transition under United Nations Peace-Keeping*, edited by Steve Heder and Judy Ledgerwood, 183–207. London: M. E. Sharpe.

Fujii, Lee Ann. 2010. "Shades of Truth and Lies: Interpreting Testimonies of War and Violence." *Journal of Peace Research* 47 (2): 231–41.

Future Forum. 2017. "Moving beyond the January 7 Narratives." https://www.futureforum.asia/.

Ghai, Yash. 2010. "Access to Land and Justice." In *Marginalized Communities and Access to Justice*, edited by Yash Ghai and Jill Cottrell, 37–59. New York: Routledge.

Gidley, Rebecca. 2018. "Trading a Theatre for Military Headquarters: Locating the Khmer Rouge Tribunal." *Contemporary Southeast Asia* 40 (2): 279–300.

———. 2019. *Illiberal Transitional Justice and the ECCC.* Palgrave Studies in the History of Genocide. Cham, Switzerland: Palgrave Macmillan.

Gillison, Douglas. 2010. "KRT Begins Investigation of Five New Regime Suspects." *Cambodia Daily*, 8 June.

———. 2011. "UN Legal Team Walk Out on Stymied KR Cases." *Cambodia Daily*, 13 June.

Giry, Stéphanie. 2012. "Necessary Scapegoats? The Making of the Khmer Rouge Tribunal." *New York Review of Books*, 23 July.

———. 2014. "The Genocide That Wasn't." *New York Review of Books*, 25 August.

Global Diligence. 2014. "Communication under Article 15 of the Rome Statute of the International Criminal Court: The Commission of Crimes against Humanity in Cambodia, July 2002 to Present." https://www.globaldiligence.com/projects-and-news/2020/cambodia-land-grabbing-icc-case.

Global Witness. 2007. "Cambodia's Family Trees: Illegal Logging and the Stripping of Public Assets by Cambodia's Elite." June. Washington, DC: Global Witness. https://www.globalwitness.org/en/reports/cambodias-family-trees/.

———. 2013. "Rubber Barons: How Vietnamese Companies and International Financiers Are Driving a Land Grabbing Crisis in Cambodia and Laos." May. London: Global Witness. https://www.globalwitness.org/en/campaigns/land-deals/rubberbarons/.

———. 2015. "The Cost of Luxury: Cambodia's Illegal Trade in Precious Wood with China." February. London: Global Witness. https://landportal.org/node/36091.

———. 2016. "Hostile Takeover: The Corporate Empire of Cambodia's Ruling Family." July. London: Global Witness. https://www.globalwitness.org/en/reports/hostile-takeover/.

Gottesman, Evan. 2004. *Cambodia after the Khmer Rouge.* Chiang Mai, Thailand: Silkworm Books.

Gready, Paul, and Simon Robins. 2017. "Rethinking Civil Society and Transitional Justice: Lessons from Social Movements and 'New' Civil Society." *International Journal of Human Rights* 21 (7): 956–75.

Grey, Rosemary. 2019. "Seen and Unseen: Sexual and Gender-Based Crimes in the Khmer Rouge Tribunal's Case 002/02 Judgment." *Australian Journal of Human Rights* 25 (3): 466–87.

Guillou, Anne Yvonne. 2012. "An Alternative Memory of the Khmer Rouge Genocide." *South East Asia Research* 20 (2): 207–26.

Hall, John A. 2009. "Court Administration at the ECCC." In *On Trial: The Khmer Rouge Accountability Process*, edited by John D. Ciorciari and Anne Heindel. Phnom Penh: Documentation Center of Cambodia.

Hamber, Brandon, and Richard Wilson. 2002. "Symbolic Closure through Memory, Reparation and Revenge in Post-conflict Societies." *Journal of Human Rights* 1 (1): 35–53.

Hammarberg, Thomas. 2001. "How the Khmer Rouge Tribunal Was Agreed." *Searching for the Truth*, October. Documentation Center of Cambodia. http://d.dccam.org/Tribunal/Analysis/How_Khmer_Rouge_Tribunal.htm.

Hansen, Thomas Obel. 2014. "The Vertical and Horizontal Expansion of Transitional Justice." In *Transitional Justice Theories*, edited by Susanne Buckley-Zistel, Teresa Koloma Beck, Christian Braun, and Friederike Mieth, 105–24. New York: Routledge.

Hassellind, Filip Strandberg, and Mikael Baaz. 2020. "Just Another Battleground: Resisting Courtroom Historiography in the ECCC." *Journal of Political Power* 13 (2): 252–67.

Hayman, Hallister, and Sam Rith. 2007. "Boeung Kak Lake Latest City Sell-Off." *Phnom Penh Post*, 9 February.

Hazan, Pierre. 2010. "Transitional Justice after September 11: A New Rapport with Evil." In *Localizing Transitional Justice: Interventions and Priorities after Mass Violence*, edited by Rosalind Shaw and Lars Waldorf, 49–65. Stanford: Stanford University Press.

Heder, Steve. 1997. "Racism, Marxism, Labelling, and Genocide in Ben Kiernan's *The Pol Pot Regime*." *South East Asia Research* 5 (2): 101–53.

———. 2002. "Hun Sen and Genocide Trials in Cambodia: International Impacts, Impunity, and Justice." In *Cambodia Emerges from the Past: Eight Essays*, edited by Judy Ledgerwood, 178–223. DeKalb: University of Northern Illinois Press.

———. 2005. "Hun Sen's Consolidation." *Southeast Asian Affairs*: 111–30.

———. 2011. "A Review of the Negotiations Leading to the Establishment of the Personal Jurisdiction of the ECCC." *Cambodia Tribunal Monitor*, 1 August. https://cambodiatribunal.org/2011/08/01/a-review-of-the-negotiations-leading-to-the-establishment-of-the-personal-jurisdiction-of-the-extraordinary-chambers-in-the-courts-of-cambodia/.

Heder, Steve, and Judy Ledgerwood. 1996a. "Politics of Violence." In *Propaganda, Politics, and Violence in Cambodia: Democratic Transition under United Nations Peacekeeping*, edited by Steve Heder and Judy Ledgerwood, 3–49. Armonk, N.: M. E. Sharpe.

———, eds. 1996b. *Propaganda, Politics, and Violence in Cambodia. Democratic Transition under United Nations Peace-Keeping.* Armonk, N.: M. E. Sharpe.

Heindel, Anne. 2016. "Managing Enormous Mass Crimes Indictments: The ECCC Severance Experiment." In *The ECCC: Assessing Their Contribution to International Criminal Law*, edited by Ignaz Stegmiller and Simon M. Meisenberg, 435–60. The Hague: T. M. C. Asser Press.

Heng, Reaksmey. 2013. "Khmer Rouge Survivor Threatens Demonstration against Opposition." Voice of America Cambodia. 5 June. https://www.voacambodia.com/a/khmer-rouge-survivor-threatens-demonstration-against-opposition/1675145.html.

Hennings, Anne. 2018. "Plantation Assemblages and Spaces of Contested Development in Sierra Leone and Cambodia." *Conflict, Security & Development* 18 (6): 521–46.

———. 2019. "The Dark Underbelly of Land Struggles: The Instrumentalization of Female Activism and Emotional Resistance in Cambodia." *Critical Asian Studies* 51 (1): 103–19.

High, Holly, James R. Curran, and Gareth Robinson. 2013. "Electronic Records of the Air War over Southeast Asia: A Database Analysis." *Journal of Vietnamese Studies* 8 (4): 86–124.

Hinton, Alexander. 1998. "A Head for an Eye: Revenge in the Cambodian Genocide." *American Ethnologist* 25 (3): 352–77.

———. 2005. *Why Did They Kill?* Berkeley: University of California Press.

———. 2011a. "Introduction." In *Transitional Justice: Global Mechanisms and Local Realities after Genocide and Mass Violence*, edited by Alexander Hinton, 1–22. New Brunswick, NJ: Rutgers University Press.

———, ed. 2011b. *Transitional Justice: Global Mechanisms and Local Realities after Genocide and Mass Violence.* New Brunswick, NJ: Rutgers University Press.

———. 2014. "Justice and Time at the Khmer Rouge Tribunal: In Memory of Vann Nath, Painter and S-21 Survivor." *Genocide Studies and Prevention: An International Journal* 8 (2): 7–17.

———. 2018. *The Justice Façade: Trials of Transition in Cambodia.* Oxford: Oxford University Press.

———. 2022. "Justice at Last for Cambodia's Killing Fields?" *Diplomat*, 21 September. https://thediplomat.com/2022/09/justice-at-last-for-cambodias-killing-fields.

Hoefinger, Heidi, Pisey Ly, and Srorn Srun. 2017. "Sex Politics and Moral Panics: LGBT Communities, Sex/Entertainment Workers and Sexually Active Youth in Cambodia." In *Routledge Handbook of Contemporary Cambodia*, 315–25. Abingdon: Routledge.

Hoffman, Diane. 1999. "Turning Power Inside Out." *International Journal of Qualitative Studies in Education* 12 (6): 671–87.

Hollander, Jocelyn A., and Rachel L. Einwohner. 2004. "Conceptualizing Resistance." *Sociological Forum* 19 (4): 533–54.

Horsington, Helen. 2004. "The Cambodian Khmer Rouge Tribunal: The Promise of a Hybrid Tribunal." *Melbourne Journal of International Law* 5 (2): 462–82.

Hughes, Caroline. 2001. "An Investigation of Conflict Management in Cambodian Villages: A Review of the Literature with Suggestions for Future Research." Letter to CDRI. https://www.academia.edu/1104516/An_Investigation_of_Conflict_Management_in_Cambodian_Villages.

———. 2003. *The Political Economy of the Cambodian Transition, 1991–2001.* New York: Routledge Curzon.

———. 2006. "The Politics of Gifts." *Journal of Southeast Asian Studies* 37 (3): 469–89.

———. 2013. "Friction, Good Governance and the Poor: Cases from Cambodia." *International Peacekeeping* 20 (2): 144–58.

———. 2015a. "Understanding the 2013 Elections in Cambodia." In "Workshop and Symposium 2013–2014," special issue, *AGLOS: Journal of Area-Based Global Studies*: 1–20.

———. 2015b. "UNTAC, Peace and Violence in Cambodia." In *The Politics of International Intervention: The Tyranny of Peace*, edited by Mandy Turner and Florian Kühn, 117–38. London: Routledge.

Hughes, Caroline, and Joakim Öjendal. 2006. "Reassessing Tradition in Times of Political Change." *Journal of Southeast Asian Studies* 37 (3): 415.

Hughes, Caroline, and Vanessa Pupavac. 2005. "Framing Post-Conflict Societies." *Third World Quarterly* 26 (6): 873–99.

Hughes, Caroline, and Kheang Un. 2011. "Cambodia's Economic Transformation: Historical and Theoretical Frameworks." In *Cambodia's Economic Transformation*, edited by Caroline Hughes and Kheang Un, 1–26. Copenhagen: NIAS Press.

Hughes, Rachel. 2006. "Fielding Genocide: Post-1979 Cambodia and the Geopolitics of Memory." Melbourne: University of Melbourne.

———. 2015. "Ordinary Theatre and Extraordinary Law at the Khmer Rouge Tribunal." *Environment and Planning D: Society and Space* 33 (4): 714–31.

———. 2018. "Reparations of the ECCC: A Brief Update." The Newsletter. International Institute for Asian Studies. https://www.iias.asia/the-newsletter/article/reparations-extraordinary-chambers-courts-cambodia-brief-update.

Human Rights Watch. 2005. "Cambodia: Opposition MP Jailed after Sham Trial." 9 August. https://www.hrw.org/node/229803/printable/print.

———. 2014. "Cambodia: Security Forces Beat Housing Rights Protesters." 14 February. https://www.hrw.org/node/252781/printable/print.

———. 2015. "At Your Own Risk: Reprisals against Critics of World Bank Group Projects." https://www.hrw.org/sites/default/files/report_pdf/worldbank0615_4up.pdf.

———. 2018. "Cambodia's Dirty Dozen: A Long History of Rights Abuse by Hun Sen's Generals." 27 June. https://www.hrw.org/report/2018/06/27/cambodias-dirty-dozen/long-history-rights-abuses-hun-sens-generals.

———. 2022. "Cambodia: 51 Opposition Politicians Convicted in Mass Trial." 14 June. https://www.hrw.org/news/2022/06/14/cambodia-51-opposition-politicians-convicted-mass-trial.

Hutt, David. 2017. "What's Next for Cambodia's Sam Rainsy?" *Diplomat*, 15 February. https://thediplomat.com/2017/02/whats-next-for-cambodias-sam-rainsy/.

Huy, Samphoas. 2019. "Translating Global Norms: The Role of NGOs in Transitional Justice in Cambodia." Edited by Julie Bernath and Ratana Ly. swisspeace Working Paper Cambodia Series. https://www.swisspeace.ch/publications/working-papers/translating-global-norms-the-role-of-ngos-in-transitional-justice-in-cambodia-2.

Jacobsen, Trude. 2005. "Paying through the Nose: Punishment in the Cambodian Past and Lessons for the Present." *South East Asia Research* 13 (2): 235–56.

Jacobsen, Trude, and Martin Stuart-Fox. 2013. "Power and Political Culture in Cambodia." Asia Research Institute Working Paper No. 200. https://ari.nus.edu.sg/wp-content/uploads/2013/05/201305-WPS-200.pdf.

Jansen, Geerteke. 2006. *Voices of Takéo: A Pilot Fear Assessment with Respect to Possible Witnesses of the ECCC.* Phnom Penh: Documentation Center of Cambodia.

Jarvis, Helen. 2014. "'Justice for the Deceased': Victims' Participation in the ECCC." *Genocide Studies and Prevention* 8 (2): 19–27.

———. 2015. "Powerful Remains." *Human Remains and Violence* 1 (2): 36–55.

———. 2016. "Trials and Tribulations: The Long Quest for Justice for the Cambodian Genocide." In *The ECCC: Assessing Their Contribution to International Criminal Law*, edited by Simon M. Meisenberg and Ignaz Stegmiller, 13–44. International Criminal Justice Series 6. The Hague: T. M. C. Asser Press.

Jeffrey, Alex. 2011. "The Political Geographies of Transitional Justice." *Transactions of the Institute of British Geographers* 36:344–59.

Jones, Briony. 2015. "Stories of 'Success': Narrative, Expertise, and Claims to Knowledge." *Canadian Journal of Law and Society* 30 (2): 293–308.

Jones, Briony, and Julie Bernath, eds. 2017. *Resistance and Transitional Justice.* New York: Routledge.

Jones, Briony, and Ulrike Lühe, eds. 2021. *Knowledge for Peace: Transitional Justice and the Politics of Knowledge in Theory and Practice.* Cheltenham, UK: Edward Elgar.

Jørgensen, Nina H. B. 2018. *The Elgar Companion to the ECCC.* Elgar Companions to International Courts and Tribunals. Cheltenham, UK: Edward Elgar.

Kagoro, Brian. 2012. "The Paradox of Alien Knowledge, Narrative and Praxis: Transitional Justice and the Politics of Agenda Setting in Africa." In *Where Law Meets Reality: Forging African Transitional Justice*, edited by Moses C. Okello, Chris Dolan, Undine Whande, Nokukhanja Mncwabe, Levis Onegi, and Stephen Oola, 4–52. Cape Town: Pambazuka Press.

Kane, Solomon. 2009. *Dictionnaire des Khmers Rouges.* Paris: Aux lieux d'être.

Kasper-Ansermet, Laurent. 2012. "Note of the International Reserve Co-investigating Judge to the Parties on the Egregious Dysfunctions within the ECCC Impeding the Proper Conduct of Investigations in Cases 003 and 004: Case Files No. 003/07-09-2009-ECCC-OCIJ and 004/07-09-2009-ECCC-OCIJ." March. http://www.eccc.gov.kh/sites/default/files/documents/courtdoc/D38_EN.PDF.

Kendall, Sara. 2011. "Donors' Justice: Recasting International Criminal Accountability." *Leiden Journal of International Law* 24 (3): 585–606.

Kent, Alexandra. 2013. "Friction and Security at the Khmer Rouge Tribunal." *SOJOURN: Journal of Social Issues in Southeast Asia* 28 (2): 299–328.

———. 2016. "Conflict Continues: Transitioning into a Battle for Property in Cambodia Today." *Journal of Southeast Asian Studies* 47 (1): 3–23.

———. 2022. "Outsourcing Outreach: 'Counter-Translation' of Outreach Activities at the ECCC." *Journal of Current Southeast Asian Affairs* 41 (1): 106–34.

Khouth, Sophak Chakrya. 2009. "Staged Killings Stir Victims' Emotions on Day of Anger." *Phnom Penh Post*, 21 May.

———. 2012. "Building Not for Evictees." *Phnom Penh Post*, 17 February.

———. 2016. "Borei Keila Evictees Mark Four-Year Anniversary." *Phnom Penh Post*, 4 January.

Kiernan, Ben. 1989. "The American Bombardment of Kampuchea, 1969–1973." *Vietnam Generation* 1 (1): 4–41.

———, ed. 1993. *Genocide and Democracy in Cambodia: The Khmer Rouge, the United Nations, and the International Community.* New Haven, CT: Yale University Southeast Asia Studies.

———. 2021. "The Pol Pot Regime's Simultaneous War against Vietnam and Genocide of Cambodia's Ethnic Vietnamese Minority." *Critical Asian Studies* 53 (3): 342–58.

Killean, Rachel. 2015. "An Incomplete Narrative: Prosecuting Sexual Violence Crimes at the ECCC." *Journal of International Criminal Justice* 13 (2): 331–52.

———. 2018a. "Constructing Victimhood at the Khmer Rouge Tribunal: Visibility, Selectivity and Participation." *International Review of Victimology* 24 (3): 273–96.

———. 2018b. *Victims, Atrocity and International Criminal Justice: Lessons from Cambodia.* London: Routledge.

Kim, Sedara. 2012. "Democracy in Action." PhD diss., School of Global Studies, University of Gothenburg.

Kimsan, Chantara. 1998. "Ranariddh Sentenced to Five Years." *Cambodia Daily*, 5 March.

Kirchenbauer, Nadine, Mychelle Balthazard, Latt Ky, Patrick Vinck, and Phuong Pham. 2013. "Victims Participation before the ECCC. Baseline Study of the Cambodian Human Rights and Development Association Civil Party Scheme for Case 002." Phnom Penh: ADHOC and Harvard Humanitarian Initiative.

Kochanski, Adam. 2018. "The 'Local Turn' in Transitional Justice: Curb the Enthusiasm." *International Studies Review* 22 (1): 26–50. https://doi.org/10.1093/isr/viy081.

———. 2021. "Framing, Truth-Telling, and the Limits of Local Transitional Justice." *Review of International Studies* 47 (4): 468–88.

Kong, Sothanarith. 2013. "Khmer Rouge Victims Sue Opposition Lawmaker." Voice of America Cambodia, 15 June. https://www.voacambodia.com/a/khmer-rouge-victims-sue-opposition-lawmaker/1682001.html.

Krever, Tor. 2014. "Unveiling (and Veiling) Politics in International Criminal Trials." In *Critical Approaches to International Criminal Law*, edited by Christine Schwöbel, 117–37. Oxon: Routledge.

Kroker, Patrick. 2010. "Transitional Justice Policy in Practice: Victim Participation in the Khmer Rouge Tribunal." *German Yearbook of International Law* 53:753–92.

Kry, Suyheang. 2014. "The Boeung Kak Development Project: For Whom and for What?" *Cambodia Law and Policy Journal* 3 (December). http://cambodialpj.org/article/the-boeung-kak-development-project-for-whom-and-for-what-poor-land-development-practices-as-a-challenge-for-building-sustainable-peace-in-cambodia/.

Kuch, Naren. 2013a. "KR Victims Delay Move to Oust President." *Cambodia Daily*, 18 June.

———. 2013b. "KR Victims Group Moves to Oust President over Partisanship." *Cambodia Daily*, 11 June.

———. 2014a. "Survivor against Inscribing Names of All S-21 Victims." *Cambodia Daily*, 7 May.

———. 2014b. "Victims Stage Protest Outside Tribunal." *Cambodia Daily*, 18 October.

Kum, Somaly. 2019. "How Do Donors Shape Transitional Justice in Cambodia." In Swisspeace Working Paper Cambodia Series 8. Bern: swisspeace; Phnom Penh: Cambodian Center for the Study of Humanitarian Law.

Lai, Daniela. 2020. *Socioeconomic Justice: International Intervention and Transition in Post-war Bosnia and Herzegovina.* Cambridge: Cambridge University Press.

Lamb, Vanessa, Laura Schoenberger, Carl Middleton, and Borin Un. 2017. "Gendered Eviction, Protest and Recovery: A Feminist Political Ecology Engagement with Land Grabbing in Rural Cambodia." *Journal of Peasant Studies* 44 (6): 1215–34.

Lao, Mong Hay. 2006. "Institutions for the Rule of Law and Human Rights in Cambodia." Asian Human Rights Commission. http://www.humanrights.asia/resources/journals-magazines/article2/focus-the-rule-of-law-human-rights-in-asia/institutions-for-the-rule-of-law-and-human-rights-in-cambodia/.

Lawreniuk, Sabina. 2020. "Intensifying Political Geographies of Authoritarianism: Toward an Anti-geopolitics of Garment Worker Struggles in Neoliberal Cambodia." *Annals of the Association of American Geographers* 110 (4): 1174–91.

Lawreniuk, Sabina, and Laruie Parsons. 2018. "For a Few Dollars More: Towards a Translocal Mobilities of Labour Activism in Cambodia." *Geoforum* 92:26–35.

Le Billon, Philippe. 2000. "The Political Ecology of Transition in Cambodia, 1989–1999: War, Peace and Forest Exploitation." *Development & Change* 31:785–905.

———. 2002. "Logging in Muddy Waters." *Critical Asian Studies* 34 (4): 563–86.

Ledgerwood, Judy. 1992. *Analysis of the Situation of Women in Cambodia.* Phnom Penh: UNICEF.

———. 1994. "UN Peacekeeping Missions." *Asia Pacific Issues* 11:1–10.

———. 1997. "The Cambodian Tuol Sleng Museum of Genocidal Crimes: National Narrative." *Museum Archaeology* 21 (1): 83–98.

———. 2002. "Understanding Cambodia: Social Hierarchy, Patron-Client Relationships and Power." Seasite, n.d. http://www.seasite.niu.edu/khmer/ledgerwood/patrons.htm.

Lee, Donald, and Sivutha Nov. 2015. "Gov't Will Not Arrest KR Suspects." *Khmer Times*, 24 March.

Lefebvre, Henri. 2009. *State, Space, World: Selected Essays.* Edited by Neil Brenner and Stuart Elden. Minneapolis: University of Minnesota Press.

Lefranc, Sandrine, Lilian Mathieu, and Johanna Siméant. 2008. "Les victimes écrivent leur histoire." *Raisons politiques* 30 (2): 5–19.

Lemonde, Marcel. 2011. "Quelles leçons tirer du procès des Khmers Rouges?" *Revue de science criminelle et de droit pénal comparé* 3 (3): 597–604.

———. 2013. *Un juge face aux Khmers Rouges.* Paris: Editions du Seuil.

LICADHO. 2007. "Human Rights in Cambodia: The Charade of Justice." A LICADHO Report. https://www.licadho-cambodia.org/reports.php?perm=113.

———. 2009. "Land Grabbing & Poverty in Cambodia: The Myth of Development." A LICADHO Report. https://www.licadho-cambodia.org/reports/files/134LICADHOREportMythofDevelopment2009Eng.pdf.

———. 2014. "Human Rights 2013: The Year in Review." A LICADHO Report. https://www.licadho-cambodia.org/reports.php?perm=194.

———. 2015. "Human Rights 2014: The Year in Review." A LICADHO Report. https://www.licadho-cambodia.org/reports.php?perm=209.

Lilja, Mona. 2010. "Discourses of Hybrid Democracy." *Asian Journal of Political Science* 18 (3): 289–309.

———. 2013. *Resisting Gendered Norms.* Farnham, UK: Ashgate.

Lilja, Mona, and Stellan Vinthagen. 2006. "A Research Network on Resistance, Power and Social Change: Mission Statement." Resistance Studies Network. https://www.resistancestudies.org/files/Missionstatement.doc.

Lobba, Paolo, and Niccolò Pons. 2020. "Rethinking the Legacy of the ECCC: Selectivity, Accountability, Ownership." *Journal of International Criminal Justice* 18 (3): 599–614.

Loughlin, Neil. 2021a. "Beyond Personalism: Elite Politics and Political Families in Cambodia." *Contemporary Southeast Asia* 43 (2): 241–64.

———. 2021b. "Chinese Linkage, Leverage, and Cambodia's Transition to Hegemonic Authoritarianism." *Democratization* 28 (4): 840–57.

Loughlin, Neil, and Sarah Milne. 2020. "After the Grab? Land Control and Regime Survival in Cambodia since 2012." *Journal of Contemporary Asia* 51 (3): 375–97.

Loughlin, Neil, and Astrid Norén-Nilsson. 2021. "Introduction to Special Issue: The Cambodian People's Party's Turn to Hegemonic Authoritarianism: Strategies and Envisaged Futures." *Contemporary Southeast Asia: A Journal of International and Strategic Affairs* 43 (2): 225–40.

Low, Sally Frances. 2023. *Colonial Law Making: The French in Cambodia.* Singapore: National University of Singapore Press.

Luco, Fabienne. 2002. "Between a Tiger and a Crocodile: Management of Local Conflicts in Cambodia: An Anthropological Approach to Traditional and New Practices." September. Phnom Penh: UNESCO.

Ly, Sok-Kheang. 2011. "Reparation in Question." *Cambodia Tribunal.* http://www.cambodiatribunal.org/assets/pdf/reports/Reparation%20in%20Question.pdf.

———. 2017. "Reconciliation Process in Cambodia: 1979–2007, Before the Khmer Rouge Tribunal." Documentation Center of Cambodia Documentation Series

No. 24. http://dccam.org/publication/reconciliation-process-in-cambodia-1979-2007-before-the-khmer-rouge-tribunal.

MacGinty, Roger. 2011. *International Peacebuilding and Local Resistance.* Basingstoke: Palgrave Macmillan.

———. 2012. "Between Resistance and Compliance." *Journal of Intervention and Statebuilding* 6 (2): 167–87.

Mack, Helen C., and Mónica S. Leonardo. 2012. "Editorial Note." *International Journal of Transitional Justice* 6 (2): 175–81.

Madlingozi, Tshepo. 2010. "On Transitional Justice Entrepreneurs and the Production of Victims." *Journal of Human Rights Practice* 2 (2): 208–28.

Mam, Kalyanee. 2001. "Evidence of Sexual Abuse during the Rule of Democratic Kampuchea." *Searching for the Truth,* no. 15 (March): 2–5. Documentation Center of Cambodia. http://d.dccam.org/Projects/Magazines/Previous%20Englis/Issue15.pdf.

Manning, Peter. 2012a. "Governing Memory: Justice, Reconciliation and Outreach at the ECCC." *Memory Studies* 5 (2): 165–81.

———. 2012b. "Legitimacy, Power and Memory at the ECCC." In *Critical Perspectives in Transitional Justice,* edited by Nicola Palmer, Phil Clark, and Danielle Granville, 217–33. Cambridge: Intersentia.

———. 2017. *Transitional Justice and Memory in Cambodia beyond the Extraordinary Chambers.* London: Routledge.

Mayer-Rieckh, Alexander. 2017. "Guarantees of Non-recurrence: An Approximation." *Human Rights Quarterly* 39 (2): 416–48.

McAuliffe, Padraig. 2011. "Hybrid Tribunals at Ten: How International Criminal Justice's Golden Child Became an Orphan." *Journal of International Law and International Relations* 7:1–65.

———. 2017a. "Reflections of the Nexus between Justice and Peacebuilding." *Journal of Intervention and Statebuilding* 11 (2): 245–60.

———. 2017b. *Transformative Transitional Justice and the Malleability of Post-conflict States.* Cheltenham, UK: Edward Elgar.

McAuliffe, Padraig, and Christine Schwöbel-Patel. 2018. "Disciplinary Matchmaking Critics of International Criminal LawMeet Critics of Liberal Peacebuilding." *Journal of International Criminal Justice* 16:985–1009.

McCargo, Duncan. 2011. "Politics by Other Means?" *International Affairs* 87 (3): 613–27.

———. 2014. "Cambodia in 2013: (No) Country for Old Men?" *Asian Survey* 54 (1): 71–77.

McEvoy, Kieran. 2018. "Travel, Dilemmas and Nonrecurrence: Observations on the 'Respectabilisation' of Transitional Justice." *International Journal of Transitional Justice* 12 (2): 185–93.

McGrew, Laura. 2009. "Re-establishing Legitimacy through the ECCC." In *Beyond Democracy in Cambodia: Political Reconstruction in a Post-conflict Society,* edited by Joakim Öjendal and Mona Lilja, 250–97. Copenhagen: NIAS Press.

———. 2011. "Pathways to Reconciliation in Cambodia." *Peace Review* 23 (4): 514–21.

———. 2018. "Hybrid Court, Hybrid Peacebuilding in Cambodia." In *Transitional Justice, International Assistance, and Civil Society*, edited by Paige Arthur and Christalla Yakinthou, 144–73. Cambridge: Cambridge University Press.

McGrew, Laura, and Scott Worden. 2017. "Lessons from Cambodia's Paris Peace Accords for Political Unrest Today." USIP Peace Brief. https://www.usip.org/publications/2017/05/lessons-cambodias-paris-peace-accords-political-unrest-today.

McPherson, Poppy. 2014. "Memorial Plan Prompts Debate about Victims and Perpetrators of Genocide." *Phnom Penh Post*, 9 May.

Meas, Sockhea, and Sokheng Vong. 2015. "Rainsy Offered a Possible Deal for Safe Return." *Phnom Penh Post*, 19 November.

Mech, Dara. 2014. "Seven Boeng Kak Protesters Arrested." *Cambodia Daily*, 10 November.

Mech, Dara, and George Wright. 2018. "The Dangers of Activism in Cambodia." New Naratif, 14 August. http://newnaratif.com/dangers-activism-cambodia/.

Mégret, Frédéric. 2016. "International Criminal Courts and Tribunals: The Anxieties of International Criminal Justice." *Leiden Journal of International Law* 29: 197–221.

Meisenberg, Simon M., and Ignaz Stegmiller, eds. 2016. *The ECCC: Assessing Their Contribution to International Criminal Law.* International Criminal Justice Series 6. The Hague: T. M. C. Asser Press.

Merry, Sally Engle. 1985. "Concepts of Law and Justice among Working Class Americans: Ideology as Culture." *Legal Studies Forum* 11:59–71.

———. 1990. *Getting Justice and Getting Even: Legal Consciousness among Working Class Americans.* Language and Legal Discourse. Chicago: University of Chicago Press.

Millar, Gearoid. 2010. "Assessing Local Experiences of Truth-Telling in Sierra Leone: Getting to 'Why' through a Qualitative Case Study Analysis." *International Journal of Transitional Justice* 4 (3): 477–96.

Millar, Gearoid, and Jesse Lecy. 2016. "Disciplinary Divides in Post-conflict Justice and Peace: Tracking If and How We Share Ideas." *Journal of Intervention and Statebuilding* 10 (3): 302–20.

Miller, Zinaida. 2008. "Effects of Invisibility: In Search of the 'Economic' in Transitional Justice." *International Journal of Transitional Justice* 2 (3): 266–91.

———. 2021. "Temporal Governance: The Times of Transitional Justice." *International Criminal Law Review* 21:848–77.

Mohan, Mahdev. 2008. "Reconstituting the 'Un-Person': The Khmer Krom and the Khmer Rouge Tribunal." *Singapore Year Book of International Law and Contributors* 12:43–55.

———. 2009. "The Paradox of Victim-Centrism: Victim Participation at the Khmer Rouge Tribunal." *International Criminal Law Review* 9 (5): 733–75.

Moon, Claire. 2006. "Narrating Political Reconciliation: Truth and Reconciliation in South Africa." *Social & Legal Studies* 15 (2): 257–75.

———. 2012. "'Who'll Pay Reparations on My Soul?' Compensation, Social Control and Social Suffering." *Social & Legal Studies* 21 (2): 187–99.

Moore, Donald S. 1998. "Subaltern Struggles and the Politics of Place: Remapping Resistance in Zimbabwe's Eastern Highlands." *Cultural Anthropology* 13 (3): 344–81.

Morgenbesser, Lee. 2018. "Misclassification on the Mekong: The Origins of Hun Sen's Personalist Dictatorship." *Democratization* 25 (2): 191–208.

Morris, Catherine. 2017. "Justice Inverted: Law and Human Rights in Cambodia." In *The Handbook of Contemporary Cambodia*, edited by Katherine Brickell and Simon Springer, 29–41. London: Routledge.

Mueller-Hirth, Natascha. 2017. "Temporalities of Victimhood: Time in the Study of Postconflict Societies." *Sociological Forum* 32 (1): 186–206.

Mueller-Hirth, Natascha, and Sandra Milena Rios Oyola, eds. 2018. *Time and Temporality in Transitional Justice and Post-conflict Societies.* Routledge Advances in Sociology 244. London: Routledge.

Muntarbhorn, Vitit. 2021. "Report of the Special Rapporteur on the Situation of Human Rights in Cambodia." A/HRC/48/79. https://ap.ohchr.org/Documents/dpage_e.aspx?si=A/HRC/48/79.

Murray, Bennett, and Sophak Chakrya Khouth. 2014. "Size Me Up: Calculating Crowds at Cambodia's Demonstrations." *Phnom Penh Post*, 3 January.

Mydans, Seth. 2006. "27 Years Later, a Formal Inquiry Begins into Khmer Rouge Atrocities." *New York Times*, 6 August.

———. 2010a. "Anger in Cambodia over Khmer Rouge Sentence." *New York Times*, 26 July.

———. 2010b. "Stampede in Cambodia Leaves Hundreds Dead." *New York Times*, 23 November, sec. World.

Nakagawa, Kasumi. 2008. "Gender-Based Violence during the Khmer Rouge: Stories of Survivors from Democratic Kampuchea (1975–1979)." Phnom Penh, Cambodia. http://gbvkr.org/wp-content/uploads/2013/02/Kasumi-GBV-Study-2007.pdf.

Natale, Katrina. 2011. "'I Could Feel My Soul Flying Away from My Body': A Study on Gender-Based Violence during Democratic Kampuchea in Battambang and Svay Rieng Provinces." Phnom Penh: Cambodian Defenders Project. http://gbvkr.org/wp-content/uploads/2013/01/Natale_K_Research_GBV_KR_ENG-web.pdf.

Neef, Andreas, Siphat Touch, and Jamaree Chiengthong. 2013. "The Politics and Ethics of Land Concessions in Rural Cambodia." *Journal of Agricultural and Environmental Ethics* 26 (6): 1085–103.

Ngoun, Kimly. 2022. "Adaptive Authoritarian Resilience: Cambodian Strongman's Quest for Legitimacy." *Journal of Contemporary Asia* 52 (1): 23–44.

Niem, Chheng. 2019. "Win-Win Monument: PM's 'Treason' or Symbol of Unity?" *Phnom Penh Post*, 2 January.

Niem, Chheng, Duong Keo, and Putheary Sin. 2011. *Behind the Darkness: Taking Responsibility or Acting under Orders?* Phnom Penh: Youth for Peace.

Norén-Nilsson, Astrid. 2015. "Cambodia at a Crossroads. The Narratives of Cambodia National Rescue Party Supporters after the 2013 Elections." *Internationales Asienforum* 46 (3–4): 261–78.

———. 2016. *Cambodia's Second Kingdom: Nation, Imagination, and Democracy.* Ithaca, NY: Cornell University Press.

———. 2021. "A Regal Authoritarian Turn in Cambodia." *Journal of Contemporary Asia* 52 (5): 1–22.

Norén-Nilsson, Astrid, and Frédéric Bourdier. 2019. "Introduction: Social Movements in Cambodia." *Journal of Current Southeast Asian Affairs* 38 (1): 3–9.

OHCHR. 2008. "Maximizing the Legacy of Hybrid Courts." New York and Geneva: United Nations. http://www.ohchr.org/Documents/Publications/HybridCourts.pdf.

———. 2018. "Assessing the Impact of Social Land Concessions on Rural Livelihood in Cambodia." https://cambodia.ohchr.org/sites/default/files/book/Assessing%20the%20Impact%20of%20Social%20Land%20Concessions%20on%20Rural%20Livelihoods%20in%20Cambodia-Eng.pdf.

Öjendal, Joakim, and Sedara Kim. 2006. "Korob, Kaud, Klach: In Search of Agency in Rural Cambodia." *Journal of Southeast Asian Studies* 37 (3): 507–26.

Öjendal, Joakim, and Mona Lilja, eds. 2009. *Beyond Democracy in Cambodia.* Copenhagen: NIAS Press.

Öjendal, Joakim, and Sivhuoch Ou. 2013. "From Friction to Hybridity in Cambodia." *Peacebuilding* 1 (3): 365–80.

Oosterveld, Valerie, and Patricia Viseur Sellers. 2016. "Issues of Sexual and Gender-Based Violence at the ECCC." In *The ECCC: Assessing Their Contribution to International Criminal Law*, edited by Simon M. Meisenberg and Ignaz Stegmiller, 321–51. The Hague: T. M. C. Asser Press.

Orentlicher, Diane. 2020. "Worth the Effort? Assessing the Khmer Rouge Tribunal." *Journal of International Criminal Justice* 18 (3):615–50.

Ortner, Sherry B. 1995. "Resistance and the Problem of Ethnographic Refusal." *Comparative Studies in Society and History* 37 (1): 173–93.

OSJI. 2006. "Memorandum to the Group of Interested States: Priority Issues for the ECCC." Open Society Justice Initiative. https://www.justiceinitiative.org/publications/priority-issues-extraordinary-chambers-courts-cambodia.

———. 2007. "Progress and Challenges at the ECCC." Open Society Justice Initiative. https://www.justiceinitiative.org/publications/new-report-open-society-justice-initiative-finds-critical-needs-khmer-rouge-tribunal.

———. 2010. "Salvaging Judicial Independence: The Need for a Principled Completion Plan for the ECCC." Open Society Justice Initiative. https://www.opensocietyfoundations.org/sites/default/files/cambodia-khmer-rouge-20101110.pdf.

———. 2011a. "Recent Developments at the ECCC. June 2011 Update." Open Society Justice Initiative. https://www.opensocietyfoundations.org/sites/default/files/cambodia-eccc-20110614.pdf.

———. 2011b. "Recent Developments at the ECCC: November 2011 Update." Open Society Justice Initiative. https://www.opensocietyfoundations.org/reports/recent-developments-extraordinary-chambers-courts-cambodia-november-2011.

———. 2012. "The Future of Cases 003/004 at the ECCC" Open Society Justice Initiative. https://www.opensocietyfoundations.org/sites/default/files/eccc-report-cases3and4-100112_0.pdf.

———. 2015. "Recent Developments at the ECCC: March 2015 Update." Open Society Justice Initiative. https://www.opensocietyfoundations.org/reports/recent-developments-extraordinary-chambers-courts-cambodia-march-2015.

———. 2020. "Dead End at Cambodia's Khmer Rouge Tribunal: Next Steps for the UN." Open Society Justice Initiative. https://www.justiceinitiative.org/newsroom/dead-end-at-cambodias-khmer-rouge-tribunal-un-must-respond.

Osman, Ysa. 2006. *The Cham Rebellion: Survivors' Stories from the Villages.* Phnom Penh: Documentation Center of Cambodia.

Owen, Taylor, and Ben Kiernan. 2006. "Bombs over Cambodia." *Walrus*, 62–69.

———. 2010. "Roots of U.S. Troubles in Afghanistan: Civilian Bombing Casualties and the Cambodian Precedent." *Asia-Pacific Journal* 8 (26). https://apjjf.org/-Taylor-Owen/3380/article.html.

———. 2015. "Making More Enemies Than We Kill? Calculating U.S. Bomb Tonnages Dropped on Laos and Cambodia, and Weighing Their Implications." *Asia-Pacific Journal* 13 (17). https://apjjf.org/Ben-Kiernan/4313.html.

Padwe, Jonathan. 2017. "Cambodia's Highlanders." In *The Handbook of Contemporary Cambodia*, edited by Katherine Brickell and Simon Springer, 134–45. Oxon: Routledge.

Pak, Kimchoeun. 2011. "A Dominant Party in a Weak State." PhD diss., Australian National University, Canberra.

Pak, Kimchoeun, Vuthy Horng, Netra Eng, Sovatha Ann, Sedara Kim, Jenny Knowles, and David Craig. 2007. "Accountability and Neo-patrimonialism in Cambodia: A Critical Literature Review." Phnom Penh: Cambodia Development Resource Institute. https://www.cdri.org.kh/publication/accountability-and-neo-patrimonialism-in-cambodia-a-critical-literature-review.

Palmer, Emma, and Sarah Williams. 2017. "A 'Shift in Attitude'? Institutional Change and Sexual and Gender-Based Crimes at the ECCC." *International Feminist Journal of Politics* 19 (1): 22–38.

Palmer, Nicola, Phil Clark, and Danielle Granville, eds. 2012. *Critical Perspectives in Transitional Justice.* Cambridge: Intersentia.

Paris, Roland. 2009. *At War's End.* Cambridge: Cambridge University Press.

Park, Clara Mi Young, and Margherita Maffii. 2015. "Landscapes of Control and Appropriation: The Missing Indigenous Woman." In *Land Grabbing, Conflict and Agrarian-Environmental Transformations: Perspectives from East and Southeast Asia.* Conference Paper No. 8. BRICS Initiatives for Critical Agrarian Studies, MOSAIC Research Project, Land Deal Politics Initiative, RCSD Chiang May University and Transnational Institute.

Path, Kosal. 2017. "Multivocal Resistance to Transitional Justice in Post-genocide Cambodia." In *Resistance and Transitional Justice*, edited by Briony Jones and Julie Bernath, 121–39. London, New York: Routledge.

Peou, Sorpong. 2000. *Intervention and Change in Cambodia: Toward Democracy?* Singapore: Institute of Southeast Asian Studies.

———. 2017. "Peace through Democracy and Justice? Legacies and Lessons from the Case of Cambodia." *Asian Journal of Peacebuilding* 5 (1): 89–110.

———. 2018. "The Politics of Survival in Cambodia: National Security for Undemocratic Control." In *National Security, State-Centricity, and Governance in East Asia*, edited by Brendan Howe, 81–106. Cham, Switzerland: Palgrave Macmillan.

Petersson, Markus. 2021. "Cambodia´s Modern Patronage System: A Brief Reflection on Historical Foundations, Contemporary Articulations, and Future Policy Formations." Future Forum Policy Brief. Phnom Penh: Future Forum.

Petit, Robert. 2010. "Lawfare and International Tribunals: A Question of Definition?" *Case Western Reserve Journal of International Law* 43 (1–2): 189–99.

Pham, Phuong, Patrick Vinck, Mychelle Balthazard, and Sokhom Hean. 2011. "After the First Trial: A Population-Based Survey on Knowledge and Perceptions of Justice and the ECCC." Berkeley: Human Rights Center, University of California. Harvard.edu. https://hhi.harvard.edu/files/humanitarianinitiative/files/after-the-first-trial.pdf?m=1612291669.

Pham, Phuong, Patrick Vinck, Mychelle Balthazard, Sokhom Hean, and Eric Stover. 2009. "So We Will Never Forget: A Population-Based Survey on Attitudes about Social Reconstruction and the ECCC." Escholarship. https://escholarship.org/uc/item/74x685xm.

Phnom Penh Post. 2017. "Live Updates: Supreme Court Rules to Dissolve CNRP." 16 November.

———. 2018. "'Day of Anger' Becomes Kingdom's Latest National Holiday." 20 February.

Poffenberger, Mark, ed. 2013. *Cambodia's Contested Forest Domain.* Honolulu: University of Hawai'i Press.

Poluda, Julian, Sineth Siv, and Sotheary Yim. 2019. "Promoting Gender Equality and Improving Access to Justice for Female Survivors and Victims of Gender-Based Violence under the Khmer Rouge Regime: Final Evaluation of the ECCC Non-Jjdicial Gender Project (Phase 2)." UN Trust Fund to End Violence against Women, VSS, and TPO. https://untf.unwomen.org/en/learning-hub/evaluations/2019/07/the-eccc-non-judicial-gender-project-phase-2.

Ponchaud, François. 2001. *Cambodge année zéro.* Paris: Kailash.

Ponniah, Kevin, and Sokheng Vong. 2014. "Tense Victory Day Expected." *Phnom Penh Post*, 7 January.

Porée, Anne-Laure. 2009a. "Les parties civiles boycottent le procès." *Procès des Khmers Rouges* (blog), 31 August. https://proceskhmersrouges.net/?p=862.

———. 2009b. "L'assemblée plénière confirme le principe de la participation des parties civiles qui restent mobilisées." *Procès des Khmers Rouges* (blog), 13 September. https://proceskhmersrouges.net/?p=871.

Power, Samantha. 2003. *"A Problem from Hell": America and the Age of Genocide.* New York: Harper Perennial.

Quigley, John. 2000. "Introduction." In *Genocide in Cambodia: Documents from the Trial of Pol Pot and Ieng Sary*, edited by Howard J. De Nike, John Quigley, and Kenneth J. Robinson, 1–18. Philadelphia: University of Pennsylvania Press.

Quinn, Kenneth. 1989. "Explaining the Terror." In *Cambodia, 1975–1978: Rendezvous with Death*, edited by Karl Jackson, 215–40. Princeton, NJ: Princeton University Press.

Rabé, Paul E. 2010. "Land Sharing in Phnom Penh and Bangkok: Lessons from Four Decades of Innovative Slum Redevelopment Projects in Two Southeast 'Asian Boom Towns.'" Worldbank. http://www.worldbank.org/content/dam/Worldbank/document/urban/places-we-live-competition-Rabe.pdf.

———. 2021. "Evaluating the Slum Redevelopment Project of Borei Keila." Urbanet. 9 March. https://www.urbanet.info/evaluating-the-slum-redevelopment-project-of-borei-keila/.

Rajagopal, Balakrishnan. 2003. *International Law from Below.* Cambridge: Cambridge University Press.

RFA. 2020. "Cambodia PM Hun Sen Using 'Thank You Peace' Campaign to Divert Attention from Abuses: Analyst." Radio Free Asia, 2 February. http://www.rfa.org/english/news/cambodia/slogan-01022020155528.html.

Richmond, Oliver, and Jason Franks. 2007. "Liberal Hubris?" *Security Dialogue* 38 (1): 27–48.

Robins, Simon. 2012. "Transitional Justice as an Elite Discourse." *Critical Asian Studies* 44 (1): 3–30.

Roht-Arriaza, Naomi. 2004. "Reparations: Decisions and Dilemmas." *Hastings International and Comparative Law Review* 27 (2): 157–219.

———. 2016. "Measures of Non-repetition in Transitional Justice: The Missing Link?" University of California, Legal Studies Research Paper Series, no. 171: 1–42.

Rubli, Sandra. 2012. "Transitional Justice: Justice by Bureaucratic Means?" swisspeace Working Paper, no. 4.

Rudi, Lisa-Marie. 2022. "Cambodia Study on Opportunities for Reparations for Survivors of Conflict-Related Sexual Violence: Left without Calla." REDRESS Trust, Kdei Karuna, Global Survivors Fund. https://redress.org/reparations-for-survivors-of-conflict-related-sexual-violence/.

Ryan, Heather, and Laura McGrew. 2016. *Performance and Perception: The Impact of the Extraordinary Chambers in the Court of Cambodia.* New York: Open Society Foundations.

Salehi, Mariam. 2022. *Transitional Justice in Process: Plans and Politics in Tunisia.* Manchester: Manchester University Press.

Saliba, Michael. 2009. "Civil Parties Boycott Start of Character Witness Testimony While Experts Offer Psychological Assessment of Duch." *Cambodia Tribunal Monitor*, 31 August. http://www.cambodiatribunal.org/wp-content/uploads/2019/07/ctm_blog_8-31-2009.pdf.

Saling, Eben. 2014. "Press Conferences Detail Triumphs, Defeats and Plans in the Aftermath of Case 002/01." *Cambodia Tribunal Monitor*, 7 August. www.cambodia

tribunal.org/2014/08/07/press-conferences-detail-triumphs-defeats-and-plans-in-the-aftermath-of-case-00201.
Sanders, Aafke. 2006. "The Evil Within: Genocide, Memory and Mythmaking in Cambodia." MA thesis, Radboud University Nijmegen.
Sanderson, John. 2001. "The Cambodian Experience." In *United Nations Peacekeeping Operations: Ad Hoc Missions, Permanent Engagement*, edited by Ramesh Thakur and Ramesh Schnabel, 155–66. Tokyo: UN University Press.
Sankey, Diana. 2016. "Recognition of Gendered Experiences of Harm at the ECCC: The Promise and the Pitfalls." *Feminist Legal Studies* 24:7–27.
Sarat, Austin. 1990. "'. . . The Law Is All Over': Power, Resistance and the Legal Consciousness of the Welfare Poor." *Yale Journal of Law & the Humanities* 2 (2): 343–79.
Saut Sok, Prathna. 2019. "Controversial Buddhist Pagoda Legalized After 22 Years." Voice of Democracy, 5 June. https://vodenglish.news/controversial-buddhist-pagoda-legalized-after-22-years/.
Savorn, Duong. 2011. *The Mystery of Sexual Violence under the Khmer Rouge Regime.* Phnom Penh: Cambodia Defenders Project.
Schabas, William. 2001. "Should Khmer Rouge Leaders Be Prosecuted for Genocide or Crimes against Humanity?" *Searching for the Truth*, no. 22 (October): 37–39. Documentation Center of Cambodia. http://d.dccam.org/Tribunal/Analysis/Debate_Genocide.htm.
Schatz, Edward. 2009. "Introduction." In *Political Ethnography: What Immersion Contributes to the Study of Power*, edited by Edward Schatz, 1–22. Chicago: University of Chicago Press.
Scheffer, David. 2012. *All the Missing Souls.* Princeton, NJ: Princeton University Press.
Schmid, Evelyne. 2015. *Taking Economic, Social and Cultural Rights Seriously in International Criminal Law.* Cambridge: Cambridge University Press.
Schoenberger, Laura, and Alice Beban. 2018. "'They Turn Us into Criminals': Embodiments of Fear in Cambodian Land Grabbing." *Annals of the Association of American Geographers* 108 (5): 1338–53.
Schwöbel, Christine, ed. 2014. *Critical Approaches to International Criminal Law.* Oxon: Routledge.
Schwöbel-Patel, Christine. 2021. *Marketing Global Justice.* Cambridge: Cambridge University Press.
Scott, James. 1972. "Patron-Client Politics and Political Change in Southeast Asia." *American Political Science Review* 66 (1): 91–113.
———. 1985. *Weapons of the Weak.* New Haven, CT: Yale University Press.
Scurrah, Natalia, and Philip Hirsch. 2015. *The Political Economy of Land Governance in Cambodia.* Ventiane: Mekong Regional Land Governance.
Seymour, Susan. 2006. "Resistance." *Anthropological Theory* 6 (3): 303–21.
Sharp, Dustin. 2018. *Rethinking Transitional Justice for the Twenty-First Century: Beyond the End of History.* Cambridge: Cambridge University Press.
Sharp, Gene. 2005. *Waging Nonviolent Struggle: 20th Century Practice and 21st Century Potential.* Boston: Extending Horizons Books.

Sirik, Savina. 2012. *Duch Final Judgment: Justice and Humanity.* Phnom Penh: Documentation Center of Cambodia.

———. 2020. "Memory Construction of Former Khmer Rouge Cadres: Resistance to Dominant Discourses of Genocide in Cambodia." *Journal of Political Power* 13 (2): 233–51.

Sisovann, Pin, and James Welsh. 2007. "CPP Marks Jan 7 'Liberation'; Others Recall 'Invasion.'" *Cambodia Daily*, 8 January.

Smirl, Lisa. 2015. *Spaces of Aid: How Cars, Compounds and Hotels Shape Humanitarianism.* London: Zed Books.

Smith, Jeff. 1998. "Rohrabacher Rebuked for Attack on Hun Sen." *Cambodia Daily*, 30 September.

Smith, Rhona. 2017. "Report of the Special Rapporteur on the Situation of Human Rights in Cambodia." *A/HRC/36/61*, 27 July. https://ap.ohchr.org/documents/dpage_e.aspx?si=A/HRC/36/61.

So, Farina. 2010. "An Oral History of Cham Muslim Women in Cambodia under the Khmer Rouge Regime." MA thesis, Ohio University.

So, Sokbunthoeun. 2010. "Land Rights in Cambodia: An Unfinished Reform." *Asia Pacific Issues* 97:1–8.

Soja, Edward W. 1989. *Postmodern Geographies: The Reassertion of Space in Critical Social Theory.* Radical Thinkers. London: Verso.

Sok, Khemara. 2020. "Khmer Rouge Victims Push for Continuation of May 20 Commemorations." Voice of America Cambodia, 14 July. https://www.voacambodia.com/a/khmer-rouge-victims-push-for-continuation-of-may-20-commemorations/5502157.html.

Sok, Leang, and Toshihiro Abe. 2019. "Participating in a National Drama: A Reflection on Local Contradictory Attitudes toward the Court Process." In *The Khmer Rouge Trials in Context*, edited by Toshihiro Abe, 195–225. Chiang Mai, Thailand: Silkworm Books.

Sokha, Cheang, and James O'Toole. 2010. "Hun Sen to Ban Ki-Moon: Case 002 Last Trial at ECCC." *Phnom Penh Post*, 27 October.

Soy, Kimsan. 2016. "Understanding Acceptance of International Justice through Duch's Sentence at the ECCC." In *After Nuremberg: Exploring Multiple Dimensions of the Acceptance of International Criminal Justice*, edited by Susanne Buckley-Zistel, Friederike Mieth, and Marjana Papa, 1–19. Nuremberg: International Nuremberg Principles Academy.

Soy, Kimsan, and Vandanet Hing. 2019. "Upholding the Right to Lawyer: Lessons Learned from the ECCC." swisspeace Working Paper Cambodia Series.

Sperfeldt, Christoph. 2014. "Broadcasting Justice: Media Outreach at the Khmer Rouge Trials." *Asia-Pacific Issues: Analysis from the East-West Center* 115 (July). https://www.eastwestcenter.org/publications/broadcasting-justice-media-outreach-the-khmer-rouge-trials.

———. 2022. *Practices of Reparations in International Criminal Justice.* Cambridge: Cambridge University Press.

Sperfeldt, Christoph, and Rachel Hughes. 2020. "The Projectification of Reparation." *Journal of Human Rights Practice* 12:545–65.

Sperfeldt, Christoph, and Jeudy Oeung. 2019. "The Evolution of Cambodian Civil Society's Involvement with Victim Participation at the Khmer Rouge Trials." In *Civil Society and Transitional Justice in Asia and the Pacific*, edited by Lia Kent, Joanne Wallis, and Claire Cronin, 85–105. Canberra: Australian National University Press.

Springer, Simon. 2013. "Violent Accumulation: A Postanarchist Critique of Property, Dispossession, and the State of Exception in Neoliberalizing Cambodia." *Annals of the Association of American Geographers* 103 (3): 608–26.

Sreang, Heng. 2006. "Justice in Cambodia: A Short Reflection on Obstacles to Implementing 'Justice' within the Context of the Law in Present-Day Cambodia." *NIAS Nytt*, 20–23 December.

Staggs Kelsall, Michelle. 2009. "Symbolic, Shambolic or Simply Sui Generis? Reflections from the Field on Cambodia's Extraordinary Chambers." *Law in Context: A Socio-legal Journal* 27 (1): 154–78.

Stammel, Nadine, Sebastian Burchert, Sopheap Taing, Estelle Bockers, and Christine Knaevelsrud. 2010. "The Survivors' Voices: Attitudes on the ECCC, the Former Khmer Rouge and Experiences with Civil Party Participation." http://www.bzfo.de/images/stories/pdf/bzfo_cambodia_report_2010.pdf.

Stanton, Gregory. 2001. "The Khmer Rouge Did Commit Genocide." *Searching for the Truth*, no. 23 (November): 32–33. Documentation Center of Cambodia. http://d.dccam.org/Tribunal/Analysis/Debate_Genocide.htm.

Stover, Eric, Mychelle Balthazard, and K. Alexa Koenig. 2011. "Confronting Duch: Civil Party Participation in Case 001 at the ECCC." *International Review of the Red Cross* 93 (882): 503–46.

Strangio, Sebastian. 2014a. "Cambodia between the End of History and the End Times of Human Rights." *Cambodia Law and Policy Journal* 3:45–60.

———. 2014b. *Hun Sen's Cambodia.* Chiang Mai: Silkworm Books.

Strangio, Sebastian, and Cheang Sokha. 2009. "Government Testimony Could Bias Khmer Rouge Trial: Prime Minister." *Phnom Penh Post*, 9 October.

Studzinsky, Silke. 2009. "Nebenklage vor den ECCC: Herausforderung und Chance oder mission impossible?" *Zeitschrift für Internationale Strafrechtsdogmatik* 1:44–50.

———. 2011. "Neglected Crimes." In *Gender in Transitional Justice*, edited by Susanne Buckley-Zistel and Ruth Stanley, 88–112. Basingstoke: Palgrave Macmillan.

Subedi, Surya P. 2010. "Report of the Special Rapporteur on the Situation of Human Rights in Cambodia." *A/HRC/15/46*, 16 September. https://ap.ohchr.org/documents/dpage_e.aspx?si=A/HRC/15/46.

———. 2012. "Report of the UN Special Rapporteur on the Situation of Human Rights in Cambodia. Addendum: A Human Rights Analysis of Economic and Other Land Concessions in Cambodia." *Doc. A/HRC/21/63/Add.1*, 24 September. https://ap.ohchr.org/documents/dpage_e.aspx?si=A/HRC/21/63/Add.1.

———. 2014. "Report of the Special Rapporteur on the Situation of Human Rights in Cambodia." *A/HRC/27/70*, 15 August. https://ap.ohchr.org/documents/dpage_e.aspx?si=A/HRC/27/70.

Subotić, Jelena. 2014. "Bargaining Justice. A Theory of Transitional Justice Compliance." In *Transitional Justice Theories*, edited by Susanne Buckley-Zistel, Teresa Koloma Beck, Christian Braun, and Friederike Mieth, 128–43. New York: Routledge.

Sun, Narin. 2019. "Bellweather Khmer Rouge Case Heads to Court on November 27." Voice of America, 26 November. http://www.voacambodia.com/a/bellwether-khmer-rouge-case-heads-to-court-on-November-27/5180364.html.

Tabeau, Ewa, and They Kheam. 2009. "Demographic Expert Report: Khmer Rouge Victims in Cambodia, April 1975–January 1979. A Critical Assessment of Major Estimates." ECCC. https://www.eccc.gov.kh/sites/default/files/documents/courtdoc/D140_1_1_Public_Redacted_EN.PDF.

Tal, Kali. 1996. *Worlds of Hurt: Reading the Literatures of Trauma*. Vol. 8. Cambridge: Cambridge University Press.

Talocci, Giorgio, and Camillo Boano. 2017. "The De-politicisation of Housing Policies: The Case of Borei Keila Land-Sharing in Phnom Penh, Cambodia." *International Journal of Housing Policy* 18 (2): 290–311.

Tarrow, Sidney. 2013. "Contentious Politics." In *The Wiley-Blackwell Encyclopedia of Social and Political Movements*, edited by David A. Snow, Donatella Della Porta, Bert Klandermans, and Doug McAdam. Malden, MA: Blackwell.

Theidon, Kimberly. 2009. "Editorial Note." *International Journal of Transitional Justice* 3 (3): 295–300.

Thun, Theara, and Duong Keo. 2021. "Ethnic Vietnamese and the Khmer Rouge: The Genocide and Race Debate." *Critical Asian Studies* 53 (3): 325–41.

Tilly, Charles. 1978. *From Mobilization to Revolution*. Reading: Addison-Wesley.

Torrens, Shannon Maree. 2016. "Allegations of Political Interference, Bias and Corruption at the ECCC." In *The ECCC: Assessing Their Contribution to International Criminal Law*, edited by Simon M. Meisenberg and Ignaz Stegmiller, 389–433. International Criminal Justice Series 6. The Hague: T. M. C. Asser Press.

Travouillon, Katrin. 2021. "From 'Sphere of Scrutiny' to 'Sphere of Opportunity': The Cambodian People's Party's Vision of International Order." *Contemporary Southeast Asia* 43 (2): 370–94.

Tyner, James, Savina Sirik, and Samuel Henkin. 2014. "Violence and the Dialectics of Landscape: Memorialization in Cambodia." *Geographical Review* 104 (3): 277–93.

Un, Kheang. 2006. "State, Society and Democratic Consolidation." *Pacific Affairs* 79 (2): 225–45.

———. 2009. "The Judicial System and Democratization in Post-conflict Cambodia." In *Beyond Democracy in Cambodia: Political Reconstruction in a Post-conflict Society*, edited by Joakim Öjendal and Mona Lilja, 70–100. Copenhagen: NIAS Press.

———. 2011. "Cambodia: Moving Away from Democracy?" *International Political Science Review* 32 (5): 546–62.

———. 2013a. "Aid Dependence in Cambodia." *Contemporary Southeast Asia: A Journal of International and Strategic Affairs* 35 (2): 284–87.

———. 2013b. "The Cambodian People Have Spoken." *New York Times*, 9 August.

———. 2019. *Cambodia: Return to Authoritarianism.* Cambridge: Cambridge University Press.

Un, Kheang, and Judy Ledgerwood. 2010. "Is the Trial of 'Duch' a Catalyst for Change in Cambodia's Courts." Asia Pacific Issues, 1 June. https://www.eastwestcenter.org/publications/trial-duch-catalyst-change-cambodias-courts.

Un, Kheang, and Sokbunthoeun So. 2011. "Land Rights in Cambodia: How Neopatrimonial Politics Restricts Land Policy Reform." *Pacific Affairs* 84 (2): 289–308.

———. 2012. "Cambodia's Judiciary: Heading for Political Judicialization?" In *The Judicialization of Politics in Asia*, edited by Björn Dressel, 184–201. New York: Routledge.

UN Development Programme. 2007. "Special Audit: Audit of Human Resources Management at the ECCC." Report No. RCM0172. United Nations Development Programme. https://www.legal-tools.org/doc/25e46e/pdf.

UN Department of Public Information. 2002. "Daily Press Briefing by the Office of the Spokesman for the Secretary-General." *United Nations Press Briefings* (blog), 8 February. https://www.un.org/press/en/2002/db020802.doc.htm.

UN General Assembly. 2003. "Resolution 57/228. Khmer Rouge Trials." A/RES/57/228. http://www.unakrt-online.org/documents/resolution-khmer-rouge-trials.

UN Group of Experts. 1999. "Report of the Group of Experts for Cambodia Established Pursuant to General Assembly Resolution 52/135." http://www1.umn.edu/humanrts/cambodia-1999.html.

UN Secretary-General. 2003. "Report of the Secretary-General on the Khmer Rouge Trials." A/57/769. UN General Assembly. http://www.unakrt-online.org/documents/report-secretary-general-khmer-rouge-trials-2.

———. 2012. "Khmer Rouge Trials: Report of the Secretary-General." A/67/380. UN General Assembly. https://www.unakrt-online.org/documents/report-secretary-general-khmer-rouge-trials1.

———. 2013. "Request for a Subvention to the ECCC: Report of the Secretary-General." A/68/532. UN General Assembly. http://www.unakrt-online.org/documents/report-secretary-general-request-subvention-extraordinary-chambers-courts-cambodia-6.

———. 2020. "Request for a Subvention to the ECCC." A/75/242. UN General Assembly. http://www.unakrt-online.org/documents/report-secretary-general-request-subvention-extraordinary-chambers-courts-cambodia.

———. 2021. "Request for a Subvention to the ECCC: Report of the Secretary-General." A/76/331. UN General Assembly. http://www.unakrt-online.org/documents/report-secretary-general-request-subvention-extraordinary-chambers-courts-cambodia-0.

Urs, Tara. 2007. "Imagining Locally-Motivated Accountability for Mass Atrocities." *Sur: International Journal on Human Rights* 7:61–99.

US Embassy, Cambodia. 2006. "KRT Judges Named: The Good, the Bad, and the Ugly (Cable 06PHNOMPENH887)." Wikileaks, 9 May. https://wikileaks.jcvignoli.com/cable_06PHNOMPENH887.

———. 2007. "Update on the ECCC; David Scheffer Coming to Cambodia (Cable 07PHNOMPENH77)." Wikileaks, 17 January. https://wikileaks.jcvignoli.com/cable_07PHNOMPENH77.

Verver, Michiel, and Heidi Dahles. 2014. "The Institutionalisation of Oknha." *Journal of Contemporary Asia* 45 (1): 48–70.

Vianney-Liaud, Mélanie. 2016. "Legal Constraints in the Interpretation of Genocide." In *ECCC: Assessing Their Contribution to International Criminal Law*, edited by Simon Meisenberg and Ignaz Stegmiller, 255–90. International Criminal Justice Series 6. The Hague: T. M. C. Asser Press.

Vong, Mun. 2022. "State Mobilization in Authoritarian Regimes: Youth Politics and Regime Legitimation in Cambodia." *Journal of East Asian Studies* 22 (2): 1–24.

Vong, Sokheng. 2014. "CPP Swings Back Hard." *Phnom Penh Post*, 8 January.

Vong, Sokheng, and Shane Worrel. 2013. "Thousands Turn Out against CNRP Deputy." *Phnom Penh Post*, 10 June.

Wallace, Julia. 2012. "Exclusive Interview with KRT Reserve Investigating Judge Laurent Kasper-Ansermet." *Cambodia Daily*, 15 February.

Werner, Alain, and Daniella Rudy. 2010. "Civil Party Representation at the ECCC: Sounding the Retreat in International Criminal Law?" *Northwestern Journal of International Human Rights* 8 (3): 301–9.

West, Lucy. 2019. "The Limits to Judicial Independence: Cambodia's Political Culture and the Civil Law." *Democratization* 26 (3): 537–53.

White, Stuart. 2014. "Anger toward Khmer Rouge Tribunal." *Phnom Penh Post*, 18 October.

Wilke, Christiane. 2013. "Remembering Complexity? Memorials for Nazi Victims in Berlin." *International Journal of Transitional Justice* 7:136–56.

Williams, Timothy. 2019. "NGO Interventions in the Post-conflict Memoryscape. The Effect of Competing 'Mnemonic Role Attributions' on Reconciliation in Cambodia." *Journal of Intervention and Statebuilding* 13 (2): 158–79.

Williams, Timothy, Julie Bernath, Boravin Tann, and Somaly Kum. 2018. "Justice and Reconciliation for the Victims of the Khmer Rouge? Victim Participation in Cambodia's TJ Process." Marburg: Center for Conflict Studies; Phnom Penh: CSHL; Bern: swisspeace. https://www.swisspeace.ch/assets/publications/downloads/Reports/af32f3c3a1/Justice-and-Reconciliation-for-the-Victims-of-the-Khmer-Rouge-Report-2018-.pdf.

Wolfe-Robinson, Maya. 2012. "Cambodia Court Hearing Khmer Rouge Trials Close to Bankruptcy." *Guardian*, 4 December.

Ye, Beini. 2014. "Transitional Justice through the Cambodian Women's Hearings." *Cambodia Law and Policy Journal* 2:23–37.

Young, Sokphea. 2019. "Protests, Regulation and Environmental Accountability in Cambodia." *Journal of Current Southeast Asian Studies* 38 (1): 33–54.

———. 2020. "Social Movements in Cambodia: Why They Succeed or Fail." *Journal of International Relations and Development* 23:899–923.

———. 2021. *Strategies of Authoritarian Survival and Dissensus in Southeast Asia: Weak Men Versus Strongmen.* Singapore: Palgrave Macmillan.

Yrigoyen Fajardo, Raquel Z., Rady Kong, and Sin Phan. 2005. *Pathways to Justice: Access to Justice with a Focus on the Poor, Women and Indigenous Peoples, Cambodia.* New York: UNDP; Phnom Penh: Cambodian Ministry of Justice.

Index

Critical Human Rights

Researching Perpetrators of Genocide
Edited by KJELL ANDERSON and ERIN JESSEE

Memory's Turn: Reckoning with Dictatorship in Brazil
REBECCA J. ATENCIO

The Khmer Rouge Tribunal: Power, Politics, and Resistance in Transitional Justice
JULIE BERNATH

Prisoner of Pinochet: My Year in a Chilean Concentration Camp
SERGIO BITAR; translated by ERIN GOODMAN; foreword and notes by PETER WINN

Legislating Gender and Sexuality in Africa: Human Rights, Society, and the State
Edited by LYDIA BOYD and EMILY BURRILL

Bread, Justice, and Liberty: Grassroots Activism and Human Rights in Pinochet's Chile
ALISON J. BRUEY

Archiving the Unspeakable: Silence, Memory, and the Photographic Record in Cambodia
MICHELLE CASWELL

Court of Remorse: Inside the International Criminal Tribunal for Rwanda
THIERRY CRUVELLIER; translated by CHARI VOSS

How Difficult It Is to Be God: Shining Path's Politics of War in Peru, 1980–1999
CARLOS IVÁN DEGREGORI; edited and with an introduction by STEVE J. STERN

After Genocide: Memory and Reconciliation in Rwanda
NICOLE FOX

Trauma, Taboo, and Truth-Telling: Listening to Silences in Postdictatorship Argentina
NANCY J. GATES-MADSEN

From War to Genocide: Criminal Politics in Rwanda, 1990–1994
ANDRÉ GUICHAOUA; translated by DON E. WEBSTER

Innocence and Victimhood: Gender, Nation, and Women's Activism in Postwar Bosnia-Herzegovina
ELISSA HELMS

Inside Rwanda's "Gacaca" Courts: Seeking Justice after Genocide
BERT INGELAERE

Practical Audacity: Black Women and International Human Rights
STANLIE M. JAMES

Amending the Past: Europe's Holocaust Commissions and the Right to History
ALEXANDER KARN

Civil Obedience: Complicity and Complacency in Chile since Pinochet
MICHAEL J. LAZZARA

Torture and Impunity
ALFRED W. MCCOY

Systemic Silencing: Activism, Memory, and Sexual Violence in Indonesia
KATHARINE E. MCGREGOR

Elusive Justice: Women, Land Rights, and Colombia's Transition to Peace
DONNY MEERTENS

Conflicted Memory: Military Cultural Interventions and the Human Rights Era in Peru
CYNTHIA E. MILTON

Historical Justice and Memory
Edited by KLAUS NEUMANN and JANNA THOMPSON

The Wars inside Chile's Barracks: Remembering Military Service under Pinochet
LEITH PASSMORE

Buried Histories: The Anti-Communist Massacres of 1965–1966 in Indonesia
JOHN ROOSA

The Human Rights Paradox: Universality and Its Discontents
Edited by STEVE J. STERN and SCOTT STRAUS

Human Rights and Transnational Solidarity in Cold War Latin America
Edited by JESSICA STITES MOR

South-South Solidarity and the Latin American Left
JESSICA STITES MOR

Remaking Rwanda: State Building and Human Rights after Mass Violence
Edited by SCOTT STRAUS and LARS WALDORF

Beyond Displacement: Campesinos, Refugees, and Collective Action in the Salvadoran Civil War
MOLLY TODD

Long Journey to Justice: El Salvador, the United States, and Struggles against Empire
MOLLY TODD

The Social Origins of Human Rights: Protesting Political Violence in Colombia's Oil Capital, 1919–2010
LUIS VAN ISSCHOT

The Soviet Union and the Gutting of the UN Genocide Convention
ANTON WEISS-WENDT

The Politics of Necessity: Community Organizing and Democracy in South Africa
ELKE ZUERN

www.ingramcontent.com/pod-product-compliance
Lightning Source LLC
Chambersburg PA
CBHW050753220425
25419CB00046B/145
9780299343606